Department for Transport

Scottish Government Executive and Welsh Assembly Government

Transport
Statistics
Great
Britain

2008

34th EDITION

December 2008

London: TSO

Department for Transport
Great Minster House
76 Marsham Street
London SW1P 4DR
Telephone 020 7944 8300

ISBN: 978-0-11-553030-2

Printed in Great Britain in December 2008 on material containing at least 75% recycled fibre.

A National Statistics publication produced by Transport Statistics: DfT
National Statistics are produced to high professional standards set out in the National Statistics Code of Practice. They undergo regular quality assurance reviews to ensure that they meet customer needs. The National Statistician maintains professional responsibility for all outputs comprising National Statistics. The United Kingdom Statistics Authority, independent of both Government and the producers of official statistics, publicly provides independent comment and advice on the National Statistics programme.

Contact Points: For general enquiries call the National Statistics Customer Enquiry Centre at: Room 1015, ONS, Government Buildings, Cardiff Road, Newport, Gwent, NP10 8XG. ☎ 0845 601 3034, fax 01633 652747 or E-mail: info@statistics.gov.uk

You can also obtain National Statistics from the United Kingdom Statistics Authority through the internet – go to www.statistics.gov.uk. For information relating to Transport Statistics go to www.dft.gov.uk/pgr/statistics

Prepared for publication by:
Tajbar Gul
Shawn Weekes

DfT is often prepared to sell unpublished data. Further information and queries concerning this publication should be directed to: Transport Statistics, 2/29, Great Minster House, 76 Marsham Street, London SW1P 4DR
☎ 020 7944 3098, Fax 020 7944 2165, E-mail: publicationgeneral.enq@dft.gov.uk

Cover photographs all courtesy of Alamy; from left to right: © Adrian Sherratt; © Nigel Lloyd; © Ashley Cooper; © Janine Wiedel Photolibrary; © Joe Fox

Contents

Transport Statistics Contacts

Logistics, Aviation & Maritime

Antonia Roberts
Chief Statistician
(Head of Profession)
☎020-7944 4280

Statisticians

Paul Swallow
National Statistics; GIS

☎020-7944 4411

Jeremy Grove
Maritime Statistics; Flag analysis of UK
seaborne trade, merchant fleet statistics; sea
passenger statistics; port traffic, finance and
manpower statistics; coastwise & inland
waterways freight statistics.

☎020-7944 4441
E-mail: maritime.stats@dft.gov.uk

Lyndsey Avery
Aviation & Airport Statistics; international
passenger survey; transport indicators;
environment statistics.

☎020-7944 4276
E-mail: aviation.stats@dft.gov.uk

Dorothy Anderson
Transport Statistics for EU & other
international bodies; international
comparisons; survey control.

☎020-7944 4442
E-mail:
inter.transport.comparisons@dft.gov.uk

Stephen Reynolds
Road Freight Statistics; continuing survey of
road goods transport; ad hoc surveys of
vehicle transport data collection and
processing unit;
Survey of international road haulage.

☎020-7944 3093
E-mail: roadfreight.stats@dft.gov.uk

Dorothy Anderson
Transport statistics publications and website
management; Local ICT management;
National Statistics.

☎020-7944 4442
E-mail: publicationgeneral.enq@dft.gov.uk

Roads & Traffic

Barbara Noble
Chief Statistician
☎020-7944 4270

Statisticians

June Bowman
Road Traffic Statistics
Roads Information Framework

☎020-7944 6573

Andy Lees
Road Traffic Statistics; national core census.
Liaison with Highways Agency. Review of core
census. Computing development. London core
traffic census; weigh-in-motion.

☎020-7944 6397
Email: roadtraff.manual@dft.gov.uk

Drew Hird
Road Traffic Statistics - Annual and quarterly
traffic estimates; manual traffic counts
and road lengths surveys.

☎020-7944 6396
E-mail: roadtraff.stats@dft.gov.uk

Eric Crane
Urban congestion monitoring and speed surveys.

☎020-7944 5383
E-mail: roadtraff.stats@dft.gov.uk

Dorothy Salathiel

Inter urban congestion monitoring and speed
surveys.

☎020-7944 6399
E-mail: roadtraff.stats@dft.gov.uk

Pat Kilbey
Road accidents; vehicle speeds; car safety;
Inter-modal passenger safety.

☎020-7944 6387
E-mail: roadacc.stats@dft.gov.uk

Travel

Anthony Boucher
Chief Statistician
☎020-7944 3079

Statisticians

Mouna Kehil
Bus & Coach Statistics: supply & demand,
income & subsidies, fares, operating costs; bus
stock; taxi statistics; assaults on public road
transport users & staff; channel tunnel
statistics.

☎020-7944 4589
E-mail: bus.statistics@dft.gov.uk

Olivia Christophersen
National Travel Survey.

☎020-7944 6594
E-mail: national.travelsurvey@dft.gov.uk

Anna Heyworth
Regional and Local Transport Statistics;
employment; census data.
Highway Maintenance Statistics; national road
maintenance condition survey; investment;
highway expenditure

☎020-7944 4746
E-mail: roadmaintenance.stats@dft.gov.uk
E-mail: subnational.stats@dft.gov.uk

Tracey Budd
Statistical Advisor & Research Co-ordinator;
Public attitudes towards transport.

☎020-7944 4892
E-mail: attitudes.stats@dft.gov.uk

Ben Coleman
Vehicle statistics statistical advice to DVLA;
VED evasion studies; road track costs.

☎020-7944 6398
E-mail: vehicles.stats@dft.gov.uk

Fax: 020-7944-2165   **Fax**: 020-7944-2164   **Fax**: 020-7944-2166

Transport Statistics Home page:
www.dft.gov.uk/pgr/statistics

Introduction

Welcome to the 34th edition of *Transport Statistics Great Britain.*

Transport Statistics Great Britain (TSGB) is a major publication within the scope of National Statistics and provides an accurate, comprehensive and meaningful picture of transport patronage in Great Britain.

All individual tables that make up TSGB are on the web-site in both PDF and EXCEL format, enabling users to manipulate the information to produce further tables or charts. The whole document is available as a PDF file (chapter by chapter) in a separate theme dedicated to TSGB (http://www.dft.gov.uk/transtat/tsgb).

The web-site also contains a great deal of other published statistical material, including (in PDF format) all of the recent bulletins produced by Transport Statistics. It also includes a list of forthcoming publications and their publication dates. In many cases, the bulletins produced during the course of the year provide the first release of data and these are subsequently consolidated into the TSGB tables.

I hope you find this publication useful and interesting. Any comments you may have on the contents and presentation would be welcome. Please send these to the address below or E-mail to publicationgeneral.enq@dft.gov.uk

Dorothy A Anderson
2/29 Great Minster House
76 Marsham Street
London, SW1P 4DR

Symbols and conventions

Unless otherwise stated, all tables refer to **Great Britain**.

Metric units are generally used.

Conversion factors:

1 kilometre	= 0.6214 mile
1 tonne	= 0.9842 ton
1 tonne-km	= 0.6116 ton-mile
1 billion	= 1,000 million
1 Gallon	= 4.546 litres
1 litre	= 0.220 gallons

Rounding of figures. In tables where figures have been rounded to the nearest final digit, there may be an apparent slight discrepancy between the sum of the constituent items and the total as shown.

Symbols. The symbols to the right have been used throughout.

..	= not available
.	= not applicable
-	= Negligible (less than half the final digit shown)
0	= Nil
*	= Sample size too small for reliable estimates
ow	= of which
{	= subsequent data is disaggregated
}	= subsequent data is aggregated
|	= break in the series
P	= provisional data
F	= forecast expenditure
e	= estimated outturn
n.e.s.	= not elsewhere specified
R	= Revised data

All statistics in this publication are National Statistics unless indicated otherwise on each table.

List of tables and charts

Section 9 - Vehicles

Section 10 - International comparisons

Transport Statistics Great Britain has been compiled by staff at DfT with contributions from the Scottish Executive, the Welsh Assembly Government and other Government Departments. Thanks go to those individuals and businesses who provided data for analysis in the tables. DfT are able to provide statistics other than those included in this annual compendium. Many of these are published separately in more specialised publications – available via the DfT website at: www.dft.gov.uk/pgr/statistics. Some unpublished material is available on request, as is a service (subject to availability of resources) providing customised analyses for clients. Potential customers should note that we do charge for these services and there are strict guidelines for maintaining confidentiality. Contact points for further details are shown at the bottom of each table.

1 Modal Comparisons:

Notes and Definitions

Passenger transport: 1.1

Buses and coaches: Passenger kilometres are derived from other survey data such as receipts, vehicle kilometres and patronage. Changes are estimated by deflating passenger receipts by the most appropriate price indices available. Because this proxy method has to be used, the series gives only a broad guide to trends.

Cars, vans, taxis, motor cycles and pedal cycles:

Estimates for cars (which include taxis), motorcycles (which include mopeds and scooters), and pedal cycles are derived from the traffic series (vehicle kilometres) shown in Table 7.2 and average occupancy rates (persons per vehicle) from the National Travel Survey (NTS).

Because of changes in methodology figures for the road traffic estimates, figures for 1993 have been shown calculated on the new and the old basis.

Occupancy rates for 1996 onwards are based on weighted NTS data. As data prior to 1996 has not been weighted, this produces a discontinuity in the data. This does not affect the underlying rate of growth.

In 2007, the occupancy rates were 1.64 for cars and taxis and 1.07 for motorcycles. As 2007 travel data from the NTS were not available at the time of publication, these figures were estimated based on the trend in previous years.

Estimates for personal use of light vans are derived from the NTS.

Rail: Rail figures include National Rail, London Underground, Glasgow Underground, public metro and light rail systems (see Table 6.2 for further details).

Air: The figures are revenue passenger kilometres on scheduled and non-scheduled domestic services on UK airlines only. They exclude air taxi services, private flying and passengers paying less than 25 per cent of the full fare on scheduled and non-scheduled services.

All modes: Figures exclude travel by water.

Passenger journeys on public transport: 1.2

The data in this table is derived from –

Bus: Returns from operators to DfT;
Rail: Office of Rail Regulation; London Underground: Transport for London; light rail and trams: operators; Air: Civil Aviation Authority.

Personal travel: 1.3, 1.4 and 1.5

These tables present some basic information from the National Travel Survey (NTS). The NTS records personal travel by residents of Great Britain along the public highway in Great Britain. It records the number of trips (a one-way course of travel for a single main purpose) and the distance travelled. All modes of transport are covered, including walking more than 50 yards. Excluded from the sample are foreign visitors and people living in communal establishments (e.g. students in halls of residence). Both of these groups are likely to make a large number of public transport trips.

In Tables 1.4 and 1.5, escort trips are those where the traveller has no purpose of his/her own, other than to escort or accompany another person, e.g. take a child to school.

In 2006, a weighting strategy was introduced to the NTS. As well as adjusting for non-response bias, the weighting strategy for the NTS also adjusts for the drop-off in the number of trips recorded by respondents during the course of the travel week. The weighting strategy has been applied to NTS data from 1995 onwards.

In 2002, the drawn sample size for the NTS was nearly trebled compared with previous years, enabling key results to be presented on a single year basis for the first time since the survey became continuous. Changes to the methodology in 2002 mean that there are some inconsistencies with data for earlier years.

Travel data from the 2007 NTS was not available at the time of publication and these tables have therefore not been updated to 2007. More details can be found at

http://www.dft.gov.uk/pgr/statistics/datatablespublications/personal/mainresults/nts2007

People entering Central London during the morning peak: 1.6

The area defined as Central London approximates to that defined as the Greater London Conurbation Centre in the Population Censuses. It is bounded by South Kensington and Paddington in the west, Marylebone Road/Euston Road in the North, Shoreditch and Aldgate in the East, Elephant and Castle and Vauxhall in the South, and includes all the main railway termini.

The survey is a count of the number of vehicle occupants (other than goods vehicles) on each road crossing the central London cordon. The cordon is situated outside the Inner Ring Road and encloses a slightly larger area than the Central London Congestion Charging Zone. Counts are conducted for one day at each of the survey points during October/November. Taxi passengers have been counted since 1996.

Results for London Underground are derived from exit counts of people leaving the Underground stations within the Central area. Since 1996, these have been taken from automatic ticket gate data. Rail passengers are counted by observers at their last station stop before the central London cordon or, in the case of long-distance operator services, on arrival at Central London rail termini. Figures for Underground exclude people transferring from surface rail.

Casualty rates: 1.7

There have been a number of small revisions to this table but these have had little effect on the comparisons of the different modes.

For rail, figures prior to 2000 are based on financial years. Changes in reporting regulations mean that serious and minor injuries are no longer collected; only casualties taken from the scene of the accident to hospital are included in these figures.

Passenger casualty rates given in the table can be interpreted as the risk a traveller runs of being injured, per billion kilometres travelled. The coverage varies for each mode of travel and the definitions of injuries and accidents are different. Thus care should be exercised in drawing comparisons between the rates for different modes.

The table provides information on passenger casualties and where possible travel by drivers and other crew in the course of their work has been excluded. Exceptions are for private journeys and those in company owned cars and vans where drivers are included.

Figures for all modes of transport exclude confirmed suicides and deaths through natural causes. Figures for air, rail and water exclude trespassers and rail excludes attempted suicides. Accidents occurring in airports, seaports and railway stations that do not directly involve the mode of transport concerned are also excluded; for example, injuries sustained on escalators or falling over packages on platforms.

The following definitions are used:

Air: Accidents involving UK registered airline aircraft in UK and foreign airspace. Fixed wing and rotary wing aircraft are included but air taxis are excluded. Accidents cover UK airline aircraft around the world not just in the UK.

Rail: Train accidents and accidents occurring through movement of railway vehicles in Great Britain. As well as national rail the figures include accidents on underground and tram systems, Eurotunnel and minor railways.

Water: Figures for travel by water include both domestic and international passenger carrying services of UK registered merchant vessels.

Road: Figures refer to Great Britain and include personal injury accidents occurring on the public highway (including footways) in which at least one road vehicle or a vehicle in collision with a pedestrian is involved and which becomes known to the police within 30 days of its occurrence. Figures include both public and private transport. More information and analyses on road accidents and casualties can be found in Section 8: Transport accidents and casualties.

Bus or coach: Vehicles equipped to carry 17 or more passengers regardless of use.

Car: Includes taxis, invalid tricycles, three and four wheel cars and minibuses. Prior to 1999 motor caravans were also included.

Van: Vans mainly include vehicles of the van type constructed on a car chassis. These are defined as those vehicles not over 3.5 tonnes maximum permissible gross vehicle weight.

Motorcycles: Mopeds, motor scooters and motor cycles (including motor cycle combinations).

Pedal cycle: Includes tandems, tricycles and toy cycles ridden on the carriageway.

Pedestrian: Includes persons riding toy cycles on the footway, persons pushing bicycles, pushing or pulling other vehicles or operating pedestrian controlled vehicles, those leading or herding animals, occupants of prams or wheelchairs, and people who alight safely from vehicles and are subsequently injured.

Travel to work: 1.8-1.9

Tables 1.8 and 1.9 use data from the October to December 2007 quarter of the Labour Force

Survey (LFS). The table is based on those people who are employed, and excludes those on Government New Deal schemes, those working from home or using their home as a working base, and those whose workplace or mode of travel to work were not known.

The questions on usual method of travel to work and usual time have been asked in each Autumn (October to December) survey since 1992. Table 1.8b gives a time series of the results from these surveys for Great Britain. The LFS is a survey of households living at private addresses in Great Britain. In spite of its large sample size (55 thousand responding households), data for some cells in Tables 1.8 and 1.9 are not shown because they fall below the 10 thousand LFS reliability threshold.

Labour Force Survey move to Calendar Quarters (CQ's): The Labour Force Survey (LFS) moved to publishing calendar quarters from May 2006. The survey previously published seasonal quarters where March-May months covered the spring quarter, June-August was summer and so forth. This has now changed to calendar quarters as part of an EU requirement for all member states to have an LFS based on calendar quarters. LFS micro data is available for January-March (Q1), April-June (Q2), July-September (Q3) and October-December (Q4). An article on the impact and issues associated with the move to calendar quarters is available at the link:

http://www.statistics.gov.uk/cci/article.asp?ID=1546

Overseas travel and tourism, and international passenger movements: 1.10-1.12

Tables 1.10-1.12 are derived from the International Passenger Survey (IPS). In this survey, which is carried out by the Office for National Statistics, a large sample of passengers are interviewed as they enter or leave the United Kingdom by the principal air and sea routes and via the Channel Tunnel. These tables are based on IPS 'main flow' interviews, i.e. United Kingdom residents returning to, and overseas residents leaving the United Kingdom. The unit of measurement is therefore the visit and not the journey, and the mode of travel for the unit is that used by a United Kingdom resident returning or by an overseas resident departing (fly cruises are an exception to this rule as they are counted as 'sea' even though United Kingdom resident interviewed will have returned by air).

Up to 1998, the results of the IPS have been supplemented with estimates of travel between the United Kingdom and the Irish Republic provided by the Irish Central Statistics Office. In Table 1.10, estimates of road and rail visits across the land border with the Irish Republic have been included with sea trips. Since 1999, IPS interviewing has been expanded to cover trips between the United Kingdom and the Irish Republic and therefore these estimates have not been necessary. The figures given here are annual totals, but quarterly as well as annual analyses are published in *Business Monitor MQ6 (Overseas Travel and Tourism)* and *Travel Trends (A report on the IPS)*, with detailed notes and definitions.

These publications are available from TSO, or through the National Statistics website. More details can be found at:

http://www.statistics.gov.uk/ssd/surveys/internat ional_passenger_survey.asp

The "European Union" category in Tables 1.11 and 1.12 includes all 25 member states. "Other Europe" in Tables 1.11 and 1.12 includes other central and Eastern Europe, North Cyprus, Faroe Islands, Gibraltar, Iceland, Norway, Switzerland (including Lichtenstein), Turkey, the former USSR and the states of former Yugoslavia. "Other areas" figures in Table 1.12 are mostly non-Europeans travelling from Europe.

Household Expenditure on Transport: 1.13

Data is shown to the nearest ten pence in line with usual Expenditure and Food Survey (EFS) practice. Data to the nearest penny may be obtained from the EFS contact point EFS@ons.gsi.gov.uk

The coding framework was changed for the 2001/02 survey onwards. The table has been amended to present data on the new European Standard Classification of Individual Consumption by Purpose (COICOP) basis.

Investment in transport: 1.14

The table attempts to define investment in a consistent manner for each mode but because of differences in the ways data are collected this is not always possible. Therefore, for some modes estimates have been made on the basis of limited or partial information. Some figures are subject to revision.

Roads: Sources for expenditure on road infrastructure include the Highways Agency, the Scottish Government, the Wales Assembly Government, local authorities and DBFO contractors. Figures for public investment in road infrastructure are for gross capital expenditure on national roads (i.e. motorways and trunk roads). Private investment in road infrastructure includes investment under Design, Build, Finance and Operate (DBFO) contracts. Expenditure on bus garages, stops, etc is not included. The source for expenditure on road vehicles is the Office for National Statistics.

It is not possible to separate all the private expenditure since 2002/03 from public expenditure due to the complex nature of funding.

Rail: The source for National Rail expenditure is the Office of Rail Regulation; Investment in rail infrastructure includes track renewals, new routes and electrification, signalling, buildings, and plant and equipment.

Other public investment in rail infrastructure and other rail rolling stock covers, and is sourced by, London Underground, Docklands Light Railway, Croydon Tramlink, Glasgow Underground, Manchester Metrolink light rail system, Midland Metro, Nottingham Express Transit, South Yorkshire Supertram and Tyne and Wear Metro. Eurotunnel PLC investment figures, including plant and materials, are included in other rail infrastructure. Similarly, Eurotunnel investment in rolling stock is included in other rail rolling stock, although not for 2006/07. The figures for other rail rolling stock also include a tentative allowance for investment in privately owned wagons of £30 million per annum.

Central and local government expenditure on transport: 1.15

This table includes central and local government expenditure on transport and excludes, where possible, private expenditure. This differs from expenditure in Table 1.14 where we attempt to capture expenditure on infrastructure but by the private sector as well as government.

As the table shows local government expenditure on transport, the grants and other financial support provided to local government to fund this expenditure have been excluded from central government expenditure to avoid double counting.

The figures shown are compiled from various government departments. Central government expenditure in England data is compiled by the Department for Transport. Local government expenditure in England is compiled by Communities and Local Government (CLG). Expenditure in Wales comes from *Welsh Transport Statistics*, produced by the National Assembly for Wales. Expenditure in Scotland

comes from *Scottish Transport Statistics*, a Scottish Government publication.

Where possible the current/resource figures exclude the cost of capital; that is the income that would have been earned if the assets had been sold and invested. This makes a considerable difference to reported spend by organisations such as the Highways Agency. For example the cost of capital charge alone for 2007/08 was given as £2.833 million in the Highway Agency Annual Report. Capital expenditure includes expenditure paid by Central Government to Agencies whether or not the funding was spent in the year awarded.

Some private corporation, such as London and Continental Railways, have been reclassified as public corporations for the purposes of the National Accounts. In such cases the expenditure included in this table only includes those funds provided by Central Government and not the total expenditure of the organisation concerned.

Some revenue such as cark parking fees gained by local authorities has been included. However receipts from items such as duties on fuel and car licensing are excluded.

Transport related employment: 1.16-1.18

Details of transport-related employment by occupation are available from the Labour Force Survey (LFS). Data shown in Table 1.16 are from Q2 2008. The Labour Force Survey (LFS) moved to publishing calendar quarters in May 2006. The survey previously published seasonal quarters where March-May months covered the spring quarter, June-August was summer and so forth. This has now changed to calendar quarters as part of an EU requirement for all member states to have an LFS based on calendar quarters. LFS micro data is available for January-March (Q1), April-June (Q2), July-September (Q3) and October-December (Q4). An article on the impact and issues associated with the move to calendar quarters is available at the link: http://www.statistics.gov.uk/cci/article.asp?ID=1546

The LFS is a survey of households living at private addresses in Great Britain. In spite of its large sample size (55 thousand responding households), data for some cells in Table 1.16 are not shown because they fall below the 10 thousand LFS reliability threshold.

Table 1.16 includes people with both main and second jobs as an employee, the self-employed, those on Government employment and training programmes, and unpaid family workers. The industry totals include those working in the following industry classifications: transport via railways, other inland transport, water transport, air transport, supporting and auxiliary transport activities and the activities of travel agents, and exclude those whose occupation was not known.

By comparison, Table 6.22 relates to local bus services only, and incorporates revisions due to late returns.

The new Standard Occupational Classification (SOC2000) has been used instead of the previous 1990 classification for editions of *Transport Statistics Great Britain* from 2001 onwards. SOC2000 is not directly comparable with the 1990 classifications, and it is therefore not possible to make direct comparisons with earlier editions.

The Short Term Employment Surveys (STES) are the primary source for employee jobs estimates. (Tables 1.17 and 1.18) The estimates of short-term change are benchmarked to the Annual Business Inquiry (ABI/1) to maintain consistency with annual employment estimates. Prior to ABI2006 the reference period was December each year; for ABI2006 the reference period changed to September.

There is a discontinuity in the employee jobs series between December 2005 and September 2006 due to improvements to the annual benchmark. Further information can be found at:

http://www.statistics.gov.uk/CCI/article.asp?ID =1802&Pos=4&ColRank=1&Rank=224

In Table 1.18, part-time is defined as not more than normally 30 hours a week; figures are actual numbers working part-time, rather than full-time equivalents.

Consumer Prices Index: transport components: 1.19a

These indices are taken from the published *Consumer Prices Index*, rebased to 1997=100 for convenience. The bus fares index includes fare changes on local and non-local buses and coaches. The four letter code used by the Office for National Statistics to identify the series in their time series data and publications has been included.

The operation of personal transport equipment includes spare parts and accessories, fuels and lubricants, maintenance and repairs, and other services. The operation of personal transport equipment, the motor running costs index used in this Table, and the all motor index in Table 1.19b from the *Retail Prices Index* is that the latter includes the purchase of vehicle. There are some other exclusions such as car insurance and vehicle excise duty but these do not have a large effect on the *Consumer Prices Index* as the weights on these are relatively small.

The two purchase of vehicles indices also differ as the index from the *Retail Prices Index* uses the purchase price of second hand cars as a proxy for the price of new cars whereas the index from the *Consumer Prices Index* uses published prices for new cars. The latter also includes the purchase of motorcycles and bicycles but the weights on these are small.

Retail Prices Index: transport components: 1.19b

These indices are taken from the published *Retail Prices Index*, rebased to 1997=100 for convenience. The all motor index includes purchase of a vehicle, maintenance, petrol and oil, and tax and insurance. See also notes on Table 1.19a.

Gross Domestic Product and Retail Prices Index deflators: 1.20

Gross Domestic Product deflators (at market prices) are calculated by reference to column YBGB of Table A1 of the *Quarterly National Accounts*. Consumer and Retail Prices Index deflators have been calculated directly from the published 'All Items' *Consumer and Retail Prices Index*.

1.1 Passenger transport: by mode: 1952-2007

Billion passenger kilometres/percentage

Year	Buses and coaches		Cars, vans and taxis		Motor cycles		Pedal cycles		All road		Rail [1]		Air (UK)		All modes [2]	
1952	92	42	58	27	7	3	23	11	180	82	38	18	0.2	0.1	218	100
1953	93	41	64	29	7	3	21	9	185	83	39	17	0.2	0.1	225	100
1954	92	40	72	31	8	3	19	8	191	83	39	17	0.3	0.1	230	100
1955	91	38	83	35	8	3	18	8	200	84	38	16	0.3	0.1	239	100
1956	89	36	91	37	8	3	16	7	204	83	40	16	0.5	0.2	245	100
1957	84	34	92	38	9	4	16	7	201	83	42	17	0.5	0.2	244	100
1958	80	31	113	44	9	4	14	5	216	84	41	16	0.5	0.2	258	100
1959	81	30	126	46	11	4	14	5	232	85	41	15	0.6	0.2	273	100
1960	79	28	139	49	11	4	12	4	241	86	40	14	0.8	0.3	282	100
1961	76	26	157	53	11	4	11	4	255	86	39	13	1.0	0.3	295	100
1962	74	25	171	57	10	3	9	3	264	87	37	12	1.1	0.4	302	100
1963	73	23	185	59	8	3	8	3	274	88	36	12	1.3	0.4	312	100
1964	71	21	214	63	8	2	8	2	301	89	37	11	1.5	0.4	340	100
1965	67	19	231	66	7	2	7	2	312	89	35	10	1.7	0.5	349	100
1966	67	18	252	68	7	2	6	2	332	90	35	9	1.8	0.5	369	100
1967	66	17	267	70	6	2	6	2	345	91	34	9	1.9	0.5	381	100
1968	64	16	279	72	5	1	5	1	353	91	33	9	1.9	0.5	389	100
1969	63	16	286	72	5	1	5	1	359	91	35	9	1.9	0.5	395	100
1970	60	15	297	74	4	1	4	1	365	91	36	9	2.0	0.5	403	100
1971	60	14	313	75	4	1	4	1	381	91	35	9	2.0	0.5	419	100
1972	60	14	327	76	4	1	4	1	395	91	34	8	2.2	0.5	431	100
1973	61	14	345	76	4	1	4	1	414	92	35	8	2.4	0.5	452	100
1974	61	14	333	76	5	1	4	1	403	91	36	8	2.1	0.5	441	100
1975	60	14	331	76	6	1	4	1	401	92	36	8	2.1	0.5	438	100
1976	58	13	348	77	7	2	5	1	418	92	33	7	2.4	0.5	452	100
1977	58	13	354	77	7	1	6	1	425	92	34	7	2.2	0.5	461	100
1978	56	12	368	78	7	1	5	1	436	92	35	7	2.7	0.6	474	100
1979	56	12	365	77	7	2	5	1	433	92	35	7	3.0	0.6	471	100
1980	52	11	388	79	8	2	5	1	453	92	35	7	3.0	0.6	491	100
1981	48	10	394	80	10	2	5	1	458	93	34	7	2.8	0.6	495	100
1982	48	10	406	81	10	2	6	1	470	93	31	6	2.9	1.0	504	100
1983	48	9	411	80	9	2	6	1	474	93	34	7	3.0	1.0	511	100
1984	48	9	432	80	9	2	6	1	495	93	35	7	3.0	1.0	534	100
1985	49	9	441	81	8	1	6	1	504	93	36	7	3.6	0.7	544	100
1986	47	8	465	82	8	1	6	1	525	93	37	7	3.7	0.7	566	100
1987	47	8	500	83	7	1	6	1	560	93	39	6	4.0	0.7	603	100
1988	46	7	536	84	6	1	5	1	595	93	41	6	4.5	0.7	640	100
1989	47	7	581	85	6	1	5	1	639	94	39	6	4.9	0.7	683	100
1990	46	7	588	85	6	1	5	1	645	93	40	6	5.2	0.8	690	100
1991	44	6	582	86	6	1	5	1	637	94	39	6	4.8	0.7	681	100
1992	43	6	583	86	5	1	5	1	635	94	38	6	4.8	0.7	678	100
1993	44	6	584	86	4	1	4	1	636	94	37	5	5.1	0.8	677	100
1993	44	6	607	87	4	1	4	1	659	94	37	5	5.1	0.7	701	100
1994	44	6	614	87	4	1	4	1	666	94	35	5	5.5	0.8	706	100
1995	43	6	618	87	4	1	4	1	669	94	37	5	5.9	0.8	712	100
1996	43	6	622	87	4	1	4	1	674	94	39	5	6.3	0.9	719	100
1997	44	6	632	86	4	1	4	1	685	93	42	6	6.8	0.9	733	100
1998	45	6	636	86	4	1	4	1	689	93	44	6	7.0	1.0	740	100
1999	46	6	642	86	5	1	4	1	697	93	46	6	7.3	1.0	751	100
2000	47	6	640	85	5	1	4	1	695	93	47	6	7.6	1.0	749	100
2001	47	6	654	85	5	1	4	1	710	93	47	6	7.7	1.0	765	100
2002	47	6	677	86	5	1	4	1	733	93	48	6	8.5	1.1	790	100
2003	47	6	673	85	6	1	5	1	731	93	49	6	9.1	1.2	789	100
2004	48	6	678	85	6	1	4	0	736	92	50	6	9.8	1.2	796	100
2005	48	6	674	85	6	1	4	1	733	92	52	7	9.9	1.2	794	100
2006	50	6	686 P	85	6	1	5	1	746 P	92	55 R	7	9.9	1.2	811 P	100
2007	50	6	689 P	84	6	1	4	1	749	92	59	7	9.5	1.2	817	100

1 Financial years. National Rail, urban metros and modern trams.
2 Excluding travel by water.

NB: See Notes and Definitions in Sections 1 and 7
for details of discontinuity in road passenger
figures from 1993 and 1996 onwards.

Bus & coach: ☎020-7944 3076
Car, m/cycle & pedal cycle: ☎020-7944 3097
Rail: ☎020-7944 3076
Air: ☎020-7944 3088
The rail and air figures in this table
are outside the scope of National Statistics
Source - Rail - ORR; Air - CAA

1.2 Passenger journeys on public transport vehicles: 1950-2007/08

For greater detail of the years 1997/98-2007/08 see Table 6.2

Millions

| Year | All local services Bus, trolleybus, or tram | Street running public transport | | | | Rail systems [1] | | | Air [2] |
		Local bus service	Non-local bus or coach	Trolley buses	Trams	National rail network	London Under-ground	Light rail, other rail & metros	Passengers on domestic flights
1950	16,445	12,734	260	1,961	1,750	1,010	695	..	..
1951	16,340	12,985	282	1,876	1,479	1,030	702	..	..
1952	16,039	13,049	297	1,783	1,207	1,017	670	..	0.7
1953	15,765	13,026	318	1,726	1,013	1,015	672	..	0.8
1954	15,597	13,059	293	1,663	875	1,020	671	..	1.0
1955	15,592	13,225	337	1,598	769	994	676	..	1.2
1956	15,169	13,059	341	1,503	607	1,029	678	..	1.4
1957	14,404	12,491	332	1,437	476	1,101	666	..	1.6
1958	13,513	11,879	337	1,257	377	1,090	692	..	1.5
1959	13,592	12,152	345	1,193	247	1,069	669	..	1.7
1960	13,313	12,166	367	990	157	1,037	674	..	2.2
1961	13,019	12,159	384	756	104	1,025	675	..	2.8
1962	12,648	12,045	382	557	46	965	668	..	3.3
1963	12,352	11,860	381	476	16	938	673	26	3.7
1964	11,881	11,497	386	368	16	928	674	27	4.2
1965	11,239	10,938	413	286	15	865	657	24	4.7
1966	10,609	10,407	419	188	14	835	667	24	5.1
1967	10,166	10,047	450	106	13	837	661	23	5.3
1968	9,779	9,699	455	68	12	831	655	21	5.0
1969	9,365	9,303	458	50	12	806	676	20	5.2
1970	8,687	8,643	467	34	10	824	672	18	5.4
1971	8,153	8,128	486	15	10	816	654	17	5.4
1972	7,912	7,901	512	1	10	754	655	16	5.9
1973	7,877	7,866	577	.	11	728	644	16	6.5
1974	7,716	7,706	597	.	10	733	636	15	6.1
1975	7,533	7,524	635	.	9	730	601	15	5.8
1976	7,149	7,141	648	.	8	702	546	11	6.1
1977	6,864	6,856	641	.	8	702	545	5	5.5
1978	6,625	6,617	680	.	8	724	568	3 [3]	6.4
1979	6,472	6,463	628	.	9	748	594	3 [3]	7.2
1980	6,224	6,216	559	.	8	760	559	13	7.2
1981	5,694	5,688	584	.	6	719	541	28	6.6
1982	5,518	5,512	579	.	6 e	630	498	51	7.0
1983	5,587	5,581	622	.	6	694	563	62	7.0
1984	5,650	5,644	587	.	6	702	672	70	8.0
1985/86 [4]	5,819	5,813	537	.	6	686	732	72	8.6
1986/87	5,500	5,494	572	.	6 e	738	769	60	9.3
1987/88	5,439	5,434	592	.	5	798	798	59	10.3
1988/89	5,357	5,352	563	.	5	822	815	66	11.6
1989/90	5,214	5,208	594	.	6	812	765	69	12.6
1990/91	4,980	4,974	619	.	6	809	775	66	13.1
1991/92	4,790	4,785	..	.	5	792	751	63	12.0
1992/93	4,599	4,594	..	.	5	770	728	68	12.0
1993/94	4,500	4,494	..	.	6	740	735	72	12.4
1994/95	4,533	4,528	..	.	5	735	764	78	13.3
1995/96	4,494	4,489	..	.	5	761	784	82	14.3
1996/97	4,459	4,455	..	.	5	801	772	87	15.3
1997/98	4,434	4,430	..	.	5	846	832	93	16.2
1998/99	4,355	4,350	..	.	4	892	866	100	16.9
1999/00	4,380	4,376	..	.	4	931	927	109	17.4
2000/01	4,424	4,420	..	.	4	957	970	134	18.2
2001/02	4,460	4,455	..	.	5	960	953	141	18.5
2002/03	4,554	4,550	..	.	4	976	942	150	20.2
2003/04	4,684	4,681	..	.	4	1,012	948	156	21.0
2004/05	4,741	4,737	..	.	4	1,045	976	168	22.7
2005/06	4,795	4,791	..	.	4	1,082	970	173	23.3
2006/07 R	5,101	5,097	..	.	3	1,151	1,040	188	23.0
2007/08	5,167	5,164	..	.	3	1,232	1,096	198	22.3

1 Light rail and metros shown here are Glasgow Subway, Nexus (opened 1980), Docklands Light Railway (1987), Manchester Metrolink (1992), Stagecoach Supertram (1994), West Midlands Metro (1999) Croydon Tramlink (2000) and Nottingham NET (2004).

2 UK airlines, domestic passengers uplifted on scheduled and non-scheduled flights. Figures are for calendar years.

3 Glasgow Subway was closed for refurbishment in 1978 and 1979.

4 Local bus series revised from 1985/86. See Public Transport Statistics Bulletin: 2006 for more details

☎020-7944 3076
Some figures in this table are outside the scope of National Statistics
Source - bus, coach, tram and rail operators

1.3 Average distance travelled per person per year by mode of travel and average trip length: 1995/97-2006

								Miles/percentage
								Percentage change from 1995/1997
	1995/1997	1998/2000	2002	2003	2004	2005	2006	to 2006
By mode (miles per person per year):								
Walking (including short walks)[1]	200	198	198	201	203	197	201	-
Bicycle	43	40	36	37	39	36	39	-9
Private hire bus	106	111	124	135	132	122	94	-11
Car/van driver	3,623	3,725	3,661	3,660	3,674	3,682	3,660	1
Car/van passenger	2,082	2,086	2,115	2,098	2,032	2,063	2,033	-2
Motorcycle/moped	35	33	35	41	38	35	34	-1
Other private (including minibuses and motorcaravans, etc.) [2]	28	32	21	28	24	34	23	-17
Bus in London	43	44	56	60	59	67	63	49
Other local bus	225	218	224	230	219	212	233	3
Non-local bus [2]	94	100	59	87	70	75	63	-34
London Underground	60	65	81	68	68	67	75	25
Surface rail	321	401	413	384	433	461	466	45
Taxi/minicab	46	63	59	55	51	60	52	13
Other public (including air, ferries, light rail, etc.) [2]	75	46	55	108	61	97	96	28
All modes	6,981	7,164	7,135	7,192	7,103	7,208	7,133	2
Percentage of mileage accounted for by car (including van/lorry)	82	81	81	80	80	80	80	.
Average trip length (miles per trip)	6.4	6.7	6.8	7.0	6.9	6.9	6.9	7

1 Short walks believed to be under-recorded in 2002 and 2003 compared with earlier years.

2 These estimates have a large sampling error because of the small samples involved.

☎020-7944 3097
Source - National Travel Survey, DfT

1.4 Trips per person per year by main mode[1] and purpose: 2006

										Trips
	Walk	Bicycle	Car driver	Car passenger	Motor-cycle	Other private	Local bus	Surface rail/under ground	Other Public	All Modes
Commuting/business	21	6	118	18	2	1	13	13	3	195
Education/escort education	44	2	22	23	-	3	11	2	1	106
Shopping	55	2	91	45	-	1	19	2	2	219
Other escort	12	-	56	26	-	-	2	-	-	97
Personal business	26	1	44	24	-	1	6	1	1	105
Leisure	48	5	98	91	1	2	13	6	7	271
Other	44	-	1	-	-	-	-	-	-	45
All purposes	249	16	430	228	3	8	65	24	14	1,037

1 Main mode is that used for the longest part of the trip.

☎020-7944 3097

1.5 Trip distance per person per year by main mode[1] and purpose: 2006

Miles

	Walk	Bicycle	Car driver	Car passenger	Motor-cycle	Other private	Local bus	Surface rail/under ground	Other Public	All Modes
Commuting/business	16	16	1,420	189	16	19	68	273	56	2,073
Education/escort education	27	3	87	76	-	27	56	25	6	306
Shopping	32	3	471	293	3	4	76	32	11	926
Other escort	7	-	300	163	-	1	7	8	2	488
Personal business	15	2	269	143	1	6	25	24	4	488
Leisure	32	15	1,101	1,156	14	62	62	223	139	2,804
Other	41	-	6	1	-	-	-	-	-	48
All purposes	170	38	3,653	2,021	34	119	292	586	218	7,133

1 Main mode is that used for the longest part of the trip.

☎020-7944 3097

1.6 People entering central London during the morning peak:[1] 1997-2007

People (thousands)

	1997	1998	1999	2000	2001	2002	2003	2004	2005	2006	2007
Public transport:											
Surface rail	435	448	460	465	468	451	455	452	473	491	502
London Underground & Docklands Light Railway [2]	341	360	362	383	377	380	339	344	344	379	397
Bus	68	68	68	73	81	88	104	116	115	116	113
Coach/minibus [3]	20	17	15	15	10	10	10	9	9	8	9
All public transport	863	892	905	935	935	929	909	921	940	994	1,020
Personal transport:											
Private car	142	140	135	137	122	105	86	86	84	78	75
Motor cycle	11	13	15	17	16	15	16	16	16	15	15
Pedal cycle	10	10	12	12	12	12	12	14	17	18	19
Taxi	9	8	8	8	7	7	7	7	8	7	6
All personal transport [4]	172	171	169	173	157	139	120	122	125	118	116
All transport [4]	1,035	1,063	1,074	1,108	1,093	1,068	1,029	1,043	1,065	1,113	1,137

1 0700-1000 hours. Surveys are conducted in October/November.
2 Excludes passengers transferring from surface rail services. Passengers transferring from surface rail services have been deducted from the gross Underground counts. The estimates of transferring passengers for 2006 have been revised using results from London Underground passenger surveys.
3 Includes commuter and tourist coaches.
4 Excludes commercial vehicles. Taxi passengers, collected since 1996 but excluded from previously published figures, have been included.

☎020-7126 4610
The figures in this table are outside the scope of National Statistics
Source - Transport for London

1.7 Passenger casualty rates by mode: [1] 1997-2006

Per billion passenger kilometres

	1997	1998	1999	2000	2001	2002	2003	2004	2005	2006	1997-06 average
Air [2]											
Killed	0.00	0.00	0.00	0.00	0.00	0.00	0.00	0.00	0.00	0.00	0.00
KSI [3]	0.00	0.00	0.02	0.00	0.00	0.00	0.00	0.01	0.00	0.00	0.00
All [4]	0.03	0.07	0.18	0.04	0.00	0.00	0.00	0.01	0.00	0.00	0.03
Rail [5,6]											
Killed	0.5	0.4	0.9	0.3	0.3	0.4	0.2	0.2	0.1	0.1	0.3
Injured	19	16	19	14	13	13	13	13	12	10	14
Water [7]											
Killed	0.0	0.7	0.4	0.4	0.4	0.0	0.0	0.0	0.3	0.3	0.2
KSI	33	41	28	52	54	49	60	43	34	39	43
Bus or coach											
Killed	0.3	0.4	0.2	0.3	0.2	0.4	0.2	0.4	0.2	0.3	0.3
KSI	12	13	12	11	11	11	10	9	7	8	10
All	196	199	202	195	191	173	175	167	146	130	177
Car [8]											
Killed	2.9	2.8	2.7	2.7	2.8	2.7	2.7	2.6	2.6	2.5	2.7
KSI	38	35	33	32	31	29	27	25	23	22	29
All	347	342	333	335	323	304	291	282	275	260	308
Van [8]											
Killed	1.0	1.0	0.9	0.9	0.9	1.0	1.0	0.8	0.6	0.6	0.9
KSI	14	14	13	12	11	11	10	8	7	6	10
All	115	113	104	100	102	96	92	76	72	68	92
Motorcycles [8]											
Killed	119	112	113	122	112	111	120	104	98	107	111
KSI	1,507	1,452	1,423	1,493	1,405	1,367	1,328	1,184	1,116	1,155	1,332
All	5,724	5,546	5,395	5,712	5,539	5,168	4,931	4,566	4,257	4,156	5,053
Pedal cycle											
Killed	45	40	42	31	33	29	26	32	33	31	34
KSI	880	838	779	666	632	555	543	550	533	527	646
All	6,036	5,798	5,599	4,953	4,512	3,874	3,838	3,964	3,739	3,494	4,546
Pedestrian											
Killed	57	50	50	49	47	42	41	35	36	36	44
KSI	651	580	564	543	521	471	424	394	384	371	487
All	2,693	2,484	2,464	2,404	2,332	2,117	1,944	1,836	1,794	1,631	2,158

1 Figures have been revised from those published in previous years,
   see Notes and Definitions for more details.
2 Passenger casualties in accidents involving UK registered airline aircraft
   in UK and foreign airspace.
3 KSI =Killed or seriously injured
4 All = Killed, seriously and slightly injured
5 Financial years up to 1999. From 2000 figures figures are based on calender year basis.
6 Passenger casualties involved in train accidents and accidents occuring through movement of railway vehicles.
   Reporting regulations changed on 1 April 1996. Since then figures are only available for passenger fatalities and injuries.
   The reporting trigger for an injury is the passenger being taken to hospital directly from the scene.
7 Passenger casualties on UK registered merchant vessels.
8 Driver and passenger casualties.

The figures for Air, Rail and Water modes
are outside the scope of National Statistics
☎ 020-7944 6595

1.8 Main mode of transport to work and mean time taken by Government Office Region and country of workplace

a) October to December 2007[1] Percentage/thousands

Area of workplace	Car, van, minibus	Motor-cycle	Bicycle	Bus, coach	Rail _ow:_ National Rail	Rail _ow:_ Other rail[2]	Rail All Rail	Walk	Number in employment[3]
North East	74	*	1	9	*	1	2	13	1,001
Tyne and Wear	70	*	*	13	*	3	4	11	471
Rest of North East	78	*	*	5	*	*	*	15	530
North West	74	1	3	8	3	-	3	11	2,744
Greater Manchester	72	*	2	10	3	*	4	10	1,050
Merseyside	70	*	*	11	6	*	6	10	459
Rest of North West	77	*	3	5	1	*	1	13	1,235
Yorkshire and the Humber	74	1	3	8	2	1	3	11	2,112
South Yorkshire	73	*	*	9	*	2	4	12	499
West Yorkshire	73	*	1	10	4	*	4	10	908
Rest of Yorks and the Humber	74	*	5	5	2	*	2	13	705
East Midlands	76	1	3	7	1	*	1	11	1,748
West Midlands	77	1	2	8	2	*	3	9	2,169
Metropolitan County	72	*	2	12	4	*	4	8	1,065
Rest of West Midlands	81	1	2	4	*	*	*	10	1,104
East of England	78	1	4	4	2	*	3	11	2,234
London	36	1	3	12	20	18	38	8	3,408
Central London	10	1	3	11	39	30	69	5	1,225
Rest of inner London	30	2	5	15	15	20	35	11	893
Outer London	64	1	2	12	6	5	11	10	1,291
South East	75	1	4	5	3	*	3	11	3,427
South West	76	1	3	5	1	*	2	12	2,212
England	69	1	3	7	5	3	8	11	21,055
Wales	80	*	2	5	2	*	2	10	1,136
Scotland	70	-	2	11	4	-	4	11	2,185
Strathclyde	69	*	2	11	7	*	8	10	897
Rest of Scotland	70	*	2	12	2	*	2	12	1,288
Great Britain	70	1	3	8	5	3	8	11	24,376

b) Great Britain: Autumn 1997 - October to December 2007[1] Percentage/minutes

	Car, van, minibus	Motor-cycle	Bicycle	Bus, coach	Rail _ow:_ National Rail	Rail _ow:_ Other rail[2]	Rail All Rail	Walk	Mean time (minutes)
Autumn 1997	71	1	4	8	3	2	6	11	24.4
Autumn 1998	71	1	3	8	4	2	6	11	24.6
Autumn 1999	70	1	3	8	4	2	6	11	24.9
Autumn 2000	70	1	3	8	4	2	6	11	25.3
Autumn 2001	70	1	3	8	4	3	7	11	25.4
Autumn 2002	71	1	3	8	4	2	6	11	25.4
Autumn 2003	71	1	3	8	4	2	6	10	25.5
Autumn 2004	71	1	3	8	4	2	6	11	25.9
Autumn 2005	71	1	3	8	4	2	7	11	25.9
October to December 2006	70	1	3	8	4	3	7	11	26.3
October to December 2007	70	1	3	8	5	3	8	11	24.3

1 The Labour Force Survey (LFS) moved to publishing calendar quarters in May 2006. The survey previously published seasonal quarters where March-May months covered the spring quarter, June-August was summer and so forth. This has now changed to calendar quarters as part of an EU requirement for all member states to have an LFS based on calendar quarters. LFS micro data is available for January-March (Q1), April-June (Q2), July-September (Q3) and October-December (Q4). An article on the impact and issues associated with the move to calendar quarters is available at the link: http://www.statistics.gov.uk/cci/article.asp?ID=1546
2 Includes light railway systems and trams.
3 Employment figures reflect only those people using the transport modes detailed, not all employed. This results in potential variations from previous years.

☎020-7944 4139
Labour Force Survey Helpline: ☎01633 455 732
Source - Labour Force Survey, ONS

1.9 Time taken to travel to work by Government Office Region of workplace: October to December 2007 [1]

Area of workplace	cumulative percentage				Mean time (minutes)
	<20 minutes	<40 minutes	<60 minutes	<90 minutes	
North East	51	87	95	99	21
Tyne and Wear	44	82	92	98	24
Rest of North East	57	92	97	99	19
North West	45	81	92	98	24
Greater Manchester	39	76	87	97	28
Merseyside	40	79	92	98	25
Rest of North West	53	87	95	99	20
Yorkshire and the Humber	44	80	91	98	25
South Yorkshire	39	79	91	98	25
West Yorkshire	41	77	90	97	27
Rest of Yorks and the Humber	50	84	92	98	23
East Midlands	48	84	94	98	22
West Midlands	44	80	91	98	25
Metropolitan County	37	75	90	97	27
Rest of West Midlands	51	85	93	98	23
East of England	48	83	92	97	24
London	17	46	66	89	44
Central London	4	26	51	83	56
Rest of inner London	19	46	67	90	43
Outer London	29	68	83	94	33
South East	46	80	90	97	25
South West	50	84	93	98	23
England	42	76	88	96	27
Wales	50	85	94	99	22
Scotland	45	80	91	97	25
Strathclyde	43	79	91	98	26
Rest of Scotland	46	80	91	97	25
Great Britain	42	77	88	96	27

1 The Labour Force Survey (LFS) moved to publishing calendar quarters in May 2006. The survey previously published seasonal quarters where March-May months covered the spring quarter, June-August was summer and so forth. This has now changed to calendar quarters as part of an EU requirement for all member states to have an LFS based on calendar quarters. LFS micro data is available for January-March (Q1), April-June (Q2), July-September (Q3) and October-December (Q4). An article on the impact and issues associated with the move to calendar quarters is available at the link: http://www.statistics.gov.uk/cci/article.asp?ID=1546

☎020 7944 4139
Labour Force Survey Helpline: ☎01633 455 732
Source - Labour Force Survey, ONS

1.10 Overseas travel: visits to and from the United Kingdom: 1997-2007

Thousands

| | | Visits to the United Kingdom [1] | | | | | | Visits abroad by United Kingdom residents [2] | | | | | |
| | | Sea/Channel Tunnel | | | | | | | Sea/Channel Tunnel | | | | |
Year	Air	With car [3]	With coach	Other [4]	Irish sea	Total Sea/ Channel Tunnel	Air	With car [3]	With coach	Other [4]	Irish sea	Total Sea/ Channel Tunnel
1997	16,858	2,504	2,198	3,297	657	8,656	30,341	7,913	2,831	2,948	1,926	15,617
1998	17,479	2,324	2,047	3,207	688	8,266	34,283	8,575	2,751	3,202	2,061	16,589
1999 [5]	17,284	2,509	1,571	4,030	.	8,110	37,510	9,309	2,857	4,205	.	16,371
2000	17,831	1,902	1,411	4,065	.	7,378	41,392	8,453	2,627	4,364	.	15,445
2001	16,054	1,670	1,415	3,697	.	6,782	43,011	8,213	2,589	4,467	.	15,269
2002	17,098	1,901	1,336	3,845	.	7,082	43,990	7,999	3,049	4,339	.	15,387
2003	17,635	1,821	1,561	3,699	.	7,080	47,101	7,860	2,068	4,395	.	14,323
2004	20,002	1,967	1,720	4,067	.	7,753	50,435	7,125	2,290	4,344	.	13,759
2005	22,043	2,017	1,801	4,109	.	7,927	53,626	6,457	2,224	4,135	.	12,815
2006	24,588	2,039	1,735	4,351	.	8,125	56,460	5,958	2,744	4,375	.	13,076
2007	25,089	2,053	1,503	4,133	.	7,689	56,329	6,506	2,246	4,370	.	13,121

1 Mode shown is that for departure from the United Kingdom.
2 Mode shown is that for return to the United Kingdom.
3 Includes motorcycles and scooters.
4 "Other" includes foot passengers, passengers with lorries and passengers with unknown vehicle type.
5 Prior to 1999, data for Irish Sea crossings were supplied separately by Irish Central Statistical Office.
  Since 1999, Irish Sea traffic is included in the IPS

☎020-7944 3088
Source - International Passenger Survey, ONS

1.11 Overseas travel by air:[1] visits to and from the UK: by area and purpose: 2007

(a) Visits to the United Kingdom: overseas residents by area of residence

Thousands

	North America	European Union [2]	Other Europe	Other areas	All areas
Business visit	921	4,214	558	817	6,510
Holiday - Independent [3]	1,183	3,782	498	1,160	6,623
Holiday - Inclusive tour [4]	156	580	81	173	990
Visiting friends and relatives	1,202	5,046	491	1,468	8,208
Miscellaneous	520	1,505	289	444	2,758
Total	3,981	15,127	1,917	4,063	25,089

(b) Visits abroad by United Kingdom residents: by area visited

Thousands

	North America	European Union [2]	Other Europe	Other areas	All areas
Business visit	868	5,008	682	985	7,543
Holiday - Independent [3]	1,823	15,814	1,243	2,437	21,318
Holiday - Inclusive tour [4]	842	10,858	1,206	2,654	15,559
Visiting friends and relatives	924	6,131	627	2,720	10,402
Miscellaneous	112	972	62	361	1,508
Total	4,569	38,783	3,820	9,157	56,329

1 Excludes passengers changing planes at UK airports.
2 "European Union" consists of 27 member states.
3 Not on a package holiday.
4 Excludes fly-cruise package holidays, which are included under 'other areas' in Table 1.12.

☎020-7944 3088
Source - International Passenger Survey, ONS

1.12 Overseas travel by sea and Channel Tunnel: visits to and from the United Kingdom by area, purpose and type of vehicle on board: 2007

Thousands

	(a) Visits to the United Kingdom by overseas residents: by area of residence				(b) Visits abroad by United Kingdom residents: by country visited			
	European Union [1]	Other Europe	Other areas	All areas	European Union [1]	Other Europe	Other areas	All areas
Business visit								
Without vehicle	440	7	58	506	633	3	2	639
Vehicle type:								
Car	215	1	3	219	348	3	0	351
Coach	116	2	4	121	124	2	0	127
Lorry	1,446	30	3	1,479	340	15	2	357
Motorcycle	7	0	0	7	0	0	0	0
Unknown	2	0	0	2	2	0	0	2
All	2,227	40	68	2,335	1,448	23	5	1,475
Holiday - Independent [2]								
Without vehicle	538	33	261	832	1,318	28	10	1,356
Vehicle type:								
Car	680	12	52	744	3,393	66	3	3,462
Coach	270	1	26	297	509	1	0	510
Lorry	6	0	0	6	3	0	0	3
Motorcycle	21	2	1	23	98	2	0	100
Unknown	5	1	0	6	11	0	1	12
All	1,521	49	340	1,909	5,332	97	14	5,443
Holiday Inclusive tour [3]								
Without vehicle	144	3	171	318	567	12	507	1,087
Vehicle type:								
Car	64	0	0	64	737	4	0	741
Coach	792	4	49	845	1,248	30	1	1,279
Lorry	0	0	0	0	0	0	0	0
Motorcycle	1	1	4	6	6	0	0	6
Unknown	3	0	0	3	4	0	-	4
All	1,004	7	224	1,235	2,562	47	508	3,117
Visiting friends and relatives								
Without vehicle	485	5	113	604	684	1	3	688
Vehicle type:								
Car	702	24	34	759	936	13	8	956
Coach	123	6	14	143	158	0	0	158
Lorry	-	0	0	-	0	0	0	0
Motorcycle	2	0	0	2	10	0	0	10
Unknown	5	0	0	5	2	0	0	2
All	1,317	34	161	1,512	1,789	13	10	1,813
Miscellaneous								
Without vehicle	241	11	47	299	217	0	0	217
Vehicle type:								
Car	212	5	5	222	871	2	0	873
Coach	94	0	2	96	173	0	0	173
Lorry	68	0	0	68	3	0	0	3
Motorcycle	7	0	0	7	7	0	0	7
Unknown	6	0	0	6	0	0	0	0
All	628	16	54	698	1,271	2	0	1,273
Total								
Without vehicle	1,849	59	650	2,558	3,420	44	522	3,987
Vehicle type:								
Car	1,873	41	94	2,008	6,285	87	11	6,383
Coach	1,396	12	95	1,503	2,212	33	1	2,246
Lorry	1,520	30	3	1,553	347	15	2	364
Motorcycle	38	3	5	45	121	2	0	123
Unknown	21	1	0	22	18	0	1	19
All	6,696	147	847	7,689	12,403	182	537	13,121

1 "European Union" consists of 27 member states.
2 Not on a package holiday.
3 Including UK residents on cruise and fly-cruise holidays under 'other areas'.

☎020-7944 3088
Source - International Passenger Survey, ONS

1.13 Household expenditure on transport: United Kingdom: 1997/98-2006

£ Per week/percentage

Transport (COICOP categories) [1]	1997/98	1998/99	1999/00	2000/01	2001/02	2002/03	2003/04	2004/05	2005/06	2006
(a) Motoring and bicycle costs										
Purchase of vehicles	20.20	23.90	23.00	23.20	25.80	26.60	28.10	25.10	23.90	23.40
New cars and vans	5.80	7.40	7.90	10.60	10.70	11.30	11.40	10.10	9.60	8.30
Second-hand cars and vans	13.40	15.90	14.30	11.80	14.40	14.50	16.00	14.10	14.00	14.50
Motorcycles and scooters	0.60	0.40	0.50	0.60	0.50	0.70	0.60	0.50	..	0.30
Other vehicles (mainly bicycles)	..	..	..	..	0.20	0.20	0.20	0.30	0.20	0.30
Bicycle purchase	0.40	0.20	0.30	0.20	..	..	..	..	..	..
Spares, accessories, repairs and servicing	6.30	6.40	6.40	6.40	7.00	7.30	6.90	7.80	8.00	8.00
Car or van	5.90	6.10	6.20	6.00	6.80	6.90	6.60	7.50	7.70	7.70
Motorcycle	0.20	0.10	0.10	0.20	0.10	0.20	0.20	0.10	0.20	0.20
Bicycle	0.20	0.20	0.20	0.10	0.10	0.20	0.10	0.10	0.20	0.20
Petrol, diesel and other motor oils:	12.60	13.00	14.40	15.80	14.80	14.80	15.00	16.20	17.50	18.20
Petrol	11.30	11.50	12.80	14.00	12.70	12.70	12.40	13.40	14.30	14.50
Diesel	1.20	1.30	1.40	1.80	2.00	2.10	2.50	2.80	3.10	3.70
Other motor oils	0.10	0.10	0.10	0.10	0.10	0.10	0.10	0.10	0.10	0.10
Other motoring costs	1.80	1.90	1.90	1.80	1.80	1.90	1.90	2.40	2.30	2.40
All motoring and bicycle costs	40.90	45.20	45.70	47.20	49.40	50.70	51.90	51.40	51.80	52.10
(b) Transport services										
Rail and tube fares:	1.40	1.90	1.80	2.00	1.90	1.80	1.90	2.00	2.10	2.20
Season tickets	0.40	0.70	0.60	0.60	0.60	0.60	0.70	0.70	0.70	0.80
Other tickets	1.00	1.20	1.20	1.40	1.30	1.20	1.20	1.30	1.40	1.40
Bus and coach fares:	1.30	1.30	1.40	1.40	1.50	1.40	1.40	1.50	1.50	1.30
Season tickets	0.30	0.30	0.30	0.30	0.30	0.40	0.40	0.40	0.40	0.40
Other tickets	1.10	1.10	1.10	1.10	1.10	1.10	1.10	1.10	1.10	0.90
Combined tickets	0.60	0.70	0.90	0.90	1.00	0.80	0.70	0.80	1.00	1.00
Season tickets	0.40	0.60	0.70	0.70	0.80	0.60	0.50	0.60	0.80	0.80
Other tickets	0.10	0.10	0.20	0.20	0.20	0.20	0.10	0.20	0.20	0.20
Air and other travel and transport:	3.80	3.70	4.00	4.30	4.10	4.50	4.80	3.80	5.40	5.50
Air fares [2]	1.30	1.00	1.00	1.30	1.20	1.50	1.90	1.00	2.50	2.20
Other transport and travel	2.60	2.70	3.00	3.00	2.90	3.00	2.80	2.90	2.90	3.30
All transport services	7.10	7.60	8.10	8.60	8.40	8.50	8.80	8.10	9.90	10.00
All transport (excluding motor vehicle insurance and taxation and boat purchase and repairs)	48.00	52.70	53.80	55.90	57.80	59.20	60.70	59.60	61.70	62.00
All household expenditure	328.80	352.20	359.40	385.70	398.30	406.20	418.10	434.40	443.40	455.90
Percentage of household expenditure on transport	*14.6*	*15.0*	*15.0*	*14.5*	*14.5*	*14.6*	*14.5*	*13.7*	*13.9*	*13.6*
Key transport expenditure totals:										
Motoring costs	46.60	51.80	52.60	55.10	58.50	61.70	62.40	62.60	63.80	62.40
Fares and other travel costs	8.10	8.30	9.20	9.50	9.50	9.70	9.60	9.50	11.10	11.10
All transport and travel	54.80	60.00	61.70	64.50	68.00	71.40	72.00	72.10	74.90	73.50
Adjusted for general inflation: 2006 prices										
Motoring costs [3]	57.50	61.00	61.00	62.10	64.30	67.10	66.00	64.30	63.80	62.40
Fares and other travel costs	10.50	9.80	10.60	10.70	10.40	10.60	10.20	9.70	11.10	11.10
All transport and travel	68.00	70.80	71.60	72.80	74.60	77.70	76.20	74.00	74.90	73.50

1 Data for 1996/97-2000/01 are based on old FES categories which
  some items excluded under COICOP, eg motor caravans
  audio equipment, helmets (See Notes and Definitions).
2 Excludes air fare component of package holidays abroad.
3 Includes expenditure on motorcycles, bicycles, boats and
  vehicle taxation and insurance (see Notes and Definitions).

☎ 020 7944 3097
Source - Expenditure and Food Survey, ONS

For further details see *Family
Spending: A Report
on the 2005/2006 Expenditure
and Food Survey*
Available at: www.statistics.gov.uk

1.14 Investment in transport: [1] 1996/97-2006/07

£ Million (outturn prices)

	1996/97	1997/98	1998/99	1999/00	2000/01	2001/02	2002/03	2003/04	2004/05	2005/06	2006/07
Road infrastructure											
Public [2]	3,583	3,267	2,957	3,071	3,344	3,643	3,955	3,621	4,079	4,313	4,756
Private	375	251	278	63	47	45	..	..	..	..	..
Total	3,958	3,518	3,235	3,134	3,391	3,688	3,955	3,621	4,079	4,313	4,756
Road vehicles [3]											
Cars and motor cycles: household	13,300	16,100	15,800	15,100	15,400	17,400	18,300	19,800	19,000	18,400	18,200
Cars and motor cycles: other	15,700	17,900	18,600	18,900	17,600	18,900	19,500	20,500	21,800	23,600	23,000
Cars and motor cycles: total	29,100	34,000	34,400	34,000	33,000	36,300	37,800	40,300	40,800	42,000	41,200
Other vehicles	6,200	6,900	7,100	7,300	7,400	7,800	7,500	8,400	9,100	9,600	9,500
Total	35,300	40,900	41,600	41,300	40,400	44,100	45,400	48,700	49,900	50,600	50,700
Rail infrastructure [4]											
National Rail	1,178	1,430	1,823	2,012	2,404	3,148	3,756	4,722	3,543	3,237	3,766
Other rail [5]	1,047	898	821	1,163	386	504	485	464	729	1,219	1,265
Total	2,225	2,328	2,644	3,175	2,790	3,652	4,241	5,186	4,272	4,456	5,031
Rail rolling stock [4]											
National Rail	47	114	176	236	554	922	566	774	897	557	326
Other rail	148	82	85	84	75	75	75	177	165	169	123
Total	195	196	261	320	629	997	641	951	1,064	726	449
Ports infrastructure [4]	150	200	240	250	205	233	236	310	202	230	..
Airports											
Public [4, 6]	171	216	140	161	163	57	71	70	62	116	..
Private [4]	463	565	542	511	566	630	784	1,373	1,434	1,662	..
Total	634	781	682	673	729	687	854	1,443	1,495	1,779	..

1 Some revisions have been made to the data since last year
2 Investment in road infrastructure includes all 'patching' but excludes local authority capital expenditure on car parks. Since 2002/03 it has not been possible to separately identify all the private expenditure from the total.
3 Source: Office for National Statistics
4 Partly based on figures for calendar years.
5 Figures for Eurotunnel unavailable for 2006/07
6 Prior to 2001/02 public airports investment includes air traffic control.

☎020-7944 3088
The figures in this table are outside the scope of National Statistics
Source - see Notes and Definitions

1.15   Central and local government expenditure on transport:[1] 2003/04-2007/08

	2003/04	2004/05	2005/06	2006/07	£ million (outturn prices) 2007/08 [2]
England	**11,011**	**10,855**	**12,138**	**13,108**	**12,705**
Central government expenditure [3, 4]	**4,025**	**3,277**	**3,837**	**4,315**	**2,784**
Capital	**1,951**	**2,122**	**2,497**	**2,832**	**1,269**
Strategic roads [5]	439	610	753	1,116	1,060
London Underground [6]	615	838	1,143	1,242	..
Channel Tunnel Rail Link [7]	897	674	601	474	209
Current / resource	**2,074**	**1,155**	**1,340**	**1,483**	**1,515**
Strategic roads [5]	1,200	1,146	1,284	1,347	1,367
London Underground [6]	867	0	0	0	0
Channel Tunnel Rail Link [7]	7	6	44	44	148
Crossrail	0	3	12	92	..
Local government expenditure	**6,986**	**7,578**	**8,301**	**8,793**	**9,921**
Capital	**2,552**	**2,904**	**3,461**	**3,480**	**4,321**
Roads	1,919	2,107	2,242	2,213	..
Car Parks	77	105	106	67	..
Public transport	547	682	1,103	1,186	..
Ports	7	4	5	10	..
Airport companies	2	7	4	4	..
Current / resource	**4,434**	**4,674**	**4,840**	**5,313**	**5,600**
Roads	2,212	2,336	2,569	2,619	..
Car Parks	-439	-456	-490	-484	..
Revenue support to public transport	2,151	2,254	2,229	2,395	..
Concessionary fares [8]	510	539	532	783	..
Scotland	**1,482**	**1,627**	**2,175**	**2,500**	**2,758**
Central government expenditure [3,4]	**773**	**857**	**1,306**	**1,620**	**1,770**
Capital - Strategic roads	**73**	**70**	**95**	**146**	**132**
Current - Strategic roads	**226**	**255**	**218**	**260**	**261**
Subsidies to rail services in Scotland [9]	188	180	542	649	679
Subsidies to other transport industries	286	352	451	565	698
Local government expenditure	**709**	**770**	**869**	**880**	**988**
Capital	**222**	**271**	**334**	**448**	**514**
Roads	138	178	243	299	..
Public transport	84	93	91	149	..
Current / resource	**487**	**499**	**535**	**432**	**474**
Roads	348	352	380	373	403
Car Parks	-24	-24	-25	-24	-28
Revenue support to public transport	72	81	85	72	91
Concessionary fares [8]	91	90	95	10	8
Wales	**500**	**549**	**619**	**819**	**869**
Central government expenditure [3]	**156**	**177**	**166**	**346**	**382**
Capital - strategic roads	**89**	**98**	**90**	**113**	**128**
Current / resource - strategic roads	**67**	**79**	**76**	**80**	**75**
Current / resource - rail [10]	..	..	..	154	179
Local government expenditure	**344**	**372**	**452**	**473**	**486**
Capital	**120**	**135**	**200**	**210**	**186**
Roads	98	111	164	181	..
Car Parks	5	3	7	9	..
Public transport	17	20	29	20	..
Current / resource	**224**	**237**	**253**	**264**	**300**
Roads	170	178	186	192	205
Car Parks	-8	-9	-9	-9	-9
Revenue support to public transport	25	27	28	29	..
Concessionary fares	37	41	48	52	..

1.15   (continued) Central and local government expenditure on transport:[1] 2003/04-2007/08

	2003/04	2004/05	2005/06	2006/07	£ million (outturn prices) 2007/08 [2]
Great Britain [11]	**16,683**	**17,054**	**18,697**	**21,714**	**21,476**
Central government expenditure [3]	**8,644**	**8,334**	**9,075**	**11,567**	**10,081**
Capital	**4,472**	**4,554**	**4,763**	**6,307**	**4,834**
Allocated to individual countries	**2,113**	**2,290**	**2,682**	**3,091**	**1,529**
Strategic roads[5]	601	778	938	1,375	1,320
London Underground	615	838	1,143	1,242	..
Channel Tunnel Rail Link [7]	897	674	601	474	209
Not allocated to individual countries	**2,359**	**2,264**	**2,080**	**3,216**	**3,305**
Rail [12]	2,262	2,182	2,005	3,128	3,238
Other roads and traffic	53	44	34	44	23
Other expenditure	44	38	42	44	45
Current / resource	**4,172**	**3,780**	**4,312**	**5,261**	**5,247**
Allocated to individual countries	**2,841**	**2,021**	**2,627**	**3,190**	**3,408**
Strategic roads[5]	1,493	1,480	1,578	1,687	1,704
Subsidies in England	875	9	56	136	148
Subsidies in Scotland	474	532	993	1,214	1,377
Subsidies in Wales	..	..	..	154	179
Not allocated to individual countries	**1,331**	**1,759**	**1,686**	**2,070**	**1,839**
Bus fuel duty rebates [13]	343	363	376	371	414
Rail [14]	610	905	714	1,039	707
Other roads and traffic	160	123	158	184	176
Air and water transport	52	40	51	59	67
Other expenditure	167	329	386	418	475
Local government expenditure	**8,039**	**8,720**	**9,622**	**10,146**	**11,395**
Capital	**2,895**	**3,310**	**3,995**	**4,138**	**5,021**
Roads	2,156	2,396	2,649	2,693	..
Car Parks	82	108	113	75	..
Public transport	648	795	1,223	1,355	..
Ports	7	4	5	10	..
Airport companies	2	7	4	4	..
Current / resource	**5,144**	**5,410**	**5,628**	**6,008**	**6,374**
Roads	2,729	2,867	3,135	3,185	..
Car Parks	-471	-489	-523	-517	..
Revenue support to public transport	2,248	2,362	2,342	2,496	..
Concessionary fares [8]	638	670	674	845	..

1   Some revisions have been made to the figures since last year. See also notes.
2   Includes provisional estimates.
3   Figures exclude grants to local authorities.
4   Net expenditure includes EU grants treated as receipts.
5   In England, funding to Highways Agency, excluding the cost of capital.
6   Capital is mainly grants and current is mainly funding for the Jubilee Line Extension.
7   This item comprises the Government Spend on the channel tunnel rail link, including money paid to London and Continental Railways (LCR). It does not include all LCR spend.
8   From 1 April 2006 residents in England who were 60 or over and eligible disabled people were guaranteed free off-peak local bus travel within the local authority in which they lived accounting for the increase in England. As of 1 April 2006, Transport Scotland assumed responsibility for Concessionary fares, accounting for the large decrease in 2006-07 provisional outturn concessionary fares figures for Local Authorities in Scotland.
9   These figures includes grants paid to Strathclyde Passenger Transport and from 2006/07 funding for Network Rail in Scotland.
10   Includes Grants to Passenger Transport Executives from 2006/07.
11   Great Britain total expenditure is not the sum of total expenditure for England, Scotland and Wales since it includes expenditure not allocated to individual countries.
12   Rail figures include direct grants to Network Rail for Great Britain to 2005/06 and England and Wales from 2006/07. Figures include a grant payment of £300 million to Network Rail in 2002/03 to facilitate the purchase of Railtrack and £700 million in 2003/04 paid directly to train operating companies that was subsequently deemed to be capital investment undertaken by Network Rail.
13   Mainly the Bus Service Operators Grant.
14   Net direct support for Passenger Rail Services and Grants to Passenger Transport Executives, Great Britain to 2005/06, England thereafter.

☎020-7944 4442
The figures in this table are outside the scope of National Statistics
Source - DfT; CLG; Scottish Government; Welsh Assembly Government; HM Treasury

1.16 People in employment in transport related occupations:[1] April to June 2008

Thousands

SOC2000[2] code	Occupation	Transport industries[3]	Other industries	All industries
1161	Transport and distribution managers	37	43	80
4134	Transport and distribution clerks	36	30	66
1232	Garage managers and proprietors	*	39	39
1226, 6212, 6219	Travel agencies and service occupations	45	49	94
3511, 3512, 8218	Air traffic controllers, pilots, operatives, etc	33	10	43
3513, 8217, 9141	Ship officers, seafarers, stevadores, dockers, etc	15	15	29
6213	Travel and tour guides	*	*	15
6214	Air travel assistants	32	*	32
6215, 8216, 3514	Rail travel assistants, operatives and train drivers	16	*	17
8213	Bus and coach drivers	116	14	130
8211	Heavy goods vehicle drivers	172	140	312
8212	Van drivers	24	189	213
8214	Taxi, cab drivers and chauffeurs	164	32	196
5231, 5233	Motor mechanics, auto engineers and electricians	20	187	207
5232, 5234	Vehicle body builders, painters and repairers	*	43	46
8135	Tyre, exhaust and windscreen fitters	*	16	16
8215	Driving instructors	*	37	39
8219	Other transport operatives	*	14	23
	Transport related occupations	731	864	1,595
	All in employment	1,337[4]	27,300	29,314

1 The Labour Force Survey (LFS) moved to publishing calendar quarters
   in May 2006. The survey previously published seasonal quarters
   where March-May months covered the spring quarter, June-August
   was summer and so forth. This will now change to calendar quarters
   as part of an EU requirement for all member states to have an LFS based on calendar quarters.
   LFS micro data will be available for January-March (Q1), April-June (Q2), July-September (Q3)
   and October-December (Q4). An article on the impact and issues associated with the move to calendar quarters
   is available at the link: http://www.statistics.gov.uk/cci/article.asp?ID=1546
2 Standard Occupation Classification 2000, see Notes and Definitions.
3 Based on 1992 Standard Industrial Classification (SIC92)
   Transport, storage and communication:
   60.1 Transport via Railway
   60.2 Other inland transport
   61   Water Transport
   62   Air transport
   63   Supporting and auxiliary transport activities; activities of travel agencies.
4 Includes non transport related occupations in transport industries

☎020 7944 4139
Labour Force Survey Helpline ☎01633 455 732
Source - Labour Force Survey, ONS

Transport Statistics Great Britain 2008

1.17 Employee jobs in transport and related industries:[1] March 1997-2008

Thousands

SIC 1992 code	Industry	1997	1998	1999	2000	2001	2002	2003	2004	2005	2006	2007	2008
60.1	Railways [2]	55	46	49	50	49	50	48	50	54	52	52	52
60.2, 60.3	Other land transport	435	443	459	455	454	460	450	458	464	477	474	488
61	Water transport	23	20	18	17	15	16	16	15	19	18	15	15
62	Air transport	68	78	85	93	90	85	88	90	85	89	88	90
63.1, 63.2, 63.4	Cargo handling, storage and other supporting activities	230	234	226	245	260	263	279	291	324	330	328	330
63.3	Travel agencies and tour operators	97	97	110	116	129	122	126	128	121	106	104	105
Total: transport industries[3]		908	918	947	975	997	996	1,008	1,032	1,066	1,073	1,061	1,080
Manufacture of transport equipment:													
34	Motor vehicles, trailers	229	236	227	221	212	206	201	196	187	172	159	158
35	Other transport equipment	148	154	162	167	171	159	150	141	140	138	140	158
50.1, 50.3-50.5	Retail distribution and filling stations	413	407	411	390	384	391	386	377	377	379	379	378
50.2	Maintenance and repair of motor vehicles	170	150	155	164	161	171	165	168	167	171	170	169
Total: transport related industries[3]		961	947	955	942	928	926	902	882	871	860	848	848
All transport and related industries and services[3]		1,869	1,864	1,902	1,918	1,925	1,922	1,909	1,914	1,937	1,933	1,909	1,928

1 The data in this table differ from those previously published. This is due to benchmarking the Annual Business Enquiry (ABI/1).
   See the note on Tables 1.17 and 1.18 in the Notes and Definitions of Section 1.
2 See Notes and Definitions.
3 Any minor discrepancies between sub categories and totals are caused by rounding.

☎01633 812079
Source - Employment, Earnings and Innovation Division, ONS

1.18 Employee jobs in transport and related industries: by sex and employment status: March 1990-2007

Thousands

SIC 1992 code	Industry	March 1990[1] Male	Female All	Part-time	March 1996 Male	Female All	Part-time	March 2006[1] Male	Female All	Part-time	March 2007 Male	Female All	Part-time
60.1	Railways[2]	155	7	1	71	13	2	42	11	2	43	9	2
60.2, 60.3	Other land transport, and via pipelines	389	27	7	379	20	6	398	78	25	392	82	27
61	Water transport	42	4	0	22	3	0	13	5	1	11	4	1
62	Air transport	36	21	2	33	26	4	53	36	10	46	42	14
63	Miscellaneous transport and storage	216	84	8	211	93	8	283	154	43	281	150	42
Total: transport industries[3]		838	143	18	717	155	20	789	283	81	773	287	86
Manufacture of transport equipment:													
34	motor vehicles, trailers	235	12	1	216	12	1	150	22	4	137	21	4
35	other transport equipment	211	18	1	136	10	1	123	15	2	124	15	3
50.1, 50.3-50.5	Retail distribution & filling stations	237	44	13	352	45	15	276	103	43	280	98	41
50.2	Maintenance & repair of motor vehicles	163	18	6	162	10	3	135	36	14	134	37	14
Total: Transport related industries[3]		846	92	21	866	77	20	684	177	64	676	172	62
All transport and related industries and services[3]		1,684	236	39	1,583	232	40	1,473	460	145	1,449	459	148

1 The data in this table differ from those previously published. This is due to benchmarking the Annual Business Enquiry (ABI/1).
   See the note on Tables 1.17 and 1.18 in the Notes and Definitions of Section 1.
2 See Notes and Definitions.
3 Any minor discrepancies between sub categories and totals are caused by rounding.

☎01633 812079
Source - Employment, Earnings and Innovation Division, ONS

1.19a   Consumer Prices Index: transport components: 1997-2007

1997=100

| | All items CPI | Motor vehicles | | | | Rail fares | Bus and coach fares | Air fares |
| | | Purchase of vehicle | Mainten- ance | Fuel and lubricants | Operation of personal transport equipment [1] | | | |
ONS Code	D7BT	D7CO	D7ED	D7EC	D7CP	D7EF	D7EG	D7EH
1997	100.0	100.0	100.0	100.0	100.0	100.0	100.0	100.0
1998	101.6	99.2	104.7	104.9	104.3	104.2	103.4	103.8
1999	102.9	96.0	109.3	113.8	110.9	107.9	107.8	105.4
2000	103.8	91.1	114.6	128.9	120.7	109.9	112.8	107.9
2001	105.0	88.1	122.4	122.3	120.3	114.5	118.0	117.6
2002	106.4	87.3	129.1	118.5	121.1	117.3	122.4	116.2
2003	107.8	86.8	138.1	122.7	127.2	118.6	128.5	110.2
2004	109.3	87.0	147.6	129.6	134.2	123.5	134.3	105.3
2005	111.5	86.1	157.5	140.8	143.7	128.2	141.8	111.1
2006	114.0	85.6	167.2	148.6	151.6	133.6	145.7	106.3
2007	116.7	85.6	175.6	153.0	157.2	140.3	152.5	108.8

1 Operation of personal transport equipment, covering motor running costs, includes
  spare parts and accessories, fuels and lubricants, maintenance and repairs and other
  services. It excludes the purchase of a vehicle, unlike the RPI all motor index given in
  Table 1.19b, and there are some other exclusions such as car insurance and vehicle
  excise duty, which are also included in the RPI, see Notes for further details.

☎020-7944 4442
Source - Consumer Prices
and Inflation Division, ONS

1.19b   Retail Prices Index: transport components: 1997-2007

1997=100

| | All items RPI | Motor vehicles | | | | | Rail fares | Bus and Coach fares |
| | | Purchase of vehicle | Mainten- ance | Petrol and oil | Tax and insurance | All motor [1] | | |
ONS Code	CHAW	DOCS	DOCT	DOCU	DOCV	CHBK	DOCW	DOCX
1997	100.0	100.0	100.0	100.0	100.0	100.0	100.0	100.0
1998	103.4	98.9	104.1	105.0	108.8	103.1	104.1	103.3
1999	105.0	94.7	108.2	113.8	117.6	105.6	107.9	107.0
2000	108.1	89.6	112.7	128.8	130.2	109.7	109.8	111.3
2001	110.0	88.3	118.2	122.2	137.0	109.1	114.0	116.0
2002	111.9	86.6	124.3	118.3	139.1	108.2	116.6	119.6
2003	115.1	84.1	131.7	122.6	145.1	109.6	118.6	124.6
2004	118.5	81.5	139.7	129.4	145.8	110.7	123.1	131.0
2005	121.9	77.3	148.2	140.8	143.9	111.4	128.1	139.6
2006	125.8	75.2	157.2	148.5	145.7	113.1	133.2	141.6
2007	131.2	73.2	165.3	152.6	152.4	114.5	140.0	149.7

1. The RPI all motor index includes purchase of a vehicle,
   maintenance, petrol and oil and tax and insurance,
   see Notes for further details.

☎020-7944 4442
Source - Consumer Prices
and Inflation Division, ONS

1.20 Gross Domestic Product, Retail Prices Index and Consumer Prices Index deflators: 1997-2007

	Calendar years to 2007 price level				Fiscal years to 2007/08 price level		
Year	GDP Factor	RPI Factor	CPI Factor	Year	GDP Factor	RPI Factor	CPI Factor
1997	1.280	1.312	1.167	1997/98	1.279	1.314	1.170
1998	1.246	1.268	1.149	1998/99	1.248	1.274	1.151
1999	1.219	1.249	1.134	1999/00	1.223	1.254	1.138
2000	1.203	1.214	1.125	2000/01	1.206	1.218	1.130
2001	1.177	1.192	1.111	2001/02	1.178	1.200	1.113
2002	1.142	1.173	1.097	2002/03	1.142	1.175	1.100
2003	1.108	1.140	1.083	2003/04	1.110	1.143	1.086
2004	1.080	1.107	1.068	2004/05	1.080	1.109	1.070
2005	1.056	1.076	1.047	2005/06	1.057	1.080	1.048
2006	1.028	1.043	1.023	2006/07	1.030	1.041	1.021
2007	1.000	1.000	1.000	2007/08	1.000	1.000	1.000

☎020-7944 4442

Sources - GDP: National Expenditure and Income Division, ONS

RPI and CPI: Consumer Prices and Inflation Division, ONS

30

2 Aviation:

Notes and Definitions

The figures for 1998-2002 in Table 2.1 differ from the time series shown in Civil Aviation Authority (CAA) *United Kingdom Airports* (annual 2007) due to CAA tables now excluding data for Sheffield City airport.

Tables 2.2a - 2.2c, and 2.8 are derived from the CAA publication *United Kingdom Airports* (annual). Thus;

TSGB table	CAA publication table N°
2.2a	4.1 and 5
2.2b	8, 10.1 and 10.2
2.2c	13.1 and 14
2.8	12.1

Table 2.3 is derived from the CAA *Punctuality Statistics*.

Tables 2.4, 2.6 and 2.11 are derived from the CAA publication *United Kingdom Airlines* (annual) and earlier volumes. Thus;

TSGB table	CAA publication table N°
2.4	1.7.1/2/3/4 and 1.8.1/2/3/4
2.6	1.11.2
2.11	1.14

CAA compiles the statistics from returns submitted by United Kingdom airlines.

Tables 2.7 and 2.12 are derived from the International Civil Aviation Organisation (ICAO) publication *Civil Aviation Statistics of the World* and from data supplied by ICAO.

Table 2.9 is derived from the CAA publication *Reportable Accidents to United Kingdom Registered Aircraft and to Foreign Registered Aircraft in United Kingdom Airspace* and from data supplied by the Civil Aviation Authority's Safety Data Unit.

Table 2.10 is derived from the CAA publication *United Kingdom Airmisses Involving Commercial Air Transport* and from data supplied by the UK Airprox Board.

Traffic at United Kingdom airports: 2.2

The table shows air transport movements (landings and take-offs of aircraft engaged in commercial air transport), terminal passengers (arrivals and departures) and cargo handled (uplifted and set down).

Domestic traffic (movements, passengers and cargo) shown is half that published in the CAA Airport Annual Reports, to remove double counting at airport of arrival and departure. The figures for individual airports have not, however, been adjusted to eliminate double counting of domestic traffic.

Terms used in Table 2.2 are defined as follows:

Air transport movements: All scheduled movements (whether loaded or empty) and loaded charter movements, but excludes empty positioning flights by scheduled aircraft and empty charter movements.

International services: These services are flown between the United Kingdom, Isle of Man or Channel Islands and points in other countries.

Scheduled services: Those performed according to a published timetable, including those supplementary thereto, available for use by members of the public.

Non-scheduled services: Air transport movements other than scheduled services.

Terminal passengers: Passengers joining or leaving an aircraft at a United Kingdom airport (a passenger who changes from one aircraft to another, carrying the same flight number, is counted as a terminal passenger both on arrival and departure). Transit passengers who arrive and depart on the same aircraft are not included.

All revenue and non-revenue passengers (who pay less than 25 per cent of the normal applicable fare) are counted as terminal passengers. Cargo excludes mail and passengers' and crews' permitted baggage, but all other property carried on an aircraft is included. Thus excess baggage is included, as are diplomatic bags. Cargo in transit through an airport on the same aircraft is excluded.

Punctuality at United Kingdom Airports: 2.3

London airports include Heathrow, Gatwick, Stansted and Luton. London City also began reporting from April 1997. Regional airports include Manchester, Birmingham and Glasgow. Newcastle and Edinburgh airports also began reporting from July 1996; the resulting discontinuity in the series is very small.

Main outputs of United Kingdom airlines: 2.4

Table 2.4 shows the carriage of revenue passengers, cargo and mail on services flown by United Kingdom airlines, scheduled and non-scheduled (but excluding air-taxi operations and sub-charter operations performed on behalf of United Kingdom airlines). Passenger kilometres are calculated by multiplying the number of revenue passengers carried on each flight stage by the stage distance. Passenger seat occupancy is calculated as passenger kilometres as a percentage of seat kilometres available.

Cargo and mail uplifted are calculated by counting each tonne of revenue cargo or mail on a particular journey once only and not repeatedly on each individual stage of the flight. Cargo and mail tonne kilometres are calculated by multiplying the number of tonnes of revenue load on each stage flight by the stage distance.

Terms used in Table 2.4 are defined as follows:

Passengers: Travellers are counted as revenue passengers if they pay at least 25 per cent of the normal applicable fare. They are counted only once on a particular flight (with one flight number) and not for each stage of that flight.

International services: These services are flown between the United Kingdom, Isle of Man or Channel Islands and points in other countries.

Domestic services: Those entirely within the United Kingdom, Isle of Man and Channel Islands.

Scheduled services: Those performed according to a published timetable, including those supplementary thereto, available for use by members of the public.

Non-scheduled services: Air transport movements other than scheduled services.

Forecasts of air traffic demand: 2.5

The forecasts show the expected number of UK and foreign passengers passing through UK airports up to 2030, after accounting for airport capacity constraints. The underlying unconstrained forecasts are based on econometric equations which specify a relationship between passenger traffic and a number of explanatory variables which determine it. The key variables determining air traffic were found to be domestic and foreign economic growth (principally GDP); air fares; trade; and exchange rates. The relationships derived from past years' data are applied to projections of future year values of the explanatory variables to calculate forecasts of air traffic. A range of forecasts is given to reflect the uncertainties inherent in long term forecasting. The range of unconstrained forecasts are processed in the DfT National Air Passenger Allocation Model which forecasts how passenger demand will split between UK airports taking account of likely future constraints on air transport movements (and thus passengers) at UK airports. The future constraints assume the increases to airport capacity supported in the 2003 White Paper.

United Kingdom airline fleet: 2.6

Table 2.6 gives information on the fleet size of selected larger United Kingdom airlines.

Activity at major airports: 2.7

Table 2.7 gives a comparison of the activity at some of the world's major airports. Airports are selected such that the largest 25 (as reported to ICAO) by number of terminal passengers are included. The ranking is only a guide as 'non-reporting' airports are excluded. Some airports which did not report in previous years have entered the table. A substantial proportion of the figures are estimated by ICAO on the basis of part-year data; the table is therefore of use only as a guide.

United Kingdom international passenger movements: 2.8

The table records the origin and destination of all revenue and non-revenue terminal passengers on air transport movement flights as reported to United Kingdom airport authorities by United Kingdom and foreign airlines. Passengers changing planes are recorded twice, on arrival and departure. Passengers carried in aircraft chartered by British government departments, and HM and other armed forces travelling in the course of their duties are excluded. Operators are required to report, in respect of each service operated, the points of uplift and discharge of each passenger. The figures record data for direct flights only, so they may not reflect a passenger's entire air journey: the point at which a passenger disembarks from a particular service may not represent the passenger's ultimate destination.

Although operators are asked to report all passenger journeys, in some cases the actual point of uplift or discharge is not recorded. In such cases, all passengers are allocated to the aircraft's origin or ultimate destination. All identifiable diversions are reallocated to the point of intended operation.

"Former USSR" includes: Albania, Armenia, Azerbaijan, Belarus, Georgia, Kazakhstan, Kyrgyzstan, Republic of Moldova, Russia, Turkmenistan, Ukraine, and Uzbekistan.
"Former Yugoslavia" includes: Bosnia-Herzegovina, Croatia, Serbia, Montenegro, and Macedonia.
"Rest of Europe" includes: Faroe Islands, and Iceland.

Casualties: 2.9

The table includes deaths, serious and minor injuries where an aircraft was engaged in airline, air taxi, general aviation (including private flights) and other commercial (including training) operations.

Terms used in Table 2.9 are defined as follows:

Airline: Public transport flights, which are subject to a United Kingdom Air Transport Licence. Also public transport flights which are not subject to a United Kingdom Air Transport Licence, but which utilise aircraft having a maximum take-off weight of 15 tonnes or more. Positioning flights are excluded. There are no rotary wing services by United Kingdom registered aircraft in foreign airspace, and no rotary wing or air taxi services by foreign registered aircraft in United Kingdom airspace.

Air Taxi: Public Transport flights which are not subject to a United Kingdom Air Transport Licence and which utilise aircraft having a maximum take-off weight of less than 15 tonnes. Positioning flights are excluded.

General Aviation: Includes executive, club and group, private and training flights, but does not include accidents to gliders, microlights, hang gliders or hot-air balloons.

Aircraft proximity: 2.10

Table 2.10 reflects the Civil Aviation Authority's practice, introduced in 1990, of including controller-reported incidents. Further, the term "airmiss" has been replaced by AIRPROX, meaning aircraft proximity hazard.

An AIRPROX is a situation in which, in the opinion of a pilot or controller, the distance between aircraft as well as their relative positions and speed have been such that the safety of the aircraft was or may have been compromised. AIRPROX can occur between various combinations of commercial, military and private

aircraft. The numbers of AIRPROX incidents involving commercial transport aircraft are shown separately in the table.

All AIRPROX reports are assessed and, following guidelines given by the International Civil Aviation Organisation, the degrees of risk involved are categorised as 'risk of collision', 'safety not assured', 'no risk of collision', and 'risk not determined'.

Employment: 2.11

Table 2.11 shows the average number of personnel employed by United Kingdom airlines in the United Kingdom and overseas. Personnel employed by companies performing solely air-taxi operations are excluded.

Passenger traffic via major international airlines: 2.12

Table 2.12 gives a comparison of the major international airlines. Airlines are selected such that the largest 25 (as reported to ICAO) by passengers uplifted are included. The ranking is only a guide as 'non-reporting' airlines are excluded.

2.1 Activity at civil aerodromes: United Kingdom: [1] 1950-2007

For greater detail of the years 1997-2007 see Table 2.2

Year	Air transport movements: aircraft landings or take-offs (thousands)	Terminal passengers (thousands)	Freight loaded plus unloaded (thousand tonnes)
1950	195	2,133	31
1951	187	2,471	44
1952	195	2,776	40
1953	214	3,419	64
1954	232	4,004	84
1955	259	4,831	113
1956	293	5,617	121
1957	329	6,600	139
1958	340	6,761	167
1959	358	7,867	226
1960	402	10,075	279
1961	447	12,249	313
1962	449	13,793	344
1963	458	15,506	360
1964	480	17,649	399
1965	508	19,918	418
1966	556	22,582	517
1967	566	24,003	488
1968	560	24,845	524
1969	591	28,064	585
1970	607	31,606	580
1971	630	34,934	532
1972	669	39,125	649
1973	719	43,125	699
1974	710	40,082	717
1975	701	41,846	638
1976	740	44,666	659
1977	759	45,927	705
1978	862	52,829	748
1979	924	56,992	797
1980	954	57,823	744
1981	927	57,771	724
1982	973	58,778	693
1983	1,019	61,109	726
1984	1,079	67,572	861
1985	1,097	70,434	850
1986	1,125	75,161	881
1987	1,193	86,041	976
1988	1,280	93,162	1,088
1989	1,375	98,913	1,151
1990	1,420	102,418	1,193
1991 [2]	1,369	95,770	1,126
1992	1,448	106,123	1,238
1993	1,484	112,277	1,376
1994	1,485	122,159	1,589
1995	1,551	129,369	1,703
1996	1,630	135,810	1,772
1997	1,703	146,657	1,943
1998	1,807	158,856	2,080
1999	1,899	168,363	2,189
2000	1,986	179,885	2,314
2001	2,028	181,229	2,146
2002	2,023	188,761	2,195
2003	2,088	199,952	2,208
2004	2,208	215,681	2,371
2005	2,333	228,214	2,363
2006	2,376	235,139	2,315
2007	2,409	240,722	2,326

1 Includes double counting of domestic traffic, unlike Table 2.2.
2 Excludes air-taxi operations from 1991.

☎020-7944 3088
The figures in this table are outside the scope of National Statistics
Source - Civil Aviation Authority

2.2 Traffic at United Kingdom airports: by type of service and operator: 1997-2007

(a) Air transport movements (aircraft landings or take-offs)											Thousands
	1997	1998	1999	2000	2001	2002	2003	2004	2005	2006	2007
International (incl. traffic to/from UK oil rigs):											
UK operators											
Scheduled	404.1	439.6	477.1	516.7	535.5	530.4	516.3	545.8	584.1	595.6	622.5
Non-scheduled	215.2	225.6	219.1	221	214.3	223.5	215.1	202.9	204	212.8	211.3
Total	619.2	665.1	696.2	737.7	749.8	753.9	731.4	748.7	788.1	808.4	833.8
Foreign operators											
Scheduled	406.1	433.9	473.9	502.9	496.2	497.7	559.7	602.6	640.3	665.9	695.7
Non-scheduled	40.25	46.18	42.2	44.55	56.08	44.88	43.76	46.72	47.76	47.37	45.38
Total	446.4	480	516.1	547.4	552.3	542.6	603.4	649.3	688	713.3	741.1
Domestic: [1,2]											
Scheduled	292	306	317	324	338	340	355	384	408	408	400
Non-scheduled	27	26	26	27	26	24	21	21	21	19	17
Total	319	332	344	351	364	363	377	405	429	427	417
UK operators total: [1,2]											
Scheduled	696	746	795	841	873	870	872	930	992	1,004	1,023
Non-scheduled	242	251	245	248	240	247	236	224	225	232	228
Total	939	997	1,040	1,089	1,114	1,117	1,108	1,154	1,217	1,236	1,251
Foreign operators	446	480	516	547	552	543	603	649	688	713	741
All operators: [1]	1,385	1,477	1,556	1,636	1,666	1,660	1,712	1,803	1,905	1,949	1,992
Selected airports: [3]											
Gatwick	227	240	245	251	244	234	234	241	252	254	259
Heathrow	429	441	449	460	458	460	457	470	472	471	476
Luton	37	44	51	56	56	55	58	64	75	79	83
Stansted	82	102	132	144	151	152	169	177	178	190	192
Birmingham	80	88	98	108	111	112	116	109	113	109	104
Bristol	30	32	33	34	41	46	50	55	61	66	59
East Midlands	36	39	39	40	41	49	54	56	54	56	61
Manchester	146	162	169	178	182	178	192	208	218	213	207
Newcastle	41	41	42	43	46	44	42	50	55	58	58
Aberdeen	82	85	78	78	83	80	77	81	89	98	103
Edinburgh	69	72	81	86	98	105	105	112	116	116	115
Glasgow	79	83	86	88	91	87	88	92	97	97	94
Belfast International	32	37	43	41	46	38	40	43	48	48	52

1 Adjusted to eliminate double counting.
2 Includes movements by foreign operators on domestic routes
3 Includes double counting.

☎020-7944 3088
The figures in this table are outside
the scope of National Statistics
Source - Civil Aviation Authority

2.2 (continued) Traffic at United Kingdom airports: by type of service and operator: 1997-2007

(b) Terminal passengers (arrivals or departures)											Millions
	1997	1998	1999	2000	2001	2002	2003	2004	2005	2006	2007
International (incl. traffic to/from oil rigs)											
UK operators											
Scheduled	41.8	46.7	50.1	54.5	53.6	54.4	56.5	63.2	69.1	72.2	77.0
Non-scheduled	28.7	31.6	32.6	33.2	34.0	33.9	33.4	32.2	30.2	29.7	28.5
Total	70.5	78.3	82.7	87.7	87.6	88.3	89.8	95.4	99.3	101.9	105.5
Foreign operators											
Scheduled	39.9	42.5	46.6	51.1	51.3	54.5	60.3	67.6	74.6	79.8	83.2
Non-scheduled	4.3	4.5	4.1	3.9	3.9	3.9	4.0	4.1	4.1	3.8	3.4
Total	44.2	47.0	50.7	55.0	55.2	58.4	64.3	71.8	78.7	83.6	86.5
Domestic: [1,2]											
Scheduled	15.7	16.5	17.3	18.4	19.0	20.8	22.7	24.1	24.9	24.7	24.2
Non-scheduled	0.3	0.2	0.2	0.2	0.2	0.2	0.2	0.2	0.2	0.2	0.2
Total	16.0	16.7	17.5	18.6	19.2	21.0	22.9	24.3	25.1	24.9	24.4
UK operators total: [1,2]											
Scheduled	57.5	63.2	67.4	72.9	72.6	75.2	79.2	87.3	94.0	96.9	101.1
Non-scheduled	29.0	31.8	32.8	33.4	34.2	34.2	33.6	32.4	30.4	29.9	28.7
Total	86.5	95.0	100.2	106.3	106.8	109.3	112.8	119.7	124.4	126.8	129.8
Foreign operators	44.2	47.0	50.7	55.0	55.2	58.4	64.3	71.8	78.7	83.6	86.5
All traffic: [1]	130.7	142.0	150.9	161.3	162.0	167.7	177.1	191.4	203.1	210.3	216.4
Selected airports:											
International:											
Gatwick	24.4	26.3	27.6	29.0	28.1	26.1	26.0	27.5	28.8	30.0	31.1
Heathrow	50.6	53.2	54.8	56.9	53.8	56.4	56.6	60.2	61.0	61.3	62.1
Luton	2.5	3.3	3.9	4.4	4.8	4.7	5.1	5.9	7.5	7.9	8.4
Stansted	4.2	5.6	8.0	10.4	11.6	13.6	16.0	18.2	19.3	21.0	21.2
Birmingham	4.8	5.4	5.8	6.3	6.5	6.7	7.5	7.5	7.8	7.5	7.6
Bristol	1.2	1.4	1.6	1.7	2.1	2.5	2.8	3.3	3.8	4.3	4.6
East Midlands	1.5	1.8	1.9	1.9	2.0	2.7	3.4	3.6	3.5	4.0	4.7
Manchester	13.3	14.6	14.7	15.5	16.3	15.9	16.4	17.7	18.7	18.6	18.7
Newcastle	1.8	2.0	2.0	2.2	2.4	2.2	2.5	3.0	3.3	3.6	3.9
Aberdeen	0.9	0.9	0.8	0.8	0.9	0.9	1.0	1.0	1.2	1.3	1.5
Edinburgh	0.9	1.0	1.3	1.5	1.8	1.8	2.0	2.2	2.3	2.7	3.4
Glasgow	2.8	3.0	3.3	3.4	3.4	3.5	3.5	3.9	4.2	4.2	4.1
Belfast International	0.7	0.8	1.0	0.9	1.0	0.9	1.0	1.2	1.4	1.5	1.8
Domestic: [3]											
Gatwick	2.4	2.7	2.8	2.9	3.0	3.4	3.9	3.9	3.9	4.1	4.0
Heathrow	7.2	7.2	7.1	7.4	6.6	6.7	6.7	6.9	6.7	6.0	5.8
Luton	0.7	0.9	1.3	1.7	1.8	1.7	1.7	1.6	1.6	1.5	1.5
Stansted	1.2	1.2	1.5	1.4	2.0	2.5	2.7	2.7	2.7	2.7	2.6
Birmingham	1.0	1.2	1.1	1.2	1.2	1.2	1.4	1.3	1.5	1.5	1.5
Bristol	0.3	0.4	0.4	0.4	0.5	0.9	1.1	1.3	1.4	1.4	1.3
East Midlands	0.4	0.4	0.4	0.3	0.3	0.5	0.8	0.8	0.7	0.7	0.7
Manchester	2.4	2.6	2.7	2.8	2.8	2.7	3.1	3.3	3.4	3.5	3.2
Newcastle	0.8	0.9	0.9	1.0	1.0	1.2	1.5	1.7	1.8	1.8	1.7
Aberdeen	1.5	1.6	1.5	1.5	1.7	1.6	1.5	1.6	1.7	1.8	1.9
Edinburgh	3.2	3.5	3.7	4.0	4.3	5.1	5.5	5.8	6.1	5.9	5.6
Glasgow	3.2	3.4	3.5	3.6	3.8	4.3	4.6	4.6	4.6	4.6	4.6
Belfast International	1.8	1.8	2.1	2.2	2.6	2.7	3.0	3.2	3.4	3.5	3.4
All traffic: [3]											
Gatwick	26.8	29.0	30.4	31.9	31.1	29.5	29.9	31.4	32.7	34.1	35.2
Heathrow	57.8	60.4	61.9	64.3	60.4	63.0	63.2	67.1	67.7	67.3	67.9
Luton	3.2	4.2	5.2	6.1	6.6	6.5	6.8	7.5	9.1	9.4	9.9
Stansted	5.4	6.8	9.5	11.8	13.6	16.0	18.7	20.9	22.0	23.7	23.8
Birmingham	5.8	6.6	6.9	7.5	7.7	7.9	8.9	8.8	9.3	9.1	9.1
Bristol	1.6	1.8	2.0	2.1	2.7	3.4	3.9	4.6	5.2	5.7	5.9
East Midlands	1.9	2.2	2.3	2.2	2.3	3.2	4.3	4.4	4.2	4.7	5.4
Manchester	15.7	17.2	17.4	18.3	19.1	18.6	19.5	21.0	22.1	22.1	21.9
Newcastle	2.6	2.9	2.9	3.2	3.4	3.4	3.9	4.7	5.2	5.4	5.6
Aberdeen	2.4	2.5	2.3	2.3	2.5	2.5	2.5	2.6	3.0	3.2	3.4
Edinburgh	4.1	4.5	5.0	5.5	6.0	6.9	7.5	8.0	8.4	8.6	9.0
Glasgow	6.0	6.4	6.8	7.0	7.2	7.8	8.1	8.6	8.8	8.8	8.7
Belfast International	2.5	2.6	3.0	3.1	3.6	3.6	4.0	4.4	4.8	5.0	5.2

2.2 (continued) Traffic at United Kingdom airports: by type of service and operator: 1997-2007

(c) Cargo handled (excl. mail and passengers' luggage)										Thousand tonnes	
	1997	1998	1999	2000	2001	2002	2003	2004	2005	2006	2007
International (incl. traffic to/from oil rigs)											
UK operators											
Scheduled	656	714	734	773	658	678	702	778	768	760	774
Non-scheduled	83	74	85	75	54	44	33	33	31	27	35
Total	739	788	819	848	712	721	735	811	800	786	809
Foreign operators											
Scheduled	954	997	1,053	1,091	1,044	1,090	1,115	1,210	1,107	1,034	1,040
Non-scheduled	148	200	216	265	279	275	240	226	320	359	371
Total	1,102	1,197	1,269	1,356	1,322	1,365	1,355	1,436	1,427	1,393	1,411
Domestic: [1]											
Scheduled	18	15	14	14	11	10	14	18	9	4	4
Non-scheduled	33	33	36	42	45	45	44	44	59	64	49
Total	50	47	50	56	56	55	59	62	68	68	53
UK operators total: [1,2]											
Scheduled	674	728	748	787	669	687	717	796	777	764	778
Non-scheduled	116	107	121	117	99	89	78	77	91	90	84
Total	790	835	870	904	768	776	794	873	868	854	862
Foreign operators	1,102	1,197	1,269	1,356	1,322	1,365	1,355	1,436	1,427	1,393	1,411
All operators: [1]	1,892	2,032	2,139	2,259	2,090	2,141	2,149	2,309	2,295	2,247	2,273
Selected airports: [3]											
Gatwick	265	274	294	319	280	243	223	218	223	212	171
Heathrow	1,156	1,209	1,265	1,307	1,180	1,235	1,223	1,325	1,306	1,263	1,311
Luton	21	26	23	33	23	20	23	26	23	18	38
Stansted	126	179	174	166	166	184	199	226	237	224	204
Birmingham	20	18	29	9	12	13	12	10	13	15	14
East Midlands	126	123	128	178	195	219	227	253	267	272	275
Kent International	2	6	23	32	36	32	43	27	8	21	28
Liverpool	25	25	25	29	23	14	12	9	9	6	4
Manchester	94	101	108	117	106	113	123	149	147	149	165
Edinburgh	8	14	18	18	16	21	25	27	30	36	19
Glasgow	11	8	9	9	6	5	5	8	9	6	4
Prestwick	34	40	41	41	43	40	40	34	29	29	32
Belfast International	25	25	26	31	32	29	30	32	38	38	38

1 Adjusted to eliminate double counting.
2 Includes freight carried by foreign operators on domestic routes.
3 Includes double counting.

☎020-7944 3088
The figures in this table are outside
the scope of National Statistics
Source - Civil Aviation Authority

2.3 Punctuality at United Kingdom Airports: Percentage of flights on time (within 15 minutes): 1997-2007

						Percentage	
	All reporting London airports		All reporting regional airports		All reporting airports	
	Scheduled	Charter	Scheduled	Charter	Scheduled	Charter
1997	71	46	80	56	74	51
1998	69	50	78	56	72	53
1999	69	49	76	53	71	51
2000	70	52	77	55	72	53
2001	71	60	77	58	73	58
2002	69	68	76	68	72	68
2003	75	73	79	74	76	74
2004	73	69	78	71	75	70
2005	71	63	77	70	73	67
2006	66	62	76	70	69	67
2007	66	63	75	69	69	66

☎020-7944 3088
The figures in this table are outside the scope of National Statistics
Source - Civil Aviation Authority

2.4 Main outputs of United Kingdom airlines: by type of service:[1] 1997-2007

(a) Aircraft kilometres flown										Million kilometres	
	1997	1998	1999	2000	2001	2002	2003	2004	2005	2006	2007
International:											
Scheduled	698	789	827	895	920	921	965	1,059	1,178	1,251	1,333
Non-scheduled	370	403	427	447	437	412	431	423	414	425	444
Total	1,068	1,192	1,254	1,342	1,357	1,333	1,396	1,483	1,592	1,677	1,778
Domestic:											
Scheduled	111	118	120	121	128	126	123	138	147	148	141
Non-scheduled	8	7	7	7	8	9	8	8	7	7	6
Total	119	125	127	129	136	135	131	146	154	155	147
All services:											
Scheduled	809	886	947	1,016	1,048	1,047	1,088	1,198	1,326	1,400	1,474
Non-scheduled	378	410	434	455	445	421	440	431	421	432	451
Total	1,187	1,297	1,381	1,471	1,493	1,468	1,528	1,629	1,746	1,831	1,925

(b) Passengers uplifted											Millions
International:											
Scheduled	40	45	48	52	51	52	56	64	71	75	80
Non-scheduled	28	31	32	33	34	34	33	32	30	29	29
Total	69	76	81	86	85	86	89	96	101	104	108
Domestic:											
Scheduled	15.9	16.6	17.1	18.0	18.2	19.8	20.8	22.5	23.1	22.9	22.1
Non-scheduled	0.3	0.3	0.2	0.2	0.3	0.3	0.3	0.2	0.2	0.2	0.2
Total	16.2	16.9	17.4	18.2	18.5	20.2	21.0	22.7	23.3	23.0	22.3
All services:											
Scheduled	56	62	65	70	69	72	76	86	94	98	102
Non-scheduled	28	31	33	33	34	34	34	32	30	30	29
Total	85	93	98	104	104	107	110	118	124	127	131

(c) Passenger kilometres flown											Billion kilometres
International:											
Scheduled	130	145	153	163	151	148	156	173	191	204	218
Non-scheduled	77	84	87	90	90	88	89	90	87	86	86
Total	206	229	240	253	241	236	245	263	278	290	305
Domestic:											
Scheduled	6.6	6.9	7.2	7.5	7.6	8.3	8.9	9.5	9.8	9.8	9.4
Non-scheduled	0.1	0.1	0.1	0.1	0.1	0.1	0.2	0.2	0.1	0.1	0.1
Total	6.8	7.0	7.3	7.6	7.7	8.5	9.1	9.8	9.9	9.9	9.5
All services:											
Scheduled	136	152	160	170	159	156	165	183	200	213	228
Non-scheduled	77	84	87	90	90	88	90	90	87	86	87
Total	213	236	248	261	249	244	254	273	287	300	314

(d) Passenger seat occupancy											Percentage
International:											
Scheduled	72.6	71.9	71.1	72.6	70.9	74.5	74.8	75.8	76.1	76.2	76.5
Non-scheduled	89.6	89.7	89.4	89.5	89.9	90.4	89.2	89.9	89.0	88.3	88.1
Total	78.1	77.5	76.8	77.9	77.0	79.7	79.5	80.1	79.7	79.4	79.5
Domestic:											
Scheduled	64.1	62.0	60.6	64.2	61.8	66.0	70.5	68.0	65.3	66.1	65.3
Non-scheduled	68.9	69.2	66.4	62.2	62.3	60.6	66.0	61.8	37.9	43.4	46.4
Total	64.2	62.1	60.7	64.9	61.8	65.9	70.4	67.9	65.0	65.9	65.1
All services:											
Scheduled	72.2	71.3	70.6	72.2	69.9	74.0	74.5	75.3	75.5	75.6	76.0
Non-scheduled	89.5	89.7	89.3	89.4	89.9	90.3	89.1	89.8	88.9	88.2	88.1
Total	77.6	76.9	76.2	77.4	75.9	79.1	79.1	79.6	79.1	78.9	79.0

2.4 (continued) Main outputs of United Kingdom airlines: by type of service:[1] 1997-2007

(e) Cargo and mail uplifted											Thousand tonnes
	1997	1998	1999	2000	2001	2002	2003	2004	2005	2006	2007
International:											
Scheduled	752	800	834	873	723	752	783	879	911	938	934
Non-scheduled	96	161	178	151	114	101	105	122	104	125 [2]	220
Total	848	960	1,012	1,024	837	853	888	1,002	1,016	1,063 [2]	1,154
Domestic:											
Scheduled	31	32	26	25	13	17	17	15	10	8	7
Non-scheduled	69	66	71	72	75	70	64	56	80	79	72
Total	99	98	97	96	88	87	81	71	90	87	79
All services:											
Scheduled	783	831	860	897	736	769	801	895	921	946	941
Non-scheduled	165	227	249	223	189	170	169	178	185	204 [2]	292
Total	948	1,059	1,109	1,120	925	939	969	1,072	1,106	1,150 [2]	1,233

(f) Cargo and mail tonne-kilometres flown											Millions
	1997	1998	1999	2000	2001	2002	2003	2004	2005	2006	2007
International:											
Scheduled	4,614	4,829	5,068	5,330	4,643	4,991	5,235	5,693	6,085	6,311	6,308
Non-scheduled	357	413	460	533	519	295	343	331	326	725 [2]	1,427
Total	4,972	5,242	5,528	5,863	5,162	5,286	5,578	6,024	6,411	7,036 [2]	7,735
Domestic:											
Scheduled	12	12	10	10	8	6.398	6	5	3	2	2
Non-scheduled	23	22	24	24	26	25.064	24	23	34	35	33
Total	35	34	34	33	34	31.462	30	29	37	37	35
All services:											
Scheduled	4,626	4,841	5,078	5,339	4,651	4,997	5,242	5,698	6,088	6,313	6,311
Non-scheduled	380	434	484	557	545	320	367	354	360	760 [2]	1,460
Total	5,006	5,275	5,562	5,896	5,196	5,317	5,608	6,053	6,449	7,073 [2]	7,770

1 Excludes sub-charter operations performed on behalf of UK airlines.

2 The increase in cargo in 2006 is due to a foreign airline registering as a UK airline in August 2006.

☎020-7944 3088

The figures in this table are outside the scope of National Statistics

Source - Civil Aviation Authority

2.5 Forecasts of air traffic demand:[1] 2004-2030

					Million terminal passengers at UK airports[2]	
	2004	**2010**	**2015**	**2020**	**2025**	**2030**
International: [3]						
Low	.	210	250	290	330	365
Mid	175	215	265	305	350	390
High	.	225	280	330	370	415
Domestic: [4]						
Low	.	50	60	70	75	85
Mid	40	50	55	70	80	90
High	.	50	55	70	85	90
Total: [5]						
Low	.	260	310	360	410	450
Mid	215	270	320	375	430	480
High	.	275	335	400	455	505

1   Forecasts of UK terminal passengers, constrained by airport capacity, as published in the November 2007 'UK Air Passenger Demand & CO_2 Forecasts' report for a base year of 2004, assuming the additional South East capacity supported in the 2003 White Paper i.e. a second runway at Stansted around 2015 and a third runway at Heathrow around 2020. The low-high range is found by using the minimum and maximum annual forecasts from the sensitivity tests reported.
2   Figures are rounded to the nearest 5 million terminal passengers.
3   Figures include international to international interlining passengers transferring at UK airports but not terminating in the UK.
4   Figures are on a different basis from those in Table 2.2(b) because passengers are counted at the airports at both ends of the journey and only includes passengers who start and end their journey in the UK. The total includes miscellaneous traffic, e.g. passengers to and from oil rigs.
5   Figures may not equal sum of international and domestic due to rounding to nearest 5 million.

The November 2007 'UK Air Passenger Demand & CO_2 Forecasts' report is available at:
http://www.dft.gov.uk/pgr/aviation/environmentalissues/ukairdemandandco2forecasts/

☎020-7944 6608
The figures in this table are outside
the scope of National Statistics
Source - International Networks Analysis
and Support Division, DfT

2.6 United Kingdom airline fleet: 1997-2007

Aircraft in service (at end of year)											Number
	1997	1998	1999	2000	2001	2002	2003	2004	2005	2006	2007
Total [1]	758	837	850	889	928	903	921	945	952	963	957
ow:											
British Airways PLC [2]	226	229	217	235	235	240	240	228	232	234	234
EasyJet Airline Company Ltd	6	9	15	17	22	32	69	94	98	103	125
Flybe Ltd [3]	18	24	28	31	31	31	33	35	35	41	88
BMI Group [4]	34	37	40	45	46	43	43	31	58	61	62
Thomsonfly Ltd [5]	27	28	28	32	31	32	32	37	42	47	48
Virgin Atlantic Airways Ltd	20	25	29	32	34	35	38	35	32	37	38
First Choice Airways Ltd [6]	16	22	25	27	29	31	32	30	32	31	32
Monarch Airlines	17	17	20	19	22	23	22	24	28	28	31
Jet2.Com Ltd [7]	13	15	15	14	14	15	21	26	23	26	29
MyTravel Airways [8]	20	21	24	31	31	34	35	31	29	25	25
Thomas Cook Airlines Ltd [9]	.	.	.	17	27	24	24	24	24	24	24
GB Airways Ltd	7	9	9	10	10	11	13	13	15	15	15
Aurigny Air Services	9	9	11	12	12	13	13	14	11	10	10
European Air Charter	15	16	13	11	13	13	13	12	13	6	4

1 Total includes only airlines who reported to the CAA in the year.
2 BA Euro Ops became part of the BA mainline fleet from 28 March 2002.
3 Prior to December 2005 known as Flybe British European.
4 Prior to 2005 data is for BMI British Midland.
 From 2005 data also includes BMI Regional and BMI Baby.
5 Prior to January 2006 known as Britannia Airways.
6 Prior to 2003 known as Air 2000.
7 Prior to January 2006 known as Channel Express.
8 Prior to 2002 known as Airtours International Airways Ltd.
9 Prior to April 2003 known as JMC Airlines Ltd.

☎020-7944 3088
The figures in this table are outside
the scope of National Statistics
Source - Civil Aviation Authority

2.7 Activity at major airports: 2007

Country	Location	Name	Terminal passengers		Freight loaded plus unloaded [1]	Commercial air transport movements	
			All (millions)	ow: International (millions)	Tonnes (thousands)	All [2] (thousands)	ow: International [3] (thousands)
USA	Atlanta	Hartsfield-Jackson International	89.4	8.9	720	994	..
USA	Chicago	O'Hare International	76.2	11.9	1,524	928	..
UK	London	Heathrow	67.9	62.1	1,311	476	416
Japan	Tokyo	Haneda	66.7	1.8	852	331	..
USA	Los Angeles	Los Angeles International	61.9	17.1	2,078	681	..
France	Paris	Charles De Gaulle	59.9	54.9	2,297	552	490
USA	Dallas	Dallas-Ft.Worth International	59.8	5.5	725	685	..
Germany	Frankfurt	Frankfurt International	54.2	47.1	2,190	492	407
China	Beijing	Capital	53.6	12.7	1,374	394	..
Spain	Madrid	Barajas	51.8	29.3	322	475	252
USA	Denver	Denver International	49.9	2.2	260	614	..
USA	New York	J. F. Kennedy International	47.8	21.8	1,596	443	140
Netherlands	Amsterdam	Schiphol	47.7	47.7	1,610	436	432
USA	Las Vegas	McCarran International	47.6	2.1	92	609	..
China	Hong Kong	Hong Kong International	47.0	47.0	3,742	296	296
USA	Houston	G. Bush Intercontinental	43.0	7.7	409	603	..
USA	Phoenix	Sky Harbor International	42.2	1.7	257	538	..
Thailand	Bangkok	Bangkok International	42.2	31.1	1,220	266	194
USA	New York	Newark International	36.4	10.7	943	444	..
USA	Orlando	Orlando International	36.4	2.3	187	359	..
USA	Detroit	Wayne County	36.1	3.1	223	467	..
USA	San Francisco	San Francisco International	35.8	8.9	563	380	..
Japan	Tokyo	Narita	35.4	34.2	2,218	191	178
Singapore	Singapore	Changi	35.2	35.2	1,895	221	221
UK	London	Gatwick	35.2	31.1	171	259	210

1 Includes mail.
2 All commercial movements including positioning and local movements.
3 International commercial air transport movements data for all world's major
   airports was not available at time of print.

☎020-7944 3088
The figures in this table are outside
the scope of National Statistics
Source - ICAO

2.8 United Kingdom international passenger movements by air: arrivals plus departures: by country of embarkation or landing: 1997-2007

Thousands

	1997	1998	1999	2000	2001	2002	2003	2004	2005	2006	2007
European Union:											
Austria	1,151	1,191	1,201	1,257	1,278	1,443	1,508	1,749	1,796	1,788	1,877
Belgium	2,338	2,673	2,858	2,864	2,686	2,343	2,277	1,863	1,711	1,626	1,624
Denmark	1,668	1,691	1,780	1,965	1,988	2,070	2,013	2,186	2,255	2,305	2,345
France	6,428	7,059	7,580	8,235	8,435	9,657	10,232	10,941	10,994	11,560	11,785
Finland	603	604	666	770	753	659	702	813	799	930	944
Germany	7,123	7,454	8,107	8,717	8,432	8,651	9,571	10,283	10,937	11,502	11,607
Greece	3,773	4,435	5,248	5,912	6,410	6,246	6,204	5,840	5,596	5,519	5,457
Irish Republic	7,781	8,522	8,966	9,295	9,293	9,813	10,163	10,862	11,789	12,356	12,259
Italy	5,233	5,895	6,454	7,033	7,456	7,654	8,913	9,677	10,713	10,571	11,207
Luxembourg	190	215	224	224	203	184	159	173	182	209	251
Netherlands	5,766	6,477	6,777	7,096	7,313	7,804	7,780	7,933	7,888	8,256	8,352
Portugal & Madeira [1]	2,887	3,178	3,443	3,607	3,752	3,967	4,022	4,256	4,540	4,745	5,339
Spain & Canary Islands	19,559	22,089	23,803	25,923	27,576	28,952	32,230	33,478	34,558	34,877	35,535
Sweden	1,589	1,877	1,896	2,032	1,958	1,976	1,993	2,253	2,321	2,290	2,267
Bulgaria	208	221	194	172	187	279	382	585	771	919	953
Cyprus	1,691	2,034	2,333	2,670	2,962	2,683	2,787	2,776	2,989	3,006	2,969
Czech Republic	490	520	541	654	736	916	1,296	2,069	2,355	2,155	2,071
Estonia	24	29	27	28	29	38	45	83	186	178	179
Hungary	325	357	398	403	383	360	375	701	1,119	1,014	960
Latvia	64	68	64	51	54	58	61	126	309	461	479
Lithuania	32	51	58	51	48	48	55	95	222	319	340
Malta	1,029	1,045	994	1,022	1,039	1,025	1,055	1,096	1,110	1,055	1,148
Poland	348	419	499	498	453	467	516	998	1,845	3,328	4,352
Romania	126	131	118	110	109	117	135	143	157	194	333
Slovak Republic	3	1	-	-	-	2	29	127	285	470	529
Slovenia	47	58	71	69	52	48	53	116	157	183	190
Total EU-15	66,089	73,361	79,003	84,930	87,534	91,419	97,768	102,308	106,079	108,534	110,851
Total EU-27	70,477	78,294	84,301	90,658	93,586	97,459	104,558	111,224	117,584	121,817	125,355
Other Europe:											
Norway	1,488	1,615	1,569	1,432	1,244	1,277	1,353	1,606	1,726	1,893	1,856
Switzerland	3,100	3,228	3,631	3,926	3,829	3,983	4,108	4,184	4,501	4,957	5,142
Gibraltar	166	183	197	208	215	227	264	309	346	329	296
Turkey	2,450	2,454	2,028	2,019	2,112	2,233	2,175	2,791	3,551	3,406	3,887
Former USSR [2]	583	603	576	667	727	814	911	1,030	1,098	1,215	1,290
Former Yugoslavia [2]	204	231	151	222	269	310	351	433	548	730	848
Rest of Europe [2]	211	240	272	329	340	268	332	403	402	436	438
Total Other Europe	8,202	8,554	8,424	8,804	8,736	9,111	9,493	10,757	12,173	12,966	13,756
Total Europe	78,678	86,849	92,724	99,463	102,322	106,570	114,050	121,980	129,757	134,783	139,112
Rest of World:											
North Africa	1,296	1,140	1,322	1,554	1,598	1,511	1,506	2,016	2,776	3,462	3,632
Southern Africa	1,220	1,371	1,438	1,510	1,588	1,584	1,602	1,768	1,733	1,771	1,818
Rest of Africa	861	854	1,009	1,129	1,163	1,310	1,336	1,588	1,719	1,829	1,973
Israel	878	925	969	967	770	630	617	659	668	672	709
Persian Gulf States	344	377	382	404	390	431	481	534	568	610	536
Saudi Arabia	385	378	350	346	297	263	229	247	205	220	257
UAE	849	926	1,056	1,324	1,524	1,795	2,022	2,535	2,881	3,256	3,736
Rest of Near and Middle East	705	777	849	913	875	907	1,002	1,238	1,372	1,470	1,625
USA	15,652	17,153	18,251	19,208	17,060	16,879	16,584	18,004	18,290	18,066	18,558
Canada	2,868	3,140	3,249	3,301	3,133	2,961	2,894	3,308	3,606	3,634	3,865
South America	474	572	587	610	523	414	379	394	379	340	395
Central America	833	825	838	862	927	884	906	1,150	1,270	1,353	1,334
Caribbean	1,235	1,399	1,635	1,744	1,692	1,657	1,763	1,895	1,828	1,903	1,948
Australia	782	900	918	916	737	693	727	874	1,211	1,169	1,211
New Zealand	173	187	194	203	154	130	202	180	189	215	344
India	973	1,012	911	911	1,017	858	960	1,073	1,579	2,329	2,486
Pakistan	376	387	413	477	486	443	517	582	654	703	684
Rest of Indian sub-continent	503	536	635	713	681	682	770	856	827	832	448
Japan	1,462	1,440	1,325	1,416	1,131	1,209	1,046	1,189	1,184	1,085	1,031
Hong Kong	1,007	1,021	996	1,081	983	1,113	1,020	1,275	1,259	1,439	1,660
Singapore	828	863	1,011	1,144	1,209	1,203	1,150	1,169	1,158	1,272	1,230
Thailand	374	446	525	575	710	715	673	718	696	673	691
Rest of Asia	1,312	1,234	1,281	1,349	1,215	1,242	1,205	1,447	1,612	1,636	1,558
Total Rest of World [3]	35,388	37,862	40,146	42,657	39,866	39,512	39,594	44,701	47,665	49,938	52,163
Oil Rigs	707	693	576	586	640	628	567	564	627	713	768
All international air passenger movements	114,773	125,404	133,446	142,706	142,827	146,711	154,211	167,245	178,049	185,434	192,042

1 Includes Azores and Cape Verde Islands.
2 See Notes & Definitions for list of countries included in group.
3 Includes Greenland.

☎020-7944 3088
The figures in this table are outside the scope of National Statistics
Source - Civil Aviation Authority

2.9 Casualties caused by aviation accidents: 1997-2007

(a) Casualties caused by accidents involving United Kingdom registered aircraft in United Kingdom airspace

	1997	1998	1999	2000	2001	2002	2003	2004	2005	2006	2007
Airline and air taxi:											
Fixed-wing:											
Crew:											
Fatal	0	0	2	1	2	0	0	0	1	0	0
Total	3	0	2	4	2	0	3	0	1	1	1
Passengers:											
Fatal	1	0	6	4	0	0	0	0	1	0	0
Total	3	1	10	4	0	0	0	0	1	0	1
Total fixed-wing [1]	6	1	12	8	2	0	3	0	2	1	3
Rotary wing:											
Crew:											
Fatal	1	1	0	0	0	2	0	0	0	2	0
Total	3	3	0	1	2	3	3	0	0	2	0
Passengers:											
Fatal	0	3	0	0	0	9	0	0	0	5	0
Total	0	5	0	2	3	11	0	0	0	5	0
Total rotary-wing [1]	3	8	0	3	6	14	3	0	0	7	0
Other (general aviation, etc.):											
Crew:											
Fatal	14	15	15	20	18	9	8	12	17	7	14
Total	44	37	53	40	50	42	46	41	52	37	36
Passengers:											
Fatal	4	6	11	7	5	3	7	7	8	0	17
Total	33	24	28	22	17	14	21	14	17	20	28
Total other [1]	79	61	82	63	68	58	68	55	70	57	64
Overall total [1]											
Fatal	20	25	34	32	25	23	15	19	25	14	31
Total	88	70	94	74	76	72	74	55	70	65	67

(b) Casualties caused by accidents involving United Kingdom registered aircraft in foreign airspace

	1997	1998	1999	2000	2001	2002	2003	2004	2005	2006	2007
Airline and air taxi:											
Fixed-wing:											
Crew:											
Fatal	0	0	2	3	0	0	0	0	0	0	0
Total	2	0	3	5	0	3	4	1	0	1	0
Passengers:											
Fatal	0	0	1	0	0	0	0	0	0	0	0
Total	4	15	43	14	0	1	1	3	0	2	0
Total fixed-wing [1]	7	15	46	19	1	4	5	4	0	4	0
Other (general aviation, etc.):											
Crew:											
Fatal	0	2	4	2	4	1	1	1	0	2	2
Total	2	2	8	3	7	1	2	4	1	2	4
Passengers:											
Fatal	0	1	1	1	2	3	1	1	0	1	0
Total	0	3	6	1	3	3	2	3	0	1	1
Total other [1]	2	5	14	4	10	4	4	7	1	3	0
Overall total [1]											
Fatal	0	3	8	6	7	4	2	2	0	3	0
Total	9	20	60	23	11	8	9	11	1	7	3

2.9 (continued) Casualties caused by aviation accidents: 1997-2007

(c) Casualties caused by accidents involving aircraft registered overseas in United Kingdom airspace

	1997	1998	1999	2000	2001	2002	2003	2004	2005	2006	2007
Airline and air taxi:											
Fixed-wing:											
Crew:											
Fatal	0	0	4	0	0	0	0	0	0	0	0
Total	0	0	5	0	0	0	0	0	1 [2]	1	0
Passengers:											
Fatal	0	0	0	0	0	0	0	0	0	0	0
Total	0	1	1	0	0	0	0	0	24 [2]	0	0
Total fixed-wing [1]	1	1	6	0	0	0	0	0	25 [2]	1	0
Other (general aviation, etc.):											
Crew:											
Fatal	1	2	0	2	5	2	4	1	1	0	2
Total	1	10	2	4	9	6	5	4	5	2	4
Passengers:											
Fatal	1	2	0	4	0	3	2	0	1	0	2
Total	1	10	1	6	4	6	5	2	5	0	4
Total other [1]	2	20	3	10	13	13	11	6	10	3	8
Overall total [1]											
Fatal	2	4	4	6	5	5	6	1	2	0	4
Total	3	21	9	10	13	13	11	6	35 [2]	4	8

1 These totals include 'third-party' casualties, not shown separately.
2 There were 25 minor injuries (1 crew and 24 passengers) in a single incident in March 2005 involving the evacuation of an aircraft.

☎020-7944 3088
The figures in this table are outside the scope of National Statistics
Source - Civil Aviation Authority

2.10 Aircraft proximity (AIRPROX): number of incidents: 1997-2007

	1997	1998	1999	2000	2001	2002	2003	2004	2005	2006	2007
Total AIRPROX civil and military:											
Risk-bearing :											
Risk of collision	36	23	23	28	33	17	14	15	19	15	9
Safety not assured	64	43	49	44	42	68	58	53	51	40	39
Total	100	66	72	72	75	85	72	68	70	55	48
No risk of collision	105	132	134	123	115	129	108	131	116	103	106
Risk not determined	3	3	2	3	5	7	1	8	2	0	0
Total AIRPROX	208	201	208	198	195	221	181	207	188	159 [1]	154
ow:											
Commercial air transport:											
Risk-bearing:											
Risk of collision	9	1	4	6	0	1	0	1	1	0	0
Safety not assured	20	14	12	8	14	7	12	7	7	6	5
Total	29	15	16	14	14	8	12	8	8	6	5
No risk of collision	67	82	83	84	65	70	54	67	78	68	60
Risk not determined	0	1	0	1	4	4	0	4	1	0	0
Total commercial air transport	96	98	99	99	83	82	66	79	87	74	65
Commercial air transport aircraft in risk-bearing AIRPROX per 100,000 hours flown in UK airspace	2.5	1.2	1.2	1.0	1.0	0.6	0.9	0.5	0.5	0.4	0.3

1 Includes one Airprox yet to be assessed.

☎020-7944 3088
The figures in this table are outside the scope of National Statistics
Source - UK Airprox Board

2.11 Employment by United Kingdom airlines: worldwide: 1997-2007

	1997	1998	1999	2000	2001	2002	2003	2004	2005	2006	Number 2007
Pilots and co-pilots	7,918	8,548	9,244	9,443	9,984	9,933	9,758	9,798	10,064	10,671	11,259
Other cockpit personnel	458	460	457	332	274	209	120	102	135	158	152
Cabin attendants	24,272	26,967	28,465	28,819	30,461	28,548	28,398	29,634	31,120	32,718	34,369
Maintenance and overhaul personnel	13,100	12,264	12,138	12,055	11,824	11,749	11,186	9,933	9,611	9,488	9,075
Tickets and sales personnel	8,369	8,929	9,643	9,100	10,062	9,074	8,168	7,706	7,312	6,555	6,258
All other personnel	29,355	30,663	32,755	31,764	31,279	27,921	27,265	26,399	26,141	25,481	24,571
Total	83,472	87,831	92,702	91,513	93,884	87,434	84,895	83,572	84,383	85,071	85,684

☎020-7944 3088
The figures in this table are outside the scope of National Statistics
Source - Civil Aviation Authority

2.12 Passenger traffic via major international airlines: 2007

Country	Airline	All scheduled traffic Passengers uplifted (millions)	All scheduled traffic Passenger kilometres (billions)	International scheduled traffic Passengers uplifted (millions)	International scheduled traffic Passenger kilometres (billions)	Charter traffic All passenger kilometres (billions)	*ow:* International passenger kilometres (billions)
United States	American	98.2	222.7	21.6	81.4	0.1	-
United States	Delta	72.9	166.2	11.4	63.2	0.3	0.1
United States	United	68.4	188.9	12.0	79.2	-	-
Germany	Lufthansa	54.2	122.1	41.3	116.8	0.1	0.1
United States	Northwest	53.7	117.3	9.9	53.5	0.2	0.1
France	Air France	50.4	128.7	31.4	117.9	0.2	0.2
Ireland	Ryanair	49.0	48.2	49.0	48.2	0.0	0.0
Japan	All Nippon Airways	49.0	59.1	4.2	20.0	0.4	0.4
United States	Continental	49.0	130.9	11.9	56.8	0.1	-
China	China Southern Airlines	47.3	70.0	3.7	10.8	0.7	0.6
Japan	JAL	47.2	85.1	11.6	56.8	1.5	1.5
United States	US Airways	42.2	70.1	5.0	18.6	-	0.0
China	China Eastern Airlines	38.9	56.6	5.5	18.0	0.6	0.4
China	Air China	34.8	66.8	5.9	28.3	0.2	0.2
United Kingdom	British Airways	32.4	112.3	27.8	110.2	-	-
United Kingdom	Easyjet	30.1	30.7	24.2	28.0	0.0	0.0
Spain	Iberia	26.7	54.2	13.0	45.5	0.0	0.0
Scandinavia	SAS	25.4	27.3	14.0	21.8	3.7	3.7
Italy	Alitalia	24.7	38.6	13.8	32.7	0.2	0.2
Australia	Qantas	24.7	82.1	8.0	57.9	0.1	-
Canada	Air Canada	23.4	74.4	11.9	53.4	0.1	0.1
Republic Of Korea	Korean Air	23.4	57.3	13.1	53.4	1.2	1.1
Netherlands	KLM	23.2	74.5	23.2	74.5	0.0	0.0
United States	America West	15.7	28.4	1.0	1.9	-	-
Malaysia	Malaysian Airlines	14.0	40.1	8.6	36.8	0.0	0.0

☎020-7944 3088
The figures in this table are outside the scope of National Statistics
Source - ICAO

2.13 Major Airports in the United Kingdom

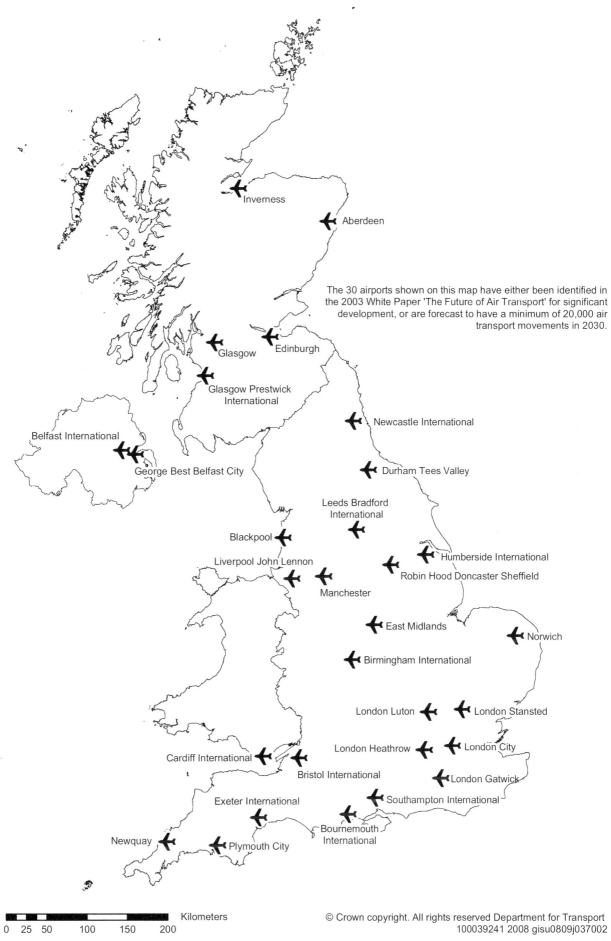

The 30 airports shown on this map have either been identified in the 2003 White Paper 'The Future of Air Transport' for significant development, or are forecast to have a minimum of 20,000 air transport movements in 2030.

Inverness

Aberdeen

Glasgow

Edinburgh

Glasgow Prestwick International

Belfast International

George Best Belfast City

Newcastle International

Durham Tees Valley

Leeds Bradford International

Blackpool

Liverpool John Lennon

Humberside International

Robin Hood Doncaster Sheffield

Manchester

East Midlands

Norwich

Birmingham International

London Luton

London Stansted

London Heathrow

London City

Cardiff International

London Gatwick

Bristol International

Southampton International

Exeter International

Newquay

Plymouth City

Bournemouth International

Kilometers

0   25   50   100   150   200

☎020-7944 3088

3 Energy and the Environment:

Notes and Definitions

Petroleum consumption: by transport mode and fuel type: 3.1

Motor spirit (All grades):
> One tonne = 299 gallons or 1,361 litres

DERV fuel (0.005% or less sulphur):
> One tonne = 264 gallons or 1,199 litres

Petroleum consumption figures are published in the *Digest of United Kingdom Energy Statistics* (DUKES) by the Department for Business, Enterprise and Regulatory Reform (BERR) at: http://www.berr.gov.uk/energy/statistics/publications/dukes/page45537.html

Road transport - Deliveries of motor spirit and DERV fuel for use in road vehicles of all kinds. As part of their work to compile the UK emissions inventory, AEA has constructed estimates for the consumption of road transport fuels by different vehicle classes. There has been a reallocation of the road transport fuel consumption between different vehicle types for years prior to 2007.

A small proportion of motor spirit and diesel (approximately 0.3 million tonnes and 0.01 million tonnes per year respectively) is not used by road vehicles, which is included in the total BERR publish for motor spirit and diesel used.

Estimates for the use of gas for road vehicles are based on information on the amounts of duty received by HM Revenue and Customs from the tax on gas used as a road fuel.

Railways - Deliveries of fuel oil, gas/diesel oil and burning oil to railways are based on estimates produced by AEA as part of their work to compile the UK Greenhouse Gas Inventory. Railway fuels include some amounts of burning oil not used directly for transport purposes.

National navigation - Fuel oil and gas/diesel oil delivered, other than under international bunker contracts, for fishing vessels, UK oil and gas exploration and production, coastal and inland shipping and for use in ports and harbours.

Air transport - Total inland deliveries of aviation turbine fuel and aviation spirit. The figures cover deliveries of aviation fuels in the United Kingdom to international and other airlines, British and foreign Governments (including armed services) and for private flying.

Energy consumption: by transport mode and source of energy: 3.2

This is the energy content of fuels delivered to consumers. The data measures the energy content of the fuels, both primary and secondary, supplied to final users. Thus it is net of fuel industry own use and conversion, transmission and distribution losses, but it includes conversion losses by final users.

Detailed data for individual fuels are converted from original units to tonnes of oil equivalent using gross calorific values and conversion factors appropriate to each category of fuel. The results are then aggregated according to the categories used in the tables. Gross calorific values represent the total energy content of the fuel, including the energy needed to evaporate the water present in the fuel.

1 tonne of oil equivalent (toe):
> = 10^7 kilocalories
> = 396.83 therms
> = 41.868 Gigajoules (GJ)
> = 11,630 Kilowatt hours (kWh).

This unit should be regarded as a measure of energy content rather than a physical quantity. There is no intention to represent an actual physical tonne of oil, and indeed actual tonnes of oil will normally have measurements in tonnes of oil equivalent which differ from units.

Gross calorific values are reviewed each year in collaboration with the fuel industries. Estimated average gross calorific values revised in 2007 for motor spirit and gas/diesel oil (DERV) are:

47.1 GJ per tonne of motor spirit
45.5 GJ per tonne of Gas/diesel oil (DERV)

For railways, data are based on estimates produced by AEA as part of their work to compile the UK Greenhouse Gas Inventory.

Petrol and diesel prices and duties per litre: 3.3

The price estimates are based on information provided by oil marketing companies and super/hypermarket chains and are representative of prices paid (inclusive of taxes) on or about the 15th of the month. Changes in fuel duty usually occur during the month in which a Budget is held. VAT is rebated to business users.

From 2005, the collection of Lead Replacement Petrol prices has been discontinued due to the low volume of sales.

The figures in Table 3.3 differ from those in Table 10.8 because of the differences in availability and timing of data collection. The international comparisons in Table 10.8 (supplied by BERR, and extracted from the IEA publication 'Energy Prices and Taxes'), are based on averages over the year, whereas Table 3.3 attempts to be as up to date as reasonably possible. The use of the term Tax in part (b) of Table 10.8 is necessary because some other European countries impose other taxes and fees on fuel. For the UK this includes just fuel duty and VAT.

Average fuel consumption: 3.4

Passenger cars: These figures are based upon fuel consumption as recorded by participants in the National Travel Survey (NTS). This is estimated by recording the start and finish points of both the fuel gauge and the milometer, and the amount of fuel put in the vehicle in the travel week.

From the 2005 survey, NTS data has been weighted for the first time, and weights have now been applied to data from 1995. Results published here for 1995 onwards may differ from previously published figures which were based on unweighted data.

In 2002, the drawn sample size for the NTS was nearly trebled compared with previous years, enabling key results to be presented on a single year basis for the first time since the survey became continuous. Changes to the methodology in 2002 mean that there are some inconsistencies with data for earlier years. Data for earlier years are shown for a three year time period because of the smaller sample sizes for individual years.

HGVs: These figures are based on fuel consumption as recorded by participants in the Continuing Survey of Road Goods Transport (CSRGT). Respondents report the amount of fuel purchased during the survey week, with the amount of fuel at the start and end of the week

assumed to balance out across the sample as a whole.

Unlike the NTS, the sample size is sufficient to report fuel consumption on a yearly basis for the whole time series. The fuel consumption figures have not been re-weighted to the population, so the figures may not be fully representative of the HGV fleet.

The HGV fuel consumption figures were revised this year and the new time series covering 1993-2007 can be found in Road Freight Statistics 2007 (http://www.dft.gov.uk/pgr/statistics/datatablespubli cations/freight/goodsbyroad/roadfreightstatistics20 07).

Average new car fuel consumption: 3.5

Chart 3.5 includes separate trends for diesel and petrol cars. These trends include all types of passenger cars registered including high performance cars, 4x4's and MPV's. The data are calculated from new registration weighted average CO_2 emissions for petrol and diesel cars and the typical carbon content of petrol and diesel. This approach accounts for the relative sales of different models of car. The registration weighted average CO_2 figures are produced to monitor trends in average petrol and diesel car CO_2 emissions from year to year. The CO_2 figures for individual vehicle models are obtained under carefully controlled laboratory conditions in order to ensure repeatability and a fair comparison between models. The actual fuel consumption achieved on the road will reflect many extraneous factors such as cold starts, different driving conditions, weather conditions, different loads carried, gradients, use of electrical accessories etc. The data shown here represents fuel economy on the current standard test used to obtain comparative data on the relative fuel economy of vehicles (a drive cycle simulating urban and extra-urban driving, effectively with a single occupant, on a level road and without heaters or lights on).

Emissions for road vehicles in urban conditions: 3.6

This table takes into account emission factors for cars, light goods vehicles, heavy goods vehicles, buses and coaches and motorcycles of different ages, and indexes them against a baseline emissions from a pre-1993 petrol car without a three-way catalyst (=100). The emission factors, in units of grammes of pollutant per kilometre travelled (g/km), are from the National Atmospheric Emissions Inventory, maintained by AEA Energy and Environment on behalf of DEFRA, and are based on the latest compilation of equations derived by the Transport Research Laboratory (TRL) relating emission factor to average vehicle speed. The equations are derived from a database of emissions measured from actual in-service vehicles, the measurements being carried out by different laboratories in the UK and the rest of Europe over different drive cycles. Particulate emissions (these are fine particles less than 10 micrometres or 0.01 millimetres diameter) are much lower from vehicles with petrol engines than they are from vehicles with diesel engines. For this pollutant, the index is against emissions from a pre-1993 diesel car (=100). Measurements have been made of emissions from vehicles of different sizes within each vehicle category. The figures shown here reflect average values of emission factors at a typical urban speed, weighted by the mix of sizes of vehicles in the fleet.

Since January 1993, all new cars have had to meet new EC emission standards. This resulted in the use of three way catalysts for petrol cars to meet those standards (EC Directive 91/441/EEC).

Table 3.7 (b) shows improved information on HGVs which is based on average fuel economy of the HGV fleet each year. However, this does not take into account the revised fuel consumption statistics published in Road Freight Statistics 2007.

Carbon dioxide emissions in the United Kingdom: 3.7

The data in Table 3.7 are presented in terms of weight of carbon dioxide emitted. To convert weight of carbon to carbon dioxide emissions, carbon figures are multiplied by a factor of 44/12.

Carbon dioxide:
Carbon dioxide is the most important greenhouse gas and is estimated to account for about two thirds of man made global warming. Although its global warming potential is much less per tonne than the other greenhouse gases it is present in the atmosphere in vastly greater quantities.

National Atmospheric Emissions Inventory (NAEI)

Emission figures, including more detail about the estimates and additional data, are published in the *Digest of Environmental Statistics*, by the Department for Environment, Food and Rural Affairs (DEFRA) at: www.defra.gov.uk/environment/statistics/Index.htm

The NAEI carbon dioxide emissions figures shown in Table 3.7, part (a) are based on the reporting guidelines of the Intergovernmental Panel on

Climate Change (IPCC). These are the guidelines used for international reporting of greenhouse gases. This system excludes international navigation and aviation bunker fuels from national totals, but these are shown as memo items separately from the national total.

Parts (b) and (c) of Table 3.7 show carbon dioxide emissions based on National Communication categories.

The table includes emissions from Crown Dependencies of Jersey, Guernsey and Isle of Man, and excludes emissions from Overseas Territories.

The main difference between "by source" and "end user" emissions comes from the treatment of emissions from combustion of fossil fuels, the largest source of carbon dioxide in the UK.
By source:
The **source** breakdown splits emissions by the sector producing them.
By end user:
The **end user** breakdown also shows emissions by the sector responsible for them, but redistributes emissions from power stations and other fuel processing industries to end users on an approximate basis according to their use of the fuel. Emissions by end user are subject to more uncertainty than emissions by source and should only be used to give a broad indication of emissions by sector.

Emissions from road transport are calculated either from a combination of total fuel consumption data and fuel properties or from a combination of drive related emission factors and road traffic data. The 2006 inventory contains a reallocation of the total road transport CO_2 between different vehicle types for years prior to 2006. This is a consequence of using revised fuel consumption factors for different classes of vehicles, particularly for HGVs.

The time series for railways for all years prior to 2006 was revised to take into account new fuel consumption data obtained from the Association of Train Operating Companies (ATOC). This resulted in an increase in emission estimates from the railway sector for each of these earlier years in the 2006 inventory.

The 3% decrease in domestic aviation emissions between 2005 and 2006 is due to a change in the aircraft fleet making domestic flights. In 2006, there was an increase in the use of Airbus A319 from Boeing 737-300 series. The Airbus is a more fuel efficient aircraft.

Further information on the UK atmospheric emissions estimates can be found at: http://www.naei.org.uk

Environmental Accounts (EA)

The Environmental Accounts provide information on the demands that UK economic activity places on the environment and on the importance of natural resources to the economy. These demands include the emission of greenhouse gases and air pollutants.

The statistics presented in the Environmental Accounts are on a **UK residents** basis, as opposed to being based on fuel purchases in the UK. This means that they measure the emissions caused by people residing in the UK, and UK-registered businesses. The principle is that this is the same basis on which the National Accounts are produced, so environmental impacts can be directly compared with economic benefits.

The UK transport industries comprise: railways, buses and coaches, tubes and trams, taxis, road freight, water transport, air transport, and transport via pipelines. The road freight industry covers road haulage companies as opposed to all types of road freight. Lorries owned by retailers for instance are allocated to the retail industry.

Further information on Environmental Accounts can be found on the Office for National Statistics (ONS) website at: http://www.statistics.gov.uk/statbase/Product.asp?vlnk=3698

The main differences between the NAEI and EA's are:

- ONS apply a cross-boundary adjustment to remove purchases by overseas residents of UK fuel, and then add purchases by UK residents of foreign fuel.
- Environmental Accounts include international aviation and shipping.
- The Environmental Accounts breaks down emissions using the Eurostat industry classification, which looks at the economic sector of the person or company responsible for the activity, rather than the activity itself.

Pollutant emissions from transport in the United Kingdom: 3.8

Emission figures, including more detail about the estimates and additional data are published in the *Digest of Environmental Statistics*, by the Department for Environment, Food and Rural Affairs (DEFRA) at:

http://www.defra.gov.uk/environment/statistics/airqual/alltables.htm

Figures shown in Table 3.8 are based on United Nations Economic Commission for Europe (UNECE) definitions. This system, like the IPCC, excludes international navigation and aviation bunker fuels from national totals, but these are shown as memo items separately from the national total.

Carbon monoxide (CO): Derived from the incomplete combustion of fuels containing carbon. It is one of the most directly toxic of substances, interfering with respiratory bio-chemistry and can affect the central nervous and cardiovascular systems. Other pollutants can exacerbate the effects. The fitting of catalytic converters to all new petrol engine vehicles made after 1992 has reduced emissions of carbon monoxide from the 1992 level.

Nitrogen oxides (NO_x) (expressed as nitrogen dioxide equivalent): A number of nitrogen compounds including nitrogen dioxide and nitric oxide are formed in the combustion of fossil fuel. Nitrogen dioxide is directly harmful to human health causing respiratory problems and can reduce lung function. Nitrogen oxides also contribute to the formation of ozone which is a harmful secondary pollutant in the lower atmosphere and also an important greenhouse gas contributing to global warming (high levels of ozone increase susceptibility to respiratory disease and irritate the eyes, nose, throat and respiratory system). Oxides of nitrogen can also have adverse effects on plants, reducing growth. In addition they contribute to acid rain. Emissions of nitrogen oxides from petrol engined vehicles have been reduced from the 1992 level as new vehicles built from 1992 onwards must comply with EC standards (normally by the fitting of a suitable catalytic converter).

Particulates (PM_{10}): Airborne particles may be measured in a number of ways. For quantifying the particles produced by transport (especially motor traffic), the most commonly used indicator relies on the use of a size-selective sampler which collects smaller particles preferentially, collecting more than 95 per cent of 5 m (0.005 millimetres) particles, 50 per cent of 10 m aerodynamic particles, and less than 5 per cent of 20 m particles. The resultant mass of material is known as PM_{10}. The road transport figures include emissions from tyre and brake wear.

Benzene: A known human carcinogen, the main source of benzene is the combustion and distribution of petrol. Some benzene evaporates directly into the atmosphere. Benzene is also emitted in a number of industrial processes. The large reduction in benzene emissions in 2000 was due to a reduction in the benzene content of petrol.

1,3–butadiene: A suspected human carcinogen, the main source of 1,3-butadiene is motor vehicle exhausts where 1,3-butadiene is formed from the cracking of higher olefines. 1,3-butadiene is also used in the production of synthetic rubber for tyres.

Lead (Pb): Of concern because of its effects on health, particularly that of children. The main sources of lead in air are from lead in petrol, coal combustion, and metal works. The maximum amount of lead permitted in petrol was reduced from 0.45 grams per litre to 0.40 in 1981 and then again in December 1985 to 0.15. A further step to reduce lead emissions from petrol was taken in 1986 when unleaded petrol was first sold in the United Kingdom. There was a rapid increase in the uptake of unleaded petrol in the 1990s followed by a ban on the general sale of leaded petrol at the end of 1999.

Sulphur dioxide (SO$_2$): An acid gas, sulphur dioxide can affect health and vegetation. It affects the lining of the nose, throat and airways of the lung, in particular, among those who suffer from asthma and chronic lung disease. The United Nations Economic Commission for Europe's (UNECE) Second Sulphur Protocol sets reduction targets for total SO$_2$ emissions of 50 per cent by the year 2000, 70 per cent by 2005 and 80 per cent by 2010 from a 1980 baseline. By 2000, the UK had achieved a 75 per cent reduction from 1980 baseline levels, 25 per cent ahead of the UNECE target level for that year. Road transport emissions have fallen by over 87 per cent since 1998 following a reduction in the sulphur content of fuel.

Aircraft noise: 3.9

Air transport movements are landings or take-offs of aircraft engaged in transport of passengers or cargo on commercial terms. All scheduled service movements (whether loaded or empty) are included, as well as charter movements transporting passengers or cargo. Air taxi movements are excluded.

The equivalent continuous sound level (Leq) is an index of aircraft noise exposure. It is a measure of the equivalent continuous sound level averaged over a 16 hour day from 0700 to 2300 hours BST and is calculated during the peak summer months mid-June to mid-September.

The contours referred to are broadly comparable with the previous Noise and Number Index (NNI) - The change was announced by the Minister for Aviation on 4 September 1990. 57dBA Leq represents the approximate onset of significant community disturbance (comparable with 35 NNI at the time), 63dBA Leq moderate disturbance and 69dBA Leq high disturbance. Leq is correlated with community response to aircraft noise, but it is recognised that the reactions of different individuals to aircraft noise can vary considerably. Changes in wind direction from year to year influence the area affected by aircraft noise.

The methodology underlying the calculation of the aircraft noise Leq contours is published in: *The CAA Leq Aircraft Noise Contour Model: ANCON Version 1* (DORA Report DR 9120), *The UK Civil Aircraft Noise Contour Model ANCON: Improvements in Version 2* (R&D Report 9842) and *The CAA Aircraft Noise Contour Model: ANCON Version 2.3* (ERCD Report 0606 - to be published).

Further information on the availability of annual contour reports for Heathrow, Gatwick and Stansted can be found on DfT website at: http://www.dft.gov.uk/pgr/aviation/environmentalissues/nec/

3.1 Petroleum consumption: by transport mode and fuel type: United Kingdom: [1] 1997-2007

Million tonnes/percentage

	1997	1998	1999	2000	2001	2002	2003	2004	2005	2006	2007 [2]
Road transport:											
Motor spirit											
Cars & Taxis	20.58	20.25	20.36	20.11	19.76	19.73	18.91	18.56	17.86	17.29	16.76
Light goods	1.27	1.20	1.02	0.89	0.78	0.67	0.58	0.51	0.44	0.44	0.42
Motorcycles	0.14	0.14	0.15	0.15	0.15	0.15	0.17	0.15	0.16	0.15	0.14
Diesel											
Cars & Taxis	2.42	2.48	2.76	2.90	3.05	3.37	3.62	3.98	4.31	4.58	4.78
Light goods	3.13	3.36	3.36	3.41	3.66	4.10	4.36	4.63	5.60	5.85	6.11
Heavy goods	7.87	7.78	8.02	8.07	8.12	8.15	8.39	8.61	8.05	8.16	8.53
Buses & Coaches	1.55	1.52	1.36	1.24	1.22	1.30	1.33	1.28	1.47	1.55	1.62
Propane	-	-	0.01	0.02	0.05	0.09	0.10	0.11	0.12	0.13	0.12
All [3]	36.96	36.73	37.03	36.79	36.78	37.55	37.46	37.84	38.01	38.14	38.47
Railways:											
Gas/diesel oil and fuel oil	0.52	0.55	0.57	0.57	0.60	0.60	0.60	0.63	0.64	0.65	0.63
Burning oil	0.01	0.01	0.01	0.01	0.01	0.01	0.01	0.01	0.01	0.01	0.01
All	0.53	0.56	0.58	0.59	0.61	0.61	0.61	0.64	0.65	0.67	0.64
Water transport:											
Gas/diesel oil	1.04	0.98	0.91	0.91	0.74	0.60	1.09	0.84	0.92	1.19	0.94
Fuel oil	0.13	0.10	0.07	0.04	0.03	0.04	0.05	0.27	0.35	0.50	0.57
All	1.16	1.09	0.98	0.95	0.78	0.65	1.14	1.11	1.27	1.69	1.51
Air:											
All aviation fuels	8.45	9.28	9.98	10.86	10.67	10.57	10.81	11.69	12.55	12.69	12.67
All petroleum used by transport [3]	47.10	47.65	48.58	49.18	48.84	49.38	50.02	51.28	52.48	53.18	53.29
All petroleum use (energy and non-energy)	79.25	78.44	77.97	77.20	76.41	76.23	77.15	79.07	80.73	79.75	76.94
Transport as a percentage of all energy and non-energy use	*59*	*61*	*62*	*64*	*64*	*65*	*65*	*65*	*65*	*67*	*69*

1 There are revisions to some of the earlier data, for details see
  "Digest of UK Energy Statistics 2008" published by BERR.
2 Figures for 2007 for road transport mode are estimated on 2006 ratios.
3 Excludes a small amount of motor spirit and diesel not used by road vehicles.

☎020-7944 4129
Source - BERR

3.2 Energy consumption: by transport mode and source of energy: United Kingdom: [1] 1997-2007

Million tonnes of oil equivalent/percentage

	1997	1998	1999	2000	2001	2002	2003	2004	2005	2006	2007
Road transport											
Petroleum	41.26	41.02	41.40	41.07	41.10	41.94	41.82	42.22	42.39	42.51	42.81
Railways											
Petroleum	0.58	0.61	0.63	0.64	0.66	0.66	0.67	0.70	0.71	0.73	0.70
Water transport											
Petroleum	1.26	1.18	1.07	1.03	0.84	0.70	1.23	1.20	1.37	1.81	1.62
Aviation											
Petroleum	9.32	10.24	11.02	11.98	11.77	11.66	11.94	12.91	13.86	14.00	13.97
All modes											
Electricity [2]	0.72	0.73	0.74	0.74	0.76	0.73	0.71	0.73	0.76	0.71	0.71
All energy used by transport	53.14	53.77	54.85	55.46	55.14	55.68	56.37	57.75	59.08	59.75	59.81
All energy used by final users	154.37	155.92	156.53	159.21	160.93	156.48	158.03	159.82	160.19	157.95	154.87
Energy used by transport as a percentage of all energy used by final users	*34*	*34*	*35*	*35*	*34*	*36*	*36*	*36*	*37*	*38*	*39*

1 There are revisions to some of the earlier data, for details see
  "Digest of UK Energy Statistics 2008" published by BERR.
2 Includes consumption at transport premises.

☎020-7944 4129
Source - BERR

3.3 Petrol and diesel prices and duties per litre: at April: 1998-2008

Pence/percentage

	April 1998	April 1999	April 2000	April 2001	April 2002	April 2003	April 2004	April 2005	April 2006	April 2007	April 2008
Lead replacement petrol[1]											
Price	72.4	77.8	84.5	78.2	77.8	81.4	81.3	88.5	..	..	..
Duty	49.3	52.9	50.9	46.8	48.8	48.8	47.1	47.1	..	..	..
VAT	10.8	11.6	12.6	11.7	11.6	12.1	12.1	13.2	..	..	..
All tax	60.0	64.5	63.5	58.5	60.4	61.0	59.2	60.3	..	..	..
All tax as a percentage of price	*83*	*83*	*75*	*75*	*78*	*75*	*73*	*68*	*..*	*..*	*..*
Unleaded petrol[2]											
Price	65.8	70.2	80.0	75.9	75.0	78.2	77.8	85.4	94.1	91.9	107.6
Duty	44.0	47.2	48.8	45.8	45.8	45.8	47.1	47.1	47.1	48.4	50.4
VAT	9.8	10.5	11.9	11.3	11.2	11.7	11.6	12.7	14.0	13.7	16.0
All tax	53.8	57.7	60.7	57.1	57.0	57.5	58.7	59.8	61.1	62.0	66.4
All tax as a percentage of price	*82*	*82*	*76*	*75*	*76*	*73*	*75*	*70*	*65*	*67*	*62*
Ultra low sulphur diesel[3]											
Price	66.8	73.2	81.1	77.3	76.9	80.9	79.2	89.6	97.6	94.7	116.6
Duty	45.0	50.2	48.8	45.8	45.8	45.8	47.1	47.1	47.1	48.4	50.4
VAT	10.0	10.9	12.1	11.5	11.5	12.0	11.8	13.3	14.5	14.1	17.4
All tax	54.9	61.1	60.9	57.3	57.3	57.9	58.9	60.4	61.6	62.5	67.7
All tax as a percentage of price	*82*	*83*	*75*	*74*	*74*	*72*	*74*	*67*	*63*	*66*	*58*

1 Prices prior to 2000 were for four star petrol
  Pump prices are broadly the same.
2 From April 2001, Premium unleaded prices represent Ultra Low Sulphur Petrol (ULSP)
  Pump prices are broadly the same.
3 Prices prior to 2000 were for diesel engined road vehicle fuel (DERV)
  Pump prices are broadly the same.

☎020-7215 6935
Source - BERR

3.4 Average fuel consumption by age and type of vehicle and type of fuel: 1995/1997 to 2006

a) Passenger cars

Miles per gallon/litres per 100 km

	1995/1997	1998/2000	2002	2003	2004	2005	2006
Petrol cars							
Up to 2 years	32	30	31	31	32	32	32
Over 2 to 6 years	31	30	31	31	31	31	31
Over 6 to 10 years	30	30	31	31	30	30	30
Over 10 years	29	28	28	29	29	30	29
All petrol cars	31	30	30	30	30	31	31
Diesel cars[1]							
Up to 2 years	43	35	40	40	41	40	39
Over 2 years	44	39	38	38	39	38	39
All diesel cars	44	38	39	39	40	39	39
Company cars[1]	34	30	35	34	36	36	35
Private cars	32	31	31	32	32	32	32
All cars (miles/gallon)	32	31	32	32	32	33	32
All cars (litres/100 km)	8.8	9.1	8.9	8.9	8.8	8.7	8.8

b) HGVs

Miles per gallon

	1996[R]	1999[R]	2002[R]	2003[R]	2004[R]	2005[R]	2006[R]
Rigid vehicles	9.9	10.3	9.8	9.5	9.8	10.0	9.7
Articulated vehicles	7.6	8.0	7.8	7.8	8.0	8.2	8.1

1 These estimates have a large sampling error because of the smaller sample sizes involved.

Cars: 020 7944 3097
HGVs: 020 7944 4261
Source - Passenger cars: National Travel Survey
HGVs - Survey of Road Goods Transport

3.5 Average New Car Fuel Consumption: 1997-2007
    (Registration-Weighted: petrol and diesel vehicles)

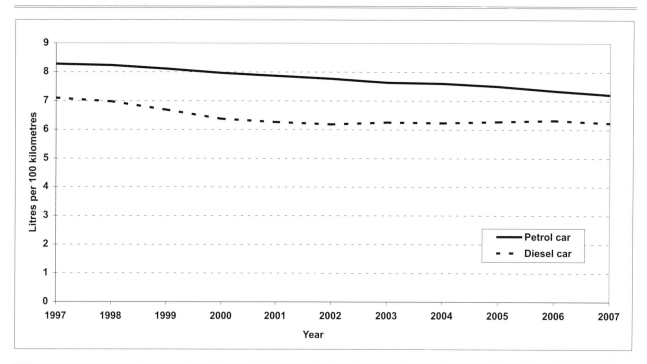

☎020-7944 4129
The figures in this graph are outside the scope of National Statistics
Source - Cleaner Fuels and Vehicles Division, DfT

3.6 Emissions for road vehicles (per vehicle kilometre) in urban conditions

Index: petrol car without three-way catalyst: pre 1993 = 100[1]

(a) Road vehicles (per vehicle kilometre) in urban conditions:			Carbon monoxide	Hydro-carbons[2]	Oxides of nitrogen	Particu-lates[3]	Carbon dioxide[4]
Petrol car without three-way catalyst	Pre-Euro I	pre 1993	100	100	100	16	100
Petrol car with three-way catalyst	Euro I	1993-1996	10	2	13	2	98
Petrol car with three-way catalyst	Euro II	1997-2000	7	2	12	-	98
Petrol car with three-way catalyst	Euro III	2001-2005	6	1	5	-	92
Petrol car with three-way catalyst	Euro IV	2006-	5	1	4	-	82
Diesel car	Pre-Euro I	pre 1993	6	10	38	100	97
Diesel car	Euro I	1993-1996	3	5	33	37	95
Diesel car	Euro II	1997-2000	2	4	33	33	93
Diesel car	Euro III	2001-2005	1	3	33	21	83
Diesel car	Euro IV	2006-	1	3	17	11	75
Petrol light goods vehicle without three-way catalyst	Pre-Euro I	pre 1994	136	96	94	19	109
Petrol light goods vehicle with three-way catalyst	Euro I	1994-1997	20	3	19	2	138
Petrol light goods vehicle with three-way catalyst	Euro II	1998-2000	5	2	17	1	146
Petrol light goods vehicle with three-way catalyst	Euro III	2001-2005	4	1	7	1	139
Petrol light goods vehicle with three-way catalyst	Euro IV	2006-	3	1	5	1	128
Diesel light goods vehicle	Pre-Euro I	pre 1994	10	19	81	187	141
Diesel light goods vehicle	Euro I	1994-1997	4	9	63	52	141
Diesel light goods vehicle	Euro II	1998-2001	4	9	60	53	143
Diesel light goods vehicle	Euro III	2002-2005	3	7	45	37	131
Diesel light goods vehicle	Euro IV	2006-	3	4	23	24	122
Heavy goods vehicle - Rigid	Pre-Euro I	pre 1993	25	118	344	277	*See table 3.6b*
Heavy goods vehicle - Rigid	Euro I	1993-1996	14	43	437	143	
Heavy goods vehicle - Rigid	Euro II	1997-2001	11	34	373	100	
Heavy goods vehicle - Rigid	Euro III	2002-2005	8	23	258	72	
Heavy goods vehicle - Rigid	Euro IV	2006-	6	17	194	16	
Heavy goods vehicle - Artics	Pre-Euro I	pre 1993	29	100	969	407	*See table 3.6b*
Heavy goods vehicle - Artics	Euro I	1993-1996	40	107	1,159	375	
Heavy goods vehicle - Artics	Euro II	1997-2001	31	88	799	260	
Heavy goods vehicle - Artics	Euro III	2002-2005	21	60	554	187	
Heavy goods vehicle - Artics	Euro IV	2006-	16	44	416	42	
Buses		pre 1993	81	90	840	399	649
Buses		1993-1996	25	67	674	202	537
Buses		1997-2001	21	48	603	132	485
Buses		2002-2005	14	33	418	95	485
Buses		2006-	12	33	292	29	470
Motorcycle (less than 50cc) - two stroke		pre 2000	236	854	2	26	42
Motorcycle (less than 50cc) - two stroke		2000-2005	24	188	1	26	19
Motorcycle (less than 50cc) - two stroke		2006-	24	188	1	26	19
Motorcycle (greater than 50cc) - two stroke		pre 2000	231	662	2	26	52
Motorcycle (greater than 50cc) - two stroke		2000-2005	119	458	2	26	41
Motorcycle (greater than 50cc) - two stroke		2006-	50	174	2	26	41
Motorcycle (greater than 50cc) - four stroke		pre 2000	206	115	9	78	52
Motorcycle (greater than 50cc) - four stroke		2000-2005	69	48	13	78	45
Motorcycle (greater than 50cc) - four stroke		2006-	29	18	13	78	45

(b) Fleet averaged CO_2 emissions for HGVs (per vehicle kilometre) in urban conditions[5]

Year	Rigid	Articulated
1990	407	677
1991	414	675
1992	414	670
1993	435	674
1994	402	635
1995	418	604
1996	410	587
1997	414	573
1998	388	543
1999	397	546
2000	402	537
2001	415	533
2002	400	533
2003	410	538
2004	433	510
2005	400	492
2006	405	493

1 Particulates index is diesel car: pre 1993 =100.
2 Figures based on non-methane hydrocarbons.
3 Legislative standards exist only for diesel vehicles.
4 Legislative standards do not apply to CO_2 emissions, but average factors
   are available for different legislative vehicle classes based on test cycle data.
   Better information on HGVs is based on average fuel economy of the HGV
   fleet each year, see Table 3.6b.
5 Based on fleet averaged fuel economy of HGVs using data from DfT survey
   of road goods transport, corrected for urban driving conditions
   for comparison with indices in Table 3.6a.

☎020-7944 4276
The figures in this table are outside
the scope of National Statistics

Source - AEA Energy and Environment

3.7 Carbon dioxide emissions in the United Kingdom: 1996-2006[1]

	1996	1997	1998	1999	2000	2001	2002	2003	2004	2005	2006	Per cent of total in 2006
(a) By IPCC source category (NAEI)[2]												Million tonnes of carbon dioxide/percentage
Transport:												
Road transport	115.2	116.6	115.9	116.8	116.0	116.0	118.4	118.2	119.4	119.9	120.3	21.7
Passenger cars	71.8	72.2	71.3	72.6	72.2	71.6	72.5	70.8	70.8	69.6	68.7	12.4
Light duty vehicles	13.4	13.9	14.4	13.8	13.6	14.0	15.1	15.6	16.3	19.1	19.9	3.6
Buses	5.1	4.9	4.8	4.3	3.9	3.8	4.1	4.2	4.0	4.6	4.9	0.9
HGVs	24.3	24.9	24.6	25.4	25.6	25.7	25.8	26.6	27.2	25.5	25.8	4.7
Mopeds & motorcycles	0.4	0.4	0.4	0.5	0.5	0.5	0.5	0.5	0.5	0.5	0.5	0.1
LPG emissions (all vehicles)	0.0	0.0	0.0	0.0	0.1	0.2	0.3	0.3	0.3	0.4	0.4	0.1
Other (road vehicle engines)	0.2	0.2	0.2	0.2	0.2	0.2	0.2	0.2	0.2	0.2	0.2	-
Other transport	7.3	7.3	7.3	7.2	7.2	6.9	6.5	8.2	8.4	9.2	10.5	1.9
Civil aviation	1.4	1.4	1.5	1.7	1.9	2.0	2.0	2.1	2.2	2.4	2.3	0.4
Railways[3]	1.7	1.7	1.8	1.8	1.8	1.9	1.9	2.0	2.1	2.1	2.2	0.4
National navigation	4.0	3.8	3.6	3.2	3.1	2.6	2.2	3.7	3.7	4.2	5.5	1.0
Other mobile sources and machinery	0.3	0.3	0.4	0.4	0.4	0.4	0.4	0.4	0.4	0.4	0.5	0.1
Total domestic transport	122.5	123.9	123.2	123.9	123.2	122.9	124.9	126.3	127.7	129.0	130.8	23.6
Net emissions all sources	571.0	548.1	549.9	540.3	548.6	559.4	542.7	554.7	555.1	555.2	554.5	100.0
Memo items[4]												
International bunkers - Aviation	21.4	22.8	25.3	27.5	30.3	29.6	29.0	29.7	32.5	35.1	35.6	.
International bunkers - Navigation	7.3	8.2	9.0	6.5	5.7	6.4	5.3	5.1	5.9	5.9	6.8	.
(b) By National Communication source category (NAEI)[2]												Million tonnes of carbon dioxide/percentage
Transport:												
Road	115.2	116.6	115.9	116.8	116.0	116.0	118.4	118.2	119.4	119.9	120.3	21.7
Aviation	1.4	1.4	1.5	1.7	1.9	2.0	2.0	2.1	2.2	2.4	2.3	0.4
Railways[3]	1.7	1.7	1.8	1.8	1.8	1.9	1.9	2.0	2.1	2.1	2.2	0.4
Railways - stationary combustion	0.5	0.5	0.5	0.5	0.4	0.5	0.4	0.1	0.04	0.04	0.04	-
Shipping	4.0	3.8	3.6	3.2	3.1	2.6	2.2	3.7	3.7	4.2	5.5	1.0
Aircraft support vehicles	0.3	0.3	0.4	0.4	0.4	0.4	0.4	0.4	0.4	0.4	0.5	0.1
Military aircraft and shipping	3.8	3.6	3.2	3.1	2.9	2.9	3.1	2.8	2.9	2.8	2.7	0.5
Transport Total	126.8	128.1	126.9	127.6	126.6	126.2	128.4	129.2	130.7	131.9	133.5	24.1
Net emissions all sources	571.0	548.1	549.9	540.3	548.6	559.4	542.7	554.7	555.1	555.2	554.5	100.0
(c) By National Communication end user category (NAEI)[5]												Million tonnes of carbon dioxide/percentage
Transport:												
Road	133.1	134.2	133.4	134.2	133.3	133.4	137.4	136.5	136.2	137.0	135.0	24.3
Aviation	1.6	1.6	1.8	2.0	2.2	2.3	2.3	2.4	2.5	2.7	2.6	0.5
Railways[3]	3.4	3.4	3.5	3.4	3.5	3.6	3.7	3.7	3.8	3.9	4.1	0.7
Railways - stationary combustion	0.6	0.5	0.5	0.5	0.5	0.5	0.4	0.1	0.05	0.05	0.05	-
Shipping	4.5	4.4	4.1	3.7	3.6	3.0	2.5	4.3	4.2	4.7	6.1	1.1
Aircraft support vehicles	0.4	0.4	0.4	0.4	0.4	0.4	0.4	0.5	0.5	0.5	0.5	0.1
Military aircraft and shipping	4.4	4.2	3.7	3.6	3.3	3.4	3.5	3.2	3.3	3.2	3.1	0.6
Transport Total	148.0	148.7	147.3	147.8	146.7	146.5	150.2	150.6	150.5	152.2	151.5	27.3
Net emissions all end users	571.0	548.1	549.9	540.3	548.6	559.4	542.7	554.7	555.1	555.2	554.5	100.0
(d) By industry code (Environmental Accounts)[6]												Million tonnes of carbon dioxide/percentage
Transport industries:												
Railways	1.7	1.8	1.9	1.9	1.9	2.0	2.0	2.0	2.1	2.2	2.2	0.4
Buses and coaches	5.7	5.5	5.5	5.0	4.6	4.3	4.8	4.8	4.7	5.3	5.5	0.9
Tubes and trams	0.6	0.5	0.6	0.5	0.5	0.5	0.4	0.1	0.1	0.1	0.1	-
Taxis operation	1.9	2.0	2.1	2.1	2.2	2.2	2.2	2.2	2.2	2.3	2.3	0.4
Freight transport by road	18.4	18.9	19.3	19.6	19.7	20.3	19.5	20.3	19.7	18.7	18.8	3.0
Transport via pipeline	0.1	0.1	0.1	0.1	0.1	0.1	0.1	0.1	0.1	0.1	0.1	-
Water transport	19.9	19.6	19.4	16.5	16.0	20.4	22.1	23.6	27.2	27.1	19.2	3.1
Air transport	26.2	27.8	31.1	33.5	37.0	36.5	35.8	37.0	39.2	42.4	43.2	6.9
All transport industries	74.6	76.2	79.8	79.3	82.0	86.3	86.8	90.1	95.3	98.0	91.4	14.6
Household use of private vehicles	59.8	60.7	60.2	61.3	60.9	61.7	63.6	62.8	63.1	62.4	61.8	9.9
Total emissions all sectors	620.5	600.3	606.2	597.4	608.8	624.3	609.3	624.4	631.7	634.4	626.3	100.0

1 Data are presented as the weight of carbon dioxide emitted.
  UK national emission estimates are updated annually and any developments in methodology are applied retrospectively to earlier years.
2 Source categories relate directly to the vehicle or other piece of equipment producing the emission. See Notes and Definitions for further details.
3 Railway emissions in the NAEI are those from diesel trains only.
4 Categories not included in the national total that is reported to the UNFCCC.
5 End user emissions now follow the 'IPCC Nomenclature for reporting' categories. End user emissions for transport include a share of the emissions from combustion of fossil fuels at power stations and other fuel processing industries. See Notes and Definitions for further details.
6 The economic sectors are based on similar concepts and classifications of industries to those used in the National Accounts. See Notes and Definitions for further details.

☎020-7944 4276
Source - AEA Energy and Environment/Defra (NAEI); Office for National Statistics (Environmental Accounts)

3.8 Pollutant emissions from transport in the United Kingdom (by source): [1] 1996-2006

	1996	1997	1998	1999	2000	2001	2002	2003	2004	2005	2006	Per cent of total in 2006
(a) Carbon monoxide (CO)												Thousand tonnes/percentage
Transport:												
Road transport	3,999	3,664	3,337	3,003	2,500	2,127	1,852	1,593	1,365	1,124	984	43.4
Passenger cars	3,353	3,065	2,785	2,526	2,108	1,802	1,584	1,360	1,169	951	830	36.6
Light duty vehicles	445	400	359	283	218	166	121	89	69	54	48	2.1
Buses	41	35	29	23	18	13	11	9	7	7	6	0.3
HGVs	70	68	66	64	60	57	53	50	48	44	42	1.9
Mopeds & motorcycles	90	95	99	108	96	90	84	85	72	68	58	2.6
Other transport	55	60	61	67	74	79	68	68	74	79	77	3.4
Civil aviation	34	39	39	46	53	59	50	46	53	56	51	2.2
Railways	11	11	12	12	13	13	12	11	12	12	12	0.5
National navigation	9	9	8	7	7	6	5	8	8	9	13	0.6
Other mobile sources[2]	1.3	1.3	1.4	1.5	1.5	1.5	1.5	1.6	1.6	1.7	1.8	0.1
All domestic transport	4,055	3,724	3,398	3,070	2,574	2,206	1,921	1,660	1,439	1,203	1,061	46.8
Total	6,151	5,678	5,273	4,926	4,230	3,880	3,338	2,932	2,689	2,388	2,268	100.0
Memo items[3]												
International bunkers - Aviation	15	15	17	18	19	18	17	18	19	20	20	.
International bunkers - Navigation	17	19	21	15	13	15	12	12	14	13	16	.
(b) Nitrogen oxides (NO$_x$)												Thousand tonnes/percentage
Transport:												
Road transport	1,068	1,014	960	900	818	749	692	636	596	549	515	32.3
Passenger cars	596	550	502	458	397	347	310	273	245	215	195	12.2
Light duty vehicles	70	70	70	67	65	64	60	59	59	58	54	3.4
Buses	59	57	55	52	48	45	43	42	38	36	36	2.3
HGVs	342	336	332	322	307	292	277	261	253	238	228	14.3
Mopeds & motorcycles	0.7	0.8	0.8	0.9	0.9	1.0	1.1	1.2	1.3	1.3	1.2	0.1
Other transport	125	124	122	119	122	111	96	129	129	143	174	10.9
Civil aviation	4.5	4.7	5.2	6.0	6.8	7.0	6.9	7.2	7.9	8.8	8.8	0.6
Railways	27	30	32	35	40	42	36	34	36	37	38	2.4
National navigation	87	84	79	71	69	56	47	82	80	92	122	7.7
Other mobile sources[2]	5.5	5.8	6.1	6.2	6.3	6.0	5.8	5.7	5.6	5.6	5.2	0.3
All domestic transport	1,193	1,138	1,082	1,019	939	860	787	764	726	692	689	43.2
Total	2,315	2,163	2,089	1,976	1,899	1,828	1,715	1,721	1,659	1,620	1,595	100.0
Memo items[3]												
International bunkers - Aviation	99	106	117	125	137	133	129	132	145	156	159	.
International bunkers - Navigation	167	187	203	147	129	145	121	116	132	132	153	.
(c) Particulates (PM$_{10}$)												Thousand tonnes/percentage
Transport:												
Road transport	51.3	47.5	45.2	43.3	38.6	37.7	36.9	36.2	35.4	33.7	32.3	21.3
Passenger cars	13.6	12.8	11.6	10.6	8.3	8.0	7.7	7.3	6.9	6.4	6.0	4.0
Light duty vehicles	9.9	10.1	10.5	11.0	10.3	10.8	11.0	11.3	11.3	10.8	10.2	6.7
Buses	4.7	3.6	2.9	2.2	1.7	1.3	1.1	1.0	0.8	0.7	0.7	0.5
HGVs	14.3	12.0	11.2	10.2	9.0	8.1	7.4	6.8	6.4	5.7	5.3	3.5
Mopeds & motorcycles	0.4	0.4	0.4	0.5	0.5	0.5	0.5	0.6	0.6	0.6	0.6	0.4
Automobile tyre & brake wear	8.3	8.5	8.6	8.8	8.8	8.9	9.1	9.2	9.4	9.4	9.5	6.3
Other transport	6.4	6.2	5.9	5.4	5.1	4.5	3.9	5.6	6.4	7.4	9.6	6.3
Civil aviation	0.1	0.1	0.1	0.1	0.1	0.1	0.1	0.1	0.1	0.1	0.1	0.1
Railways	0.7	0.7	0.8	0.8	0.8	0.9	0.7	0.6	0.6	0.7	0.7	0.4
National navigation	5.2	4.8	4.4	3.9	3.7	3.0	2.6	4.4	5.2	6.2	8.3	5.5
Other mobile sources[2]	0.5	0.5	0.6	0.6	0.6	0.5	0.5	0.5	0.5	0.5	0.5	0.3
All domestic transport	57.7	53.6	51.1	48.7	43.7	42.2	40.8	41.8	41.9	41.1	41.9	27.6
Total	233	224	209	197	184	177	155	154	153	150	152	100.0
Memo items[3]												
International bunkers - Aviation	1.3	1.4	1.6	1.7	1.9	1.8	1.8	1.8	2.0	2.2	2.2	.
International bunkers - Navigation	14.5	17.0	17.3	12.4	10.5	10.9	9.3	9.5	10.9	11.5	13.2	.
Road transport resuspension[4]	18.2	18.6	19.0	19.3	19.4	19.7	20.2	20.3	20.7	20.7	21.0	.
(d) Benzene												Thousand tonnes/percentage
Transport:												
Road transport[5]	25.7	22.8	19.8	17.0	5.6	5.2	4.6	4.0	3.4	2.9	2.6	18.0
Passenger cars	21.7	19.1	16.5	14.1	4.8	4.4	3.9	3.4	2.9	2.4	2.2	15.2
Light duty vehicles	1.6	1.4	1.3	1.0	0.3	0.3	0.2	0.2	0.2	0.2	0.2	1.1
Buses	-	-	-	-	-	-	-	-	-	-	-	-
HGVs	-	-	-	-	-	-	-	-	-	-	-	0.1
Mopeds & motorcycles	0.9	0.9	0.9	1.0	0.2	0.3	0.3	0.3	0.2	0.2	0.2	1.2
Gasoline evaporation	1.4	1.3	1.1	0.9	0.2	0.2	0.1	0.1	0.1	0.1	0.1	0.4
Other transport	0.9	0.9	0.9	0.9	0.9	0.8	0.7	0.9	1.0	1.1	1.2	8.6
Civil aviation	-	-	-	-	-	-	-	-	-	-	-	0.2
Railways	0.4	0.4	0.4	0.4	0.4	0.5	0.4	0.4	0.5	0.5	0.5	3.6
National navigation	0.5	0.5	0.4	0.4	0.4	0.3	0.3	0.5	0.5	0.5	0.7	4.8
Other mobile sources[2]	-	-	-	-	-	-	-	-	-	-	-	0.1
All domestic transport	26.6	23.7	20.7	17.8	6.4	6.0	5.3	4.9	4.4	4.0	3.8	26.6
Total	41.2	38.0	34.2	30.9	18.4	17.5	16.2	15.6	15.2	14.5	14.4	100.0
Memo items[3]												
International bunkers - Aviation	0.1	0.1	0.1	0.1	0.1	0.1	0.1	0.1	0.1	0.1	0.1	.
International bunkers - Navigation	0.9	1.1	1.2	0.8	0.7	0.8	0.7	0.7	0.8	0.7	0.9	.

3.8 (Continued) Pollutant emissions from transport in the United Kingdom (by source): [1] 1996-2006

	1996	1997	1998	1999	2000	2001	2002	2003	2004	2005	2006	Per cent of total in 2006
(e) 1,3-butadiene												Thousand tonnes/percentage
Transport:												
Road transport	6.7	5.9	5.2	4.5	3.8	3.2	2.7	2.2	1.9	1.6	1.4	55.4
Passenger cars	4.4	3.9	3.3	2.8	2.3	1.9	1.5	1.2	0.9	0.7	0.6	22.3
Light duty vehicles	0.4	0.3	0.3	0.2	0.2	0.2	0.1	0.1	0.1	0.1	0.1	2.9
Buses	0.4	0.3	0.3	0.2	0.2	0.1	0.1	0.1	0.1	0.1	0.1	2.9
HGVs	1.3	1.2	1.1	1.0	0.9	0.8	0.8	0.7	0.7	0.6	0.6	22.8
Mopeds & motorcycles	0.2	0.2	0.2	0.2	0.2	0.2	0.2	0.2	0.1	0.1	0.1	4.5
Other transport	0.2	0.2	0.2	0.2	0.2	0.2	0.2	0.2	0.2	0.2	0.2	8.8
Civil aviation	-	-	-	-	-	-	-	-	-	-	-	0.9
Railways	0.1	0.2	0.2	0.2	0.2	0.2	0.2	0.2	0.2	0.2	0.2	7.6
National navigation	0.0	0.0	0.0	0.0	0.0	0.0	0.0	0.0	0.0	0.0	0.0	0.0
Other mobile sources[2]	-	-	-	-	-	-	-	-	-	-	-	0.3
All domestic transport	6.9	6.1	5.4	4.7	4.0	3.4	2.9	2.4	2.1	1.8	1.6	64.2
Total	8.2	7.3	6.5	5.9	5.1	4.4	3.8	3.4	3.0	2.7	2.5	100.0
Memo items[3]												
International bunkers - Aviation	0.1	0.1	0.1	0.1	0.1	0.1	0.1	0.1	0.1	0.1	0.1	.
International bunkers - Navigation	0.0	0.0	0.0	0.0	0.0	0.0	0.0	0.0	0.0	0.0	0.0	.
(f) Lead (Pb)												Tonnes/percentage
Transport:												
Road transport[6]	892	782	573	301	2.2	2.0	2.0	2.0	2.0	2.1	2.1	1.9
Passenger cars	831	731	537	284	1.5	1.3	1.2	1.2	1.2	1.3	1.3	1.2
Light duty vehicles	55.5	45.4	31.9	14.4	0.2	0.2	0.2	0.2	0.3	0.3	0.3	0.3
Buses	0.1	0.1	0.1	0.1	0.1	0.1	0.1	0.1	0.1	0.1	0.1	0.1
HGVs	0.4	0.4	0.4	0.4	0.4	0.4	0.4	0.4	0.4	0.4	0.4	0.4
Mopeds & motorcycles	5.2	4.8	3.6	2.1	-	-	-	-	-	-	-	-
Other transport	0.5	0.5	0.5	0.5	0.5	0.4	0.4	0.5	0.6	0.7	0.8	0.8
Civil aviation	-	-	-	-	-	-	-	-	-	-	-	-
Railways	0.1	0.1	0.1	0.1	0.1	0.2	0.2	0.2	0.2	0.2	0.2	0.2
National navigation	0.4	0.3	0.3	0.3	0.3	0.2	0.2	0.3	0.4	0.4	0.6	0.5
Other mobile sources[2]	-	-	-	-	-	-	-	-	-	-	-	-
All domestic transport	893	782	574	302	2.6	2.4	2.4	2.5	2.6	2.7	2.9	2.7
Total	1,316	1,153	849	493	163	155	142	129	134	117	106	100.0
Memo items[3]												
International bunkers - Aviation	0.4	0.4	0.4	0.5	0.5	0.5	0.5	0.5	0.6	0.6	0.6	.
International bunkers - Navigation	1.0	1.2	1.2	0.9	0.7	0.7	0.6	0.7	0.8	0.8	0.9	.
(g) Sulphur dioxide (SO$_2$)												Thousand tonnes/percentage
Transport:												
Road transport	38.3	28.3	23.3	14.3	6.7	4.2	3.8	3.8	3.5	3.0	2.7	0.4
Passenger cars	15.7	17.3	12.6	11.9	5.4	3.0	2.6	2.6	2.4	2.1	2.0	0.3
Light duty vehicles	5.9	3.4	3.4	1.0	0.5	0.4	0.4	0.4	0.4	0.4	0.3	-
Buses	2.9	1.1	0.7	0.1	0.1	0.1	0.1	0.1	0.1	0.1	0.1	-
HGVs	13.8	6.4	6.5	1.1	0.6	0.6	0.7	0.7	0.6	0.5	0.4	0.1
Mopeds & motorcycles	0.1	0.1	0.1	0.1	-	-	-	-	-	-	-	-
Other transport	31.8	29.7	27.6	24.4	22.6	19.0	16.9	27.2	34.0	40.1	53.3	7.9
Civil aviation	0.3	0.5	0.5	0.4	0.4	0.5	0.4	0.5	0.6	0.6	0.7	0.1
Railways	1.5	1.5	1.6	1.6	1.5	1.4	1.7	1.9	1.9	1.9	2.0	0.3
National navigation	29.7	27.4	25.1	22.1	20.3	16.8	14.5	24.4	31.1	37.2	50.2	7.4
Other mobile sources[2]	0.3	0.3	0.3	0.3	0.3	0.3	0.3	0.4	0.4	0.4	0.4	0.1
All domestic transport	70.1	58.0	50.8	38.7	29.2	23.2	20.7	30.9	37.5	43.2	56.1	8.3
Total	2,003	1,661	1,633	1,209	1,198	1,095	978	967	812	688	676	100.0
Memo items[3]												
International bunkers - Aviation	5.4	7.2	8.1	6.1	6.9	7.5	6.1	7.2	8.5	9.1	11.0	.
International bunkers - Navigation	93.9	110.7	111.2	79.1	66.3	67.3	58.3	60.2	69.6	74.6	85.3	.

1 UK national emission estimates are updated annually and any developments in
   methodology are applied retrospectively to earlier years.
2 Includes machinery.
3 Categories not included in the national total that is reported to UNECE.
4 Resuspension of particles caused by the turbulence of passing vehicles. Not included in totals for PM$_{10}$
   to avoid double-counting, but is important in reconciling roadside concentration measurements.
5 Reduction in road transport benzene emissions in 2000 mainly due to reduction in benzene content of petrol.
6 Reduction in road transport lead emissions in 2000 is mainly due to a ban on the general sale of leaded petrol.

☎020-7944 4276
Source - AEA Energy & Environment/Defra

3.9 Aircraft noise: population affected by noise around airports: 1997-2007

(a) Heathrow	1997	1998	1999	2000	2001	2002	2003	2004	2005	2006	2007
Air transport movements (thousands)	429.2	441.2	449.5	459.7	457.6	460.3	457.1	469.8	472.0	470.9	475.79
Area (sq kms) within:											
57 Leq contour	158.3	163.7	155.6	135.6	117.4	126.9	126.9	117.4	117.2	117.4	119.6
63 Leq contour	53.8	55.4	53.9	48.2	41.2	43.8	43.8	40.3	39.1	38.4	37.6
69 Leq contour	23.2	22.8	21.9	19.0	14.1	16.4	15.6	13.3	12.4	11.9	12.2
Population (thousands) within:											
57 Leq contour	300.0	341.0	331.6	275.2	240.4	258.3	263.7	239.7	251.7	258.0	251.9
63 Leq contour	84.2	82.2	91.2	71.9	54.9	64.2	64.6	55.9	51.8	51.2	45.1
69 Leq contour	13.8	15.5	13.8	11.5	6.8	8.6	8.0	5.7	3.9	3.6	3.7
(b) Gatwick											
Air transport movements (thousands)	227.3	240.2	244.7	251.2	244.0	233.6	234.5	241.2	252.0	254.4	258.9
Area (sq kms) within:											
57 Leq contour	85.9	76.8	71.4	71.9	55.9	45.2	46.1	48.0	49.3	46.7	49.0
63 Leq contour	30.4	28.2	26.4	26.4	19.6	15.8	16.5	16.7	16.9	15.6	16.3
69 Leq contour	10.3	9.7	8.9	9.0	6.0	4.6	4.8	4.8	5.1	4.6	4.9
Population (thousands) within:											
57 Leq contour	12.6	9.0	7.8	8.7	5.2	3.5	4.2	4.5	4.7	4.5	4.8
63 Leq contour	2.0	1.4	1.4	1.4	0.8	0.5	0.6	0.6	0.7	0.6	0.6
69 Leq contour	0.4	0.3	0.3	0.2	0.1	0.1	0.1	0.1	0.1	-	-
(c) Stansted											
Air transport movements (thousands)	82.2	102.2	132.3	143.6	150.6	152.4	169.2	176.8	178.0	190.0	191.5
Area (sq kms) within:											
57 Leq contour	52.1	64.5	52.3	52.4	32.1	31.7	33.3	29.9	27.4	29.3	30.8
63 Leq contour	17.7	22.3	20.5	20.4	11.6	11.3	11.7	9.9	8.7	8.6	8.9
69 Leq contour	6.6	8.7	7.9	7.6	3.6	3.4	3.5	2.8	2.4	2.3	2.5
Population (thousands) within:											
57 Leq contour	6.0	7.6	4.4	5.7	2.3	2.0	2.3	2.9	2.0	2.0	2.5
63 Leq contour	0.9	1.3	1.4	1.3	0.4	0.3	0.5	0.3	0.3	0.3	0.3
69 Leq contour	0.2	0.3	0.2	0.2	0.1	0.1	-	-	-	-	-
(d) Manchester											
Air transport movements (thousands)	145.7	161.8	169.3	177.6	182.1	177.5	191.5	208.5	218.0	213.0	206.5
Area (sq kms) within:											
57 Leq contour	51.6	53.5	48.5	46.4	43.4	40.3	39.1	39.6	40.2	37.7	37.5
63 Leq contour	17.2	16.9	17.6	15.8	14.6	12.8	13.3	13.7	14.3	13.0	12.4
69 Leq contour	6.5	6.1	5.9	5.0	4.8	4.2	4.4	4.6	4.8	4.6	4.4
Population (thousands) within:											
57 Leq contour	45.6	44.7	53.5	48.4	44.9	38.7	40.6	40.9	41.6	39.2	36.8
63 Leq contour	9.5	10.1	11.9	9.4	6.4	4.5	5.8	5.1	5.6	4.0	3.5
69 Leq contour	2.4	2.0	1.9	1.2	0.5	0.5	0.6	0.6	0.6	0.2	0.1
(e) Birmingham											
Air transport movements (thousands)	79.8	88.2	98.4	108.4	111.0	112.3	116.0	109.2	113.0	108.7	104.5
Area (sq kms) within:											
57 Leq contour	..	35.3	..	19.0	..	14.8	..	16.2	..	16.8	..
63 Leq contour	..	12.3	..	6.2	..	4.4	..	5.1	..	5.2	..
69 Leq contour	..	4.5	..	1.7	..	1.2	..	1.3	..	1.4	..
Population (thousands) within:											
57 Leq contour	..	65.6	..	33.7	..	23.7	..	26.2	..	26.8	..
63 Leq contour	..	16.5	..	5.5	..	2.6	..	3.8	..	3.6	..
69 Leq contour	..	2.5	..	0.1	..	-	..	-	..	-	..
(f) Luton											
Air transport movements (thousands)	36.9	43.6	50.8	55.5	56.0	55.0	58.4	64.2	75.4	78.8	83.3
Area (sq kms) within:											
57 Leq contour	17.8	15.8	19.6	17.6	10.6	10.9	12.2	12.8	13.5	14.9	15.4
63 Leq contour	6.9	5.5	7.3	6.6	3.5	3.6	4.0	4.2	4.2	4.8	5.1
69 Leq contour	2.5	2.0	2.5	2.4	1.2	1.2	1.3	1.3	1.3	1.5	1.6
Population (thousands) within:											
57 Leq contour	5.5	5.8	7.4	8.1	2.3	2.4	3.2	3.8	2.6	3.0	4.4
63 Leq contour	1.2	1.1	1.2	1.7	-	0.1	0.1	0.1	0.1	0.1	0.1
69 Leq contour	0.0	0.0	0.0	0.0	0.0	0.0	0.0	0.0	0.0	0.0	0.0

☎020-7944 4276
The figures in this table are outside
the scope of National Statistics
Source - Noise contour data - Major UK airports
Air transport movements - Civil Aviation Authority

4 Freight:

Notes and Definitions

Freight transport by mode: 4.1 – 4.3

Road: These figures include the activity of goods vehicles over 3.5 tonnes gross vehicle weight and light goods vehicles up to that weight. The estimates for heavy goods vehicles are derived from the Continuing Survey of Road Goods Transport (CSRGT) and, for light goods vehicles, from surveys carried out in 1976, 1987, 1992/93, and from 2003 to 2005 with data being interpolated for the intervening years. The light goods vehicle component of Table 4.2 has been allocated to the appropriate commodity group. In previous years it had been assumed that it should all be in the 'miscellaneous' category. Figures for 2005 onwards are therefore not strictly comparable with those previously published for earlier years.

Rail: Figures up to 1962 include free-hauled (Departmental *i.e.* goods carried by British Rail for its own purposes) traffic on revenue-earning trains (the inclusion of this traffic in 1962 would have increased the figure). Figures for rail from 1991 are for each financial year.

Water: Figures from 1972 onwards are not comparable with earlier years. From 1972, water includes all UK coastwise and one-port freight movements by sea, and inland waterway traffic. Earlier years include only GB coastwise traffic and internal traffic on waterways controlled by British Waterways.

Pipeline: Pipeline estimates are for oil pipelines only (excluding offshore pipelines); data differ from those in the International Comparisons section as the latter exclude pipelines less than 50 kilometres long. The increase between 1989 and 1990 is largely due to changes in coverage.

Air: Domestic air freight within the United Kingdom, while sometimes important in terms of speed of delivery, is insignificant in volume; in 2006, domestic air freight amounted to only 37 million tonne kilometres (see Table 2.4(f)).

Road freight transport by goods vehicles over 3.5 tonnes gross weight: 4.4-4.6

The data in these tables are derived from the Continuing Survey of Road Goods Transport.

Estimates are of domestic freight activity by GB-registered heavy goods vehicles over 3.5 tonnes gross vehicle weight. These vehicles pay the goods vehicle rates of Vehicle Excise Duty, are subject to goods vehicle 'plating' and annual testing, and require a goods operator's licence. They currently account for some 93 per cent of road freight activity, with the rest being carried by light goods vehicles up to 3.5 tonnes gross vehicle weight.

In Table 4.5, freight activity is measured in terms of the weight of goods (tonnes) handled, taking no account of the distance they are carried; this is termed 'goods lifted'. The measure in Table 4.4 is 'goods moved' (tonne kilometres) which does take account of distance. 'Goods moved', for each loaded journey, is the weight of the load multiplied by the distance it is carried. 'Goods moved' is therefore a better measure of the work done by heavy goods vehicles. In both tables activity is shown by 'mode of working', 'gross weight of vehicle' and 'commodity'.

In Tables 4.4 and 4.5 'Crude minerals' comprises *sand, gravel and clay* and *other crude minerals*. 'Building materials' comprises *cement* and *other building materials*.

The vehicle weight groups reflect some of the operating controls on goods vehicles. For rigid vehicles the maximum allowed gross vehicle weights are:

- 18 tonnes on 2 axles
- 26 tonnes on 3 axles
- 32 tonnes on 4 axles

For articulated vehicles the general limits are:

- 38 tonnes on 4 axles
- 40 tonnes on 5 axles

- 44 tonnes on 6 axles

'Mode of working' relates to whether goods are being carried on either a hire or reward or own account basis. The former relates to the carriage of goods owned by people other than the operator; the latter covers goods carried by operators in the course of their own trade or business.

The tonnes lifted and tonne kilometres estimates shown in these tables are not directly comparable to those of heavy goods vehicle kilometres derived from the traffic census in Table 7.2. Therefore, any analysis such as calculating average load (tonne kilometres/ vehicle kilometres) should use estimates published in *Road Freight Statistics 2007* which is available from DfT, available at:

http://www.dft.gov.uk/pgr/statistics/datatabl espublications/freight/goodsbyroad/

The estimates are derived from the Continuing Survey of Road Goods Transport (CSRGT) which in 2007 was based on an average weekly returned sample of some 320 heavy goods vehicles. The samples are drawn from the vehicle licence records held by the Driver and Vehicle Licensing Agency (DVLA). Questionnaires are sent to the registered keepers of the sampled vehicles asking for details of its activity during the survey week. The estimates are grossed to the vehicle population and, and at the overall national level have a three per cent margin of error (at 95 per cent confidence level). Further details and results are published in *Road Freight Statistics 2007*, and previously in *Transport of Goods by Road in Great Britain*.

Methodological changes

A key component of National Statistics outputs is a programme of quality reviews carried out at least every five years to ensure that such statistics are fit for purpose and that their quality and value continue to improve. A quality review of the Department for Transport's road freight surveys, including the CSRGT, was carried out in 2003. A copy of the report can be accessed at

http://www.statistics.gov.uk/nsbase/method s_quality/quality_review/downloads/NSQR3 0FinalReport.doc

The quality review made a number of recommendations about the CSRGT. The main methodological recommendation was that, to improve the accuracy of survey estimates, the sample strata should be amended to reflect current trends in vehicle type, weight and legislative groups. These new strata are described more fully in the survey report. For practical and administrative reasons, changes were also made to the sample selection methodology. These changes have resulted in figures from 2004 onwards not being fully comparable with those for 2003 and earlier years. Detailed comparisons should therefore be made with caution.

International Roads Goods Transport: 4.7-4.9

These tables show the international activity of United Kingdom registered vehicles. The statistics for GB registered vehicles are derived from the International Road Haulage Survey (IRHS), which has been conducted by the Department for Transport (and its predecessors) since 1979 in order to comply with EC Regulation 1172/98 (which replaced EC Directive 78/546 and 89/462). The Regulation requires each member state to compile statistics of the international road haulage carried out by its own goods vehicles as well as national haulage (see Tables 4.4 and 4.5).

The IRHS is carried out by asking hauliers who undertake international work to report the details of recently completed international trips travelling to mainland Europe or the Irish Republic via roll-on/roll-off ferry services or through the Channel Tunnel. Details of the sampling scheme are available from DfT.

The sample is grossed up quarterly in stages: the results, by each ferry route, are grossed to total route traffic; figures are then re-grossed to the grand total of United Kingdom powered vehicles on all ferry routes and the Channel Tunnel, to allow for routes not sampled. The ferry totals are obtained from the associated quarterly 'Ro-Ro survey'. Vehicles registered to hauliers operating in Northern Ireland are covered by the CSRGT (NI). Since 2004, this survey has been expanded to cover international activity including that across the Irish land boundary. Details of this activity are shown in Table 4.9.

A substantial amount of traffic goes by unaccompanied trailers (as well as in the foreign powered vehicles) for which statistics are not obtained in this survey. In particular, trade across the North Sea is mainly carried on unaccompanied trailers. Freight carried in foreign vehicles is not included in the IRHS (or CSRGT) tables. Other EU countries, being subject to the same Regulation, obtain comparable statistics which are published by Eurostat.

The goods classification, *Nomenclature Statistiques de Transport* (NST), the classification of commodities for transport statistics used in the European Union, is a hierarchical structure which divides the 176 headings of the classification into 10 chapters and 52 main groups. At present it is only practicable to disaggregate the IRHS data by 'chapter' - apart from showing separately the two main components of chapter 9.

In Table 4.9, only 'bilateral' traffic is shown, that is traffic between the United Kingdom and another country in either United Kingdom vehicles or in those registered in that other country. The figures exclude 'cross trade', i.e. trade in vehicles registered other than in the country of loading or unloading.

Freight Traffic: 4.10

This table summarises the performance of the freight business in terms of freight 'lifted' (measured in tonnes) and freight 'moved' (measured in tonne-kilometres). Freight 'moved' takes account of the distance the goods are carried.

Freight data exclude all parcels traffic by coaching trains (but see below) and all departmental traffic (i.e. goods carried by Network Rail for its own purposes) whether carried on revenue-earning trains or on special departmental trains.

Following the move of BR's bulk freight operations to the private sector there have been some changes in the way estimates of freight traffic have been compiled. In particular, the method of estimating tonne kilometres is different with the result that recent estimates are not consistent with those for earlier periods. Some revisions have been made to the series. The freight moved series now has a full commodity breakdown with the inclusion of parcels.

The freight lifted series has also been revised, in this case from 1999/00. Further details can be found in *National Rail Trends* published each quarter, by the Office of Rail Regulation (ORR).

Roll-on/roll-off: 4.11 and 4.12

Statistics on the number of lorries and unaccompanied trailers travelling from Great Britain to mainland Europe and Ireland are compiled from quarterly returns provided by roll-on/roll-off ferry operators and Eurotunnel. (Unaccompanied trailers are not carried by Eurotunnel.) The results are broken down by country of vehicle registration, by country of disembarkation and by GB port group. Separate figures are given for powered vehicles and unaccompanied trailers. The statistics presented in Tables 4.11 and 4.12 refer to vehicle travelling to mainland Europe only and exclude those to Ireland.

Powered vehicles comprise rigid vehicles, lorries with semi-trailers (articulated units) and lorries with drawbar trailers. (Some vehicles under 3.5 tonnes gross vehicle weight are also included). Unaccompanied trailers are trailers and semi-trailers not accompanied on the ferry by a powered unit. Up to 1978 inward traffic was also recorded, but because it was similar to outward traffic the data requirement was discontinued to save respondent effort.

The estimates for 2004 to 2007 have been revised. Information on these revisions can be found in the bulletin *"Road Goods Vehicles Travelling to Mainland Europe: 2007"*. More detailed analyses are provided in the Department's quarterly publication *Road Goods Vehicles Travelling to Mainland Europe*, available on the Department's website:

http://www.dft.gov.uk/pgr/statistics/datatablespublications/freight/secroadseur/

4.1 Domestic freight transport: by mode: 1953-2007
For greater detail of the years 1997-2007 see Table 4.3

Year	Goods moved (billion tonne kilometres)					Goods lifted (million tonnes)				
	Road	Rail [1]	Water	Pipe-line	All modes	Road	Rail [1]	Water	Pipe-line	All modes
1953	32	37	20	0	89	889	294	52	2	1,237
1954	35	36	20	0	91	940	288	52	2	1,282
1955	38	35	20	0	93	1,013	279	50	2	1,344
1956	38	35	22	0	95	1,009	281	55	2	1,347
1957	37	34	21	0	92	985	279	55	2	1,321
1958	41	30	21	0	92	1,078	247	53	2	1,380
1959	46	29	21	0	96	1,164	238	53	3	1,458
1960	49	30	20	0	99	1,211	252	54	4	1,521
1961	53	29	22	1	105	1,260	242	56	6	1,564
1962	55	26	24	1	106	1,268	232	58	7	1,565
1963	57	25	25	1	108	1,407	239	60	15	1,721
1964	66	26	25	1	118	1,560	243	61	18	1,882
1965	69	25	25	1	120	1,590	232	62	26	1,910
1966	73	24	26	2	125	1,641	217	61	31	1,950
1967	75	21	25	2	123	1,651	204	57	32	1,944
1968	79	23	25	2	129	1,707	211	59	32	2,009
1969	83	23	24	3	133	1,658	211	59	36	1,964
1970	85	25	23	3	136	1,610	209	57	39	1,915
1971	86	22	22	4	134	1,582	198	52	49	1,881
1972	88	21	29 [2]	4	142	1,629	177	117 [2]	45	1,968
1973	90	23	31	5	149	1,660	196	122	50	2,028
1974	90	22	31	5	148	1,537	176	117	50	1,880
1975	92	21	28	6	147	1,511	175	108	52	1,846
1976	96	21	30	6	153	1,515	176	113	53	1,857
1977	98	20	41	9	168	1,429	171	122	75	1,797
1978	100	20	48	10	178	1,503	171	133	83	1,890
1979	103	20	56	10	189	1,499	169	140	85	1,893
1980	93	18	54	10	175	1,395	154	137	83	1,769
1981	94	18	53	9	174	1,299	154	129	75	1,657
1982	95	16	59	10	179	1,389	142	137	78	1,746
1983	96	17	60	10	183	1,358	145	143	82	1,728
1984	100	13	60	10	183	1,400	79	140	88	1,707
1985	103	15	58	11	187	1,452	122	142	89	1,805
1986	105	17	55	10	187	1,473	140	144	79	1,836
1987	113	17	54	11	195	1,542	141	142	83	1,908
1988	130	18	59	11	219	1,758	150	156	99	2,163
1989	138	17	58	10	223	1,812	146	155	93	2,206
1990	136	16	56	11 [3]	219	1,749	140	152	121 [3]	2,162
1991	130	15	58	11	214	1,600	136	144	105	1,985
1992	127	15	55	11	208	1,555	122	140	106	1,923
1993	135	14	51	12	211	1,615	103	134	125	1,977
1994	144	13	52	12	221	1,689	97	140	161	2,087
1995	150	13	53	11	227	1,701	101	143	168	2,113
1996	154	15	55	12	236	1,730	102	142	157	2,131
1997	157	17	48	11	234	1,740	105	142	148	2,135
1998	160	17 [4]	57	12	246	1,727	102	149	153	2,131
1999	158	18	59	12	246	1,664	97 [4]	144	155	2,060
2000	159	18	67	11	256	1,693	96	137	151	2,077
2001	159	19	59	12	248	1,682	94	131	151	2,058
2002	159	19	67	11	256	1,734	87	139	146	2,106
2003	162	19	61	11	252	1,753	89	133	141	2,116
2004	163 [5]	20	59	11	253	1,863 [5]	100 [R,6]	127	158	2,248
2005	163 [5]	22 [7]	61	11	257	1,868 [5]	105 [R,7]	133	168	2,275
2006	167 [R,5]	22 [R]	52	11	251	1,940 [R,5]	108	126	159	2,333
2007	173 [5]	21	51	10	255	2,001 [5]	102 [8]	126	146	2,376

1 From 1991 figures for rail are for financial years 1991/92 etc.
2 Figures from 1972 onwards are not comparable with earlier years. From 1972, water includes all UK coastwise and one-port freight movements by sea, and inland waterway traffic. Earlier years inlcude only GB coastwise traffic and internal traffic on BWB waterways.
3 The increase compared to the corresponding figure for 1989 is largely due to changes in coverage.
4 Figures for goods moved by rail are on a new basis from 1998. Figures for goods lifted by rail have a break in the series from 1999.
5 See footnote 2 Table 4.4.
6 Break in the series, increase largely due to changes in coverage.
7 Break in the series, because figures from 2005 onwards include some of the tonnes lifted by GB railfreight
8 Break in the series, because coal data was not supplied by GB Railfreight prior to 2007-08.

Rail: ☎020-7944 8874
Road: ☎020-7944 3180
Water: ☎020-7944 3087
Pipeline: ☎020-7215 2718
The rail figures in this table are outside the scope of National Statistics
Source - Rail - ORR
Pipeline - BERR

4.2 Domestic freight moved: by commodity: 2007

Billion tonne kilometres/percentage

Commodity group (NST[3] Chapter)	Road[1] Billion tonne-kms	Percentage	Rail[2] Billion tonne-kms	Percentage	Pipeline Billion tonne-kms	Percentage
0 Agricultural products and live animals	12.5	7	..	..	0	0
1 Foodstuffs and animal fodder	39.2	23	..	..	0	0
2 Solid mineral fuels	1.6	1	7.7	36	0	0
3 Petroleum products	5.1	3	1.6	7	10.2	100
4 Ores and metal waste	1.8	1	..	..	0	0
5 Metal products	8.0	5	1.8	9	0	0
6 Crude and manufactured minerals and building materials	26.8	15	2.8	13	0	0
7 Fertilisers	1.5	1	..	..	0	0
8 Chemicals	8.4	5	..	..	0	0
9 Machinery, transport equipment, manufactured articles and miscellaneous articles	68.2	39	..	..	0	0
All commodities	173.1	100	21.2	100	10.2	100

1 All goods vehicles, including those up to 3.5 tonnes gross vehicle weight.
2 Figures for rail are for financial years e.g. 2007/08.
  Rail categories do not all match those recorded by ORR,
  so the components do not sum to the total.
3 Standard EC classification for transport. See Notes.

Rail: ☎020-7944 8874
Road: ☎020-7944 3180
Water: ☎020-7944 3087
Pipeline: ☎020-7215 2718
The rail figures in this table are
outside the scope of National Statistics
Source - Rail - ORR
Pipeline - BERR

4.3 Domestic freight transport: by mode: 1997-2007

(a) Goods moved										Billion tonne kilometres/percentage	
	1997	1998	1999	2000	2001	2002	2003	2004	2005	2006	2007
Petroleum products											
Road [1]	5.8	5.2	5.0	6.4	5.8	5.2	5.5	5.7	5.5	5.6 [R]	5.1
Rail [2]	..	1.6	1.5	1.4	1.2	1.2	1.2	1.2	1.2	1.5 [7]	1.6
Water [3]	38.3	45.2	48.6	52.7	43.5	51.7	46.9	46.9	47.2	37.8	36.4
ow: coastwise	33.8	36.4	33.3	26.0	23.1	24.2	23.3	26.6	30.3	22.7	25.0
Pipeline	11.2	11.7	11.6	11.4	11.5	10.9	10.5	10.7	10.8	10.8	10.2
All modes	55.3 [4]	63.7	66.7	71.9	62.0	69.0	64.1	64.5	64.7	55.8	53.3
Coal and coke											
Road [1]	2.7	2.0	2.2	1.5	2.1	1.5	1.5	1.2	1.5	1.3 [R]	1.6
Rail [2]	4.4	4.5	4.8	4.8	6.2	5.7	5.8	6.7	8.3	8.6 [7]	7.7
Water [3]	0.6	0.5	0.5	0.2	0.5	0.3	0.5	0.3	0.4	0.5	0.5
All modes	7.7	7.0	7.5	6.5	8.8	7.5	7.9 [R]	8.5	10.2	10.4	9.8
Other traffic											
Road [1]	148.9	153.1	150.5	151.5	150.6	152.7	154.7	155.6	156.4	159.7 [R]	166.4
Rail [2]	12.5	11.2	11.9	11.9	12.0	11.7	11.9	12.5	12.2	11.8 [7]	11.9
Water [3]	9.2	11.2	9.6	14.6	14.8	15.2	13.5	12.3	13.3	13.5	13.9
All modes	170.6	175.5	172.0	178.0	177.4	179.6	180.0	180.4	181.9	185.0	192.2
All traffic											
Road [1]	157.4	160.3	157.7	159.4	158.5	159.4	161.7	162.5 [5]	163.4 [5]	166.7 [R,5]	173.1 [5]
Rail [2]	16.9	17.3	18.2	18.1	19.4	18.5	18.9	20.4	21.7	21.9 [7]	21.2
Water [3]	48.1	56.9	58.7	67.4	58.8	67.2	60.9	59.45	60.8698	51.8	50.8
Pipeline	11.2	11.7	11.6	11.4	11.5	10.9	10.5	10.7	10.8	10.8	10.2
All modes	233.6	246.2	246.2	256.3	248.2	256.0	252.0	253.0	256.8	251.3	255.3
Percentage of all traffic											
Road [1]	67	65	64	62	64	62	64	64	64	66 [R]	68
Rail [2]	7	7	7	7	8	7	7	8	8	9	8
Water [3]	21	23	24	26	24	26	24	23	24	21	20
Pipeline	5	5	5	4	5	4	4	4	4	4	4
All modes	100	100	100	100	100	100	100	100	100	100	100

(b) Goods lifted										Million tonnes/percentage	
Petroleum products											
Road [1]	73	61	61	75	74	59	64	67	70	69 [R]	71
Rail [2]	..	..	..	..	..	..	..	..	..	..	..
Water [3]	69	76	72	72	60	67	64	62.99	66	57	56
ow: coastwise	52	55	52	40	34	36	35	37.79	42	34	35
Pipeline	148	153	155	151	151	146	141	158	168	159	146
All modes[4]	290	290	288	298	285	272	269	288	304	285	274
Coal and coke											
Road [1]	37	26	28	22	21	17	22	14	21	17 [R]	24
Rail [2]	50	45	36 [8]	35	40	34	35	43 [7]	48 [7,8]	49 [7]	43 [9]
Water [3]	4	3	3	3	3	2	2	1	2	2	2
All modes	91	70	75	60	64	53	59	67	72	68	69
Other traffic											
Road [1]	1,630	1,640	1,575	1,596	1,587	1,658	1,667	1,782	1,777	1,854 [R]	1,906
Rail [2]	55	57	61 [8]	60	55	53	54	57 [7]	58 [7,8]	59 [7]	59 [9]
Water [3]	69	70	70	62	68	70	67	63	65	66	68
All modes	1,754	1,767	1,706	1,718	1,710	1,781	1,788	1,902	1,901	1980	2,032
All traffic											
Road [1]	1,740	1,727	1,664	1,693	1,682	1,734	1,753	1,863 [5]	1,868 [5]	1,940 [R,5]	2,001 [5]
Rail [2]	105	102	97 [8]	96	94	87	89	100 [6]	105 [7,8]	108 [7]	102 [9]
Water [3]	142	149	144	137	131	139	133	127	133	126	126
Pipeline	148	153	155	151	151	146	141	158	168	159	146
All modes	2,135	2,131	2,060	2,077	2,058	2,106	2,116	2,249	2,275	2,333	2,376
Percentage of all traffic											
Road [1]	81	81	81	82	82	82	83	83	82	83 [R]	84
Rail [2]	5	5	5	5	5	4	4	4	5	5	4
Water [3]	7	7	7	7	6	7	6	6	6	5	5
Pipeline	7	7	8	7	7	7	7	7	7	7	6
All modes	100	100	100	100	100	100	100	100	100	100	100

1 All goods vehicles, including those up to 3.5 tonnes gross vehicle weight.
  See Notes and Definitions.
2 Figures for rail are for financial years eg 1997/98 etc
3 Figures for water are for UK traffic.
4 Excludes rail.
5 See footnote 2 Table 4.4.
6 See footnote 6 Table 4.1
7 There have been revisions to data since the last TSGB publication
8 There is a break in the series between 2003-04 and 2004-05, due to a change in the method
  of data collection
9 There is a break in the series between 2006-07 and 2007-08 because coal data was not supplied by GB Railfreight prior to 2007-08.

Rail: ☎020-7944 8874
Road: ☎020-7944 3180
Water: ☎020-7944 3087
Pipeline: ☎020-7215 2718
The rail figures in this table are
outside the scope of National Statistics
Source - Rail - ORR
Pipeline - BERR

4.4 Freight transport by road: goods moved by goods vehicles over 3.5 tonnes:[1] 1997-2007

Billion Tonne Kilometres

(a) By mode of working	1997	1998	1999	2000	2001	2002	2003	2004 [2]	2005 [2]	2006[R,2]	2007 [2]
Mainly public haulage	112.2	114.3	110.9	113.0	114.7	110.6	114.3	110.8	109.7	112.1	115.6
Mainly own account	37.4	37.6	38.3	37.5	34.7	39.2	37.4	41.4	43.0	43.5	45.9
All modes	149.6	151.9	149.2	150.5	149.4	149.8	151.7	152.2	152.7	155.6	161.5
(b) By gross weight of vehicle											
Rigid vehicles:											
Over 3.5 tonnes up to 17 tonnes	19.2	17.8	17.9	15.8	13.1	11.9	10.1	9.1	8.1	7.2	5.8
Over 17 tonnes up to 25 tonnes	4.7	4.2	4.3	4.8	5.7	6.3	6.8	7.9	8.3	8.6	9.5
Over 25 tonnes	14.3	14.7	15.3	15.4	15.6	17.3	18.3	18.9	20.3	20.8	22.5
All rigids	38.1	36.6	37.5	36.0	34.5	35.6	35.2	35.9	36.7	36.6	37.8
Articulated vehicles:											
Over 3.5 tonnes up to 33 tonnes	14.3	14.4	14.0	14.0	12.8	9.9	8.8	7.0	6.3	6.1	5.6
Over 33 tonnes	97.1	100.9	97.7	100.4	102.1	104.4	107.7	109.4	109.7	112.9	118.1
All artics	111.4	115.3	111.7	114.4	114.9	114.3	116.5	116.4	116.0	119.0	123.7
All vehicles:											
Over 3.5 tonnes up to 25 tonnes	24.3	22.5	22.7	21.3	19.3	18.7	17.3	17.3	16.7	16.3	15.7
Over 25 tonnes	125.2	129.4	126.5	129.2	130.1	131.1	134.4	134.9	136.0	139.3	145.8
All weights	149.6	151.9	149.2	150.5	149.4	149.8	151.7	152.2	152.7	155.6	161.5
(c) By commodity											
Food, drink and tobacco	40.8	42.5	41.5	44.3	41.4	43.1	42.2	41.7	40.6	42.0	45.1
Wood, timber and cork	3.5	3.6	3.8	3.7	3.9	3.8	4.1	4.5	4.7	4.1	3.3
Fertiliser	1.3	1.2	1.4	1.2	1.2	1.2	1.2	0.8	1.1	0.8	0.9
Crude minerals	13.6	13.3	12.7	12.4	13.0	13.9	13.8	14.1	14.8	15.4	16.0
Ores	1.7	1.1	1.3	1.2	1.2	1.1	1.2	1.4	1.7	1.4	1.8
Crude materials	2.1	2.6	2.6	2.6	2.3	2.7	2.3	3.3	2.4	2.7	2.6
Coal and coke	2.7	2.0	2.2	1.5	2.1	1.5	1.5	1.2	1.5	1.3	1.6
Petrol and petroleum products	5.8	5.2	5.0	6.4	5.8	5.2	5.5	5.7	5.5	5.7	5.1
Chemicals	8.2	7.9	7.4	6.8	7.2	6.5	6.8	6.3	7.6	6.2	7.0
Building materials	11.1	10.7	10.6	10.6	11.7	10.9	12.0	12.1	10.9	11.5	11.6
Iron and steel products	7.9	7.7	6.8	6.8	5.7	5.3	5.4	5.4	5.2	4.7	6.4
Other metal products n.e.s.	1.5	1.7	1.7	1.7	1.4	1.5	1.5	1.9	2.1	2.1	2.0
Machinery and transport equipment	8.4	9.1	8.7	9.1	8.9	8.5	8.7	8.9	9.3	9.4	9.5
Miscellaneous manufactures n.e.s.	14.2	15.9	15.7	15.1	15.4	16.2	15.8	16.3	15.5	16.3	16.4
Miscellaneous articles n.e.s. (incl. commodity not known)	26.8	27.5	27.9	27.1	28.2	28.4	29.5	28.8	29.8	31.7	32.2
All commodities	149.6	151.9	149.2	150.5	149.4	149.8	151.7	152.2	152.7	155.6	161.5

1 Rigid vehicles or articulated vehicles (tractive unit and trailer) with gross vehicle weight over 3.5 tonnes.

2 Figures for 2004 onwards are not fully comparable with those for 2003 and earlier years.
  Detailed comparisons should therefore be made with caution. See Notes and Definitions.

☎020-7944 3180

4.5 Freight transport by road: goods lifted by goods vehicles over 3.5 tonnes:[1] 1997-2007

Million tonnes

(a) By mode of working	1997	1998	1999	2000	2001	2002	2003	2004 [2]	2005 [2]	2006 [R,2]	2007 [2]
Mainly public haulage	1,044	1,041	991	1,038	1,052	1,019	1,053	1,101	1,079	1,127	1,145
Mainly own account	599	589	576	556	529	608	590	643	667	685	724
All modes	1,643	1,630	1,567	1,593	1,581	1,627	1,643	1,744	1,746	1,813	1,869
(b) By gross weight of vehicle											
Rigid vehicles:											
Over 3.5 tonnes up to 17 tonnes	294	268	254	229	203	188	159	160	135	130	109
Over 17 tonnes up to 25 tonnes	120	106	86	87	86	90	100	113	118	120	130
Over 25 tonnes	380	401	408	424	443	491	506	539	559	598	629
All rigids	793	776	748	741	733	768	765	812	812	849	868
Articulated vehicles:											
Over 3.5 tonnes up to 33 tonnes	124	125	113	107	97	81	69	60	51	50	50
Over 33 tonnes	726	729	706	746	751	778	809	872	883	914	952
All artics	850	854	819	852	848	859	878	932	934	964	1,001
All vehicles:											
Over 3.5 tonnes up to 25 tonnes	419	382	346	325	294	283	265	277	257	256	245
Over 25 tonnes	1,224	1,248	1,221	1,268	1,287	1,343	1,378	1,467	1,489	1,557	1,624
All weights	1,643	1,630	1,567	1,593	1,581	1,627	1,643	1,744	1,746	1,813	1,869
(c) By commodity											
Food, drink and tobacco	342	346	333	346	321	339	333	351	339	360	373
Wood, timber and cork	26	27	28	26	28	28	32	42	36	30	29
Fertiliser	10	9	11	10	9	11	12	7	14	7	9
Crude minerals	329	327	297	308	298	333	327	364	370	380	390
Ores	25	18	20	16	16	17	21	22	23	19	22
Crude materials	17	20	20	18	20	21	19	25	22	23	23
Coal and coke	37	26	28	22	21	17	22	14	21	17	24
Petrol and petroleum products	73	61	61	75	74	59	64	67	70	69	71
Chemicals	53	53	47	49	50	41	47	46	53	48	48
Building materials	156	161	159	165	165	167	165	185	169	180	175
Iron and steel products	55	54	48	49	44	39	41	43	42	41	47
Other metal products n.e.s.	16	18	17	16	14	14	16	19	19	21	20
Machinery and transport equipment	71	73	67	69	70	68	66	70	76	79	83
Miscellaneous manufactures n.e.s.	90	96	91	97	97	105	98	111	109	112	113
Miscellaneous articles n.e.s. (incl. commodity not known)	343	342	340	328	353	367	379	378	384	426	440
All commodities	1,643	1,630	1,567	1,593	1,581	1,627	1,643	1,744	1,746	1,813	1,869

1 Rigid vehicles or articulated vehicles (tractive unit and trailer) with gross vehicle weight over 3.5 tonnes.
2 Figures for 2004 onwards are not fully comparable with those for 2003 and earlier years.
  Detailed comparisons should therefore be made with caution. See Notes and Definitions.

☎020-7944 3180

4.6 Freight transport by road: length of haul by goods vehicles over 3.5 tonnes:[1] 1997-2007

Million tonnes

(a) Goods lifted	1997	1998	1999	2000	2001	2002	2003	2004 [2]	2005 [2]	2006[R,2]	2007 [2]
Not over 100 kilometres	1,157	1,132	1,073	1,093	1,083	1,129	1,132	1,223	1,228	1,286	1,320
Over 100 kilometres	487	497	494	501	496	498	509	521	518	527	549
All distances	1,643	1,630	1,567	1,593	1,581	1,627	1,643	1,744	1,746	1,813	1,869

(b) Goods moved										Billion tonne - kilometres	
Not over 100 kilometres	39.7	38.6	36.9	38.1	36.8	38.8	39.4	41.7	42.9	44.4	45.9
Over 100 kilometres	109.9	113.3	112.3	112.4	112.6	111.0	112.0	110.6	109.8	111.1	115.6
All distances	149.6	151.9	149.2	150.5	149.4	149.8	151.7	152.2	152.7	155.6	161.5

(c) Average length of haul by gross weight of vehicle											Kilometres
Rigid vehicles:											
Over 3.5 tonnes up to 17 tonnes	65	66	68	69	65	63	63	57	60	55	53
Over 17 tonnes up to 25 tonnes	39	40	50	56	67	70	68	70	71	72	73
Over 25 tonnes	38	37	37	36	35	35	36	35	37	35	36
All rigids	48	47	50	49	47	46	46	44	45	43	44
Articulated vehicles:											
Over 3.5 tonnes up to 33 tonnes	116	115	124	131	132	122	128	118	121	122	113
Over 33 tonnes	134	138	138	135	136	134	133	125	124	123	124
All artics	131	135	136	134	136	133	133	125	124	123	124
All vehicles	91	93	95	94	94	92	92	87	87	86	86

1 Rigid vehicles or articulated vehicles (tractive unit and trailer) with gross vehicle weight over 3.5 tonnes.
2 Figures for 2004 onwards are not fully comparable with those for 2003 and earlier years.
  Detailed comparisons should therefore be made with caution. See Notes and Definitions

☎020-7944 3180

4.7 International road haulage by United Kingdom registered powered vehicles over 3.5 tonnes gross vehicle weight: goods carried: by country of loading or unloading:[1] 2007

Country	Outward journey				Inward journey			
	Tonnes (thousand)	Per cent	Tonne-kms (million)	Per cent	Tonnes (thousand)	Per cent	Tonne-kms (million)	Per cent
Austria	9	-	14	-	12	-	17	-
Belgium	884	17	416	10	1,327	22	645	14
Denmark	13	-	10	-	4	-	5	-
Finland	-	-	-	-	-	-	-	-
France	1,871	37	1,276	30	2,456	40	1,369	31
Germany	636	12	582	14	620	10	547	12
Greece	13	-	37	1	3	-	9	-
Irish Republic	335	7	133	3	138	2	49	1
Italy	263	5	415	10	292	5	449	10
Luxembourg	55	1	32	1	50	1	29	1
Netherlands	492	10	289	7	628	10	363	8
Portugal	8	-	18	-	7	-	16	-
Spain	364	7	670	16	453	7	829	19
Sweden	22	-	33	1	3	-	5	-
EU15 (excl. United Kingdom)	4,966	97	3,926	93	5,994	98	4,331	97
Bulgaria	0	0	0	0	0	0	0	0
Cyprus	5	-	16	-	3	-	9	-
Czech Republic	4	-	5	-	4	-	5	-
Estonia	0	0	0	0	0	0	0	0
Hungary	2	-	5	-	1	-	1	-
Latvia	0	0	0	0	0	0	0	0
Lithuania	12	-	0	0	0	0	0	0
Malta	0	0	0	0	0	0	0	0
Poland	5	-	10	-	-	-	1	-
Romania	1	-	3	-	1	-	3	-
Slovakia	3	-	6	-	0	0	0	0
Slovenia	-	-	-	-	-	-	-	-
New Member States[2]	32	1	45	1	9	-	20	-
European Union	4,998	98	3,970	94	6,002	98	4,350	97
Switzerland	59	1	70	2	87	1	101	2
Norway	1	-	1	-	0	0	0	0
Other countries	61	1	179	4	5	-	13	-
All countries	5,119	100	4,222	100	6,094	100	4,464	100

1 Excludes vehicles travelling between Northern Ireland and the Republic of Ireland only, i.e. where the whole journey is confined to the island of Ireland.

2 New Member State countries that joined the EU since 1 May 2004.

☎020-7944 4261

4.8 International road haulage by United Kingdom registered powered vehicles over 3.5 tonnes gross weight by type of transport and commodity:[1] 2007

(a) Outward journey

Commodity group (NST[2] Chapter)	Total traffic				ow: Hire or reward			
	Tonnes (thousand)	Per cent	Tonne-kms (million)	Per cent	Tonnes (thousand)	Per cent	Tonne-kms (million)	Per cent
0 Agricultural products and live animals	166	3	108	3	164	3	106	3
1 Foodstuffs and animal fodder	990	19	941	22	947	19	907	22
2 Solid mineral fuels	24	-	12	-	24	-	12	-
3 Petroleum products	36	1	20	-	36	1	20	-
4 Ores and metal waste	20	-	11	-	20	-	11	-
5 Metal products	162	3	148	4	162	3	148	4
6 Crude and manufactured minerals and building materials	66	1	58	1	66	1	58	1
7 Fertilisers	3	-	2	-	3	-	2	-
8 Chemicals	573	11	452	11	570	11	450	11
9 Miscellaneous	1,695	33	1,369	32	1,637	33	1,312	32
ow:								
Machinery & engines	836	16	718	17	804	16	675	16
Leather & textiles	514	10	450	11	500	10	442	11
All unclassified	1,384	27	1,101	26	1,378	28	1,097	27
All commodities	5,119	100	4,222	100	5,006	100	4,123	100

(b) Inward journey

Commodity group (NST[2] Chapter)	Total traffic				ow: Hire or reward			
	Tonnes (thousand)	Per cent	Tonne-kms (million)	Per cent	Tonnes (thousand)	Per cent	Tonne-kms (million)	Per cent
0 Agricultural products and live animals	531	9	457	10	510	9	442	10
1 Foodstuffs and animal fodder	1,855	30	1,184	27	1,814	30	1,163	27
2 Solid mineral fuels	21	-	15	-	21	-	15	-
3 Petroleum products	23	-	18	-	23	-	18	-
4 Ores and metal waste	22	-	12	-	22	-	12	-
5 Metal products	82	1	48	1	82	1	48	1
6 Crude and manufactured minerals and building materials	144	2	174	4	144	2	174	4
7 Fertilisers	3	-	1	-	3	-	1	-
8 Chemicals	372	6	256	6	372	6	256	6
9 Miscellaneous	1,568	26	1,289	29	1,538	26	1,246	28
ow:								
Machinery & engines	765	13	609	14	743	12	576	13
Leather & textiles	469	8	357	8	461	8	348	8
All unclassified	1,473	24	1,009	23	1,467	24	1,005	23
All commodities	6,094	100	4,464	100	5,995	100	4,381	100

1 Excludes vehicles travelling between Northern Ireland and the Republic of Ireland only, i.e. where the whole journey is confined to the island of Ireland.

2 Standard EC classification for transport. See Notes.

☎020-7944 4261

73

4.9 Bilateral[1] traffic, between the United Kingdom and European Union countries, in vehicles registered in the United Kingdom and the corresponding European Union country: [2,3] 2006

Thousand tonnes/percentage

Country of loading/unloading	Goods loaded in the United Kingdom			Goods unloaded in the United Kingdom		
	In UK vehicles[R]	In vehicles registered in the country of unloading	UK hauliers' share (percentage)	In UK vehicles[R]	In vehicles registered in the country of loading	UK hauliers' share (percentage)
Austria	25	98	20	18	219	8
Belgium	1,026	438	70	1,884	860	69
Denmark	2	70	3	13	154	8
Finland	-	1	37	1	8	14
France	2,239	2,096	52	2,697	3,266	45
Germany	887	1,116	44	992	1,765	36
Greece	17	60	22	0	191	0
Irish Republic	10,569	4,344	71	2,838	3,232	47
Italy	435	..	..	481	..	..
Luxembourg	78	11	88	56	51	52
Netherlands	679	1,014	40	1,132	2,202	34
Portugal	18	140	11	8	213	4
Spain	437	839	34	580	2,212	21
Sweden	71	2	98	12	8	61
EU15[3] (excl. United Kingdom)	16,483	10,228	62	10,714	14,382	43
Cyprus	8	1	91	5	2	72
Czech Republic	4	228	2	3	481	1
Estonia	0	11	0	0	13	0
Hungary	3	134	2	1	244	-
Latvia	-	5	8	0	12	0
Lithuania	0	61	0	0	103	0
Malta	3	..	..	6	..	..
Poland	17	501	3	12	990	1
Slovakia	0	60	0	0	93	0
Slovenia	0	26	0	0	164	0
New Member States[3,4]	36	1,027	3	27	2,101	1
European Union[3]	16,519	11,255	59	10,741	16,483	39

1 Excluding 'cross trade', i.e. trade in vehicles registered elsewhere than in the country of loading or unloading.   ☎020-7944 4261
2 All figures are for 2006, as these are the most recent available for foreign vehicles.
  2007 data for UK vehicles is shown on table 4.7.
3 2006 data for Italy were incomplete and no data were supplied by Malta.
4 New Member State countries that joined the EU since 1 May 2004.

4.10   National railways freight: 1997/98-2007/08

(a) Freight moved by commodity

Billion tonne-kilometres

	1997/98	1998/99 [1]	1999/00	2000/01	2001/02	2002/03 [2]	2003/04 [2]	2004/05 [2]	2005/06 [2]	2006/07 [2]	2007/08
Coal	4.4	4.5	4.8	4.8	6.2	5.7	5.8	6.7	8.3	8.6	7.7
Metals	..	2.1	2.2	2.1	2.4	2.6	2.4	2.6	2.2	2.0	1.8
Construction	..	2.1	2.0	2.4	2.8	2.5	2.7	2.9	2.9	2.7	2.8
Oil and petroleum	..	1.6	1.5	1.4	1.2	1.2	1.2	1.2	1.2	1.5	1.6
Other traffic	12.5	7.1	7.6	7.4	6.7	6.6	6.8	7.0	7.1	7.1	7.2
All traffic	16.9	17.3	18.2	18.1	19.4	18.5	18.9	20.3	21.7	21.9	21.2

(b) Freight lifted by commodity

Million tonnes

	1997/98	1998/99	1999/00 [3]	2000/01	2001/02	2002/03	2003/04	2004/05 [4,5]	2005/06 [4,6]	2006/07 [4]	2007/08 [7]
Coal	50.3	45.3	35.9	35.3	39.5	34.0	35.2	43.3	47.6	48.7	43.3
Metals	..	..	..	..	..	..	..	..	..	..	..
Construction	..	..	..	..	..	..	..	..	..	..	..
Oil and petroleum	..	..	..	..	..	..	..	..	..	..	..
Other traffic	55.1	56.8	60.6	60.3	54.5	53.0	53.7	56.8	57.7	59.5	59.1
All traffic	105.4	102.1	96.5	95.6	93.9	87.0	88.9	100.1	105.3	108.21	102.4

1 Revised series on new basis from 1998/99, see Notes and Definitions.
2 Goods moved data from 2002/03 onwards have been revised since the last TSGB publication
3 Break in series from 1999/2000, see Notes and Definitions.
4 Goods lifted data from 2004/05 onwards have been revised since the last TSGB publication.
5 Break in series with most of the increase due to changes in data collection method.
6 Break in the series from 2005/06 as some GB Railfreight tonnes lifted now included.
7 Break in series from 2007/08 as GB Railfreight coal data now included.

4.11 Roll-on/roll-off ferry and Channel Tunnel traffic; road goods vehicles outward to mainland Europe: by country of registration: 1997-2007

Thousands

	1997	1998	1999	2000	2001	2002	2003	2004[R]	2005[R]	2006[R]	2007
Powered vehicles:											
United Kingdom	543.2	544.3	562.7	544.8	517.6	493.3	473.9	440.6	417.8	405.9	399.7
Austria	5.3	10.1	14.7	17.1	42.0	45.8	42.9	39.0	36.4	30.9	34.5
Belgium }	53.6	72.7	96.7	114.1	119.3	121.4	104.3 {	121.7	116.7	107.8	112.5
Luxembourg								3.7	3.7	3.9	5.0
Denmark	5.5	7.3	8.7	9.5	12.0	16.9	13.7	25.8	23.0	22.6	22.3
Finland	0.1	0.6	0.7	0.9	3.1	2.0	1.1	0.2	0.3	0.6	0.6
Germany	39.3	52.4	73.1	111.5	132.0	148.2	155.7	233.2	213.9	211.6	218.4
France	234.2	272.4	319.1	338.8	352.4	363.1	363.2	224.3	214.0	204.8	197.2
Greece	2.6	1.9	2.6	2.9	2.6	2.8	3.6	10.7	9.5	8.3	7.6
Irish Republic	32.3	38.8	44.7	48.5	46.6	44.6	30.8	59.5	56.2	56.6	55.8
Italy	30.4	35.3	45.8	67.8	91.1	127.8	132.4	99.2	92.5	87.8	81.7
Netherlands	107.0	125.4	153.3	185.1	187.5	186.3	210.2	263.8	251.6	244.0	251.9
Spain	45.1	56.3	67.7	81.8	93.9	102.2	105.9	134.2	128.5	129.2	124.8
Sweden	8.9	10.3	1.0	1.4	1.8	1.8	1.4	1.5	1.4	1.8	1.7
Portugal	5.1	6.7	9.2	10.7	10.2	11.0	9.4	26.5	24.5	25.9	26.1
EU15 (excluding United Kingdom)	569.5	690.2	837.3	990.0	1,094.5	1,173.9	1,174.6	1,243.4	1,172.2	1,135.7	1,140.2
Cyprus	..	..	0.1	0.2	0.1	0.2	0.2	0.1	0.1	0.1	0.1
Czech Republic	..	..	5.4	5.2	6.8	7.8	13.1	27.5	46.1	57.8	70.0
Estonia	..	..	0.0	0.1	0.2	0.3	0.3	1.3	1.4	2.2	2.7
Hungary	..	..	6.9	8.0	11.1	12.4	12.7	22.3	43.9	60.7	79.5
Latvia	..	..	0.3	0.3	0.1	0.2	0.2	0.4	1.0	1.4	1.6
Lithuania	..	..	0.9	1.4	1.0	0.7	1.6	5.5	11.8	21.7	29.2
Malta	..	..	0.2	0.3	0.3	0.3	0.2	0.2	0.2	0.2	0.2
Poland	..	..	7.0	10.4	12.5	12.0	14.2	58.2	100.3	146.6	204.5
Slovakia	..	..	0.2	0.2	0.4	1.0	2.4	9.4	18.1	29.6	37.2
Slovenia	..	..	1.5	1.9	3.5	4.7	4.7	8.6	11.6	16.5	19.3
Romania	..	..	..	..	..	..	8.3	10.4	15.6	19.2	25.9
Bulgaria	..	..	..	..	..	..	8.6	8.3	11.0	7.9	12.5
NMS[1,2]	..	.. {	22.5	28.0	36.2	39.5	49.5	152.3	261.0	363.9	482.8
Other countries in Europe and elsewhere	28.0	35.4 {	24.9	24.9	43.2	76.7	97.6	50.6	79.5	106.5	95.9
Unknown	5.7	4.8	6.3	17.7	20.5	18.1	19.1	10.0	10.4	9.2	10.9
All countries	1,146.4	1,274.8	1,453.7	1,605.4	1,711.9	1,801.5	1,814.7	1,896.9	1,940.8	2,021.2	2,129.5
Unaccompanied trailers	740.0	737.5	737.8	712.9	686.4	726.0	780.4	787.5	762.8	786.6	810.8
Powered vehicles and unaccompanied trailers	1,886.4	2,012.3	2,191.4	2,318.3	2,398.3	2,527.5	2,595.1	2,684.4	2,703.6	2,807.8	2,940.2

1 Data for 2004 - 2007 includes 12 New Member State countries as at 1st January 2007 (Includes Romania and Bulgaria)

2 Data for 1997 - 2003 includes the 10 states that joined the EU in 2004 (omits Romania and Bulgaria).

☎0207-944 4131

4.12 Roll-on/roll-off ferry and Channel Tunnel traffic: road goods vehicles outward to mainland Europe:[1] 1997-2007

(a) By country of disembarkation[2]

Thousands

	1997	1998	1999	2000	2001	2002	2003	2004 [R]	2005 [R]	2006 [R]	2007
Powered vehicles:											
Belgium	169	132	132	152	144	144	76	88	100	87	100
France	854	1,024	1,210	1,330	1,435	1,520	1,601	1,651	1,693	1,789	1,883
Netherlands	110	103	107	119	125	128	129	149	139	136	138
Others	13	15	4	4	8	9	7	8	8	10	9
All countries	1,146	1,275	1,454	1,605	1,712	1,802	1,815	1,897	1,941	2,021	2,129
Unaccompanied trailers:											
Belgium	276	267	289	263	251	263	266	240	240	247	227
France	101	86	64	57	57	47	54	54	50	41	46
Netherlands	263	281	279	281	275	312	344	366	350	369	378
Others	100	104	107	112	103	105	116	127	123	130	160
All countries	740	738	738	713	686	726	780	787	763	787	811
All vehicles	1,886	2,012	2,191	2,318	2,398	2,527	2,595	2,684	2,704	2,808	2,940

(b) By Great Britain port area[3,4,5]

Thousands

	1997	1998	1999	2000	2001	2002	2003	2004 [R]	2005 [R]	2006 [R]	2007
Powered vehicles:											
North Sea	142	132	129	144	152	155	157	174	166	161	162
Strait of Dover	891	1,018	1,207	1,350	1,446	1,531	1,525	1,589	1,646	1,740	1,846
English Channel	114	124	117	112	114	116	132	133	129	121	121
All ports	1,146	1,275	1,454	1,605	1,712	1,802	1,815	1,897	1,941	2,021	2,129
Unaccompanied trailers:											
North Sea	575	601	641	634	610	667	730	732	702	733	751
Strait of Dover	109	91	53	44	43	30	22	27	32	33	35
English Channel	56	46	44	36	33	29	28	28	28	21	25
All ports	740	738	738	713	686	726	780	787	763	787	811
All vehicles	1,886	2,012	2,191	2,318	2,398	2,527	2,595	2,684	2,704	2,808	2,940

1 For details of revisions to the figures for the years 2004 to 2007 see DfT Statistical Bulletin 'Roads Goods Vehicles travelling to Mainland Europe: 2007

2 For Channel Tunnel traffic, France is the country of disembarkation.

3 North Sea: all ports on east coast north of and including the Thames estuary.

4 Dover Strait: Dover, Folkestone, Ramsgate and the Channel Tunnel.

5 English Channel: all ports on south coast, west of Folkestone.

☎020-7944 4131

5 Maritime:

Notes and Definitions

Ports traffic: 5.2 - 5.5, 5.6 and 5.7

These tables relate to foreign, coastwise and one-port traffic through ports in the United Kingdom.

More details are available in the annual Transport Statistics Report *Maritime Statistics,* published by The Stationery Office, and also available free on the DfT web site.

The data are derived as follows:

(a) from 2000,

(i)   detailed quarterly returns from shipping lines or their agents of all freight traffic at major UK ports;

(ii)   quarterly returns of inwards and outwards weight and units by port authorities or other undertakings at major ports;

(iii) annual returns of inwards and outwards traffic only by port authorities or other undertakings at minor ports.

(b) prior to 2000,

(i)   detailed annual traffic returns made by port authorities or other undertakings at major ports;

(ii)   annual returns of inwards and outwards traffic from port authorities or other undertakings at minor ports

The major ports include all ports with cargo volumes of at least 1 million tonnes in 2001 (2 million tonnes under the previous system between 1995 and 1999) and a few other smaller ports. The breakdowns of traffic for 1995 and later years in the tables include major ports traffic and are supplemented by estimates for the minor ports.

Definitions used:
Port groups: For statistical purposes, ports of Great Britain are grouped geographically as shown in map 5.9.

Weights: All weights reported for port and waterborne freight statistics include crates and other packaging. The tare weights of containers and other items of transport equipment are excluded.

Foreign traffic: Traffic between ports in the United Kingdom (Great Britain and Northern Ireland), and foreign countries, that is

countries outside Great Britain, Northern Ireland, the Isle of Man and the Channel Islands.

Domestic traffic: The sum of coastwise and one-port traffic.

Coastwise traffic: Goods loaded or unloaded at ports in the United Kingdom, and transported to or from another port in the United Kingdom.

One-port traffic: One-port traffic comprises:

- dredged sand, gravel, etc. landed at a port for commercial purposes;
- traffic to and from off-shore installations. Fuel shipped to oil rigs is included in 'Other traffic - outwards'; and
- material shipped for dumping at sea.

Container and roll-on traffic (commonly known as 'unitised' traffic): Includes road goods vehicles, unaccompanied trailers and other goods carried on roll-on/roll-off shipping services, containers carried on all types of shipping services and rail wagons and barges carried on ships. Goods carried on 'unitised' services constitute a subset of total traffic and are reported in Tables 5.4 and 5.5.

Coastwise routes: Coastwise routes (Table 5.6) are the ferry services between mainland Great Britain and Northern Ireland, the Isle of Man, the West of Scotland island of Lewis (between Ullapool and Stornoway), the Orkneys and Shetlands, and the Channel Islands. Short ferry routes between Scottish islands, and those across river estuaries and to the Isle of Wight, are excluded. Only in the case of ferry routes between mainland Great Britain and the Orkneys and Shetlands is traffic counted at both ends of the route. In other cases, traffic is counted at the mainland Great Britain port only.

Domestic waterborne freight traffic: 5.8 and 5.10

These tables present estimates of goods lifted (tonnes) and goods moved (tonne -kilometres) in the United Kingdom by coastal shipping (coastwise and one-port traffic) and on inland waters. The data are based on annual studies for DfT by MDS- Transmodal.

The definitions of inland waters were devised for the first survey of waterborne transport carried out in 1980, and slightly updated in 2004. The definitions were produced from the perspective of measuring freight traffic travelling on inland waters, which could travel by another surface mode within the UK. There are two boundary definitions used to measure the amount of traffic:

Inland waterways: all water areas available for navigation that lie inland of a boundary defined as the most seaward point of any estuary which might reasonably be bridged or tunnelled - this is taken to be where the width of water surface area is both less than 3 km at low water and less than 5 km at high water on spring tides.

Inland waters: all waters within the *Smooth Water Line*, that is, the outermost limit of Category D waters in the Martime and Coastguard Agency (MCA) inland waters classification, "tidal rivers and estuaries where significant wave height could not be expected to exceed 2m at any time". This is generally much further seaward than the inland waterways boundary. Prior to 2004 a broadly similar limit was used - the summer boundary of the Partially Smooth Water Area (PSWA) - waters within this limit are known as *sheltered waters*.

For the purpose of estimating tonnes and tonne-kilometres, all traffic *wholly within* inland waters (ie internal traffic) is counted. Tonnes is then simply tonnes lifted, and tonne-kilometres is tonnes lifted multiplied by the distance travelled.

Traffic which crosses the inland waters boundary and which also goes upstream of the inland waterways boundary, is counted as well; but traffic which is essentially *seagoing traffic* to and from major *seaboard* ports is specifically excluded.

Where traffic is included, tonnes is then tonnes lifted and tonne-kilometres is tonnes lifted multiplied by the distance travelled but calculated from the point at which the vessel crosses the *inland waterways* boundary.

Detailed statistics for 2007 are available in the annual Statistics Bulletin, *Waterborne Freight in the UK 2007*, and further details of the inland waterway network in freight use, its wharves and its craft, in the occasional report *Waterborne Freight Benchmark Report 2007*, both published by DfT and available on the DfT web site.

United Kingdom International sea passenger movements: 5.11 and 5.12

These tables have been compiled from statistics collected monthly from shipping operators by DfT and cover travel between the UK and other countries. Domestic passengers are excluded. The figures do include drivers of lorries, coaches and other vehicles. Short sea routes in these tables are generally routes between the UK and Belgium, Denmark, Faroe Isles, Finland, France, Germany, Ireland, Netherlands, Norway, Spain and Sweden.

United Kingdom and Crown Dependency registered trading vessels: 5.13

Until the end of 1986, United Kingdom registered fleet figures were derived from DfT records of trading vessels of 500 gross tons or over registered at ports in the United Kingdom, the Channel Islands and the Isle of Man. A different ship type classification was also in use. For 1986 only, for purposes of comparison, it shows figures from both sources giving the composition of the fleet on the basis of both the 'old' and 'new' ship type classifications.

The United Kingdom owned and registered merchant fleets: 5.14 and 5.15

The figures given in these tables are derived from Lloyd's Register-Fairplay data and cover trading vessels of 500 gross tons or above. Table 5.15 covers vessels owned by UK companies wherever the vessels are registered, while Table 5.14 covers vessels registered in the United Kingdom and Crown Dependencies (Isle of Man, Channel Islands), excluding those owned by the Government.

The figures for both fleets exclude offshore supply vessels, non-cargo vessels, tugs, fishing vessels, dredgers, river and other non seagoing vessels. For more data and background information see the Transport Statistics Report, *Maritime Statistics 2007*, available from The Stationery Office and the DfT web site.

Gross tonnage: Under the International Convention on the Tonnage Measurement of Ships, 1969 gross tonnage (gt) is defined as the following function of the total volume of all enclosed spaces in the ship (V), in cubic metres:

$$GT = K_1V$$
where $K_1 = 0.2 + 0.02 \log_{10} V$.

Deadweight tonnes: The term deadweight tonnes, or 'dwt', is a measurement of the weight of cargo, stores, fuel, passengers and crew carried by the ship when loaded to her maximum summer loadline.

Tankers: Include oil, gas, chemical and other specialised tankers.

Bulk carriers: Large and small carriers including combination - ore/oil and ore/bulk/oil - carriers. *Specialised carriers:* Includes vessels such as livestock carriers, car carriers and chemical carriers.

Fully cellular container: Figures include only container vessels of this type.

Ro-Ro: These are for passenger and cargo Ro-Ro vessels.

Other general cargo vessels: These include reefer vessels, general cargo/passenger vessels, and single and multi-deck general cargo vessels.

Passenger vessels: These are cruise liner and other passenger vessels.

UK shipping industry revenue and expenditure from international activities: 5.16

The revenue and expenditure figures in this table are derived from the results of annual inquiries carried out by the Chamber of Shipping (CoS). The United Kingdom shipping industry is defined as United Kingdom resident companies which own or operate ships irrespective of their flag of registry.

This includes companies, which are United Kingdom subsidiaries of overseas parent companies, and excludes overseas resident subsidiaries of United Kingdom companies.

This treatment arises from the primary purpose of the CoS inquiries, which is to provide estimates for the sea transport account of the United Kingdom Balance of Payments. In the Balance of Payments the revenue from overseas resident subsidiary companies is treated as investment income, not part of the sea transport account.

International activities cover the activities of ships either owned by the United Kingdom industry or operated by the industry on charter. The activities covered are:

- carriage of UK imports and exports;
- carriage of trade between two foreign countries (cross trades);
- carriage of passengers on international ferry routes and sea cruises;
- chartering ships to overseas operators.

The passenger revenue series includes revenue from overseas residents only and is consistent with data published in *The Pink Book* (United Kingdom Balance of Payments). Associated expenditure includes:

- payment for bunkers uplifted abroad;

- disbursements in overseas ports: cargo handling, port dues, crews' expenses, agency fees, light dues etc.;
- charter payments to overseas ship owners.

Marine accident casualties: 5.17

The data refer to accidents to persons on UK registered merchant vessels of greater than or equal to 100gt only, including accidents during access. The information is derived from incidents reported in compliance with the Merchant Shipping (Accident Reporting and Investigation) Regulations (SI 2005 No. 881).

HM Coastguard Statistics: 5.18

HM Coastguard, part of the Maritime and Coastguard Agency (MCA), initiates and co-ordinates Civil Maritime Search and Rescue operations within the UK Search and Rescue Region (UKSRR).

Machinery and equipment failure, the inability to cope when the weather deteriorates, diving incidents and failure to inform relatives or other agents ashore when likely to be overdue have been the major causes of SAR incidents.

Definitions of terms used are:

Commercial vessels: All Merchant Vessels (including ferries and cruise ships), tugs, barges, dredgers, offshore installations, tenders, supply vessels, support vessels, research vessels, cable layers, mega-yachts, hovercraft etc.

Fishing vessels: All registered fishing vessels.

Pleasure craft: Yachts (except mega-yachts), sailing dinghies, cabin cruisers, speedboats, diving support boats, sail training craft, square riggers, rowing boats and inflatable craft. From 1994 data also includes canoes/kayaks, sailboards and jet-skis (personal watercraft) previously included in 'others'.

Incidents to persons: Includes man-overboard, divers, swimmers, missing persons, persons cut off by tides, persons stuck on cliffs, etc.

Medical evacuations: Incidents where injured persons taken from vessels at sea to shore for medical treatment, or injured cliff walkers evacuated to hospital, etc.

Others: Includes incidents involving military vessels, military aircraft, civilian aircraft, animal rescue, etc.

Distress reports: Includes all Distress, Urgency, Pyrotechnic and EPIRB/ELT signals and those reports subsequently found to be false alarms or hoaxes.

5.1 United Kingdom ports:[1] foreign, coastwise and one-port traffic: 1965-2007

Million tonnes

Year	Foreign			Coastwise			One-port			Total		
	Imports	Exports	All	Inwards	Outwards	All	Inwards	Outwards [2]	All	Inwards	Outwards	All
Great Britain												
1965	153.4	35.7	189.1	54.1	60.4	114.5	7.2	8.5	15.7	214.7	104.6	319.2
1966	157.1	38.2	195.3	54.2	59.7	113.9	6.8	8.5	15.3	218.1	106.4	324.5
1967	161.7	38.0	199.7	53.1	56.9	110.0	6.6	8.5	15.1	221.4	103.4	324.8
1968	175.6	41.7	217.3	51.1	56.6	107.7	7.8	8.5	16.3	234.5	106.8	341.3
1969	185.5	43.3	228.8	52.1	56.9	109.0	8.3	8.5	16.8	245.9	108.7	354.6
1970	196.2	48.0	244.2	51.8	56.2	108.0	9.2	8.6	17.8	257.2	112.8	370.0
1971	202.0	48.7	250.7	46.0	52.0	98.0	10.9	8.6	19.5	258.9	109.3	368.2
1972	205.0	49.7	254.7	45.4	51.8	97.2	16.0	8.8	24.8	266.4	110.3	376.7
1973	219.5	53.5	273.0	46.4	57.3	103.7	13.9	8.9	22.8	279.8	119.7	399.5
1974	211.1	51.1	262.2	48.5	56.9	105.4	13.1	10.1	23.2	272.7	118.1	390.8
1975	175.3	50.2	225.5	41.5	48.9	90.4	13.0	11.2	24.2	229.8	110.3	340.1
1976	180.0	62.8	242.8	41.1	50.9	92.0	14.4	11.2	25.6	235.5	124.9	360.3
1977	158.2	77.6	235.8	44.1	56.3	100.4	21.7	12.3	34.0	224.0	146.2	370.2
1978	152.8	90.7	243.5	47.5	62.2	109.7	26.5	12.8	39.3	226.8	165.7	392.4
1979	157.1	107.5	264.6	52.7	67.0	119.7	29.5	12.9	42.4	239.3	187.5	426.8
1980	131.2	117.1	248.3	57.4	67.7	125.1	24.6	14.0	38.6	213.2	198.8	412.0
United Kingdom												
1980	133.4	117.5	250.8	64.8	69.8	134.6	24.6	14.0	38.6	222.8	201.3	424.1
1981	125.7	126.1	251.8	60.2	68.2	128.4	22.3	13.6	35.8	208.2	207.8	416.1
1982	122.9	130.7	253.6	67.2	71.3	138.5	24.6	13.4	37.9	214.7	215.4	430.1
1983	121.9	136.8	258.7	68.9	71.3	140.1	26.6	13.0	39.6	217.5	221.1	438.5
1984	143.5	142.1	285.5	64.2	66.3	130.5	28.5	12.3	40.9	236.3	220.7	456.9
1985	143.3	148.2	291.5	63.2	66.3	129.6	28.1	13.7	41.8	234.7	228.2	462.9
1986	150.6	150.7	301.3	60.9	63.7	124.6	27.2	13.4	40.6	238.7	227.8	466.5
1987	154.9	151.0	305.9	59.8	61.2	121.0	31.8	12.9	44.7	246.6	225.0	471.6
1988	169.7	142.2	311.9	66.3	65.1	131.3	34.2	14.6	48.8	270.2	221.9	492.1
1989	174.6	127.5	302.1	64.1	64.8	128.9	35.0	14.8	49.8	273.7	207.1	480.9
1990	183.5	136.2	319.6	61.0	61.5	122.3	34.1	15.9	50.0	278.4	213.6	492.0
1991	182.1	143.2	325.3	61.7	62.8	124.4	29.8	15.1	44.9	273.6	221.0	494.6
1992	182.6	150.2	332.8	58.2	60.8	119.0	29.0	14.9	43.9	269.8	225.9	495.7
1993	189.5	157.5	346.9	59.4	62.0	121.5	23.8	14.0	37.8	272.7	233.5	506.2
1994	190.1	179.0	369.1	63.3	64.8	128.1	28.6	12.4	41.0	281.9	256.2	538.1
1995	190.3	178.8	369.1	67.9	72.1	140.0	26.7	12.4	39.1	284.9	263.3	548.2
1996	192.7	175.8	368.5	69.9	75.3	145.2	25.1	12.4	37.5	287.7	263.5	551.2
1997	205.7	179.3	385.0	67.5	72.0	139.5	21.8	12.2	34.0	295.0	263.5	558.5
1998	209.3	181.7	390.9	70.7	71.9	142.7	26.1	8.8	34.9	306.1	262.4	568.5
1999	203.6	184.4	387.9	67.0	71.1	138.1	36.4	3.2	39.6	307.0	258.7	565.6
2000	220.9	193.1	414.0	57.4	61.9	119.3	38.0	1.7	39.8	316.3	256.7	573.1
2001	238.4	180.4	418.7	57.3	54.9	112.2	33.3	2.2	35.4	328.9	237.5	566.4
2002	220.9	178.2	399.1	57.8 R	57.3	115.2 R	41.7	2.0	43.7	320.5 R	237.5	557.9 R
2003	229.3	174.0	403.3	56.9 R	56.1	113.0 R	37.2	1.7	39.0	323.4 R	231.9	555.3 R
2004	250.4	169.6	420.0	58.3 R	59.7	117.9 R	33.4	1.4	34.8	342.1 R	230.6	572.8 R
2005	262.3	163.7	426.0	61.4 R	64.9	126.2 R	30.4	1.9	32.3	354.0 R	230.5	584.5 R
2006	278.9	160.6	439.5	56.7 R	56.5	113.2 R	29.0	1.6	30.6	364.7 R	218.6	583.3 R
2007	273.3	164.5	437.9	57.6	57.2	114.8	26.9	2.0	28.9	357.8	223.7	581.5

1 Great Britain only prior to 1980.
2 Estimated prior to 1974.

☎020-7944 3087

5.2 United Kingdom ports: foreign, coastwise and one port traffic by type of cargo: 1997-2007

											Thousand tonnes
	1997	1998	1999	2000	2001	2002	2003	2004	2005	2006	2007
Foreign traffic											
Liquid bulk traffic											
Imports	61,060	61,346	56,528	70,788	74,495	62,811	66,447	75,897	76,988	85,530	83,442
Exports	104,654	106,041	110,591	118,509	110,321	107,516	100,772	95,974	87,995	82,883	84,563
All	165,714	167,387	167,120	189,297	184,816	170,327	167,218	171,871	164,983	168,412	168,005
Dry bulk traffic											
Imports	68,208	68,333	65,219	65,652	77,360	67,575	72,644	76,625	87,546	92,846	85,936
Exports	19,596	20,840	18,905	19,739	17,206	18,026	20,559	18,098	18,010	18,113	17,725
All	87,805	89,173	84,124	85,391	94,565	85,600	93,203	94,722	105,557	110,959	103,661
Container and roll-on traffic											
Imports	58,822	61,191	64,272	64,753	65,721	68,371	69,199	75,520	77,431	80,288	84,519
Exports	48,805	49,029	49,616	49,323	47,334	47,313	47,291	49,869	51,045	52,801	54,418
All	107,628	110,220	113,889	114,076	113,054	115,685	116,490	125,390	128,476	133,089	138,937
Semi-bulk traffic											
Imports	16,097	16,878	15,967	17,174	17,059	18,523	17,284	18,413	16,766	16,706	17,016
Exports	5,142	4,897	4,519	4,411	3,737	3,613	3,848	4,342	5,287	5,299	6,511
All	21,239	21,775	20,486	21,584	20,796	22,136	21,131	22,755	22,054	22,005	23,527
Conventional traffic											
Imports	1,506	1,531	1,595	2,500	3,730	3,645	3,699	3,990	3,529	3,555	2,399
Exports	1,100	854	735	1,145	1,786	1,705	1,535	1,314	1,393	1,456	1,321
All	2,607	2,385	2,330	3,645	5,515	5,349	5,234	5,304	4,922	5,012	3,720
All foreign traffic											
Imports	205,694	209,279	203,581	220,866	238,364	220,924	229,273	250,445	262,261	278,925	273,312
Exports	179,298	181,661	184,367	193,127	180,383	178,173	174,003	169,597	163,731	160,552	164,539
All	384,992	390,940	387,948	413,993	418,747	399,097	403,276	420,042	425,992	439,477	437,851
Coastwise traffic											
Liquid bulk traffic											
Inwards	49,981	51,514	48,164	36,677	37,008	38,631 R	36,901 R	39,183 R	41,261 R	35,429 R	36,440
Outwards	53,753	52,622	51,966	41,696	36,049	37,535	35,371	38,788	42,477	33,941	34,893
All	103,734	104,136	100,131	78,373	73,058	76,166 R	72,273 R	77,971 R	83,738 R	69,370 R	71,333
Dry bulk traffic											
Inwards	6,678	7,599	6,792	8,243	8,032	7,245	7,956	6,453	6,717	7,914	6,861
Outwards	6,963	7,882	7,229	8,201	7,112	7,785	8,438	7,814	8,366	8,675	7,761
All	13,642	15,480	14,021	16,444	15,144	15,030	16,395	14,268	15,083	16,589	14,622
Container and roll-on traffic											
Inwards	10,522	11,236	11,542	12,186	11,797	11,539 R	11,458 R	12,253 R	12,910 R	12,872 R	13,434
Outwards	10,786	10,660	11,396	11,506	11,064	11,341	11,426	12,026	12,995	12,988	13,785
All	21,307	21,895	22,938	23,692	22,861	22,880 R	22,884 R	24,280 R	25,905 R	25,860 R	27,219
Semi-bulk traffic											
Inwards	166	176	203	247	364	324	373	320	217	351	479
Outwards	188	477	221	311	570	546	544	519	565	373	443
All	354	653	424	558	934	870	917	838	783	725	922
Conventional traffic											
Inwards	161	212	274	96	74	99	194	73	278	167	345
Outwards	314	306	285	139	131	124	368	518	451	482	328
All	475	518	559	236	206	223	562	591	729	649	673
All coastwise traffic											
Inwards	67,508	70,736	66,975	57,448	57,276	57,838 R	56,883 R	58,282 R	61,382 R	56,734 R	57,559
Outwards	72,004	71,946	71,098	61,853	54,926	57,331	56,147	59,665	64,854	56,459	57,210
All	139,512	142,682	138,073	119,302	112,202	115,168 R	113,030 R	117,947 R	126,237 R	113,193 R	114,769

5.2 (continued) United Kingdom ports: foreign, coastwise and one port traffic by type of cargo - 1997-2007

Thousand tonnes

	1997	1998	1999	2000	2001	2002	2003	2004	2005	2006	2007
One-port traffic											
Liquid bulk traffic											
Inwards	6,871	10,587	20,220	24,937	18,245	25,886	22,328	19,152	16,169	14,171	10,816
Outwards	8,560	4,365	126	485	647	693	563	361	421	336	494
All	15,431	14,951	20,346	25,422	18,892	26,579	22,892	19,513	16,590	14,506	11,310
Dry bulk traffic											
Inwards	14,123	14,436	15,051	12,503	14,362	15,197	14,389	13,821	13,476	14,189	15,311
Outwards	106	98	41	41	68	67	70	28	52	32	67
All	14,229	14,534	15,092	12,544	14,430	15,264	14,460	13,849	13,529	14,221	15,378
Non-oil traffic with UK off-shore installations											
Inwards	851	1,063	1,136	589	643	606	490	414	724	672	801
Outwards	3,515	4,332	3,019	1,199	1,452	1,234	1,112	995	1,470	1,249	1,395
All	4,366	5,394	4,155	1,789	2,095	1,840	1,602	1,409	2,194	1,921	2,196
All one-port traffic											
Inwards	21,844	26,085	36,407	38,030	33,250	41,688	37,208	33,388	30,369	29,031	26,928
Outwards	12,181	8,794	3,186	1,725	2,167	1,994	1,745	1,383	1,944	1,617	1,956
All	34,026	34,880	39,593	39,755	35,417	43,682	38,953	34,771	32,313	30,648	28,884
Foreign and domestic traffic											
Liquid bulk traffic											
Inwards	117,912	123,446	124,913	132,402	129,748	127,328 [R]	125,676 [R]	134,232 [R]	134,417 [R]	135,129 [R]	130,699
Outwards	166,967	163,028	162,684	160,690	147,017	145,744	136,706	135,123	130,894	117,159	119,950
All	284,879	286,474	287,597	293,092	276,765	273,072 [R]	262,382 [R]	269,355 [R]	265,311 [R]	252,289 [R]	250,649
Dry bulk traffic											
Inwards	89,009	90,367	87,062	86,398	99,754	90,016	94,990	96,899	107,739	114,949	108,109
Outwards	26,666	28,820	26,175	27,981	24,386	25,878	29,067	25,940	26,429	26,820	25,553
All	115,675	119,187	113,237	114,379	124,140	115,894	124,057	122,839	134,168	141,769	133,661
Container and roll-on traffic											
Inwards	69,344	72,427	75,814	76,939	77,518	79,910 [R]	80,657 [R]	87,774 [R]	90,341 [R]	93,160 [R]	97,953
Outwards	59,591	59,689	61,013	60,829	58,398	58,654	58,717	61,896	64,040	65,789	68,203
All	128,935	132,115	136,827	137,768	135,915	138,565 [R]	139,374 [R]	149,669 [R]	154,381 [R]	158,949 [R]	166,156
Semi-bulk traffic											
Inwards	16,263	17,054	16,170	17,421	17,423	18,847	17,657	18,733	16,984	17,057	17,495
Outwards	5,330	5,374	4,740	4,721	4,307	4,159	4,392	4,860	5,853	5,672	6,954
All	21,593	22,428	20,910	22,142	21,730	23,006	22,049	23,593	22,836	22,729	24,449
Conventional traffic											
Inwards	1,667	1,744	1,869	2,596	3,804	3,744	3,893	4,063	3,807	3,722	2,744
Outwards	1,414	1,159	1,020	1,284	1,917	1,828	1,903	1,832	1,843	1,938	1,649
All	3,082	2,903	2,889	3,880	5,721	5,572	5,796	5,895	5,651	5,660	4,393
Non-oil traffic with UK off-shore installations											
Inwards	851	1,063	1,136	589	643	606	490	414	724	672	801
Outwards	3,515	4,332	3,019	1,199	1,452	1,234	1,112	995	1,470	1,249	1,395
All	4,366	5,394	4,155	1,789	2,095	1,840	1,602	1,409	2,194	1,921	2,196
All foreign and domestic traffic											
Inwards	295,046	306,100	306,963	316,344	328,890	320,450 [R]	323,364 [R]	342,115 [R]	354,012 [R]	364,690 [R]	357,800
Outwards	263,484	262,402	258,651	256,706	237,477	237,497	231,896	230,645	230,529	218,627	223,704
All	558,530	568,502	565,614	573,050	566,366	557,947 [R]	555,260 [R]	572,760 [R]	584,541 [R]	583,318 [R]	581,504

☎020-7944 3087

5.3 United Kingdom ports: foreign and domestic traffic by port: 1997-2007

Thousand tonnes

	1997	1998	1999	2000	2001	2002	2003	2004	2005	2006	2007
Aberdeen	4,013	3,786	3,368	3,377	3,845	3,645	3,233	3,888	4,609	4,663	5,131
Ayr	499	346	229	283	274	241	291	401	418	419	553
Barrow	261	275	247	231	225	279	241	206	151	145	192
Barry	384	433	445	597	586	547	457	403	443	515	456
Belfast	12,344	12,510	12,862	12,484	13,402	12,825	13,201	13,559	13,500	13,514	13,416
Berwick	143	139	135	146	110	89	134	89	76	94	83
Blyth	801	1,135	807	933	761	786	885	892	915	1,147	1,464
Boston	1,235	1,258	1,179	1,265	847	766	1,035	705	767	834	836
Bridgwater	69	67	59	84	104	86	101	105	106	91	50
Brightlingsea	153	140	142	65	248	76	125	138	118	97	103
Bristol	7,041	7,710	7,615	9,647	10,895	10,083	11,439	10,759	11,206	12,261	11,178
Cairnryan	2,227	2,504	2,437	2,283	2,014	2,099	2,328	2,849	3,274	3,145	3,163
Cardiff	2,857	2,452	2,661	2,699	2,739	2,209	2,287	2,504	2,450	2,873	3,057
Clyde (incl. Ardrossan)	7,494	8,127	8,495	7,224	11,069	9,733	9,214	11,507	15,737	14,981	12,063
Colchester	380	330	207	163	-	-	-	-	-	-	-
Coleraine	23	21	7	21	45	54	54	53	67	55	74
Cowes IOW	238	310	412	434	480	213 [R]	281 [R]	193 [R]	179 [R]	235 [R]	266
Cromarty Firth	3,971	4,456	2,336	2,329	2,145	2,658	3,501	3,208	3,325	3,206	3,502
Dover	19,073	17,690	19,387	17,434	19,074	20,212	18,796	20,753	21,145	23,805	25,144
Dundee	1,124	1,061	1,072	1,047	1,101	1,103	1,016	1,058	1,222	1,202	1,035
Exmouth (incl. Exeter)	46	52	-	-	-	-	-	-	-	-	-
Falmouth	431	484	398	598	471	406	438	352	570	697	753
Felixstowe	28,881	30,025	31,466	29,686	28,354	25,119	22,282	23,413	23,144	24,370	25,685
Fishguard	420	387	395	421	341	408	474	522	513	597	572
Fleetwood	1,362	1,106	1,368	1,530	1,608	1,521	1,624	1,662	1,635	1,670	1,772
Folkestone	347	634	462	560	251	-	112	77	94	13	25
Forth	43,102	44,400	45,396	41,143	41,607	42,202	38,752	34,892	34,218	31,556	36,681
Fowey	1,538	1,624	1,451	1,527	1,535	1,453	1,447	1,330	1,270	1,103	1,121
Garston	588	572	522	472	462	443	433	511	532	570	515
Glensanda	4,401	5,140	5,217	5,899	5,471	5,846	5,322	5,189	5,439	6,004	7,050
Gloucester & Sharpness	414	410	427	598	541	564	552	539	498	458	490
Goole	2,760	2,648	2,650	2,711	2,633	2,265	1,913	2,174	2,623	2,215	2,281
Great Yarmouth	1,577	1,865	1,216	757	666	711	778	607	763	950	900
Grimsby & Immingham	47,991	48,387	49,757	52,501	54,831	55,731	55,931	57,616	60,686	64,033	66,279
Harwich	3,523	3,281	4,059	3,990	2,623	3,495	4,330	4,264	4,221	4,176	3,784
Heysham	4,069	3,585	3,370	3,723	3,824	3,705	4,083	3,539	3,676	4,014	3,586
Holyhead	2,951	3,407	3,437	3,444	3,229	3,288	3,329	3,945	4,147	4,153	3,468
Hull	10,047	10,249	10,119	10,722	10,586	10,298	10,529	12,443	13,363	12,785	12,497
Inverness	769	763	783	724	714	686	727	726	665	671	684
Ipswich	1,956	2,184	2,391	2,925	2,924	3,336	3,888	3,557	3,578	3,505	2,797
King's Lynn	855	883	945	1,069	873	1,019	1,052	718	1,008	613	578
Lancaster	121	126	112	135	117	130	156	115	111	146	123
Larne	3,153	3,389	4,032	4,508	3,520	4,295	4,319	4,984	5,496	5,489	5,464
Lerwick	687	559	486	521	979	653	616	590	622	541	615
Littlehampton	181	128	173	188	210	224	174	93	61	71	72
Liverpool	30,841	30,357	28,913	30,421	30,288	30,413	31,684	32,233	33,775	33,550	32,258
London	55,692	57,311	52,206	47,892	50,654	51,185	51,028	53,289	53,843	51,911	52,739
Londonderry	1,138	1,127	1,216	1,133	1,060	1,065	1,172	1,392	1,151	1,690	1,934
Lowestoft	378	269	456	439	319	309	370	242	242	323	237
Manchester	7,939	7,409	7,825	7,687	7,879	6,279	6,088	6,634	7,222	8,049	8,079
Medway	13,803	15,528	13,973	15,292	14,853	14,840	15,619	14,535	15,470	18,957	15,417
Milford Haven	34,518	28,783	32,187	33,768	33,792	34,543	32,737	38,452	37,547	34,307	35,496
Mistley Quay	217	217	144	150	163	116	116	135	155	160	174
Montrose	616	561	614	721	675	728	798	777	697	640	582
Mostyn	320	326	359	310	309	871	944	656	203	180	154
Neath	525	506	474	466	504	369	383	416	406	464	420
Newhaven	1,241	1,012	461	578	998	863	949	929	876	1,046	1,003
Newport	2,974	2,628	2,532	2,673	2,980	3,111	2,790	3,448	3,971	3,846	2,843
Orkney	10,483	16,156	16,998	22,798	18,407	18,812	14,422	17,934	14,534	11,249	10,592
Par	605	549	605	558	485	479	348	337	315	209	58

5.3 (continued) United Kingdom ports: foreign and domestic traffic by port: 1997-2007

Thousand tonnes

	1997	1998	1999	2000	2001	2002	2003	2004	2005	2006	2007
Perth	161	240	242	266	218	176	144	159	139	148	144
Peterhead	819	2,818	2,209	1,123	1,339	1,343	1,051	676	928	947	790
Plymouth	1,773	1,310	1,671	1,799	1,877	1,854	2,053	2,167	2,308	2,452	2,486
Poole	1,768	1,700	1,581	1,296	1,819	1,798	1,640	1,754	1,712	1,806	1,405
Port Talbot	13,050	13,302	11,821	11,725	8,271	4,971	7,819	8,555	8,573	8,659	9,052
Portsmouth	4,543	4,527	4,317	4,521	4,282	4,365	4,222	4,940	4,931	4,205	3,961
Ramsgate	2,208	1,869	1,207	1,237	1,432	1,848	1,789	1,702	1,872	1,704	2,015
River Ouse	582	412	247	302	197	181	236	238	217	234	282
River Trent	2,587	2,360	2,193	2,450	2,396	2,346	2,309	2,329	1,924	2,062	2,207
Rivers Hull and Humber	7,562	10,197	8,830	9,015	7,846	8,902	10,025	9,242	9,843	9,774	9,370
Seaham	608	521	493	506	536	314	459	434	505	530	554
Shoreham	1,812	1,811	1,708	1,762	1,804	1,786	1,725	1,686	1,828	1,797	1,989
Silloth	147	155	231	168	141	134	155	168	170	171	180
Southampton	33,053	34,259	33,289	34,773	35,689	34,156	35,773	38,431	39,947	40,556	43,815
Stranraer	1,794	1,780	1,690	1,506	1,404	1,273	1,274	1,277	1,165	1,222	1,231
Sullom Voe	32,082	31,109	37,680	38,204	31,166	29,376	26,360	23,939	20,541	19,447	16,573
Sunderland	1,305	999	1,037	934	1,021	928	1,020	1,117	920	904	1,024
Sutton Bridge	844	913	846	817	695	669	746	571	534	593	609
Swansea	3,674	3,137	1,650	1,014	1,261	1,069	848	721	695	634	683
Tees and Hartlepool	51,249	51,454	49,316	51,473	50,842	50,447	53,842	53,819	55,790	53,348	49,779
Teignmouth	665	665	654	657	660	641	641	569	595	683	639
Tyne	2,083	2,136	2,210	2,391	2,469	2,656	2,763	2,973	3,357	4,077	4,613
Wallasea	87	120	128	146	149	165	175	176	196	233	221
Warrenpoint	1,344	1,563	1,715	1,676	1,480	1,826	1,880	1,967	2,436	2,307	1,999
Whitby and Scarborough	75	65	62	39	-	-	-	4	-	-	-
Whitehaven	-	-	-	-	-	-	2	-	-	-	-
Whitstable	387	306	153	170	189	159	129	103	81	121	79
Wisbech	46	61	59	50	54	59	49	57	75	112	63
Workington	565	623	563	636	418	430	258	180	246	200	182
Other ports	3,864	4,313	4,118	4,412	5,014	4,589	4,543	4,269	3,961	4,131	4,016
England	361,563	367,560	357,652	363,212	366,645	362,409 R	370,138 R	378,872 R	392,286 R	400,573 R	399,085
Wales	62,307	56,150	56,578	57,892	54,734	52,020	52,613	60,051	59,310	56,673	56,598
Scotland	115,069	124,713	130,100	130,512	123,820	122,156	110,535	110,444	108,890	101,587	101,952
Great Britain	538,939	548,423	544,330	551,616	545,199	536,585 R	533,287 R	549,367 R	560,486 R	558,833 R	557,636
Northern Ireland	19,591	20,079	21,284	21,434	21,167	21,363	21,973	23,393	24,055	24,485	23,868
All UK ports	558,530	568,502	565,614	573,050	566,366	557,947 R	555,260 R	572,760 R	584,541 R	583,318 R	581,504

☎020-7944 3087

5.4 United Kingdom ports: foreign and domestic unitised traffic: [1] 1997-2007

(a) Units	1997	1998	1999	2000	2001	2002	2003	2004	2005	2006	Thousands 2007
Containers on Lo-Lo and conventional services [2,3]	3,518	3,722	3,918	4,325	4,464	4,506	4,533	4,919	4,754	4,883	5,381
Containers on Ro-Ro service	514	528	550	-	-	-	-	-	-	-	-
Road goods vehicles	3,124	3,206	3,182	3,118	3,317	3,479	3,547	3,857	3,906	4,183	4,295
Unaccompanied trailers	2,304	2,312	2,533	2,742	2,687	2,760	2,781	2,734	2,840	2,944	2,989
Rail wagons, shipborne port to-port trailers and barges [3]	-	-	-	361	344	348	374	383	665	668	744
All main freight units	9,459	9,769	10,182	10,546	10,811	11,094	11,235	11,893	12,165	12,678	13,408
Other unitised freight:											
Import/export vehicles	2,934	3,135	3,251	3,095	3,313	3,662	3,736	3,953	3,978	3,906	4,022
Other units	..	..	..	277	225	167	163	145	208	186	244
All freight units	12,393	12,904	13,433	13,918	14,349	14,923	15,133	15,991	16,351	16,770	17,674
(b) Tonnage											Thousand tonnes
Containers on Lo-Lo and conventional services [2,3]	45,442	46,680	49,600	51,613	51,814	51,178	51,413	56,502	53,949	54,493	60,718
Containers on Ro-Ro service	7,884	8,830	8,800	-	-	-	-	-	-	-	-
Road goods vehicles [4]	71,057	71,802	73,519	35,852	37,706	39,119 [R]	38,759 [R]	42,896 [R]	44,854 [R]	46,592 [R]	48,233
Unaccompanied trailers	..	..	..	38,408	35,678	36,843	37,361	38,087	38,600	39,658	38,534
Rail wagons, shipborne port to-port trailers and barges [3]	-	-	-	6,166	4,846	5,294	5,505	5,483	10,064	10,837	11,099
All main freight units	124,383	127,312	131,919	132,039	130,043	132,434 [R]	133,038 [R]	142,969 [R]	147,468 [R]	151,580 [R]	158,583
Other unitised freight:											
Import/export vehicles	3,503	3,812	3,965	4,083	4,023	4,693	4,839	5,268	5,400	5,566	5,932
Other unitised freight	1,050	992	942	1,646	1,849	1,437	1,497	1,433	1,513	1,803	1,641
All unitised traffic	128,935	132,115	136,827	137,768	135,915	138,565 [R]	139,374 [R]	149,669 [R]	154,381 [R]	158,949 [R]	166,156

1 Includes estimates for traffic at minor ports. ☎020-7944 3087

2 From 2000, containers on Ro-Ro services are mainly classified to rail wagons, shipborne port-to-port trailers and barges.

3 More accurate recording of container/shipborne port-to-port trailers movements from 2005 means that figures for 2005 onwards are not directly comparable with 2000-2004; in 2005 approximately 300,000 container units were reported under rail wagons, shipborne port-to-port trailers and barges, which would previously have been erroneously reported under the Containers on Lo-Lo and conventional services.

4 Including unaccompanied trailers prior to 2000.

5.5 United Kingdom ports: foreign and domestic main freight units by port: [1,2] 1997-2007

(a) Units										Thousand units
	1997	1998	1999	2000	2001	2002	2003	2004	2005	2006	2007
Aberdeen	8	10	10	12	39	40	42	45	51	49	50
Belfast	419	448	456	471	444	422	448	470	472	488	500
Boston	22	20	16	17	4	3	7	11	11	4	7
Bristol	20	21	27	32	49	57	60	69	73	64	63
Cairnryan	142	170	171	157	165	179	193	211	231	237	240
Cardiff	23	25	24	29	29	24	28	33	34	42	28
Clyde	65	55	59	53	48	33	45	36	36	37	43
Cromarty Firth	5	6	5	4	1	-	-	-	-	-	-
Dover	1,593	1,499	1,652	1,625	1,774	1,856	1,786	1,982	2,047	2,325	2,364
Felixstowe	2,029	2,150	2,246	2,330	2,247	2,058	1,817	1,936	1,945	2,095	2,281
Fishguard	31	31	32	34	27	33	36	40	47	54	53
Fleetwood	92	91	108	116	125	120	126	125	131	134	147
Forth	64	63	66	79	90	117	143	165	171	168	164
Goole	69	67	68	70	70	51	18	27	61	44	36
Grimsby and Immingham	391	411	449	478	560	637	747	718	732	777	835
Harwich	219	212	215	246	199	258	323	404	408	330	322
Heysham	261	273	275	259	257	253	324	240	250	281	250
Holyhead	163	191	193	185	208	215	231	272	296	315	337
Hull	310	318	303	324	293	298	327	358	376	385	409
Ipswich	-	2	6	37	65	88	106	114	93	89	39
Larne	274	299	311	301	317	345	339	365	385	390	402
Liverpool	566	590	667	737	769	724	747	810	837	878	946
London	678	768	852	831	827	912	890	948	962	951	1,130
Manchester	1	1	-	1	-	-	-	1	7	3	1
Medway	260	333	326	324	310	325	314	377	413	354	307
Milford Haven	28	46	53	55	61	58	61	68	71	84	94
Newhaven	30	24	1	-	9	24	37	31	34	50	39
Newport	4	4	3	-	-	-	-	-	-	-	-
Orkney	11	11	12	4	16	22	22	22	22	21	34
Plymouth	9	8	7	6	7	7	8	11	13	12	14
Poole	86	82	81	73	70	75	73	67	69	75	79
Portsmouth [3]	310	302	288	292	327	328	331	323	305	291	298
Ramsgate	128	100	60	83	95	135	147	143	153	152	148
Shoreham	-	-	-	-	-	-	-	-	-	-	-
Southampton [3]	593	559	604	713	745	793	849	894	857	904	1,111
Stranraer	148	146	146	155	139	122	117	127	105	112	116
Swansea	23	22	21	14	6	4	5	5	7	4	-
Tees & Hartlepool	235	237	207	234	213	219	228	226	232	254	275
Tyne	23	30	31	24	35	51	47	55	47	50	59
Warrenpoint	61	67	65	68	63	68	65	68	94	104	104
Other ports of UK	64	79	66	71	108	142	145	97	87	71	83
England	7,960	8,143	8,525	8,896	9,071	9,272	9,323	9,876	10,064	10,509	11,171
Wales	273	318	326	318	342	397	430	438	455	498	512
Scotland	473	493	499	492	574	590	628	676	695	689	718
Great Britain	8,705	8,955	9,350	9,706	9,987	10,259	10,382	10,991	11,214	11,696	12,402
Northern Ireland	754	814	832	840	824	835	853	903	951	982	1,007
All ports of UK	9,459	9,769	10,182	10,546	10,811	11,094	11,235	11,893	12,165	12,678	13,408

1 Includes containers, road goods vehicles, unaccompanied trailers,
 rail wagons, shipborne port to port trailers and barges only.
2 Includes estimates of traffic at minor ports.
3 Excludes traffic to and from the Isle of Wight.

(continued) 5.5 United Kingdom ports: foreign and domestic main freight units by port: [1,2] 1997-2007

(b) Tonnage									Thousand tonnes of goods		
	1997	1998	1999	2000	2001	2002	2003	2004	2005	2006	2007
Aberdeen	75	90	88	102	235	261	272	309	343	309	328
Belfast	5,580	5,928	6,068	5,727	5,944	5,658	5,926	6,095	6,258	6,406	6,637
Boston	342	270	238	229	47	39	87	85	111	59	56
Bristol	233	307	370	457	695	770	810	942	1,030	993	1,092
Cairnryan	2,225	2,502	2,436	2,116	1,834	1,915	2,138	2,662	3,062	2,948	2,979
Cardiff	259	283	239	290	307	247	205	238	248	265	235
Clyde	729	533	530	779	534	346	426	406	370	398	469
Cromarty Firth	40	44	45	30	10	-	-	-	-	-	-
Dover	18,587	17,162	18,782	17,017	18,627	19,694	18,261	20,170	20,663	23,341	24,582
Felixstowe	28,200	29,321	30,859	28,881	27,388	24,250	21,439	22,547	22,717	24,076	25,601
Fishguard	415	382	391	417	336	405	470	518	506	594	568
Fleetwood	1,362	1,106	1,368	1,469	1,542	1,470	1,561	1,599	1,615	1,648	1,763
Forth	940	900	985	607	832	1,687	2,077	2,383	2,351	2,398	2,572
Goole	1,215	1,071	980	966	920	684	294	383	887	636	559
Grimsby and Immingham	6,758	7,107	7,592	7,928	9,142	9,993	11,793	11,290	11,879	12,487	13,342
Harwich	2,587	2,485	3,211	3,121	1,992	2,858	3,517	4,030	3,582	3,539	3,194
Heysham	3,862	3,390	3,199	3,471	3,422	3,352	3,745	3,232	3,303	3,699	3,289
Holyhead	2,655	3,116	3,148	3,019	2,896	2,974	2,981	3,596	3,768	3,794	3,128
Hull	4,364	4,524	4,452	4,771	4,145	4,156	4,502	4,799	4,971	4,983	5,245
Ipswich	4	35	83	414	712	1,039	1,294	1,410	1,151	1,096	453
Larne	3,132	3,372	4,016	4,159	3,211	4,020	3,957	4,692	5,168	5,127	5,221
Liverpool	7,003	7,723	8,429	9,429	9,513	8,856	9,494	10,382	10,873	11,200	11,967
London	8,631	10,444	10,282	10,711	10,986	12,015	12,233	14,355	14,590	14,485	15,062
Manchester	5	9	6	8	-	-	-	20	23	5	3
Medway	3,414	4,205	3,984	4,142	3,572	3,556	3,280	3,796	4,269	3,506	2,975
Milford Haven	370	567	712	717	797	760	794	886	1,059	1,086	1,224
Newhaven	587	326	20	-	251	300	450	416	468	687	560
Newport	39	37	44	-	-	1	9	6	2	7	3
Orkney	144	101	105	91	84	129	69	115	114	115	149
Plymouth	160	118	92	78	76	69	78	110	148	137	157
Poole	1,077	1,043	1,012	602	1,048	1,118	902	1,021	1,041	1,120	990
Portsmouth [3]	3,764	3,765	3,639	3,771	3,549	3,400	3,312	3,874	3,757	2,884	3,108
Ramsgate	2,170	1,834	1,096	1,187	1,356	1,848	1,758	1,668	1,842	1,648	1,971
Shoreham	-	-	-	-	1	3	2	1	1	-	-
Southampton [3]	5,845	4,710	5,430	6,396	6,724	7,030	7,299	7,894	7,799	8,327	10,617
Stranraer	1,794	1,780	1,690	1,505	1,404	1,273	1,273	1,277	1,165	1,222	1,231
Swansea	186	174	159	100	31	39	50	51	75	36	5
Tees & Hartlepool	3,771	4,304	3,969	4,930	3,362	3,388	3,441	3,382	3,657	3,876	4,153
Tyne	261	322	333	433	434	510	518	514	486	470	634
Warrenpoint	945	1,033	1,088	1,160	1,046	1,196	1,205	1,363	1,837	1,646	1,513
Other ports of UK	655	889	749	808	1,039	1,126 [R]	1,120 [R]	451 [R]	279 [R]	326 [R]	952
England	104,606	106,247	109,933	111,006	109,789	110,120 [R]	109,820 [R]	117,704 [R]	120,571 [R]	124,589 [R]	131,490
Wales	3,924	4,559	4,693	4,543	4,498	5,179	5,337	5,535	5,658	5,782	5,163
Scotland	6,196	6,173	6,122	5,444	5,555	6,262	6,793	7,580	7,976	8,030	8,560
Great Britain	114,726	116,979	120,747	120,993	119,842	121,561 [R]	121,950 [R]	130,819 [R]	134,205 [R]	138,402 [R]	145,213
Northern Ireland	9,657	10,332	11,172	11,046	10,201	10,873	11,088	12,150	13,263	13,178	13,370
All ports of UK	124,383	127,312	131,919	132,039	130,043	132,434 [R]	133,038 [R]	142,969 [R]	147,468 [R]	151,580 [R]	158,583

1 Includes containers, road goods vehicles, unaccompanied trailers,
  rail wagons, shipborne port to port trailers and barges only.
2 Includes estimates of traffic at minor ports.
3 Excludes traffic to and from the Isle of Wight.

☎020-7944 3087

5.6 United Kingdom ports: accompanied passenger vehicles on foreign and coastwise routes:[1] 1997-2007

Thousand vehicles

(a) Cars	1997	1998	1999	2000	2001	2002	2003	2004	2005	2006	2007
France	4,839	4,453	3,954	3,524	3,619	3,727	3,669	3,720	3,449	3,563	3,734
Belgium	235	87	244	260	115	120	111	112	124	129	132
Netherlands	337	351	405	422	383	420	390	379	336	330	290
Germany	43	44	40	22	27	32	19	24	23	-	-
Irish Republic	780	886	854	876	833	878	879	837	773	751	781
Denmark	24	25	27	23	26	27	22	23	21	48	26
Scandinavia and Baltic	52	52	36	26	15	36	44	31	39	19	21
of which:											
Norway	..	..	..	14	6	15	29	9	20	9	21
Sweden	..	..	..	11	8	20	15	21	18	10	-
Spain	84	83	84	83	93	104	80	81	94	85	88
All overseas routes	6,395	5,982	5,644	5,235	5,111	5,344	5,213	5,207	4,861	4,927	5,072
Channel Tunnel [2]	*2,319*	*3,351*	*3,260*	*2,784*	*2,530*	*2,336*	*2,279*	*2,101*	*2,047*	*2,046*	*2,142*
Coastwise routes by ship: [3]											
Northern Ireland [4]	1,175	1,179	1,282	1,108	1,078	1,082	1,104	1,138	1,054	1,007	1,089
Isle of Man	85	98	137	140	136	166	159	157	75	147	183
Orkney and Shetland [4]	120	122	127	128	104	125	155	156	163	170	196
Channel Islands	172	103	112	159	162	179	128	111	104	90	89
Other	35	34	34	36	39	42	44	48	48	47	49
All coastwise routes	1,588	1,536	1,692	1,570	1,520	1,594	1,591	1,611	1,444	1,461	1,605
All cars	7,982	7,518	7,336	6,806	6,631	6,939	6,804	6,818	6,305	6,388	6,677

(b) Buses and coaches	1997	1998	1999	2000	2001	2002	2003	2004	2005	2006	2007
France	178	166	167	157	153	155	141	152	128	114	110
Belgium	4	3	3	2	2	1	4	4	4	3	4
Netherlands	8	8	7	7	6	8	7	5	8	7	7
Germany	-	-	-	-	-	-	-	1	-	-	-
Irish Republic	18	19	18	19	16	17	16	16	17 [R]	15	15
Denmark	-	-	-	-	-	-	-	1	-	-	-
Scandinavia and Baltic	1	1	1	-	-	1	1	1	1	-	-
Spain	1	1	1	-	1	1	1	1	1	1	1
All overseas routes	211	198	196	187	178	183	169	181	159	142	137
Channel Tunnel [2]	*65*	*96*	*82*	*79*	*75*	*72*	*72*	*63*	*77*	*67*	*65*
Coastwise routes by ship: [3]											
Northern Ireland [4]	16	15	14	15	14	16	17	17	15	15	15
Isle of Man	1	1	1	1	1	1	1	-	-	-	-
Orkney and Shetland [4]	-	-	-	-	-	-	1	1	1	1	1
Channel Islands	-	-	-	-	-	-	-	-	-	1	-
Other	-	-	-	-	-	-	-	-	1	-	-
All coastwise routes	17	16	16	16	16	17	19	18	16	18	16
All buses and coaches	228	214	212	203	194	201	188	199	175	159	153

1 Includes estimates for traffic at minor ports.
2 Shown here for comparison but not included in total.
3 Excludes traffic to the Isle of Wight.
4 Vehicles counted at both ends of route.

☎020-7944 3087

5.7 United Kingdom ports: accompanied passenger vehicles on foreign and coastwise routes by port:[1] 1997-2007

Thousand vehicles

	1997	1998	1999	2000	2001	2002	2003	2004	2005	2006	2007
Cars:											
Belfast	413	400	454	437	397	400	403	406	315	316	328
Cairnryan	169	183	182	151	140	153	139	137	140	134	156
Dover	3,332	3,047	2,758	2,433	2,396	2,466	2,418	2,507	2,470	2,648	2,838
Fishguard	162	178	187	194	180	183	157	156	144	140	152
Forth	-	-	-	-	-	28	43	44	43	28	31
Harwich	282	256	273	285	272	280	254	244	207	182	119
Heysham	43	52	121	123	97	86	75	76	67	83	94
Holyhead	401	481	454	500	464	488	501	481	465	452	480
Hull	174	205	215	217	197	186	167	165	173	176	189
Larne	169	187	196	155	149	164	175	174	206	199	232
Liverpool	89	130	125	37	133	148	162	162	129	135	160
Medway	-	-	-	-	-	-	-	-	-	-	-
Milford Haven	143	124	119	130	114	117	118	111	97	101	120
Newhaven	152	136	78	73	76	78	90	91	44	74	91
Orkney	47	49	51	50	40	49	62	64	67	69	99
Plymouth	180	178	178	175	176	192	187	189	194	176	183
Poole	274	202	163	176	200	234	216	186	119	126	141
Portsmouth [2]	918	939	973	934	976	1,011	915	891	770	666	610
Ramsgate	282	21	-	-	-	-	-	3	11	29	27
Southampton	-	-	-	-	-	-	-	-	-	-	-
Stranraer	396	372	338	270	248	257	239	275	239	250	257
Swansea	48	48	45	41	38	41	41	40	36	29	-
Tyne	62	71	98	73	63	121	123	113	112	113	103
Other ports	245	260	326	351	274	258	319	301	260	262	270
All cars	7,982	7,518	7,336	6,806	6,631	6,939	6,804	6,818	6,305	6,388	6,677
Buses and coaches:											
Dover	165	154	157	148	145	148	125	128	108	106	105
Holyhead	12	13	12	13	12	12	12	12	13	12	12
Portsmouth	11	11	10	8	7	7	15	24	20	8	4
Other ports	40	36	33	33	30	33	35	35	34	33	32
All buses and coaches	228	214	212	203	194	201	188	199	175	159	153

1 Includes estimates for traffic at minor ports.

☎020-7944 3087

5.8 Waterborne transport within the United Kingdom: 1997-2007

(a) Goods moved — Billion tonne-kilometres

	1997	1998	1999	2000	2001	2002	2003	2004	2005	2006	2007
UK inland waters traffic											
Non-seagoing traffic											
Internal	0.2	0.2	0.2	0.2	0.2	0.2	0.2	0.2	0.2	0.2	0.1
Seagoing traffic (by route)											
Coastwise	0.2	0.2	0.2	0.2	0.2	0.2	0.2	0.2	0.2	0.2	0.2
Foreign	1.3	1.3	1.3	1.0	1.1	1.1	1.0	1.0	1.1	1.1	1.2
One-port	0.3	0.3	0.3	0.2	0.3	0.3	0.2	0.2	0.2	0.2	0.2
Total	1.9	2.0	1.9	1.7	1.8	1.7	1.6	1.5	1.6	1.7	1.7
Coastwise traffic											
between UK ports [1]	40.4	45.0	40.6	36.5	34.1	35.1	33.3	35.4	39.4	32.4	34.5
One-port traffic											
of UK ports [1]	5.7	10.0	16.2	29.7	23.3	30.8	26.4	22.9	20.3	18.2	15.0
All traffic [1,2]	48.1	56.9	58.7	67.4	58.8	67.2	60.9	59.4	60.9	51.8	50.8

(b) Goods lifted [1] — Million tonnes

	1997	1998	1999	2000	2001	2002	2003	2004	2005	2006	2007
UK inland waters traffic											
Non-seagoing traffic											
Internal	4.8	4.3	4.3	4.3	4.3	4.0	3.2	2.6	3.4	3.6	3.4
Seagoing traffic (by route)											
Coastwise	8.2	9.6	8.7	9.3	8.8	6.8	7.4	7.2	8.6	8.5	8.0
Foreign	34.6	35.3	33.9	30.8	33.4	32.0	31.8	30.1	32.0	34.0	34.9
One-port	10.9	8.2	7.0	4.5	7.0	6.2	5.0	4.7	4.8	4.9	5.7
Total	58.5	57.3	53.8	49.0	53.5	49.0	47.4	44.6	48.7	51.0	52.0
Coastwise traffic											
between UK ports [1]	71.1	77.3	73.0	63.1	58.5	59.5	58.5	59.8	65.1	58.1	58.8
One-port traffic											
of UK ports [1]	31.3	32.6	33.3	39.3	35.1	43.7	39.0	34.8	32.3	30.6	28.9
All traffic [1,2]	141.8	149.4	144.5	137.4	131.3	139.1	132.5	127.2	132.8	126.3	125.9

1 More accurate recording of the origin and destination of crude oil
  traffic from 2000 onwards has meant that figures for coastwise
  and one-port traffic are not directly comparable with previous years.
2 The 'All traffic' figures in part (a) from 2000 onwards and in part (b)
  for all years are calculated by the addition of the totals for coastwise
  traffic, one-port traffic, and the internal and foreign components of inland waters traffic.

☎020-7944 3087

5.9   Principal ports, port groups and freight waterways

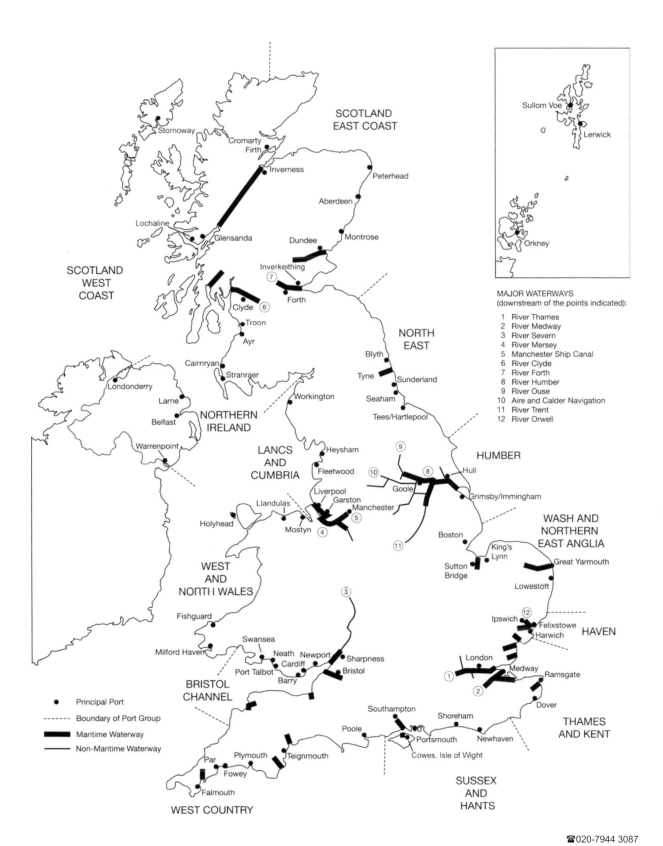

SCOTLAND
EAST COAST

Stornoway

Cromarty
Firth

Inverness

Peterhead

Aberdeen

Lochaline

Glensanda

Montrose

SCOTLAND
WEST
COAST

Dundee

Inverkeithing
⑦

Forth

Clyde ⑥

Troon

Ayr

NORTH
EAST

Blyth

Cairnryan

Stranraer

Tyne

Sunderland

Londonderry

Larne

Belfast

Workington

NORTHERN
IRELAND

Seaham

Tees/Hartlepool

Warrenpoint

LANCS
AND
CUMBRIA

Heysham

Fleetwood

⑨

HUMBER

Liverpool

Garston

Hull

Llandulas

Manchester

⑩

Goole

⑧

Grimsby/Immingham

Holyhead

Mostyn ④

⑤

WASH AND
NORTHERN
EAST ANGLIA

WEST
AND
NORTH WALES

Boston

⑪

King's
Lynn

Great Yarmouth

Fishguard

③

Sutton
Bridge

Lowestoft

Milford Haven

Swansea

Neath Newport

Cardiff

Sharpness

Ipswich ⑫

Felixstowe

Harwich

HAVEN

BRISTOL
CHANNEL

Port Talbot

Barry

Bristol

London

Medway

Ramsgate

①

②

Dover

Southampton

Shoreham

THAMES
AND KENT

Poole

Portsmouth

Newhaven

Cowes, Isle of Wight

Par Plymouth

Teignmouth

SUSSEX
AND
HANTS

Fowey

Falmouth

WEST COUNTRY

Sullom Voe

Lerwick

Orkney

MAJOR WATERWAYS
(downstream of the points indicated):

1   River Thames
2   River Medway
3   River Severn
4   River Mersey
5   Manchester Ship Canal
6   River Clyde
7   River Forth
8   River Humber
9   River Ouse
10 Aire and Calder Navigation
11 River Trent
12 River Orwell

• Principal Port
---- Boundary of Port Group
▬ Maritime Waterway
— Non-Maritime Waterway

☎ 020-7944 3087

93

5.10 Traffic on major rivers and other inland waterway routes: 2001-2007

	Internal Traffic							Seagoing Traffic						
(a) Goods moved												**Billion tonne-kilometres**		
	2001	2002	2003	2004	2005	2006	2007	2001	2002	2003	2004	2005	2006	2007
River Thames	0.10	0.10	0.11	0.09	0.09	0.09	0.08	0.71	0.67	0.60	0.53	0.61	0.67	0.74
River Medway	-	-	-	-	-	-	-	0.04	0.04	0.05	0.04	0.03	0.04	0.04
River Severn	-	-	-	-	-	-	-	0.01	0.01	0.01	0.01	0.01	0.01	0.01
River Mersey	-	-	-	-	-	-	-	0.12	0.09	0.09	0.10	0.10	0.11	0.11
Manchester Ship Canal	0.01	0.01	0.01	0.01	0.01	0.01	0.01	0.11	0.09	0.09	0.09	0.09	0.09	0.08
River Clyde	-	-	-	-	-	-	-	0.07	0.05	0.06	0.05	0.07	0.06	0.09
River Forth	-	-	-	-	-	-	-	0.20	0.18	0.18	0.18	0.18	0.18	0.17
River Humber	0.01	0.01	0.01	0.01	0.02	0.01	0.01	0.24	0.23	0.21	0.22	0.22	0.21	0.22
River Ouse	-	0.01	0.01	0.01	0.01	0.01	-	0.04	0.03	0.03	0.04	0.05	0.04	0.04
Aire and Calder Nav'n	0.03	0.02	0.01	0.01	0.01	0.01	0.01	-	-	-	-	-	-	-
River Trent	0.02	0.02	0.02	0.02	0.02	0.02	-	0.03	0.03	0.03	0.03	0.03	0.03	0.03
River Orwell	-	-	-	-	-	-	-	0.05	0.06	0.07	0.06	0.06	0.06	0.05
All above waterways	0.18	0.17	0.17	0.15	0.16	0.16	0.12	1.63	1.50	1.43	1.35	1.45	1.50	1.59
All waterways	0.19	0.18	0.18	0.15	0.17	0.16	0.14	1.65	1.51	1.44	1.37	1.46	1.52	1.60
(b) Goods lifted												**Million tonnes**		
River Thames	1.95	2.09	2.02	1.54	1.81	2.09	1.94	18.50	17.16	16.03	14.19	17.13	18.67	20.06
River Medway	0.47	0.58	0.56	0.37	0.44	0.35	0.24	2.01	2.38	2.74	2.02	1.45	2.13	2.22
River Severn	-	-	-	-	0.21	0.19	0.26	0.54	0.56	0.55	0.54	0.50	0.46	0.49
River Mersey	0.28	0.23	0.22	0.23	0.24	0.32	0.3	6.99	5.51	5.08	5.63	6.13	6.57	6.42
Manchester Ship Canal	0.28	0.23	0.22	0.23	0.24	0.32	0.3	6.99	5.51	5.08	5.63	6.13	6.57	6.42
River Clyde	-	0.01	-	-	-	-	-	1.61	1.29	1.34	1.29	1.59	1.53	2.08
River Forth	-	-	-	-	-	-	-	9.59	8.53	8.58	8.52	8.47	8.49	8.28
River Humber	0.22	0.40	0.35	0.44	0.58	0.44	0.34	6.11	5.53	5.29	5.51	5.79	5.32	5.67
River Ouse	0.37	0.41	0.43	0.37	0.52	0.43	0.29	2.83	2.45	2.15	2.41	2.84	2.45	2.56
Aire and Calder Nav'n	1.57	1.06	0.50	0.37	0.40	0.40	0.30	-	-	-	-	-	-	-
River Trent	0.33	0.30	0.26	0.26	0.25	0.24	0.17	2.61	2.35	2.31	2.33	1.92	2.06	2.21
River Orwell	-	-	-	-	-	-	-	2.92	3.34	3.90	3.56	3.58	3.51	2.80
All waterways [1]	4.26	3.96	3.18	2.60	3.40	3.56	3.36	49.23	44.99	44.21	42.02	45.33	47.42	48.65

1 Where goods are carried on more than one inland
  waterway route, the tonnage lifted is counted on
  each route travelled. The 'All Waterways' figures
  exclude all such double counting.

☎020-7944 4131

5.11 United Kingdom international sea passenger movements by country of embarkation or landing:[1] 1997-2007

Thousands

	1997	1998	1999	2000	2001	2002	2003	2004	2005	2006	2007
Ro-Ro ferry passengers on short sea routes											
Belgium	2,075	1,749	1,592	1,507	1,379	1,129	740	739	778	748	751
Denmark	190	195	188	164	156	132	88	97	91	89	96
France	26,975	23,912	22,454	19,755	19,485	20,555	19,077	18,565	16,834	16,925	17,377
Germany	240	246	222	188	164	161	92	117	98	1	1
Irish Republic	4,066	4,606	4,343	4,234	3,882	3,880	3,802	3,656	3,380	3,221	3,291
Netherlands	1,961	1,768	1,939	2,031	2,026	2,209	2,094	2,002	1,848	1,897	1,636
Norway	172	188	208	225	230	241	235	231	200	149	153
Spain	388	373	346	320	355	341	308	310	378	372	357
Sweden	190	186	87	89	73	73	81	75	79	59	5
Other Europe	-	4	3	3	4	3	7	7	8	6	1
Total	36,258	33,226	31,381	28,517	27,753	28,726	26,523	25,799	23,693	23,465	23,668
Passengers on long sea journeys [2]	29	23	26	26	27	32	25	40	52	58	68
Passengers on cruises beginning or ending at UK ports [3]	..	..	445	461	469	540	702	767	935	1,013 R	1,064
All international passengers [4]	36,288	33,249	31,852	29,003	28,249	29,298	27,250	26,605	24,680	24,537 R	24,800

1 For details of Channel Tunnel passenger numbers please see Table 6.8.
2 Details of foreign ports of call were not collected after 2004.
3 Cruise passengers, like other passengers, are included at both departure.
   and arrival if their journey begins and ends at a UK seaport.
4 Excluding cruise passengers in 1997 and 1998.

☎020-7944 4121

5.12 United Kingdom international sea passenger movements by port and port area:[1] 1997-2007

Thousands

	1997	1998	1999	2000	2001	2002	2003	2004	2005	2006	2007
Ro-Ro ferry passengers on short sea routes [2]											
Thames and Kent											
London	-	12	16	15	14	13	11	14	13	12	11
Ramsgate	1,836	161	50	76	88	117	137	148	193	214	233
Dover	21,236	19,330	18,324	16,078	15,857	16,329	14,631	14,275	13,359	13,799	14,258
Folkestone	776	905	653	440	5	-	-	-	-	-	-
All Thames and Kent	23,848	20,408	19,043	16,609	15,964	16,459	14,780	14,437	13,566	14,025	14,503
South Coast											
Newhaven	750	621	337	313	337	379	397	361	167	270	329
Portsmouth	3,391	3,509	3,487	3,176	3,344	3,406	3,116	3,077	2,631	2,166	2,084
Southampton	1	-	-	-	-	-	-	5	3	-	-
Poole	418	414	472	455	586	620	623	520	398	479	469
Weymouth	-	53	56	60	-	8	15	20	21	18	19
Plymouth	649	642	627	583	583	631	603	617	636	564	575
All South Coast	5,209	5,240	4,980	4,587	4,851	5,044	4,754	4,600	3,856	3,498	3,476
West Coast											
Swansea	150	158	133	124	122	121	118	116	100	81	-
Milford Haven	546	512	495	463	388	387	384	378	321	333	379
Fishguard	815	810	830	832	687	662	645	614	590	584	597
Holyhead	2,457	2,775	2,541	2,518	2,380	2,371	2,333	2,262	2,173	2,057	2,138
Mostyn	-	-	-	-	5	44	48	10	-	-	-
Liverpool	97	343	337	293	298	291	269	270	190	162	173
Fleetwood	1	-	-	-	-	-	-	-	-	-	-
Other ports	-	9	7	4	3	4	5	5	5	4	3
All West Coast	4,066	4,606	4,343	4,234	3,882	3,880	3,802	3,656	3,380	3,221	3,291
East Coast											
Lerwick	3	7	6	6	6	7	13	14	11	10	1
Forth	-	-	-	-	-	105	195	192	183	112	110
Tyne	365	466	626	667	745	816	829	767	699	648	638
Hull	1,006	1,027	1,022	972	1,006	1,041	994	976	964	1,017	1,010
Grimsby and Immingham	12	10	9	12	13	38	43	43	44	49	63
Ipswich	-	-	-	5	6	6	6	7	8	8	4
Felixstowe	77	77	78	86	80	58	19	19	19	16	15
Harwich	1,672	1,384	1,272	1,335	1,196	1,268	1,085	1,085	959	857	553
Other ports	-	2	2	3	4	3	3	3	4	4	4
All East Coast	3,134	2,973	3,016	3,086	3,056	3,342	3,188	3,106	2,891	2,722	2,398
All port areas	36,258	33,226	31,381	28,517	27,753	28,726	26,523	25,799	23,693	23,465	23,668
Passengers on long sea journeys	29	23	26	26	27	32	25	40	52	58	68
Passengers on cruises beginning or ending at UK ports [3]	..	..	445	461	469	540	702	767	935	1,013 R	1,064
of which:											
Southampton	..	..	211	281	295	331	438	476	637	658	716
Dover	..	..	136	119	100	120	139	154	141	188	175
Harwich	..	..	70	43	68	69	97	91	84	104	104
Other ports	..	..	28	17	4	20	28	46	71	64 R	69
All international passengers [4]	36,288	33,249	31,852	29,003	28,249	29,298	27,250	26,605	24,680	24,537 R	24,800

1 For details of Channel Tunnel passenger numbers please see Table 6.8.

2 See Notes and Definitions.

3 Cruise passengers, like other passengers, are included at both departure.
  and arrival if their journey begins and ends at a UK seaport.

4 Excluding cruise passengers in 1997 and 1998.

☎020-7944 4121

5.13 United Kingdom and Crown Dependency registered trading vessels of 500 gross tons and over: summary of tonnage by type on old classification: 1950-1986 and on new classification: 1986-2007

For greater detail of the years 1997-2007 see Table 5.14

End of year	Passenger 000 Gt	Cargo liners 000 Gt	Container 000 Gt	Tramps 000 Gt	Bulk carriers 000 Gt	Tankers 000 Gt	Total 000 Gt	Total Number[2]
1950	2,936	5,949	-	..	4,366	3,946	17,198	3,092
1951	2,992	5,933	-	..	4,084	4,187	17,196	3,056
1952	2,935	6,063	-	..	3,836	4,430	17,264	3,014
1953	2,825	6,066	-	..	3,939	4,637	17,467	3,016
1954	2,998	6,007	-	..	3,965	5,046	18,016	3,041
1955	3,012	6,080	-	..	3,979	5,138	18,208	3,041
1956	3,013	6,300	-	..	3,841	5,329	18,484	3,041
1957	2,958	6,540	-	..	3,696	5,638	18,833	3,031
1958	2,843	6,545	-	..	3,837	6,021	19,245	3,007
1959	2,749	6,605	-	..	3,706	6,745	19,805	2,950
1960	2,814	6,568	-	..	3,762	7,058	20,202	2,902
1961	2,771	6,294	-	..	4,143	7,288	20,497	2,808
1962	2,495	6,133	-	..	4,441	7,486	20,554	2,689
1963	2,342	5,939	-	..	4,328	7,788	20,396	2,538
1964	2,244	5,936	-	..	4,444	7,804	20,428	2,473
1965	2,115	5,894	-	..	4,687	7,685	20,382	2,401
1966	1,971	5,898	..	2,666	2,130	7,857	20,522	2,319
1967	1,709	5,576	..	2,521	2,661	7,908	20,375	2,181
1968	1,605	5,398	..	2,173	2,974	8,580	20,730	2,058
1969	1,245	5,452	194	1,904	3,265	10,215	22,274	2,002
1970	1,230	5,233	418	1,621	3,710	11,849	24,061	1,977
1971	1,101	4,444	683	1,425	4,219	13,304	25,177	1,875
1972	1,010	3,895	1,162	1,222	6,152	13,500	26,940	1,798
1973	920	3,749	1,346	1,060	7,366	14,665	29,106	1,776
1974	855	3,656	1,365	1,027	7,694	16,199	30,795	1,767
1975	748	3,330	1,363	958	8,022	17,069	31,489	1,682
1976	661	3,148	1,349	910	8,030	15,742	29,839	1,573
1977	654	2,923	1,624	882	8,181	15,797	30,061	1,545
1978	614	2,546	1,827	743	7,174	15,173	28,078	1,421
1979	606	2,248	1,651	613	6,555	13,558	25,232	1,305
1980	617	1,992	1,600	554	6,428	14,578	25,769	1,275
1981	604	1,589	1,600	470	5,985	11,870	22,117	1,118
1982	582	1,340	1,580	409	5,101	10,221	19,233	985
1983	602	1,099	1,543	372	3,911	8,367	15,894	866
1984	636	893	1,572	349	3,398	7,463	14,312	777
1985	616	728	1,489	335	2,851	6,191	12,208	693
1986	588	564	1,369	244	1,864	3,083	7,711	545

End of year	Passenger 000 Gt	Other cargo 000 Gt	Ro-Ro 000 Gt	Container 000 Gt	Specialised carriers 000 Gt	Bulk carriers 000 Gt	Tankers 000 Gt	Total 000 Gt	Total Number[2]
1986	259	510	561	1,369	95	2,003	3,249	8,046	546
1987	259	410	591	1,335	132	1,322	3,010	7,059	506
1988	259	332	586	1,335	128	1,301	2,661	6,603	482
1989	242	277	510	1,368	122	1,253	2,252	6,025	450
1990	269	257	555	1,275	118	828	2,210	5,512	427
1991	271	242	604	1,091	99	489	2,166	4,963	409
1992	276	174	632	1,015	100	446	2,188	4,831	363
1993	272	145	657	1,017	124	293	2,161	4,670	344
1994	281	212	874	1,236	110	294	2,481	5,488	360
1995	360	282	910	1,326	52	485	2,346	5,761	365
1996	360	269	1,068	1,110	49	819	2,383	6,057	377
1997	361	254	1,093	1,113	49	831	3,407	7,108	392
1998	358	307	1,123	1,379	49	854	2,977	7,048	416
1999	363	293	1,161	1,502	103	761	3,253	7,436	421
2000	762	321	1,332	2,140	151	844	3,971	9,521	471
2001	746	502	1,431	2,362	151	946	4,516	10,653	534
2002	945	570	1,617	3,303	100	1,491	4,472	12,497	610
2003	1,130	825	1,637	4,548	121	1,729	5,991	15,982	723
2004	711	830	1,608	5,072	165	2,302	6,214	16,902	754
2005	539	885	1,589	5,539	345	2,926	6,978	18,801	795
2006	472	936	1,466	5,900	604	2,839	7,536	19,753	814
2007	627	763	1,534	6,304	925	3,050	7,401	20,603	816

1 See Notes for brief explanation of change in classification.
2 Number of vessels (units).

☎020-7944-4119
The figures in this table are outside the scope of National Statistics
Source - Lloyds Register - Fairplay

5.14   United Kingdom and Crown Dependency registered trading vessels of 500 gross tons and over: summary of tonnage by type of vessel: 1997-2007 (end of year)

	1997	1998	1999	2000	2001	2002	2003	2004	2005	2006	2007
Number:											
Tankers	133	145	141	141	166	195	224	244	263	273	268
Bulk carriers	27	26	22	26	28	34	38	49	60	58	63
Specialised carriers	11	11	15	16	16	13	13	14	16	21	26
Fully cellular container	39	45	51	67	71	99	137	146	160	170	177
Ro-Ro (passenger and cargo)	89	92	94	105	110	118	120	118	113	108	110
Other general cargo	81	86	87	100	127	131	169	169	172	174	160
Passenger	12	11	11	16	16	20	22	14	11	10	12
All vessels	392	416	421	471	534	610	723	754	795	814	816
Gross tonnage (thousand tons):											
Tankers	3,407	2,977	3,253	3,971	4,516	4,472	5,991	6,214	6,978	7,536	7,401
Bulk carriers	831	854	761	844	946	1,491	1,729	2,302	2,926	2,839	3,050
Specialised carriers	49	49	103	151	151	100	121	165	345	604	925
Fully cellular container	1,113	1,379	1,502	2,140	2,362	3,303	4,548	5,072	5,539	5,900	6,304
Ro-Ro (passenger and cargo)	1,093	1,123	1,161	1,332	1,431	1,617	1,637	1,608	1,589	1,466	1,534
Other general cargo	254	307	293	321	502	570	825	830	885	936	763
Passenger	361	358	363	762	746	945	1,130	711	539	472	627
All vessels	7,108	7,048	7,436	9,521	10,653	12,497	15,982	16,902	18,801	19,753	20,603
Thousand deadweight tonnes:											
Tankers	6,119	5,163	5,737	7,069	7,885	7,567	9,446	9,660	11,112	11,920	11,540
Bulk carriers	1,519	1,563	1,404	1,545	1,738	2,782	3,245	4,375	5,580	5,409	5,791
Specialised carriers	29	29	47	65	65	44	48	59	109	181	272
Fully cellular container	1,224	1,543	1,682	2,365	2,597	3,691	5,124	5,663	6,241	6,673	7,160
Ro-Ro (passenger and cargo)	337	364	366	474	522	607	605	591	574	535	554
Other general cargo	335	414	402	430	706	799	1,121	1,126	1,193	1,265	1,039
Passenger	55	56	58	98	95	111	131	92	76	70	82
All vessels	9,618	9,132	9,695	12,045	13,608	15,602	19,719	21,566	24,885	26,053	26,438

☎020-7944 4119
The figures in this table are outside
the scope of National Statistics
Source - Lloyds Register - Fairplay

5.15 Shipping: United Kingdom owned trading vessels of 500 gross tons and over: summary of tonnage by type of vessel: 1997-2007 (end of year)

	1997	1998	1999	2000	2001	2002	2003	2004	2005	2006	2007
Number:											
Tankers	123	127	124	133	114	113	124	145	144	149	143
Bulk carriers	35	29	29	29	38	35	43	51	60	60	63
Specialised carriers	11	10	14	10	10	10	9	9	11	17	19
Fully cellular container	60	62	57	73	77	72	92	78	75	91	101
Ro-Ro (passenger and cargo)	85	91	99	103	103	105	109	106	102	98	105
Other general cargo	156	148	153	139	116	115	124	138	146	146	158
Passenger	16	19	17	16	18	20	26	15	19	18	23
All vessels	486	486	493	503	476	470	527	542	557	579	612
Gross tonnage (thousand tons):											
Tankers	2,704	2,408	1,565	2,952	2,579	2,620	3,601	4,497	4,139	4,668	5,246
Bulk carriers	1,408	1,230	825	904	1,845	1,772	1,913	2,287	2,753	2,614	2,786
Specialised carriers	43	42	192	53	100	100	82	81	261	594	798
Fully cellular container	1,626	1,841	1,641	2,240	2,525	2,509	3,552	3,035	3,297	4,254	4,893
Ro-Ro (passenger and cargo)	827	991	1,145	1,260	1,355	1,423	1,589	1,472	1,404	1,334	1,445
Other general cargo	654	526	546	492	409	570	793	940	912	963	1,070
Passenger	548	541	585	604	636	725	1,092	588	919	915	1,088
All vessels	7,809	7,577	6,499	8,505	9,449	9,720	12,622	12,900	13,685	15,341	17,327
Thousand deadweight tonnes:											
Tankers	5,048	4,411	2,662	5,205	4,646	4,690	5,529	6,687	6,054	6,080	6,474
Bulk carriers	2,575	2,254	1,479	1,636	3,495	3,377	3,594	4,300	5,345	4,922	5,228
Specialised carriers	30	29	80	32	45	45	42	40	90	189	241
Fully cellular container	1,672	1,948	1,774	2,433	2,734	2,785	3,993	3,349	3,708	4,758	5,491
Ro-Ro (passenger and cargo)	243	285	349	423	414	454	543	514	504	478	513
Other general cargo	887	713	735	660	569	807	1,113	1,323	1,233	1,296	1,464
Passenger	90	86	86	80	82	87	130	64	117	114	139
All vessels	10,546	9,727	7,164	10,469	11,985	12,245	14,945	16,277	17,052	17,836	19,551

☎020-7944 4119
The figures in this table are outside
the scope of National Statistics
Source - Lloyds Register - Fairplay

5.16 United Kingdom shipping industry: international revenue and expenditure: 1997-2007

(a) Revenue

£ Million

	1997	1998	1999	2000	2001	2002	2003	2004	2005	2006	2007
Dry cargo and passenger vessels: (including ferries)											
Freight on:											
Imports	484	482	522	484	541	534	501	547	619	390 [1]	423
Exports	416	322	375	400	406	481	525	444	544	530 [1]	552
Cross-trades	1,614	1,602	1,511	1,453	1,609	1,844	2,069	3,380	4,122	1,600 [1]	1,424
Total freight revenue	2,514	2,406	2,408	2,337	2,556	2,859	3,095	4,371	5,285	2,520	2,399
Charter receipts	147	109	99	148	106	129	196	676	963	1,086	1,564
Passenger revenue	697	462	463	630	488	569	993	846	608	444	430
Total revenue	3,358	2,977	2,970	3,115	3,150	3,557	4,284	5,893	6,856	4,050	4,393
Wet (tankers and liquefied gas carriers):											
Freight on:											
Imports	24	29	20	3	46	47	44	48	52	79	87
Exports	68	60	59	98	82	96	126	173	174	130	142
Cross-trades	536	442	350	458	497	420	742	1,305	1,194	1,222	1,395
Total freight revenue	628	531	429	559	625	563	912	1,526	1,420	1,431	1,624
Charter receipts	68	70	87	104	336	162	247	472	748	603	554
Total revenue	696	601	516	663	961	725	1,159	1,998	2,168	2,034	2,178
All vessels:											
Freight on:											
Imports	508	511	542	487	587	581	545	595	671	469	510
Exports	484	382	434	498	488	577	651	617	718	660	694
Cross-trades	2,150	2,044	1,861	1,911	2,106	2,264	2,811	4,685	5,316	2,822	2,819
Total freight revenue	3,142	2,937	2,837	2,896	3,181	3,422	4,007	5,897	6,705	3,951	4,023
Charter receipts	215	179	186	252	442	291	443	1,148	1,711	1,689	2,118
Passenger revenue	697	462	463	630	488	569	993	846	608	444	430
Total revenue	4,054	3,578	3,486	3,778	4,111	4,282	5,443	7,891	9,024	6,084	6,571

(b) Expenditure

£ Million

	1997	1998	1999	2000	2001	2002	2003	2004	2005	2006	2007
Dry cargo operations:											
Bunkers	216	149	165	288	321	377	429	537	701	463	255
Other disbursements	1,780	1,367	1,060	1,143	1,284	1,618	1,646	1,962	2,759	1,405	1,373
Charter payments	282	239	146	173	335	255	236	692	577	317 [1]	106
Total expenditure	2,278	1,755	1,371	1,604	1,940	2,250	2,311	3,191	4,037	2,185	1,734
Wet cargo operations:											
Bunkers	100	70	81	141	146	134	171	195	319	278	399
Other disbursements	124	150	132	115	141	135	284	276	523	236	408
Charter payments	161	181	89	172	176	140	184	359	636	655	721
Total expenditure	385	401	302	428	463	409	639	830	1,478	1,169	1,528
All cargo operations:											
Bunkers	316	219	246	429	467	511	600	732	1,020	741	654
Other disbursements	1,904	1,517	1,192	1,258	1,425	1,753	1,930	2,238	3,282	1,641	1,781
Charter payments	443	420	235	345	511	395	420	1,051	1,213	972	827
Total expenditure	2,663	2,156	1,673	2,032	2,403	2,659	2,950	4,021	5,515	3,354	3,262

1 Following a restructuring in the UK shipping industry trading in dry freight and in chartering-in of dry vessels fell significantly during 2006.

☎ 020-7533 6081

Source - ONS

5.17 Marine accident casualties:[1] 1997-2007
(United Kingdom registered merchant vessels of 100 gt and over only)

(a) Deaths of passengers and crew members by cause											Number
	1997	1998	1999	2000	2001	2002	2003	2004	2005	2006	2007
Deaths from accidents to vessels	0	1	0	0	0	0	0	0	0	0	3
Deaths from accidents on board- other than accidents to vessels	2	1	2	2	1	4	1	3	2	2	9
Deaths Person Overboard	3	2	3	2	3	1	2	1	1	2	0
Total	5	4	5	4	4	5	3	4	3	4	12

(b) Deaths and injuries to passengers by type of injury											
Death	0	2	1	1	1	0	0	0	1	1	0
Fractures	85	108	66	88	111	110	138	113	78	82	79
Cuts, lacerations, bruising	4	2	4	10	11	9	11	10	14	13	8
Dislocations	3	2	3	4	4	10	9	7	6	3	8
Strains	2	1	3	1	3	0	10	5	1	3	1
Other Injuries	0	5	3	33	7	5	18	10	7	12	9
Total	94	120	80	137	137	134	186	145	107	114	105

(c) Deaths and injuries to crew members by type of injury											
Death	5	2	4	3	3	5	3	4	2	3	12
Fractures - major	30	24	16	11	6	25	27	24	20	26	18
Other fractures	46	44	46	55	65	53	54	45	42	31	47
Cuts, lacerations, bruising	85	84	56	80	75	72	78	85	67	62	65
Strained back	44	57	47	23	28	29	36	45	29	19	18
Other strains, sprains, hernias etc	60	35	46	43	52	48	36	37	34	36	28
Other injuries	57	84	73	86	67	70	54	67	53	54	55
Total	327	330	288	301	296	302	288	307	247	231	243

1 This latest table contains revisions to various years between 2000 and 2006.

☎023 8039 5500
The figures in this table are outside
the scope of National Statistics
Source - MAIB, DfT

For further details see the *Annual Report* by the
Marine Accident Investigation Branch. Available at:
www.maib.gov.uk

5.18 HM Coastguard statistics: search and rescue operations: United Kingdom:[1,2] 1997-2007

Number

	1997	1998	1999	2000	2001	2002	2003	2004	2005	2006	2007
Incidents involving vessels where assistance rendered:											
Commercial vessels	886	308	458	537	569	597	512	961	1,207	672	..
Fishing vessels	850	715	624	647	670	627	589	521	624	360	..
Pleasure craft	4,545	3,328	3,334	3,267	3,529	3,679	3,748	3,924	4,101	2,933	..
Incidents involving persons where assistance rendered:											
Incidents involving persons	2,365	1,359	1,202	1,693	1,872	2,241	2,436	2,169	3,237	2,169	..
Medical evacuations	958	370	427	403	473	460	585	481	513	458	..
Reports received:											
Distress reports	2,257	1,627	2,548	2,353	2,208	2,357	..	..	..	..	..
Hoaxes	..	269	258	221	206	260	232	301	406	529	691
Number of persons involved in incidents where assistance rendered:											
Persons assisted	16,884	14,366	17,535	14,717	16,487	19,984	25,118	21,929	22,477	23,113	..
Persons rescued	..	4,685	5,215	5,217	4,852	5,851	5,689	4,947	4,790	4,809	..
Lives lost	251	249	251	236	284	319	316	364	376	360	313
Total number of incidents where assistance rendered	..	6,328	6,581	6,703	7,242	7,604	8,070	8,056	7,252	6,592	..
Total number of incidents	..	11,553	12,220	12,016	12,514	13,395	13,849	14,240	16,754	17,185	18,180

1 HM Coastguard revised its statistical collection and collation procedures in 1998 and again in a phased programme between 2003 and 2005. Continuing ongoing refinements to the data collection, recording and analyses may make comparisons with previous years difficult. e.g. A change to data collection procedures in 2006 has resulted in a fall in the number of vessels recorded as 'assisted'.
2 Due to industrial action by some HM Coastguard staff, figures for 2007 are incomplete.

☎023 8032 9487
The figures in this table are outside the scope of National Statistics
Source - MCA

6 Public Transport:

Notes and Definitions

National Rail/London Underground passenger traffic: 6.1

The figures shown for national rail passenger traffic during 1919 and 1923 include all journeys on those 'London Railways' subsequently taken over by the London Passenger Transport Board in 1933. Additionally, in 1919 a journey using the services of more than one company was reported by each of them, with consequent duplication in the figures. The figures for journeys on the London Underground from 1948 include those originating on the former British Railways network (approximately 70 million journeys in 1948), and on those lines transferred to the London Transport Passenger Executive on 1 January 1948 (estimated at 62 million journeys in 1947).

Electrified route: Pre 1947 figures refer to track length, not route length, and include electrified sidings. In 1947, there were 3,370 electrified track kilometres.

National Railways passenger journeys and kilometres: Figures from 1986 are assessed on the All Purpose Ticket Issuing System (APTIS) and are not comparable with earlier years. The rail series for passenger data changes after privatisation in 1994, with possible double counting of some journeys where a route is shared with more than one operator. Both series have been revised from 1999/00. More detail is given in sections 6.3 and 6.4.

London Underground passenger kilometres: From 1965, passenger kilometres are those actually travelled. Prior to 1965, a different method of estimation was used, leading to slight overestimates of the order of 0.1 billion passenger kilometres per year.

Rail systems: 6.2

National Rail

Data up to 1994/95 show services by the former British Rail. From 1995/96 data these show the transition to services provided by the privatised passenger train operators on the national network.

London Underground

Summary data are shown here. Further detail appears in Table 6.7.

Glasgow Underground

The series shown is for the underground loop line which serves Glasgow. Suburban rail services in Strathclyde PTE are excluded.

Docklands Light Railway

The series shows the growth of the DLR. The Lewisham extension under the Thames at Greenwich was completed in 1999. A new line for London City Airport opened in December 2005. A further extension to Woolwich Arsenal is currently under construction.

Tyne and Wear Metro

The system has been extended in stages. Heworth to South Shields was opened on 24th March 1984. The extension from Bankfoot to Callerton and Newcastle Airport opened in November 1991. The 24km extension from Pelaw to Sunderland and South Hylton opened in March 2002. Part of that route shares some stations with national rail services.

Blackpool Trams

The traditional Victorian street-running tramway serves Blackpool Unitary Authority and Fleetwood, Lancashire.

Manchester Metrolink

Converted and extended from suburban rail, in 1991/92, 26 kilometres and 16 stations were transferred from the national network to the light rail system. It has a mix of segregated track and on-street running. Metrolink was opened in 1992, with the first section running between Bury and Manchester Victoria Station. The Eccles extension opened in 2000.

Sheffield Supertram

The Supertram was opened in 1994 between Sheffield and Meadowhall. Further lines came into service from Malin Bridge to Halfway and Cathedral to Herdings Park. In December 1997, operations were transferred to Stagecoach Plc.

Midland Metro

This rapid transit system was constructed by the Altram consortium, making use of former rail alignments. The line from Wolverhampton to Birmingham Snow Hill opened in 1999.

Croydon Tramlink

A modern three line tram network in south London, opened in May 2000. It is operated by FirstGroup for TfL.

Nottingham NET

NET is a modern street running tram system running north-south through the city. It runs parallel to suburban rail north of the centre. It was opened in March 2004.

National Rail receipts and passenger traffic: 6.3 and 6.4

Passenger Revenue: Passenger revenue includes all ticket revenue and miscellaneous charges associated with passenger travel e.g. car park charges. For journeys involving some travel on London Underground, receipts have been apportioned appropriately. Revenue does not include government support or grants.

Passenger Kilometres: Estimates of passenger kilometres are made from ticket sales. Travel on season tickets assumes appropriate factors for the number of journeys per ticket. Results are compiled in respect of 13 four week periods per year, so quarterly figures are derived from these.

There is some underestimation of passenger journeys and kilometres from 1997/98. This is because, for technical reasons, the passenger kilometres represented by certain new ticket types were not being captured by the operators' ticket system.

The figures were reviewed and revised by the Strategic Rail Authority (SRA) to include best estimates for this missing element. This exercise was backdated to the start of 1999/00, and is now repeated annually by the Office of Rail Regulation (ORR), who have taken over responsibility for rail statistics. Passenger revenue data are unaffected by these adjustments.

For the passenger kilometres series, new methodologies were applied in 2003/04 and in 2007/08 to improve the categorisation of ticket type. Further details can be found in *National Rail Trends Yearbook,* published by ORR (previously the responsibility of the SRA).

Route and station/depots open to traffic: 6.5

In 1991/92, 16 stations transferred from the national network to Manchester Metrolink. From 1994/95 the number of stations shown include only those on the national network. Eighteen other stations, mainly on the London Underground, are included in the figures for earlier years.

Recent revisions to the 'length of route' infrastructure series represented in Table 6.5 reflect improvements in the technology used to measure route kilometres. Up until 2003/04 the data were collected on a semi-manual basis from various systems. From 2004-05 the principal track engineers' database, GEOGIS, has been used. The apparent drop from 2004/05 to 2005/06 does not reflect an actual reduction in route km open for traffic but is due to improvements in data collection and data quality that resulted in a restatement of route length. 2007/08 data are not consistent with earlier years as a new methodology has been introduced because of revisions to route classification data.

Public Performance Measure (PPM): 6.6

The PPM was introduced in 2000 by the then Shadow Strategic Rail Authority, replacing the Passengers' Charter as a means of measuring passenger train performance. Unlike the Charter measure that only covered particular services, PPM covers all scheduled services and combines the previously individual punctuality and reliability results into a single performance measure. PPM is measured against the planned timetable, which makes allowance for specific delays (e.g. engineering works), which might differ from the previously published timetable. Table 6.6 shows the Charter results for years in which it applied, and also PPM results from the time it was introduced. Passenger Charter figures are displayed regularly by individual train operators.

London Underground: 6.7

Data obtained from the London Underground Directors Report and Accounts each year up to 2002/03. Responsibility for the Underground transferred to Transport for London in July 2003. TfL's *Annual Report* provides further detail.

Traffic receipts data are provided by TfL in 13 four week periods per year. These include revenue from car parking and penalty fares. Season ticket journeys are those estimated to have been made in each year, irrespective of when the ticket was sold. The cost per train kilometre includes renewals and depreciation. It excludes reorganisation and restructuring costs within TfL.

Other income includes property rents received, and commercial advertising receipts.

The number of stations is for those currently owned and operated by London Underground. Some suburban stations on the national rail network in London are also served by London Underground trains but are managed by the local rail franchise holder.

Channel Tunnel: 6.8

The Channel Tunnel opened for freight traffic in June 1994 and for passenger services in November of that year. Passenger shuttle services opened in December. Four different types of service operate through the Channel Tunnel as follows:

- *Freight Shuttles*: carrying road freight vehicles between Folkestone and Calais.
- *Tourist Shuttles*: carrying passenger vehicles between Folkestone and Calais.
- *Freight Trains*: through freight trains between Great Britain and Europe.
- *Eurostar Trains*: carrying passengers between London, France and Belgium.

Commercial traffic is fare-paying traffic using the tunnel. *Non-commercial traffic* is non-fare-paying traffic (e.g. staff and authorised agents). Figures for 1996/97 and 1997/98 were affected by a fire on 16 November 1996 which suspended services on both freight and tourist shuttles. Tourist shuttle resumed services on 10 December 1996 with full freight services resuming in June 1997.

Bus and coach industry: 6.9-6.16

Tables for the bus and coach industry refer to the activities of all holders of Public Service Vehicle (PSV) operators' licences. These vehicles are generally classified in the Bus Tax Class. An operator wishing to run bus or coach services is normally required to possess a PSV licence. However, certain vehicles and types of service are exempt from licensing and are excluded from the tables, such as community buses and local services operated by taxis. Taxis are generally classified in the Private Light Goods tax class, with private cars, so they are excluded from the PSV tables. Most of the information in these tables, which mainly refer to local bus services, is derived from annual returns made to DfT by a sample of holders of PSV operators' licences.

A local bus service is a stopping service available to the general public, where the route is registered with the Traffic Commissioner, which is eligible for Bus Service Operators Grant.

Bus and coach services which comprise contract, private hire, tours, excursions and express journeys are generally classified as "non-local" or "other" work. Some services,

such as long distance coach services, might contain a mixture of local work and non-local express work.

Some important changes have been made to the legal framework under which the industry operates.

Outside London:

- from 1 April 1986, the Passenger Transport Authorities in metropolitan areas were subjected to precept control
- local bus services outside London were deregulated on 26 October 1986, introducing on-the-road competition
- widespread privatisation of public sector bus operations took place from 1986. There are fewer bus operators in the public sector.

Within London:

- responsibility for London (Regional) Transport transferred from the former Greater London Council to the Secretary of State for Transport from 29 June 1984. On 1 April 1985, a separate operating subsidiary, London Buses Ltd, was established
- progressive tendering of local bus services in London was introduced in July 1985
- the former operating divisions of London Buses Ltd were privatised by the end of 1994
- from July 2000, Transport for London (TfL) was established as a successor body to London Transport, with strategic control of local buses through the Greater London Authority (GLA) under an elected Mayor of London.

Outside London, after bus deregulation in 1986, general subsidy was no longer feasible as most services were provided on a purely commercial basis, with on-the-road competition for routes.

Public transport support was restricted to unprofitable but socially necessary services, the operation of which was generally put out to tender.

In London, nearly all local bus services are operated by the private sector under contract to TfL. Bus routes, once awarded to a contractor after a tendering process, are then protected from on-the-road competition.

Bus and coach vehicle kilometres: 6.9

Service kilometres operated are measured by DfT's annual sample PSV survey of operators, and, for the bus contractors in London, by TfL. The majority of local bus service kilometres are run on a commercial basis. Subsidised local service kilometres are around a fifth of the local service total. Non-local service kilometres comprise long distance coaching, private hire, school contract work, excursions and tours.

Bus and coach stock: 6.10

After deregulation many large buses were replaced by smaller ones. In recent years, with the emphasis on passenger accessibility, more full size, low floor single deck buses have entered service. Operators have been buying more new vehicles, which has increased the fleet size and reduced the overall age of the PSV fleet.

Passenger receipts: 6.11

Receipts comprise amounts paid by, or for, all passengers carried. They include payments for season tickets and travel passes, and concessionary fare reimbursement from local authorities. Receipts exclude public transport support, Rural Bus Subsidy Grant (RBSG) and Bus Service Operator Grant (BSOG, formerly Fuel Duty Rebate).

Local authorities and passenger transport authorities run concessionary fare schemes for groups such as the elderly, the disabled and children. From April 2006, schemes in England must offer, as a minimum, free off-peak bus travel to elderly and disabled residents in their local area. Local authorities reimburse operators for revenue lost as a result of their participation in concessionary fare schemes after taking account of any income from the extra travel generated. The reimbursement should be seen as an incentive to the passenger to travel more. The operators should not lose, or gain, revenue through such schemes. From April 2008, the scheme has been extended across England to allow elderly and disabled residents to travel anywhere in England, in line with the national schemes already in place in Scotland and Wales.

Staff employed: 6.12

There was a fall in staff employed in the mid 1990s reflecting the widespread use of driver-only buses and the contracting out of an increased proportion of activities such as fleet maintenance. In recent years, as the bus fleet has grown, staff numbers have increased. Staff members may have more than one role, so the tables show those classified according to their main occupation.

Local passenger journeys by area: 6.13

These are collected through DfT's annual sample PSV survey of operators and, for London, from TfL. They are a count of

boardings of each vehicle, so a trip which requires a change from one bus to another would show two boardings. TfL obtains data on boardings from on-bus surveys. This information is useful as a check on DfT's annual PSV survey results for the capital. Over the last year, further bus patronage data have been obtained from local authorities, which they have used in their Local Transport Plans. This extra information has allowed DfT to revise its series of boardings. The main change has been an adjustment which gives a reduction in the allocation to London, with an increase in the surrounding counties.

Local authority support: 6.14

Public transport support, also known as "revenue support" covers forms of local authority current expenditure on public transport (not concessionary fare reimbursement). It includes payments to operators for the operation of subsidised services, and local authority administrative costs associated with bus operations, such as the tendering process itself and publicity. The Transport Act 1985 restricted support to unprofitable "socially necessary" services.

Subsidised bus services are run under contract to local transport authorities, usually following competitive tendering. Outside London, from 1998/99, Rural Bus Subsidy Grant (RBSG) has been paid by central government to many local authorities to encourage bus service provision in their more rural parts. RBSG is therefore included in the support table. In London, support takes a different form, as nearly all bus services are run on a commercial basis, under contract to TfL. Contracts for particular routes are awarded to operators after competitive tendering. The contract payments take into account the high level of service provision required in London, including services that run later in the evenings and at weekends.

Local bus fares indices: 6.15

Information required for the calculation of the index of local bus fares is obtained from a DfT survey of a panel of bus operators, who account for about 85 per cent of receipts from passengers on local bus services. Operators supply information about the size of each fare change, each quarter. Indices for groups of operators in different areas of GB are obtained by averaging changes, using weights based on receipts from passengers from DfT's PSV annual survey (receipts used for the index exclude concessionary fare reimbursement from local authorities). The DfT local bus fares index is a small part of the Retail Prices Index.

The index is intended to measure the change in the average cost to the fare-paying passenger. In practice, as the operators select the basket of fare changes to report each quarter and as cash-less transactions become more common (e.g. pre-paid travel passes) the index can only give a broad guide to fare changes. Also, fare changes outside London are frequent, so adjustments must be made to the index each quarter. Bus fare changes in London usually take place once a year, in January.

There is a trend towards simpler fare structures, with operators charging flat fares or zoned fares, and the use of pre-payment through stored value tickets, which speed up boarding. Introduction of free concessionary fares in England have affected the fares index for 2006/07, showing an effective drop in the fares paid by passengers.

Operating costs per local bus kilometre: 6.16

Costs per bus kilometre are higher in London and metropolitan areas than elsewhere. Greater traffic congestion, more frequent services and the need to use larger buses for busy services all contribute to higher costs.

Other costs, such as the cost of tendering and publicity associated with bus services, borne by local authorities or TfL rather than the operators, are not shown in this table.

Taxi industry: 6.17

A taxi, or hackney carriage, is a vehicle with fewer than 9 passenger seats which is licensed to "ply for hire" (i.e. it may stand at ranks or be hailed in the street by members of the public). This distinguishes taxis from Private Hire Vehicles (PHVs), which must be booked in advance through an operator and may not ply for hire (taxis may also be pre-booked). Taxis must normally be hired as a whole (i.e. separate fares are not charged to each passenger). However, taxis may charge separate fares when a sharing scheme is in operation, when they are run as a bus under a special PSV operators' licence or when pre-booked (PHV operators may also charge passengers separately if they share a journey).

In England and Wales, taxis and PHVs are licensed by district or borough councils, unitary authorities or, in London, the Public Carriage Office (PCO) which is part of TfL. The licensing authority is usually the body which sets taxi fares, although fare changes may be requested by the taxi trade. PHV fares are set by the operator. TfL is implementing the Private Hire Vehicles (London) Act 1998 for the licensing of

London PHV operators, drivers and vehicles. PHV operators in London must be licensed.

Taxi and PHV use has grown so there has been a large increase in the numbers of licensed taxis and PHVs.

The data on vehicles and drivers come from several sources. The London figures are from data held by TfL in the PCO. The statistics relating to provincial England and Wales come from surveys of district councils and unitary authorities.

6.1 Rail: length of national railway [1] route at year end, and passenger travel by national railway [1] and London Underground: 1900-2007/08

For greater detail of the years 1997/98-2007/08 see Table 6.2

| Year | Length of National Rail route (kilometres) | | | National Rail | | London Underground | |
	Total route	Electrified [2] route	Open to Passenger traffic	Passenger journeys (million)	Passenger kilometres (billion)	Passenger journeys (million)	Passenger kilometres (billion)
1900	29,783	..	..	..	..	..	..
1919	32,420	1,321	..	2,064	..	..	..
1923	32,462	1,122	..	1,772	..	..	..
1928	32,565	1,901	..	1,250	..	..	..
1933	32,345	2,403	..	1,159	..	..	..
1938	32,081	3,378	..	1,237	30.6	492	..
1946	31,963	..	..	1,266	47.0	569	..
1947	31,950	1,455	..	1,140	37.0	554	5.4
1948	31,593	1,455	..	1,024	34.2	720	6.2
1949	31,500	1,489	..	1,021	34.0	703	6.1
1950	31,336	1,489	..	1,010	32.5	695	6.0
1951	31,152	1,487	..	1,030	33.5	702	5.6
1952	31,022	1,508	..	1,017	32.9	670	5.4
1953	30,935	1,508	..	1,015	33.1	672	5.4
1954	30,821	1,577	..	1,020	33.3	671	5.7
1955	30,676	1,577	23,820	994	32.7	676	5.6
1956	30,618	1,624	23,612	1,029	34.0	678	5.5
1957	30,521	1,621	23,532	1,101	36.4	666	5.4
1958	30,333	1,622	23,621	1,090	35.6	692	5.3
1959	29,877	1,799	22,632	1,069	35.8	669	5.1
1960	29,562	2,034	22,314	1,037	34.7	674	5.2
1961	29,313	2,234	22,043	1,025	33.9	675	5.1
1962	28,117	2,511	20,785	965	31.7	668	4.9
1963	27,330	2,556	20,328	938	30.9	674	4.9
1964	25,735	2,659	18,781	928	32.0	674	4.9
1965	24,011	2,886	17,516	865	30.1	657	4.7
1966	22,082	3,064	16,359	835	29.7	667	4.8
1967	21,198	3,241	15,904	837	29.1	661	4.8
1968	20,080	3,182	15,242	831	28.7	655	4.7
1969	19,470	3,169	15,088	805	29.6	676	5.0
1970	18,989	3,162	14,637	824	30.4	672	5.1
1971	18,738	3,169	14,484	816	30.1	654	5.2
1972	18,417	3,178	14,499	754	29.1	655	5.3
1973	18,227	3,462	14,375	728	29.8	644	5.2
1974	18,168	3,647	14,373	733	30.9	636	5.2
1975	18,118	3,655	14,431	730	30.9	601	4.8
1976	18,007	3,735	14,407	702	28.4	546	4.4
1977	17,973	3,767	14,413	702	29.3	545	4.3
1978	17,901	3,716	14,396	724	30.0	568	4.5
1979	17,735	3,718	14,412	748	30.7	594	4.5
1980	17,645	3,718	14,394	760	30.3	559	4.2
1981	17,431	3,729	14,394	719	29.7	541	4.1
1982	17,229	3,753	14,371	630	27.2	498	3.7
1983	16,964	3,750	14,375	695	29.5	563	4.3
1984/85	16,816	3,798	14,304	701	29.5	672	5.4
1985/86	16,752	3,809	14,310	686	30.4	732	6.0
1986/87	16,670	4,154	14,304	738 [3]	30.8 [3]	769	6.2
1987/88	16,633	4,207	14,302	798	32.4	798	6.3
1988/89	16,599	4,376	14,309	822	34.3	815	6.3
1989/90	16,587	4,546	14,318	812	33.3	765	6.0
1990/91	16,584	4,912	14,317	809	33.2	775	6.2

6.1 (continued) Rail: length of national railway [1] route at year end, and passenger travel by national railway [1] and London Underground: 1900-2007/08

For greater detail of the years 1997/98-2007/08 see Table 6.2

| Year | Length of National Rail route (kilometres) | | | National Rail | | London Underground | |
	Total route	Electrified [2] route	Open to Passenger traffic	Passenger journeys (million)	Passenger kilometres (billion)	Passenger journeys (million)	Passenger kilometres (billion)
1991/92	16,588	4,886	14,291	792	32.5	751	5.9
1992/93	16,528	4,910	14,317	770	31.7	728	5.8
1993/94	16,536	4,968	14,357	740	30.4	735	5.8
1994/95	16,542	4,970	14,359	735	28.7	764	6.1
1995/96	16,666	5,163	15,002	761	30.0	784	6.3
1996/97	16,666	5,176	15,034	801	32.1	772	6.2
1997/98	16,656	5,166	15,024	846	34.7	832	6.5
1998/99	16,659	5,166	15,038	892	36.3	866	6.7
1999/00	16,649	5,167	15,038	931 [4]	38.5 [4]	927	7.2
2000/01	16,652	5,167	15,042	957	38.2	970	7.5
2001/02	16,652	5,167	15,042	960	39.1	953	7.5
2002/03	16,670	5,167	15,042	976	39.7	942	7.4
2003/04	16,493	5,200	14,883	1,012	40.9	948	7.3
2004/05	16,116 [5]	5,200 [5]	14,328 [5]	1,045	41.8	976	7.6
2005/06	15,810	5,205	14,356	1,082	43.2	970	7.6
2006/07	15,795	5,250	14,353	1,151 [R]	46.2 [R]	1,040	8.0
2007/08	15,814 [6]	5,250 [6]	14,484 [6]	1,232	49.0	1,096	8.4

1 From 1994/95 route length is for the former Railtrack.
'From 1995/96 data are for National Rail, former British Rail and
'Train Operating Companies. Excludes rail routes managed by PTEs.
2 Pre 1947 figures refer to track length, not route length,
    and include electrified sidings.   In 1947 electrified track kilometres totalled 3,370.
3 Break in series. From 1986/87 figures include an element of double counting,
    as a journey involving more than one operator is scored against each operator.
    This contrasts with former British Rail data for which a through ticket journey was counted only once.
4 Break in series due to a change in methodology.
5 Break in series due to a change in methodology.
6 Break in series due to a change in methodology.

☎Rail: 020-7944 8874
☎London Underground: 020-7944 3076
The figures in this table are outside
the scope of National Statistics
Sources - ORR,
London Underground

6.2 Rail systems: 1997/98-2007/08

(a) Passenger journeys — Millions

	1997/98	1998/99	1999/00	2000/01	2001/02	2002/03	2003/04	2004/05	2005/06	2006/07	2007/08
National Rail network [1]	846	892	931	957	960	976	1,012	1,045	1,082	1,151 R	1,232
London Undergound	832	866	927	970	953	942	948	976	970	1,040	1,096
Glasgow Underground	14	15	15	14	14	13	13	13	13	13	14
Docklands Light Railway	21	28	31	38	41	46	48	50	54	64	67
Tyne & Wear Metro [2]	35	34	33	33	33	37	38	37	36	38	40
Blackpool Trams [3]	5	4	4	4	5	4	4	4	4	3	3
Manchester Metrolink [4]	14	13	14	17	18	19	19	20	20	20	20
Sheffield Supertram	9	10	11	11	11	12	12	13	13	14	15
Midland Metro [5]	.	.	5	5	5	5	5	5	5	5	5
Croydon Tramlink [6]	.	.	.	15	18	19	20	22	23	25	27
Nottingham NET [7]	.	.	.	.	.	.	-	8	10	10	10
All light rail	98	104	113	138	146	154	160	172	177	192	201
All rail	1,776	1,862	1,971	2,065	2,059	2,072	2,119	2,193	2,229	2,383	2,529

(b) Passenger kilometres — Millions

	1997/98	1998/99	1999/00	2000/01	2001/02	2002/03	2003/04	2004/05	2005/06	2006/07	2007/08
National Rail network	34,700	36,280	38,472	38,179	39,141	39,678	40,906 R	41,762	43,211	46,218 R	49,007
London Undergound	6,479	6,716	7,171	7,470	7,451	7,367	7,340	7,606	7,586	7,947	8,352
Glasgow Underground	45	47	47	46	44	43	43	43	42	42	46
Docklands Light Railway	103	144	172	200	207	232	235	245	257	301	326
Tyne & Wear Metro	249	238	230	229	238	275	284	283	279	295	313
Blackpool Trams	..	..	13	13	15	14	11	12	11	10	9
Manchester Metrolink	88	117	126	152	161	167	169	204	206	208	210
Sheffield Supertram	34	35	37	38	39	40	42	44	44	42	44
Midland Metro	.	.	50	56	50	50	54	52	54	51	51
Croydon Tramlink	.	.	.	96	99	100	105	112	117	128	141
Nottingham NET	.	.	.	.	.	.	2	37	42	43	44
All Light rail	519	581	675	830	854	920	945	1,033	1,052	1,120	1,185
All rail	41,698	43,577	46,318	46,479	47,446	47,965	49,191	50,401	51,849	55,285	58,544

(c) Passenger revenue — £ million (at current prices)

	1997/98	1998/99	1999/00	2000/01	2001/02	2002/03	2003/04	2004/05	2005/06	2006/07	2007/08
National Rail network	2,821	3,089	3,368	3,413	3,548	3,663	3,901	4,158	4,493	5,012 R	5,555
London Undergound	899	977	1,058	1,129	1,151	1,138	1,161	1,241	1,309	1,417	1,525
Glasgow Underground	9	9	10	10	10	10	10	11	11	13	13
Docklands Light Railway	14	20	22	29	32	36	37	40	46	54	62
Tyne & Wear Metro	22	23	24	24	25	29	31	33	34	38	32
Blackpool Trams	5	4	4	4	5	5	4	4	4	5	4
Manchester Metrolink	14	..	..	18	20	20	21	22	23	24	22
Sheffield Supertram	6	6	7	7	8	10	9	11	10	13	11
Midland Metro	.	.	..	3	4	5	5	5	6	6	4
Croydon Tramlink	.	.	.	12	13	15	16	18	19	20	15
Nottingham NET	.	.	.	.	.	.	..	6	7	8	7
All Light rail	69	63	68	108	117	130	135	151	161	180	171
All rail	3,789	4,128	4,493	4,650	4,815	4,931	5,197	5,550	5,963	6,609	7,251

(d) Route kilometres open for passenger traffic — Number

	1997/98	1998/99	1999/00	2000/01	2001/02	2002/03	2003/04	2004/05	2005/06	2006/07	2007/08
National Rail network [8]	15,024	15,038	15,038	15,042	15,042	15,042	14,883	14,328	14,356	14,353	14,484
London Undergound	392	392	408	408	408	408	408	408	408	408	408
Glasgow Underground	11	11	11	11	11	11	11	11	10	10	10
Docklands Light Railway	22	22	26	26	26	26	26	26	30	31	55
Tyne & Wear Metro	59	59	59	59	78	78	78	78	78	78	78
Blackpool Trams	18	18	18	18	18	18	18	18	18	18	18
Manchester Metrolink	31	31	39	39	39	39	39	39	39	39	42
Sheffield Supertram	29	29	29	29	29	29	29	29	29	29	29
Midland Metro	.	.	20	20	20	20	20	20	20	20	20
Croydon Tramlink	.	.	.	28	28	28	28	28	28	28	28
Nottingham NET	.	.	.	.	.	.		14	14	15	14	14
All Light rail	170	170	202	230	249	249	263	263	268	267	294
All rail	15,586	15,600	15,648	15,680	15,699	15,699	15,554	14,999	15,032	15,028	15,186

6.2 (continued) Rail systems: 1997/98-2007/08

(e) Stations or stops served
Number

	1997/98	1998/99	1999/00	2000/01	2001/02	2002/03	2003/04	2004/05	2005/06	2006/07	2007/08
National Rail network	2,495	2,499	2,503	2,508	2,508	2,508	2,507	2,508	2,510	2,520	2,516
London Undergound	269	269	274	274	274	274	274	274	274	273	268
Glasgow Underground	15	15	15	15	15	15	15	15	15	15	15
Docklands Light Railway	29	29	34	34	34	34	34	34	38	34	39
Tyne & Wear Metro	46	46	46	46	58	58	58	58	59	59	60
Blackpool Trams	124	124	124	124	124	124	124	124	124	121	121
Manchester Metrolink	26	26	36	36	36	37	37	37	37	37	37
Sheffield Supertram	46	47	47	47	48	48	48	48	48	48	48
Midland Metro	.	.	23	23	23	23	23	23	23	23	23
Croydon Tramlink	.	.	.	38	38	38	38	38	38	39	38
Nottingham NET	.	.	.	.	.	.	23	23	23	23	23
All Light rail	286	287	325	363	376	377	400	400	406	399	404
All rail	3,050	3,055	3,102	3,145	3,158	3,159	3,181	3,182	3,190	3,192	3,188

(f) Loaded train or tram kilometres
Millions

	1997/98	1998/99	1999/00	2000/01	2001/02	2002/03	2003/04	2004/05	2005/06	2006/07	2007/08
National Rail network [9]	376.3	405.1	418.4	427.2	435.9	443.3	446.2	458.4	463.2	463.5	..
London Undergound	62.1	61.2	63.1	63.8	65.4	65.9	68.5	69.5	68.8	69.8	70.5
Glasgow Underground	1.1	1.1	1.2	1.2	1.2	1.1	1.1	1.1	1.2	1.2	1.2
Docklands Light Railway	2.4	2.6	2.9	2.9	2.9	3.2	3.4	3.3	3.4	4.4	4.4
Tyne & Wear Metro	4.8	4.8	4.8	4.7	4.7	6.3	6.3	5.6	5.5	5.8	6.2
Blackpool Trams	1.2	1.2	1.2	1.2	1.3	1.1	0.9	0.8	0.8	0.9	0.7
Manchester Metrolink	3.2	3.4	3.6	4.4	4.5	4.6	4.6	4.4	4.4	3.8	4.0
Sheffield Supertram	2.7	2.4	2.4	2.4	2.4	2.5	2.5	2.4	2.4	2.4	2.4
Midland Metro	.	.	.	1.9	1.6	1.7	1.7	1.6	1.7	1.6	1.5
Croydon Tramlink	.	.	.	2.1	2.4	2.5	2.5	2.4	2.4	2.5	2.2
Nottingham NET	.	.	.	.	.	.	0.2	1.0	1.2	1.2	1.2
All Light rail	15.4	15.5	16.1	20.8	21.0	23.0	23.2	22.8	23.0	23.8	24.0
All rail	453.8	481.8	497.6	511.8	522.3	532.2	537.9	550.6	555.0	557.1	..

(g) Passenger carriages or tramcars
Number

	1997/98	1998/99	1999/00	2000/01	2001/02	2002/03	2003/04	2004/05	2005/06	2006/07	2007/08
National Rail network [10]	..	..	..	..	..	..	..	..	..	..	..
London Undergound	3,886	3,923	3,954	3,954	3,954	3,954	3,959	3,959	4,070	4,070	4,070
Glasgow Underground	41	41	41	41	41	41	41	41	41	41	44
Docklands Light Railway	70	70	70	70	74	94	94	94	94	94	94
Tyne & Wear Metro	90	90	90	90	90	90	90	90	90	90	102
Blackpool Trams	77	77	75	81	75	76	76	76	76	75	78
Manchester Metrolink	26	26	32	32	32	32	32	32	32	32	34
Sheffield Supertram	25	25	25	25	25	25	25	25	25	25	28
Midland Metro	.	.	16	16	16	16	16	16	16	16	23
Croydon Tramlink	.	.	24	24	24	24	24	24	24	24	26
Nottingham NET	.	.	.	.	.	.	15	15	15	15	16
All Light rail	329	329	373	379	377	398	413	413	413	412	445
All rail	..	..	..	..	..	..	..	..	..	..	..

1 Franchised train operating companies from February 1996 following rail privatisation.
2 Tyne & Wear Metro extension to Sunderland opened in March 2002.
3 Blackpool Trams shown as a self-contained system.
4 Transfer of 20 stations from the rail network to Manchester Metrolink.
5 Midland Metro opened in 1999.
6 Croydon Tramlink opened in 2000.
7 Nottingham Express Transit opened in March 2004.
8 Breaks in series due to changes in methodology (see notes and definitions section 6.5)
9 Figure for 2007/08 not yet available
10 No data available for National Rail leased rolling stock after rail privatisation.

☎London Underground: 020-7944 3076
☎Rail: 020-7944 8874
The National Rail and Underground figures in this
table are outside the scope of National Statistics
Source - Network Rail, former Railtrack, ORR, TfL,
light rail operators and PTEs

6.3 National railways: receipts:[1] 1996/97-2007/08

£ Million

	1997/98	1998/99	1999/00	2000/01	2001/02	2002/03	2003/04[2]	2004/05	2005/06	2006/07[3]	2007/08[4]
All Passenger Operators											
Ordinary fares	2,048	2,242	2,463	2,463	2,585	2,693	2,890	3,088	3,323	3,714	4,120
Season tickets	773	847	905	950	964	970	1,011	1,071	1,170	1,298	1,434
All tickets (current prices)	2,821	3,089	3,368	3,413	3,548	3,663	3,901	4,158	4,493	5,012	5,555
All tickets (2007/08 prices)	3,608	3,854	4,119	4,115	4,178	4,183	4,329	4,490	4,750	5,158	5,555

1 Includes British Rail services and those provided by private operators.
   Adjusted to 2007/08 prices using the GDP market price deflator.
2 Break in series due to change in methodology.
3 Revisions made to figures previously published for 2006/07
4 Break in series due to change in methodology.

☎020-7944 8874
The figures in this table are outside
the scope of National Statistics
Source - ORR

6.4 Passenger kilometres on national railways:[1] 1997/98-2007/08

Billions

	1997/98	1998/99	1999/00[2]	2000/01	2001/02	2002/03	2003/04	2004/05	2005/06	2006/07[3]	2007/08[4]
All Passenger Operators:											
Ordinary fare	25.3	26.4	28.0	27.2	28.1	28.4	28.9	29.4	30.0	32.9	33.9
Season ticket	9.3	9.8	10.4	10.9	11.0	11.3	12.0	12.4	13.2	13.3	15.1
All tickets	34.7	36.3	38.5	38.2	39.1	39.7	40.9	41.8	43.2	46.2	49.0

1 Estimates of passenger kilometres are derived from ticket sales.
   Travel on season tickets assumes appropriate factors for the
   number of journeys made per ticket.
2 Break in series due to change in methodology (see notes and definitions Section 6)
3 Revisions made to figures previously published for 2006/07
4 Break in series due to change in methodology (see notes and definitions Section 6)

☎020-7944 8874
The figures in this table are outside
the scope of National Statistics
Source - ORR

6.5 National railways: route and stations open for traffic at end of year: 1997/98-2007/08

Kilometres/number

	1997/98	1998/99	1999/00	2000/01	2001/02	2002/03	2003/04	2004/05[2]	2005/06	2006/07	2007/08
Route open for traffic:											
Electrified	5,166	5,166	5,167	5,167	5,167	5,167	5,200	5,200	5,205	5,250	5,250
Non-electrified	11,490	11,493	11,482	11,485	11,485	11,503	11,293	10,916	10,605	10,545	10,564
All routes:	16,656	16,659	16,649	16,652	16,652	16,670	16,493	16,116	15,810	15,795	15,814
Open for passenger traffic	15,024	15,038	15,038	15,042	15,042	15,042	14,883	14,328	14,356	14,353	14,484
Open for freight traffic only	1,632	1,621	1,610	1,610	1,610	1,610	1,610	1,788	1,454	1,442	1,330
Passenger stations: [1]	2,495	2,499	2,503	2,508	2,508	2,508	2,507	2,508	2,510	2,520	2,516

1 The number of stations shown are those on the national network.
   Metro stations and stations shared with London Underground are excluded.
2 Break in series due to change in methodology (see notes and definitions Section 6)
3 Break in series due to change in methodology (see notes and definitions Section 6)

☎020-7944 8874
The figures in this table are outside
the scope of National Statistics
Source - Network Rail, formerly Railtrack

6.6 National railways: punctuality and reliability: 1997/98-2007/08

Percentage

	1997/98	1998/99	1999/00	2000/01	2001/02	2002/03	2003/04	2004/05	2005/06	2006/07	2007/08
Public Performance Measure (PPM)[1]	89.7	87.9	87.8	79.1	78.0	79.2	81.2	83.6	86.4	88.1	89.9
Punctuality	92.5	91.5	91.9	..	..	..	..	..	..	..	..
Reliability	98.9	98.8	98.8	..	..	..	..	..	..	..	..

1 The PPM is a measure of the percentage of
   trains arriving on time, combining punctuality
   and reliability. It replaced the former
   Passenger's Charter measures from June 2000.

☎020-7944 8874
The figures in this table are outside the scope of National Statistics
Source - ORR

6.7 London Underground: 1997/98-2007/08

	1997/98	1998/99	1999/00	2000/01	2001/02	2002/03	2003/04	2004/05	2005/06	2006/07	2007/08
Passenger Journeys (millions)											
Ordinary [1]	448	463	477	486	491	495	491	486	460	519	581
Season ticket	384	403	450	484	462	446	457	490	510	521	515
All journeys	832	866	927	970	953	942	948	976	970	1,040	1,096
Passenger kilometres (millions)	6,479	6,716	7,171	7,470	7,451	7,367	7,340	7,606	7,586	7,947	8,352
Receipts (£ million)											
Ordinary [1]	510	546	579	610	636	628	625	663	679	782	880
Season ticket	389	430	479	519	515	510	536	578	629	635	645
Traffic receipts	899	976	1,058	1,129	1,151	1,138	1,161	1,241	1,308	1,417	1,525
Traffic receipts at 2007/08 prices [2]	1,150	1,218	1,294	1,361	1,355	1,299	1,289	1,340	1,383	1,458	1,525
Costs (£ million)											
Rail operations [3,4]	681	869	962	1,115	1,341	1,628	..	..	..	..	..
Other operations	15	18	33	42	30	36	..	..	..	..	..
Depreciation, renewals, severance [3]	315	267	299	341	344	336	..	..	..	..	..
All costs (current prices)	1,010	1,154	1,294	1,497	1,715	2,000	..	..	..	..	..
All costs 2007/08 prices [2]	1,292	1,440	1,583	1,805	2,020	2,284	..	..	..	..	..
Loaded train kilometres (millions)	62	61	63	64	65	66	69	69	69	70	70
Passenger place kilometres (billions)	56	55	57	57	58	58	..	..	..	..	..
Receipts per journey (£)	1.08	1.13	1.14	1.16	1.21	1.21	1.22	1.27	1.35	1.36	1
Receipts per jny at 2007/08 prices [2]	1.38	1.41	1.40	1.40	1.42	1.38	1.36	1.37	1.43	1.40	1
Costs per train kilometre (£)	16	19	21	23	26	31	..	..	..	..	..
Costs per km at 2007/08 prices [2]	21	24	25	28	31	35	..	..	..	..	..
Average no. passengers per train	104	110	114	117	114	113	107	110	110	114	118
Loss before grants and tax (£ m)	111	178	236	368	564	863	..	..	..	..	..
Loss at 2007/08 prices [2]	142	222	289	444	665	985	..	..	..	..	..
Operational data (number)											
Rail staff	15,892	16,032	16,462	16,956	18,679	17,214	..	..	..	..	..
Stations	269	269	274	274	274	274	274	274	274	273	268
Rail carriages	3,886	3,923	3,954	3,954	3,954	3,954	3,959	3,959	4,070	4,070	4,070
Route kilometres	392	392	408	408	408	408	408	408	408	408	408

1 Ordinary journeys include daily travelcards and those where concessionary fares apply.
2 Adjustment to 2006/07 values using the GDP Deflator. 'Other' income no longer available on
  the same basis as previously published.
3 From 1998/99, following a change in London Underground's accounting policy, expenditure
  that had previously been treated as renewals was either charged to the cost of operations or
  capitalised as an addition to fixed assets.
4 The cost of rail operations includes most of the costs of London Underground's PFI
  and PPP contracts that are delivering a modernised tube network.

020-7944 3076
The figures in this table are
outside the scope of National Statistics
Source - Transport for London

6.8   Channel Tunnel: traffic to and from Europe: 1997-2007

											Thousands
	1997 [1]	1998	1999	2000	2001	2002	2003	2004	2005	2006	2007
Vehicles carried on Le Shuttle:											
Passenger	2,383	3,448	3,342	2,864	2,605	2,408	2,351	2,165	2,124	2,089	2,207
Freight	268	705	839	1,133	1,198	1,231	1,285	1,281	1,309	1,296	1,415
All vehicles	2,651	4,153	4,181	3,997	3,803	3,639	3,636	3,446	3,433	3,385	3,622
Passengers on Eurostar and Le Shuttle	14,653	18,405	17,550	17,018	16,313	15,252	14,699	15,064	15,527	15,501	16,164
Through-train freight tonnes	2,925	3,141	2,865	2,947	2,447	1,487	1,743	1,889	1,588	1,569	1,214

1 Figures for 1997 were affected by a fire on 16 November 1996.
  Tourist shuttle resumed services on 10 Dec 1996 with full
  freight services resuming on 15 June 1997.

☎020-7944 8874
The figures in this table are outside
the scope of National Statistics
Source - Eurotunnel, Eurostar and EWS International

6.9 Bus and coach services: vehicle kilometres: 1997/98-2007/08

(a) Local bus services by area — Millions

	1997/98	1998/99	1999/00	2000/01	2001/02	2002/03	2003/04	2004/05	2005/06	2006/07	2007/08
London	362	358	362	371	381	404	444	457	461	465	475
English metropolitan are	697	684	661	654	646	630	596	575	565	584	604
English other areas	1,083	1,123	1,160	1,134	1,102	1,088	1,069	1,077	1,070	1,141	1,207
England	2,142	2,165	2,183	2,158	2,129	2,122	2,109	2,109	2,096	2,190	2,286
Scotland	368	358	363	369	368	374	369	357	357	377	399
Wales	117	118	123	126	126	123	113	116	120	116	116
Great Britain	2,628	2,642	2,670	2,653	2,622	2,619	2,590	2,581	2,573	2,682	2,801
All outside London	2,266	2,284	2,308	2,282	2,241	2,215	2,146	2,124	2,112	2,217	2,326

(b) Local bus services outside London by area — Millions

	2005/06			2006/07			2007/08		
	Comm-ercial	Sub-sidised	Total	Comm-ercial	Sub-sidised	Total	Comm-ercial	Sub-sidised	Total
English metropolitan are	483	82	565	512	72	584	516	89	604
English other areas	799	271	1,070	867	274	1,141	920	287	1,207
Scotland	296	61	357	301	76	377	301	98	399
Wales	85	35	120	79	37	116	87	29	116
All outside London	1,663	449	2,112	1,759	459	2,218	1,823	504	2,326

(c) All services — Millions

	1997/98	1998/99	1999/00	2000/01	2001/02	2002/03	2003/04	2004/05	2005/06	2006/07	2007/08
Local bus services	2,628	2,642	2,670	2,653	2,622	2,619	2,590	2,581	2,573	2,682	2,801
Other (non-local) service	1,558	1,590	1,451	1,507	1,479	1,336	1,398	1,343	1,395	1,284	1,511
All services	4,186	4,232	4,121	4,160	4,101	3,955	3,988	3,924	3,968	3,967	4,312

☎020-7944 3076

6.10 Bus and coach services: vehicle stock: 1997/98-2007/08

Thousands

	1997/98	1998/99	1999/00	2000/01	2001/02	2002/03	2003/04	2004/05	2005/06	2006/07	2007/08
Single deckers:											
up to 16 seats	10.5	10.9	11.5	10.8	11.3	11.7	14.2	14.4	15.6	13.0	11.9
17-35 seats	13.6	14.4	13.9	15.0	13.0	12.9	..	..	..	..	0.0
36 plus seats	34.9	36.4	37.5	37.5	39.2	37.9	..	..	..	..	..
All single deckers[1]	59.0	61.7	62.9	63.3	63.5	62.5	63.7	64.0	65.5	63.8	64.1
All double deckers	17.1	17.0	16.8	16.0	16.0	16.3	16.5	16.6	15.5	16.2	16.3
All vehicles [2]	76.2	78.7	79.7	79.2	79.5	78.8	80.1	80.6	81.0	80.0	80.4

1 "Single deckers", in this context, includes minibuses and coaches as well as single-decker buses
2 Public Service Vehicles in tax classes 34 and 38. Taken from DfT's annual surveys.

☎020-7944 3076

6.11 Bus and coach services: passenger receipts (Including concessionary fare reimbursement): 1996/97-2006/07

(a) Local bus services by area (current prices)											£ Million
Area	1996/97	1997/98	1998/99	1999/00	2000/01	2001/02	2002/03	2003/04	2004/05	2005/06	2006/07
London	561	599	626	652	674	695	715	767	871	939	1,003
English metropolitan areas	672	719	718	704	747	764	786	815	846	907	914
English other areas	866	906	930	972	1,038	1,074	1,135	1,281	1,311	1,424	1,709
England	2,099	2,224	2,274	2,328	2,459	2,533	2,635	2,863	3,029	3,270	3,626
Scotland	290	296	300	314	332	321	354	358	381	385	424
Wales	83	81	85	88	99	98	105	105	110	114	124
Great Britain	2,472	2,601	2,659	2,731	2,890	2,952	3,094	3,326	3,519	3,769	4,173
All outside London	1,911	2,002	2,033	2,078	2,216	2,257	2,379	2,559	2,648	2,830	3,170
(b) All services at current prices											£ Million
Local bus services	2,472	2,601	2,659	2,731	2,890	2,952	3,094	3,326	3,519	3,769	4,173
Other (non-local) services[2]	1,067	1,144	1,260	1,390	1,556	1,606	1,535	1,586	1,603	..	..
All services	3,539	3,745	3,919	4,121	4,446	4,558	4,629	4,912	5,122	..	..
(c) All services at 2007/08 prices [1]											£ Million
Local bus services	3,159	3,328	3,317	3,339	3,485	3,476	3,533	3,692	3,801	3,983	4,297
Other (non-local) services	1,363	1,464	1,572	1,700	1,876	1,891	1,753	1,760	1,731	..	..
All services	4,522	4,792	4,890	5,039	5,361	5,367	5,286	5,452	5,532	..	..

1 Prices for the series are adjusted for general inflation to 2007/08 prices, using the GDP market price deflator. ☎020-7944 3076
2 Passenger receipts for non-local services are no longer collected.

6.12 Bus and coach services: staff employed: 1997/98-2007/08

											Thousands
Staff	1997/98	1998/99	1999/00	2000/01	2001/02	2002/03	2003/04	2004/05	2005/06	2006/07	2007/08
Drivers & crew	108.7	113.6	117.1	116.8	117.9	118.0	122.0	126.0	126.0	127.3	131.9
Maintenance	19.9	20.0	19.8	19.6	20.8	19.3	19.7	20.6	20.1	20.3	20.9
Other	17.3	18.1	17.9	19.5	21.5	17.9	20.7	20.0	20.4	20.0	21.0
All staff [1]	145.9	151.6	154.8	156.0	160.2	155.2	162.4	166.6	166.5	167.6	173.8

1 The full-time equivalents of all part time staff and all ☎020-7944 3076
  working proprietors are classified according to their main occupation.

6.13 Local bus services: passenger journeys by area:[1] 1997/98-2007/08

											Millions
Area	1997/98	1998/99	1999/00	2000/01	2001/02	2002/03	2003/04	2004/05	2005/06	2006/07	2007/08
London	1,281	1,266	1,294	1,347	1,422	1,527	1,692	1,802	1,881	1,993	2,090
English metropolitan areas	1,292	1,256	1,213	1,203	1,196	1,182	1,162	1,128	1,111	1,141	1,121
England: other areas	1,286	1,286	1,297	1,292	1,263	1,255	1,233	1,210	1,204	1,336	1,319
England	3,859	3,808	3,804	3,842	3,881	3,964	4,087	4,140	4,196	4,470	4,530
Scotland	448	424	455	458	466	471	478	479	477	506	513
Wales	122	118	117	119	108	115	116	118	118	122	122
Great Britain	4,430	4,350	4,376	4,420	4,455	4,550	4,681	4,737	4,791	5,097	5,164
All outside London	3,149	3,084	3,082	3,073	3,033	3,023	2,989	2,935	2,910	3,104	3,074

1 Previous years figures have been revised (See notes and definitions of Section 6) ☎020-7944 3076

6.14 Local bus services: Local authority support by area: 1997/98-2007/08

(a) Concessionary fare reimbursement: by area (current prices)											£ Million
	1997/98	1998/99	1999/00	2000/01	2001/02	2002/03	2003/04	2004/05	2005/06	2006/07	2007/08
London	110	113	124	126	129	129	137	135	157	167	..
English metropolitan areas	176	176	185	189	190	184	188	188	189	257	..
England: other areas	104	103	106	108	122	123	132	132	141	289	..
England	390	393	415	423	441	436	457	455	487	712	..
Scotland	39	42	41	35	39	60	86	85	114	154	..
Wales	8	8	10	11	13	30	37	41	48	48	..
All Great Britain	437	451	466	470	483	526	580	581	650	914	..
All outside London	327	338	341	344	354	397	442	446	493	747	..

(b) Public transport support: by area (current prices)											£ Million
London [1]	1	12	10	57	201	368	516	546	596	625	..
English metropolitan areas	98	109	109	104	110	106	113	104	116	128	..
England: other areas	86	110	127	133	147	170	196	212	240	253	..
England	185	231	246	294	458	644	825	862	952	1,007	..
Scotland	23	22	25	28	33	35	36	38	45	47	..
Wales	9	11	14	16	20	21	25	27	28	30	..
All Great Britain	218	265	284	337	511	700	885	927	1,026	1084	..
All outside London	217	253	274	280	310	332	369	381	430	459	..

(c) All Great Britain at 2007/08 prices [1]											
Concessionary fare reimbursement	542	546	553	550	552	583	625	609	668	910	..
Public transport support	270	320	337	394	584	776	954	972	1,054	1084	..

1 Adjusted for general inflation to 2007/08 prices using the GDP deflator.   ☎020-7944 3076

6.15 Local bus services: fare indices by area: 1997/98-2007/08

											1995=100
Area	1997/98	1998/99	1999/00	2000/01	2001/02	2002/03	2003/04	2004/05	2005/06	2006/07	2007/08
London	109.4	113.8	117.2	117.3	115.5	114.8	116.9	126.8	139.7	151.5	159.5
English metropolitan areas	112.8	117.9	123.5	128.6	135.5	140.7	146.7	153.3	166.0	168.3	178.3
English other areas	112.0	117.3	122.6	129.2	136.1	142.4	149.0	155.9	166.2	159.5	168
England	111.5	116.4	121.4	125.8	130.3	134.3	139.4	147.2	159.4	160.1	169.1
Scotland	116.2	121.2	124.1	129.1	131.1	133.8	136.1	140.0	143.9	151.0	155.7
Wales	109.6	116.0	121.9	128.4	135.7	142.3	147.2	153.7	159.9	169.7	177.8
Great Britain	112.1	117.1	121.8	126.4	130.6	134.5	139.2	146.5	157.5	159.0	167.6
All outside London	112.9	118.2	123.2	129.0	135.1	140.4	146.0	152.3	162.2	160.7	169.1
Retail Prices Index	106.5	109.9	111.6	114.9	116.6	119.1	122.4	126.2	129.5	134.4	139.9

☎020-7944 4139

6.16 Local bus services: operating costs per vehicle-kilometre: 1996/97-2006/07

(a) At current prices										Pence per vehicle kilometre [1]	
	1996/97	1997/98	1998/99	1999/00	2000/01	2001/02	2002/03	2003/04	2004/05	2005/06	2006/07
London [2]	154	152	155	157	168	178	203	210	221	238	251
English PTE areas	94	90	90	92	101	105	105	114	118	130	148
English other areas	74	76	79	81	87	94	89	100	94	98	111
England	91	92	94	96	105	111	114	127	128	138	151
Scotland	73	74	77	73	78	84	80	80	86	90	100
Wales	65	71	74	74	76	77	84	83	82	86	93
Great Britain	88	89	91	92	100	105	108	118	120	129	141
All outside London	79	81	84	82	89	95	92	99	98	105	118

(b) At 2007/08 prices [3]										Pence per vehicle kilometre [1]	
London [2]	197	194	193	192	203	210	232	233	239	251	258
English PTE areas	120	115	112	113	122	124	120	126	127	137	152
English other areas	95	97	99	99	105	111	102	110	102	104	114
England	116	118	117	117	127	131	130	141	138	145	155
Scotland	93	95	96	89	94	99	91	89	93	95	103
Wales	83	91	92	90	92	91	96	92	89	91	95
Great Britain	112	114	114	113	121	124	123	131	130	136	145
All outside London	101	104	105	100	107	112	105	110	106	111	121

1 Net of Bus Service Operators Grant. Includes depreciation of vehicles.
2 Routes operated under contract to Transport for London
   on the London bus network and other scheduled local services.
3 Adjusted for general inflation to 2007/08 prices using the GDP Deflator.

☎020-7944 3076

6.17 Taxis: vehicles, drivers and fares: England and Wales: 1997-2007/08

										Thousands/Index	
	1997	1998	1999	2000	2001	2002	2003/04	2004/05	2005/06	2006/07	2007/08
London											
Number of licensed taxis [1]	18.9	19.4	19.2	20.9	20.5	20.5	20.8	20.7	21.4	21.6	21.8
Number of licensed drivers	22.3	22.7	23.3	23.7	24.5	24.5	24.8	24.7	24.7	24.6	24.7
Taxi fare index 1995=100 [2]	109	113	118	125	140	150	..	..	..	..	..
Private Hire Vehicles	..	..	..	..	..	..	..	32.4	39.9	44.4	46.9
Outside London											
Number of licensed taxis [1]	36.5	..	42.1	..	42.6	..	46	47	..	52	..
Number of licensed drivers [3]	83.2	..	98.2		96.4	..	48	48	..	47	..
Taxi fare index 1995=100 [2]	109	116	122	..	130	..	..	..	..	..	..
Private Hire Vehicles	66.2	..	..	..	..	..	80.8	..	..	85.7	..

1 Data for London are from TfL. Outside London they are from surveys of
   district councils and unitary authorities.
2 Fare changes are not collected each year. Fare rises usually
   take place in the spring in London, or at various times of the
   year outside London, so these indices can only give a guide.
3 Dual licensing of drivers for both taxis and PHVs may have overstated the figures from 1994 to 2001.

☎020-7944 3076

7 Roads and Traffic:

Notes and Definitions

Road traffic: 7.1, 7.2, 7.3 and 7.4

Special Note

Quality Review
1. The Department has undertaken a *Quality Review* of its road traffic estimates, under National Statistics guidelines. The report of this *Quality Review* was published in January 2007 and is available from the UK Statistical Authority website:

http://www.statistics.gov.uk/about/data/methodology/quality/reviews/transport.asp

Methodological Note
2. A revised short paper (*How National Traffic Estimates are Made*) outlining the full methodology used by the Department to calculate traffic estimates is now available online and from: Department for Transport, Statistics Roads 2 Division, Zone 3/17, Great Minster House, 76 Marsham Street, London SW1P 4DR.

Local Authority level statistics
3. Estimates of road traffic statistics at local authority level, together with corresponding figures for casualties in road accidents, are available on the DfT web site.

The local authority level traffic figures may differ to any figures produced by local authorities using local data and different methodologies. These traffic figures are less robust than the regional and national totals and are not designated as National Statistics.

Revisions to data
4. The road traffic and length estimates for 2006 have been revised. This is as a result of updates to the minor road lengths as well as the expansion factors and growth rates used to calculate major road estimates.

5. There are step changes in the minor road length figures in 2004 and 2006 due to changes in the base data. In 2004, amendments were made to the data for private roads in Scotland which had been incorrectly recorded as public roads. Since 2006, minor road length estimates have been made using Ordnance Survey's Integrated Transport Network (ITN) dataset, rather than the OSCAR dataset. This change in methodology leads to an increase in minor road lengths due to the greater accuracy of ITN.

End of Special Note

The total activity of traffic on the road network in Great Britain is measured in vehicle kilometres. In Table 7.2, road traffic is given by vehicle class and year. The traffic for each year is a function of the length of the public road network (kilometres) and the traffic flow (vehicles).

The Department produces estimates of annual average daily flow (AADF) for each link of the major road network. They are produced using 12-hour manual data counts from a large number of sites and traffic profiles derived from automatic counters at about 190 sites. The AADFs are available from www.dft.gov.uk/matrix

The definitions for the vehicle types included in the traffic census are given below:

All motor vehicles: All vehicles except pedal cycles.

Cars and taxis: Includes passenger vehicles with nine or fewer seats, three-wheeled cars and four wheel-drive 'sports utility vehicles'. Cars towing caravans or trailers are counted as one vehicle. The definition used for traffic statistics therefore differs from that used in the vehicle licensing statistics shown in tables 9.1-9.8.

Heavy goods vehicles (HGV): Includes all goods vehicles over 3.5 tonnes gross vehicle weight.

Rigid HGV with two axles: Includes all rigid heavy goods vehicles with two axles. Includes tractors (without trailers), road rollers, box vans and similar large vans. A two axle motor tractive unit without trailer is also included.

Rigid HGV with three axles: Includes all non-articulated goods vehicles with three axles irrespective of the position of the axles. Excludes two axle rigid vehicles towing a single axle caravan or trailer. Three axle motor tractive units without a trailer are also included.

Rigid HGV with four or more axles: Includes all non-articulated goods vehicles with four axles, regardless of the position of the axles. Excludes two or three axle rigid vehicles towing a caravan or trailer.

Articulated heavy goods vehicles: When a heavy goods vehicle is travelling with one or more axles raised from the road (sleeping axles or hobos) then the vehicle is classified into the class of the number of axles on the road, and not to the class of the total number of axles. Articulated goods vehicles with three and four axles are merged into one category, as they are not differentiated during manual traffic counts.

Articulated HGV with three axles (or with trailer): Includes all articulated goods vehicles with three axles. The motor tractive unit will have two axles and the trailer one. Also included in this class are two axle rigid goods vehicles towing a single axle caravan or trailer.

Articulated HGV with four axles (or with trailer): Includes all articulated vehicles with a total of four axles regardless of the position of the axles, i.e. two on the tractive unit with two on the trailer, or three on the tractive unit with one on the trailer. Also includes two axle rigid goods vehicles towing two axle close coupled or drawbar trailers.

Articulated HGV with five axles (or with trailer): This includes all articulated vehicles with a total of five axles regardless of the position of the axles. Also includes rigid vehicles drawing close coupled or drawbar trailers where the total axle number equals five and articulated vehicles where the motor tractive unit has more than one trailer and the total axle number equals five.

Articulated HGV with six or more axles (or with trailer): This includes all articulated vehicles with a total of six or more axles regardless of the position of the axles. Also includes rigid vehicles drawing close coupled or drawbar trailers where the total axle number equals six or more and articulated vehicles where the motor tractive unit has more than one trailer and the total axle number equals six or more.

Larger buses and coaches: Includes all public service vehicles and works buses over 3.5 tonnes gross vehicle weight.

Light vans: Goods vehicle not exceeding 3.5 tonnes gross vehicle weight. Includes all car-based vans and those of the next largest carrying capacity such as transit vans. Also included are ambulances, pickups and milk floats.

Motorcycles etc: Includes motorcycles, scooters and mopeds and all motorcycle or scooter combinations.

Pedal cycles: Includes all non-motorised cycles.

Forecasts of Road Traffic: 7.5

The forecasts in Table 7.5 are taken from the modelling and analytical work undertaken by the National Transport Model that lay behind the Department's publication entitled 'Road Transport Forecasts for England 2007'. The forecasts show traffic growth in England, disaggregated by vehicle type. The figures in the table are based to 2003 = 100. Further details of the Department's National Transport Model, the forecasts paper and separate forecasts for each English region can be found on the DfT web site. Full details of the Plan and underlying assumptions are given in Transport 2010: The 10 Year Plan and Background Analysis. A technical paper describing the improvements to the 1997 NRTF modelling framework will be made available shortly.
http://www.dft.gov.uk/pgr/economics/ntm/

Road network: 7.6, 7.8 and 7.9

The lengths of major roads are obtained from the major roads database maintained by the Department for Transport using information from the Government Offices, local authorities, the Scottish Government, the Welsh Assembly Government and Ordnance Survey. Road length information for minor 'B', 'C' and unclassified roads are obtained from Ordnance Survey roads data (the Integrated Transport Network dataset), local authorities, the Scottish Government and the Welsh Assembly Government. All figures given in tables 7.8 and 7.9 are road lengths at the 1st April of each year. The road definitions are as follows:

Major roads: Include motorways and all class 'A' roads. These roads usually have high traffic flows and are often the main arteries to major destinations.

Motorways (built under the enabling legislation of the *Special Roads Act 1949,* now consolidated in the *Highways Acts of 1959 and 1980*): Are major roads of regional and urban strategic importance, often used for long distance travel. They are usually three or more lanes in each direction and generally have the maximum speed limit of 70mph.

'A' Roads: Can be **trunk** or **principal** roads. These are often described as the 'main' roads and tend to have heavy traffic flows though not as high as motorways.

Trunk roads (designated by the Trunk roads Acts 1936 and 1946): Major roads comprising the national network of through routes. The network contains both motorways (which legally are special roads reserved for certain classes of traffic), and all-purpose roads (which are open to all classes of traffic). All-purpose trunk roads are class 'A' roads as are most principal roads, see below. It is very common for inter-urban stretches of a given road to be classed as an all purpose trunk road, with one or more urban stretches of the same (with the same road number) classified as principal.

In England, the trunk road highway authority is the Secretary of State for Transport, though certain responsibilities are delegated to the Highways Agency. The trunk road highway authority in Scotland is the Scottish Government, and the highways authority in Wales is the Welsh Assembly Government.

Non-trunk roads: Roads for which local authorities are highway authorities. The Secretary of State, the Scottish Government, and the Welsh Assembly Government have power to classify non-trunk roads in agreement with the local highway authority. Non-trunk roads are therefore either classified or unclassified, the former being of two types, principal and non-principal. The classified principal roads are class 'A' roads, except for a few local authority motorways, and are of regional and urban strategic importance. The non-principal roads are those which distribute traffic to urban and regional localities. The non-principal classified roads are sub-divided into 'B' and 'C' classes. Unclassified roads are those in the least important categories, i.e. local distributor and access roads.

Minor Roads: These are 'B' and 'C' classified roads and unclassified roads (all of which are maintained by the local authorities), as referred to above. Class III (later 'C') roads were created in April 1946. 'B' roads in urban areas can have relatively high traffic flows, but are not regarded as being as significant as 'A' roads, though in some cases may have similarly high flows. They are useful distributor roads often between towns or villages. 'B' roads in rural areas often have markedly low traffic flows compared with their 'A' road counterparts. 'C' Roads are regarded as of lesser importance than either 'B' or 'A' roads, and generally have only one carriageway of two lanes and carry less traffic. They can have low traffic flows in rural areas. Unclassified roads include residential roads both in urban and rural situations and rural lanes, the latter again normally having very low traffic flows. Most unclassified roads will have only two lanes, and in rural areas may only have one lane with "passing bays" at intervals to allow for two-way traffic flow.

Urban roads: Are major and minor roads within an urban area with a population of 10,000 or more. The definition is based on the 2001 Communities and Local Government definition of Urban Settlements. The definition for 'urban settlement' is in *Urban and rural area definitions: a user guide* which can be found on the Communities and Local Government web site.
Rural roads: Are major and minor roads outside urban areas (these urban areas have a population of more than 10,000 people).

Private Roads: Are included in the major roads as these private roads (usually toll roads, tunnels or bridges) are accessible to the general public, whereas private minor roads, not usually being accessible to the general public, are not included.

Vehicle speeds: 7.10 and 7.11

The types of vehicle analysed in the urban and non-urban survey are motor cycles, cars, cars towing, LGVs, buses/coaches, rigid 2 axles HGVs, rigid 3 and rigid 4 axles HGVs, 4 axles articulated HGVs and 5 or more axles articulated HGVs. The automatic counters identify rigid 2 axles lorries but cannot distinguish between vehicles weighing less than 7.5 tonnes gross and those weighing more. The weight of this type of vehicle determines its speed limit on non-urban roads. Consequently it is impossible to tell how many rigid 2 axles HGVs are speeding. (For further details of speed limits for different types of vehicle on different classes of non-built up road, see Annex B of *Vehicle Speeds* bulletin, produced by Transport Statistics DfT).

Non-urban roads (Table 7.10): The speeds indicated are average traffic speeds from 27 motorway sites, 7 dual carriageway sites and 26 single carriageway sites.

Urban roads (Table 7.11): Speed measurements were taken from 26 sites with speed limits of 30 mph and from 10 sites with speed limits of 40 mph.

Congestion on the Strategic Road Network in England: 7.12

The Strategic Road Network (SRN) in England consists of motorways and trunk 'A' roads (dual and single carriageway) that are managed by the Highways Agency, as well as the M6 Toll.

For monitoring purposes, the network has been split into 103 recognisable routes (for instance the A46 from Leicester to Lincoln). Each route has 2 directions, so there is a total of 206 route-directions. Currently 91 of the 103 routes are used to monitor network performance due to data quality considerations on the remaining 12 routes.

The Department monitors reliability using the average vehicle delay on the slowest 10% of journeys on the SRN. This indicator is used to measure performance against the Department's Public Service Agreement (PSA). For the Spending Review 2004, there was target to improve reliability between the baseline year ending July 2005 and the year ending March 2008. For the Comprehensive Spending Review 2007, the baseline is the year ending March 2008. The measure will be monitored until March 2011, though there is no specific numerical target.

Average vehicle delay is derived from the difference between observed journey times and a reference journey time (the time that could theoretically be achieved when the traffic is free flowing), weighting by traffic flows for each route of the network. The slowest 10% of journeys are selected for each 15-minute departure time between 6am and 8pm for each day of the week, on each of the 91 routes. The indicator therefore reflects journeys experienced on all types of route on all days at all times of the day.

The data used for the measure are from the Highways Agency's Traffic Information System, which brings together journey time and traffic flow data from several different sources.

Details of the methodology used for the measure are provided online:
http://www.dft.gov.uk/pgr/statistics/datatablespublications/roadstraffic/speedscongestion/congestiononthestrategicroad5359

Regional expenditure on roads: 7.13

Whereas the figures in Table 1.15 relate to net expenditure, those in Table 7.13 relate to gross expenditure. For this reason, and because of certain differences in coverage (in particular the treatment of professional and technical services), England totals differ from those in Table 1.16.

The local roads figure for new construction/ improvement plus structural maintenance includes expenditure on technical surveys. These figures include both expenditure recorded on local authority capital expenditure returns and also structural maintenance recorded on the revenue returns. Structural maintenance includes reconstruction, overlay, resurfacing, patching, surface dressing, drainage, footways, bridges, earthworks and fences. Routine maintenance includes verge maintenance, sweeping, gullies, signals, signs and marking. Winter maintenance includes salting, snow clearance and the maintenance and operation of ice detection equipment.

Figures for motorways and trunk roads are not directly comparable with previously published

data for years earlier than 2001/02, as the Highways Agency is now using a resource accounting system. The introduction of the new accounting systems has led to changes in categorisation and slight adjustments to the way some figures are calculated.

Road construction tender price index: 7.14

The overall index provides a measure of the change in tender prices for road construction in Great Britain. Since the end of June 1992, it has been based on bills of quantities for the winning tenders for new contracts with a works cost of £1 million or more. (Before that date the cut off was £250,000.) The index includes all HA national road - and local authority principal road - new build projects, and maintenance projects of appropriate value. The published annual figures are the derived from a quarterly series produced published by the Building Cost Information Service of the Royal Institution of Chartered Surveyors for Construction Market Intelligence Division of the Department for Business, Enterprise and Regulatory Reform.

For each project a price relative is produced by re-pricing, using 1990 prices, after making an adjustment for preliminary and balancing items, the quantifiable items in the bill of quantities. Then the total adjusted cost of the quantifiable items at current prices is divided by their total adjusted cost at 1990 prices, over all contracts, in order to calculate the project price relative. A value-weighted index calculated by combining the price relatives of a single quarter's contracts, often relatively few in number, would be over-sensitive to tender prices of individual large schemes. For this reason a smoothed quarterly series is produced based on adjustment factors for type of work, location and contract size

Road Tax Revenue: 7.15

Information on fuel tax revenues is collected by HMRC. Information on vehicle excise duty is collected by the Driver and Vehicle Licensing Agency (DVLA) and reported in financial returns and the motor tax account. These figures do not include revenues from trade plates but do include revenue from duties that are subsequently refunded. Vehicle numbers are averages based on quarterly analyses and therefore differ from the end year estimates given in section three.

Latest estimates on the level of revenue loss from vehicle excise duty evasion is available from a DfT report – 'Vehicle Excise Duty Evasion 2007' or at

'Vehicle Excise Duty Evasion 2007' or at www.dft.gov.uk/pgr/statistics/datatablespublicat ions/vehicles/excisedutyevasion

New road construction and improvements: 7.16

Start figures from 1996/97 onwards include schemes under Design, Build Finance and Operate (DBFO) contracts. These contracts, which are a part of the Private Finance Initiative, involve the private sector in the provision and improvement of sections of trunk road, or in a few cases of motorway, and in the management of both their own works and contiguous stretches of road over a lengthy period. The private sector provides the funding and is reimbursed by Government through payments linked to usage and performance.

In 1997/98, there were no new starts for any national schemes (including PFI schemes see above) that involved the construction of additional lane kilometres. This reflected policy decisions taken by the previous and present governments. There were no completions in 2001/02.

7.1 Road traffic by type of vehicle: 1949-2007
For greater detail for the years 1997-2007 see Table 7.2

Billion vehicle-kilometres

Year	Cars and taxis	Motor cycles etc	Larger buses & coaches	Light vans [1]	Goods vehicles [2]	All motor vehicles	Pedal cycles
1949	20.3	3.1	4.1	6.5	12.5	46.5	23.6
1950	25.6	4.4	4.1	7.8	11.2	53.1	19.9
1951	29.3	5.6	4.2	8.2	11.7	58.9	20.8
1952	30.6	6.0	4.2	8.7	11.3	60.8	22.9
1953	33.4	6.7	4.2	9.1	11.5	64.9	20.8
1954	37.2	6.9	4.2	9.3	12.2	69.7	18.8
1955	42.3	7.5	4.2	9.8	13.2	77.0	18.2
1956	46.2	7.4	4.2	10.0	13.0	80.8	16.2
1957	45.2	8.3	4.0	10.3	12.5	80.3	16.1
1958	55.4	8.4	3.9	11.9	13.5	93.0	14.1
1959	62.2	9.8	4.0	13.7	14.6	104.2	13.6
1960	68.0	10.0	3.9	15.0	15.3	112.3	12.0
1961	76.9	9.7	4.0	16.4	15.5	122.4	10.9
1962	83.7	8.7	4.0	16.6	15.4	128.3	9.3
1963	91.4	7.6	4.0	17.6	15.7	136.3	8.2
1964	105.7	7.5	4.0	17.7	17.4	152.3	8.0
1965	115.8	6.7	3.9	19.0	17.3	162.7	7.0
1966	126.5	6.0	3.9	19.0	17.5	172.9	6.3
1967	135.1	5.2	3.8	18.7	17.2	180.0	5.6
1968	142.7	4.7	3.8	18.9	17.6	187.7	5.0
1969	147.9	4.2	3.8	19.3	17.4	192.5	4.6
1970	155.0	4.0	3.6	20.3	17.6	200.5	4.4
1971	165.1	3.9	3.6	21.3	18.1	212.0	4.3
1972	174.7	3.7	3.6	22.2	18.4	222.5	3.9
1973	184.0	3.9	3.5	23.3	19.3	234.0	3.7
1974	180.0	4.2	3.3	23.6	18.6	229.7	3.8
1975	181.6	5.1	3.2	23.5	18.3	231.7	4.4
1976	190.4	6.3	3.3	24.2	19.2	243.5	5.0
1977	194.1	6.2	3.2	24.5	18.8	246.8	6.1
1978	202.4	6.1	3.3	25.2	19.5	256.5	5.1
1979	201.5	6.4	3.3	25.1	19.6	255.9	4.6
1980	215.0	7.7	3.5	26.1	19.7	271.9	5.1
1981	219.5	8.9	3.5	26.2	18.9	276.9	5.4
1982	227.3	9.2	3.5	26.0	18.4	284.5	6.4
1983	231.2	8.3	3.7	26.1	18.8	288.1	6.4
1984	244.0	8.1	3.9	27.5	19.6	303.1	6.4
1985	250.5	7.4	3.7	28.6	19.6	309.7	6.1
1986	264.4	7.1	3.7	30.0	20.1	325.3	5.5
1987	284.6	6.7	4.1	32.7	22.3	350.5	5.7
1988	305.4	6.0	4.3	36.2	23.8	375.7	5.2
1989	331.3	5.9	4.5	39.7	25.5	406.9	5.2
1990	335.9	5.6	4.6	39.9	24.9	410.8	5.3
1991	335.2	5.4	4.8	41.7	24.5	411.6	5.2
1992	338.0	4.5	4.6	41.2	23.8	412.1	4.7
1993 [3]	338.1	3.8	4.6	41.6	24.3	412.3	4.0
1994	345.0	3.8	4.6	43.3	24.8	421.5	4.0
1995	351.1	3.7	4.9	44.5	25.4	429.7	4.1
1996	359.9	3.8	5.0	46.2	26.2	441.1	4.1
1997	365.8	4.0	5.2	48.6	26.9	450.3	4.1
1998	370.6	4.1	5.2	50.8	27.7	458.5	4.0
1999	377.4	4.5	5.3	51.6	28.1	467.0	4.1
2000	376.8	4.6	5.2	52.3	28.2	467.1	4.2
2001	382.8	4.8	5.2	53.7	28.1	474.4	4.2
2002	392.9	5.1	5.2	55.0	28.3	486.5	4.4
2003	393.1	5.6	5.4	57.9	28.5	490.4	4.5
2004	398.1	5.2	5.2	60.8	29.4	498.6	4.2
2005	397.2	5.4	5.2	62.6	29.0	499.4	4.4
2006 [4]	402.6	5.2	5.4	65.2	29.1	507.5	4.6
2007	404.1	5.6	5.7	68.2	29.4	513.0	4.2

1 Not exceeding 3,500 kgs gross vehicle weight, post 1982
2 Over 3,500 kgs gross vehicle weight, post 1982.
3 Data for 1993 onwards are not directly comparable with the figures for 1992 and earlier.
4 Data for 2006 have been revised. See paragraph 4 of the notes and definitions for further detail.

☎020-7944 3095

7.2 Road Traffic: by type of vehicle: 1997-2007

Billion vehicle kilometres

	1997	1998	1999	2000 [1]	2001 [2]	2002	2003	2004	2005	2006 [5]	2007
Cars and taxis	365.8	370.6	377.4	376.8	382.8	392.9	393.1	398.1	397.2	402.6	404.1
Motor cycles etc	4.0	4.1	4.5	4.6	4.8	5.1	5.6	5.2	5.4	5.2	5.6
Larger buses and coaches	5.2	5.2	5.3	5.2	5.2	5.2	5.4	5.2	5.2	5.4	5.7
Light vans [3]	48.6	50.8	51.6	52.3	53.7	55.0	57.9	60.8	62.6	65.2	68.2
Goods vehicles [4]											
2 axles rigid	11.0	11.1	11.6	11.7	11.5	11.6	11.7	11.7	11.5	11.3	11.1
3 axles rigid	1.6	1.9	1.7	1.7	1.8	1.8	1.8	1.9	1.9	1.9	2.0
4 or more axles rigid	1.5	1.6	1.5	1.5	1.5	1.5	1.6	1.6	1.7	1.7	1.8
3 and 4 axles artic	3.2	3.0	3.0	2.7	2.5	2.3	2.2	2.2	2.0	1.9	1.8
5 axles artic	7.1	7.3	7.2	6.7	6.4	6.4	6.2	6.5	6.4	6.6	6.6
6 or more axles artic	2.5	2.9	3.3	4.1	4.5	4.8	5.0	5.4	5.5	5.7	6.1
All	26.9	27.7	28.1	28.2	28.1	28.3	28.5	29.4	29.0	29.1	29.4
All motor vehicles	450.3	458.5	467.0	467.1	474.4	486.5	490.4	498.6	499.4	507.5	513.0
Pedal cycles	4.1	4.0	4.1	4.2	4.2	4.4	4.5	4.2	4.4	4.6	4.2

1 The decline in the use of cars and taxis in 2000 was due to the fuel dispute.　☎020-7944 3095
2 Figures affected by the impact of Foot and Mouth disease during 2001.
3 Not exceeding 3,500 kgs gross vehicle weight.
4 Over 3,500 kgs gross vehicle weight.
5 Data for 2006 have been revised. See paragraph 4 of the notes and definitions for further detail.

7.3 Motor vehicle traffic: by road class: 1997-2007

Billion vehicle kilometres

	1997	1998	1999	2000 [1]	2001 [2]	2002	2003	2004	2005	2006 [6]	2007
Motorways	82.1	85.7	87.8	88.4	90.8	92.6	93.0	96.6	97.0	99.4	100.6
Rural 'A' roads: [3]											
Trunk [5]	62.5	63.3	64.7	64.2	65.9	64.6	61.5	59.7	58.0	59.2	58.6
Principal [5]	64.1	65.4	66.0	65.8	67.4	71.8	77.7	81.6	83.3	84.4	84.9
All rural 'A' roads	126.6	128.7	130.7	130.0	133.3	136.4	139.3	141.3	141.3	143.6	143.5
Urban 'A' roads: [4]											
Trunk [5]	13.8	13.8	14.0	14.0	7.6	7.4	6.7	6.0	5.5	5.6	5.4
Principal [5]	67.1	67.5	67.9	67.7	74.2	74.8	75.1	76.8	76.2	76.9	75.9
All urban 'A' roads	80.9	81.3	81.9	81.7	81.8	82.2	81.7	82.8	81.7	82.5	81.3
All Major roads	289.6	295.7	300.4	300.0	305.9	311.2	314.0	320.7	320.1	325.5	325.4
Minor roads:											
Minor rural roads	60.0	60.4	61.3	61.5	61.6	64.5	64.4	65.9	66.8	69.3	72.0
Minor urban roads	100.7	102.4	105.3	105.5	106.9	110.8	111.9	112.0	112.5	112.7	115.5
All minor roads	160.7	162.8	166.6	167.0	168.5	175.3	176.4	177.9	179.3	182.0	187.5
All roads	450.3	458.5	467.0	467.1	474.4	486.5	490.4	498.6	499.4	507.5	513.0

1 The decline in the use of cars and taxis in 2000 was due to the fuel dispute.　☎020-7944 3095
2 Figures affected by the impact of Foot and Mouth disease during 2001.
3 Rural roads: Major and minor roads, from 1993 onwards, are defined as being outside an urban area (see definition below).
4 Urban roads: Major and minor roads, from 1993 onwards, are defined as within an urban area with a population
   of 10,000 or more. These are based on the 2001 urban settlements. The definition for 'urban settlement' is in
   Urban and rural area definitions: a user guide which can be found on the Communities and Local Government
   web site at:
   http://www.communities.gov.uk/publications/planningandbuilding/urbanrural
5 Figures for trunk and principal 'A' roads in England, from 2001 onwards, are affected by the detrunking programme.
6 Data for 2006 have been revised. See paragraph 4 of the notes and definitions for further detail.

7.4 Road traffic: by type of vehicle and class of road: 2007

Billion vehicle kilometres

	Cars and taxis	Motor cycles etc.	Larger buses and coaches	Light vans²	Goods vehicles¹ Rigid by number of axles			Articulated by number of axles			All Goods vehicles	All motor vehicles	Pedal cycles
					2	3	4 or more	3 + 4	5	6 or more			
Motorways:	74.9 -	0.4	0.6	12.4	3.1	0.5	0.5	0.8	4.0	3.3	12.3 -	100.6	.
Rural 'A' roads: ³													
Trunk ⁴	44.4 -	0.4	0.4	7.6	1.8	0.3	0.3	0.4	1.5	1.5	5.8 -	58.6	-
Principal ⁴	67.7 -	0.8	0.6	11.1	2.1	0.4	0.5	0.3	0.7	0.7	4.7 -	84.9	0.1
All rural 'A' roads:	112.1 -	1.2	1.0	18.7	3.9	0.7	0.8	0.7	2.2	2.3	10.5 -	143.5	0.1
Urban 'A' roads: ⁵													
Trunk ⁴	4.3 -	0.0	0.0	0.7	0.1	0.0	0.0	0.0	0.1	0.1	0.4 -	5.4	-
Principal ⁴	62.1 -	1.0	1.2	9.3	1.4	0.2	0.3	0.1	0.2	0.2	2.5 -	75.9	0.6
All urban 'A' roads:	66.3 -	1.0	1.2	9.9	1.6	0.2	0.3	0.1	0.3	0.3	2.8 -	81.3	0.6
Minor roads:													
Minor rural roads	56.2 -	0.9	0.8	12.2	1.2	0.3	0.2	0.1	0.1	0.1	2.0 -	72.0	0.9
Minor urban roads	94.6 -	2.1	2.2	14.9	1.3	0.2	0.1	0.1	0.0	0.1	1.7 -	115.5	2.7
All minor roads:	150.8 -	3.0	3.0	27.2	2.5	0.5	0.3	0.1	0.1	0.2	3.7 -	187.5	3.5
All roads:	404.1 -	5.6	5.7	68.2	11.1	2.0	1.8	1.8	6.6	6.1	29.4 -	513.0	4.2

1 Over 3,500 kgs gross vehicle weight.
2 Not exceeding 3,500 kgs gross vehicle weight.
3 Rural roads: Major and minor roads, from 1993 onwards, are defined as being outside an urban area.
4 Figures for trunk and principal 'A' roads in England are affected by the detrunking programme.
5 Urban roads: Major and minor roads, from 1993 onwards, are defined as within an urban area with a population of 10,000 or more. These are based on the 2001 urban settlements. The definition for 'urban settlement' is in *Urban and rural area definitions: a user guide* which can be found on the Communities and Local Government web site at:
http://www.communities.gov.uk/publications/planningandbuilding/urbanrural
NB: Versions of this table for the years 1993-2006 are available from the DfT website at:
http://www.dft.gov.uk/pgr/statistics/datatablespublications/roadstraffic

☎020-7944 3095

7.5 Forecasts of road traffic in England and vehicles in Great Britain:¹ 2010-2025

Index: 2000 = 100 ¹

	2003	2010	2015	2025
Vehicle kilometres: England:				
Cars and taxis	100	111	120	127
Goods vehicles ²	100	104	106	112
Light goods vehicles	100	117	134	167
Buses and coaches	100	100	100	100
All motor traffic (except two wheelers)	100	111	121	131
Car ownership: Great Britain:				
Cars per person	100	107	110	116
Number of cars	100	111	119	133

1 The traffic forecasts are central forecasts taken from the Department's Road Transport Forecasts for England 2007. The paper also contains: a forecast range reflecting uncertainties in the key forecasting assumptions that affect travel demand; and a break down of the forecasts by region.
2 Over 3.5 tonnes gross vehicle weight.
3 Car Ownership Data is taken from TEMPRO (Ver 5.4)

☎020-7944 6197
The figures in this table are outside of the scope of National Statistics
Source - Integrated Transport, Economics

7.6 Roads lengths: Great Britain: 1914-2007

For greater detail for the years 1997-2007 see Table 7.8 or 7.9.

Kilometres

Year	Trunk	Class 1 or principal	Class 2 or B	Class 3 or C	Unclassified	All	ow: motorways		
							Trunk	Principal	Total
1914	..	..	..	.	..	284,843	.	.	.
1923	.	37,383	23,720	.	224,265	285,369	.	.	.
1928	.	40,457	25,244	.	221,996	287,697	.	.	.
1933	.	42,784	26,786	.	215,842	285,412	.	.	.
1938	4,953	39,276	27,418	.	217,799	289,446	.	.	.
1943	7,176	37,305	28,532	.	..	..	.	.	.
1947	13,181	31,410	28,498	77,768	143,735	294,592	.	.	.
1951	13,275	31,435	28,481	78,346	145,929	297,466	.	.	.
1952	13,274	31,484	28,471	78,340	147,002	298,570	.	.	.
1953	13,284	31,464	28,485	78,364	148,161	299,758	.	.	.
1954	13,309	31,519	28,469	78,409	149,305	301,012	.	.	.
1955	13,309	31,553	28,479	78,505	150,863	302,710	.	.	.
1956	13,309	31,656	28,398	78,565	152,297	304,226	.	.	.
1957	13,311	31,762	28,333	78,615	153,998	306,018	.	.	.
1958	13,372	31,714	28,329	78,621	155,583	307,620	.	.	.
1959	13,401	31,744	28,329	78,653	158,573	310,700	13	.	13
1960	13,580	31,765	28,334	78,718	160,106	312,502	153	.	153
1961	13,628	31,780	28,357	78,740	161,667	314,171	209	10	219
1962	13,654	31,797	28,349	78,785	163,064	315,649	233	10	243
1963	13,745	31,860	28,337	78,829	166,611	319,382	312	10	322
1964	13,885	31,902	28,368	78,837	168,463	321,455	470	10	480
1965	13,993	31,971	28,392	78,855	170,357	323,568	557	10	566
1966	14,030	32,053	28,376	78,858	171,865	325,182	616	13	629
1967	14,159	32,543	..	279,479 [1]	..	326,180	747	11	761 [2]
1968	14,354	32,536	..	281,288 [1]	..	328,178	869	11	884 [2]
1969	14,439	32,533	107,254 [3]	..	166,089	320,315	946	18	964
1970	14,463	32,584	107,285 [3]	..	168,152	322,484	1,022	35	1,057
1971	14,668	32,737	107,388 [3]	..	169,872	324,665	1,235	35	1,270
1972	15,060	32,825	107,404 [3]	..	172,428	327,717	1,609	60	1,669
1973	15,011	32,859	27,409	79,791	172,060	327,131	1,660	70	1,730
1974	15,119	32,942	27,500	80,062	173,443	329,036	1,776	92	1,869
1975	15,240	33,088	27,606	80,156	173,949	330,039	1,881	94	1,975
1976	15,502	33,225	27,812	80,512	175,794	332,846	2,062	93	2,155
1977	15,223	33,598	27,875	80,693	177,874	335,263	2,131	106	2,237
1978	14,820	34,199	27,874	80,545	178,826	336,264	2,287	107	2,394
1979	14,805	34,430	27,866	80,599	180,278	337,978	2,340	116	2,455
1980	14,949	34,187	28,151	80,736	181,610	339,633	2,445	111	2,556
1981	14,915	34,656	28,232	80,398	184,119	342,320	2,524	123	2,647
1982	14,901	34,700	28,451	80,358	185,531	343,942	2,561	131	2,692
1983	14,972	34,819	28,537	80,327	187,121	345,776	2,609	132	2,741
1984	15,057	34,862	29,036	80,123	188,511	347,589	2,678	108	2,786
1985	15,014	34,908	29,042	80,460	189,276	348,699	2,705	108	2,813
1986	15,359	34,969	29,121	80,360	191,267	351,076	2,820	101	2,920
1987	15,394	35,089	29,766	80,004	192,442	352,695	2,874	101	2,975
1988	15,472	35,041	29,681	80,165	193,957	354,315	2,891	102	2,992
1989	15,618	35,131	29,706	80,542	195,606	356,602	2,903	92	2,995
1990	15,666	35,226	29,838	80,716	196,588	358,034	2,993	77	3,070
1991	15,356	35,649	30,106	81,073	197,783	359,966	3,033	68	3,102
1992	15,358	35,712	30,227	81,334	199,679	362,310	3,063	71	3,133
1993 [4]	14,819	34,514	30,229	83,816	221,461	384,839	3,139	72	3,211
1994	14,815	34,574	30,225	83,931	222,012	385,557	3,170	72	3,242
1995	14,840	34,732	30,221	84,046	222,562	386,401	3,197	72	3,269
1996	14,967	34,522	30,217	84,162	223,115	386,983	3,253	45	3,298
1997	15,131	34,603	30,213	84,277	223,668	387,893	3,333	45	3,378
1998	15,058	34,758	30,209	84,392	224,225	388,641	3,376	44	3,421
1999	15,102	34,916	30,205	84,509	224,783	389,515	3,404	45	3,449
2000	15,123	34,951	30,200	84,624	225,339	390,237	3,422	45	3,467
2001	14,800 [5]	35,330 [5]	30,196	84,742	225,901	390,969	3,431	45	3,476
2002	14,112	36,040	30,192	84,858	226,462	391,663	3,433	45	3,478
2003	13,047	37,083	30,188	84,976	227,048	392,342	3,432	46	3,478
2004	12,625	37,567	30,178 [6]	84,223 [6]	223,082 [6]	387,674 [6]	3,478	46	3,523
2005	12,148	38,028	30,189	84,459	223,184	388,008	3,466	54	3,519
2006	12,219	38,097	30,018 [6]	84,469 [6]	229,605 [6]	394,409 [6]	3,503	53	3,555
2007	12,201	38,101	30,265	84,423	229,889	394,879	3,518	41	3,559

1 Includes 'B' and unclassified roads.
2 Includes other motorways i.e. those not at the time allocated to either the Department for Transport or local authorities.
3 Includes 'C' roads.
4 A number of minor revisions have been made to the lengths of major roads from 1993 onwards.
5 Figures for trunk and principal 'A' roads in England, from 2001 onwards, are affected by the detrunking programme.
6 New information from 2004 and from 2006 has enabled better estimates of Minor Road lengths to be made - see notes and definitions.

☎020-7944 3095

7.7 Motorway and trunk road network of England, Scotland and Wales: March 2008

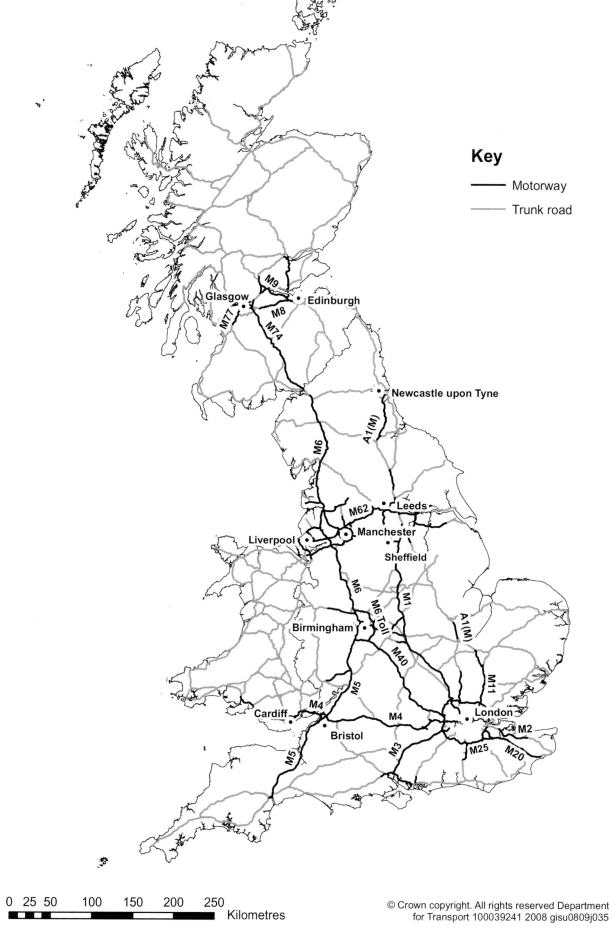

Key
— Motorway
— Trunk road

0 25 50 100 150 200 250 Kilometres

7.8 Public road length: by road type: [1] 1997-2007

Kilometres

	1997	1998	1999	2000	2001	2002	2003	2004	2005	2006 [6]	2007
Trunk motorway	3,333	3,376	3,404	3,422	3,431	3,433	3,432	3,478	3,466	3,503	3,518
Principal motorway	45	44	45	45	45	45	46	46	54	53	41
Rural 'A' roads: [2]											
Trunk [3]	10,690	10,585	10,611	10,627	10,607	9,973	9,027	8,641	8,239	8,277	8,258
Principal [3]	24,636	24,783	24,852	24,866	24,915	25,559	26,498	26,889	27,312	27,336	27,346
All rural 'A' roads:	35,326	35,369	35,463	35,493	35,522	35,532	35,525	35,530	35,550	35,612	35,603
Urban 'A' roads: [4]											
Trunk [3]	1,108	1,096	1,087	1,074	762	705	587	506	444	446	425
Principal [3]	9,923	9,931	10,019	10,040	10,370	10,436	10,539	10,632	10,663	10,696	10,714
All urban 'A' roads:	11,031	11,027	11,106	11,114	11,132	11,141	11,127	11,138	11,107	11,143	11,139
Minor rural roads: [5]											
B roads	24,594	24,586	24,579	24,570	24,562	24,554	24,547	24,640	24,639	24,574	24,795
C roads	73,312	73,405	73,500	73,593	73,688	73,783	73,878	73,363	73,581	73,548	73,480
Unclassified	110,915	111,132	111,350	111,568	111,787	112,006	112,231	109,561	109,426	115,250	115,365
All minor rural roads	208,820	209,123	209,429	209,731	210,037	210,343	210,656	207,565	207,646	213,371	213,641
Minor urban roads: [5]											
B roads	5,618	5,622	5,626	5,630	5,633	5,638	5,641	5,538	5,550	5,445	5,470
C roads	10,966	10,986	11,009	11,031	11,054	11,076	11,098	10,859	10,878	10,921	10,942
Unclassified	112,754	113,093	113,432	113,772	114,114	114,456	114,816	113,520	113,757	114,355	114,524
All minor urban roads	129,338	129,702	130,068	130,432	130,802	131,169	131,556	129,917	130,186	130,721	130,936
All major roads	49,735	49,816	50,018	50,074	50,130	50,152	50,130	50,192	50,176	50,310	50,302
All minor roads: [5]	338,158	338,825	339,496	340,163	340,838	341,512	342,212	337,482	337,832	344,092	344,577
All roads	387,893	388,641	389,515	390,237	390,969	391,663	392,342	387,674	388,008	394,402	394,879

1 A number of minor revisions have been made to the lengths of major roads from 1993 onwards.
2 Rural roads: Major and minor roads, from 1993 onwards, are defined as being outside an urban area.
3 Figures for trunk and principal 'A' roads in England, from 2001 onwards, are affected by the detrunking programme.
4 Urban roads: Major and minor roads, from 1993 onwards, are defined as within an urban area with a population
  of 10,000 or more. These are based on the 2001 urban settlements. The definition for 'urban settlement' is in
  Urban and rural area definitions: a user guide which can be found on the Communities and Local
  Government web site at:
  http://www.communities.gov.uk/publications/planningandbuilding/urbanrural
5 New information from 2004 and from 2006 has enabled better estimates of minor road lengths to be made - see notes and definitions
6 Data for minor roads in 2006 have been revised. See paragraph 4 of the notes and definitions for further detail.

☎020-7944 3095

7.9 Public road length: by class of road and country: 2007

Kilometres

	England	Wales	Scotland	Great Britain
Motorways:				
Trunk	2,970	141	407	3,518
Principal	41	-	-	41
Dual Carriageway:				
Trunk urban [1,2]	200	19	50	269
Trunk rural [1,3]	2,430	329	459	3,218
Principal urban [1,2]	2,361	104	185	2,650
Principal rural [1,3]	1,613	97	89	1,799
Single Carriageway:				
Trunk urban [1,2]	89	29	38	156
Trunk rural [1,3]	1,597	1,170	2,273	5,040
Principal urban [1,2]	7,059	371	634	8,064
Principal rural [1,3]	16,926	2,047	6,574	25,547
B roads [4]	19,963	2,982	7,320	30,265
C roads [4]	64,207	9,797	10,419	84,423
Unclassified roads [4]	181,983	16,775	31,131	229,889
Total	301,440	33,861	59,578	394,879

1 Figures for trunk and principal 'A' roads in England, from 2001 onwards, are affected by the detrunking programme. ☎020-7944 3095
2 Urban roads: Major and minor roads, from 1993 onwards, are defined as within an urban area with a population
   of 10,000 or more. These are based on the 2001 urban settlements. The definition for 'urban settlement' is in
   Urban and rural area definitions: a user guide which can be found on the Communities and Local
   Government web site at:
   http://www.communities.gov.uk/publications/planningandbuilding/urbanrural
3 Rural roads: Major and minor roads, from 1993 onwards, are defined as being outside an urban area.
4 New information from 2004 and from 2006 has enabled better estimates of minor road lengths to be made - see notes and definitions

7.10 Vehicle speeds on non-built-up roads by road type and vehicle type: Great Britain: 2007

per cent

| | | | | | | Heavy goods vehicles [5] | | | | |
| | | | | | | Rigid | | | Articulated | |
(a) Motorways [1]	Motor-cycles [7]	Cars	Cars towing	Light Goods [4]	Buses/ Coaches	2 axles [6]	3 axles	4 axles	4 axles	5+ axles
Under 50 mph	5	4	12	4	5	7	11	13	7	8
50-59 mph	23	12	53	15	46	50	81	85	89	90
60-64 mph	8	12	20	13	33	12	7	1	2	1
65-69 mph	12	18	10	17	7	11	1	0	1	0
70-74 mph	14	20	4	19	5	9	0	0	1	0
75-79 mph	14	16	1	15	3	6	0	0	0	0
80-89 mph	18	15	0	14	2	4	0	0	0	0
90 mph and over	7	3	0	3	0	1	0	0	0	0
Speed limit (mph)	70	70	58	70	60	61	54	54	54	54
Percentage more than 10 mph over limit	25	18	5	17	3	n/a	0	1	1	0
Average speed (mph)	70	70	58	70	60	61	54	54	54	54
Number observed (thousands)	3,243	423,289	2,934	63,161	3,536	27,665	2,625	1,645	7,778	40,387
(b) Dual carriageways [2]										
Under 30 mph	0	0	1	0	0	0	0	0	1	0
30-39 mph	1	0	1	0	1	1	2	1	1	1
40-49 mph	5	3	16	3	9	9	20	19	18	15
50-59 mph	20	15	50	17	54	47	69	77	76	82
60-64 mph	9	16	17	15	25	13	7	1	2	1
65-69 mph	13	20	9	19	6	11	1	0	1	0
70-79 mph	29	33	5	32	5	14	1	1	1	0
80 mph and over	23	12	0	13	1	4	0	0	0	0
Speed limit (mph)	70	70	60	70	60	n/a	50	50	50	50
Percentage more than 10 mph over limit	23	12	6	13	6	n/a	9	3	5	2
Average speed (mph)	69	69	56	68	58	60	53	53	53	53
Number observed (thousands)	399	45,106	378	5,708	328	2,197	264	186	425	2,076
(c) Single carriageways [3]										
Under 20 mph	1	0	2	0	1	1	1	1	1	0
20-29 mph	3	2	7	3	3	3	6	6	5	2
30-39 mph	11	16	20	16	20	19	25	26	23	23
40-49 mph	30	41	48	40	50	45	50	46	48	49
50-59 mph	28	30	22	30	24	26	17	21	22	25
60-64 mph	9	6	2	6	2	3	0	0	1	1
65-69 mph	6	2	0	3	0	1	0	0	0	0
70 mph and over	12	2	0	2	0	1	0	0	0	0
Speed limit (mph)	60	60	50	60	50	n/a	40	40	40	40
Percentage more than 10 mph over limit	12	2	2	2	3	n/a	18	21	23	26
Average speed (mph)	53	48	43	48	45	46	43	43	44	45
Number observed (thousands)	543	51,337	617	6,355	434	2,456	337	247	455	2,455

1 Average vehicle speeds from 27 motorway sites.
2 Average vehicle speeds from 7 dual carriageway sites.
3 Average vehicle speeds from 26 single carriageway sites.
4 Goods vehicles 3.5 tonnes gross weight and under.
5 Goods vehicles over 3.5 tonnes gross weight.
6 Speed limit depends on loading which cannot be determined.
7 Motorcycles include mopeds and other types of two wheeled motor vehicles.

☎020-7944 6397

7.11: Vehicle speeds on built-up roads by speed limit and vehicle type: Great Britain: 2007

(a) 30 mph speed limit roads [1]   per cent

| | Motor-cycles [3] | Cars | Cars towing | Light goods [4] | Buses/ Coaches | Heavy goods vehicles [5] | | | | |
| | | | | | | Rigid | | | Articulated | |
						2 axles	3 axles	4 axles	4 axles	5+ axles
Under 20 mph	10	6	7	8	11	10	9	6	7	4
20-29 mph	39	44	50	41	63	45	49	44	48	50
30-34 mph	26	30	32	30	20	28	32	36	32	36
35-39 mph	14	13	9	15	5	12	8	11	10	9
40-44 mph	6	4	2	5	1	4	1	2	2	1
45-49 mph	3	1	0	1	0	1	0	0	0	0
50 mph and over	2	0	0	1	0	1	0	0	0	0
Percent over 35 mph	26	19	11	22	7	18	10	14	13	11
Average speed (mph)	31	30	29	30	27	29	29	30	29	30
Number observed (thousands)	646	58,529	142	5,756	591	1,740	119	128	88	178

(b) 40 mph speed limit roads [2]   per cent

| | Motor-cycles [3] | Cars | Cars towing | Light goods [4] | Buses/ Coaches | Heavy goods vehicles [5] | | | | |
| | | | | | | Rigid | | | Articulated | |
						2 axles	3 axles	4 axles	4 axles	5+ axles
Under 20 mph	4	3	4	4	4	5	4	3	6	3
20 - 29 mph	12	13	19	14	16	16	16	12	14	14
30 - 34 mph	21	27	29	25	31	26	24	21	24	23
35 - 39 mph	28	32	32	31	35	30	36	38	35	40
40 - 44 mph	18	15	13	16	10	14	15	19	15	16
45 - 49 mph	10	6	3	7	2	5	3	5	4	3
50 - 59 mph	6	2	1	3	1	2	1	1	2	1
60 mph and over	2	0	0	1	0	0	0	0	0	0
Percent over 45 mph	18	9	4	11	3	8	4	7	6	4
Average speed (mph)	38	36	34	36	34	35	35	36	35	36
Number observed (thousands)	815	52,868	231	6,137	557	1,970	231	186	199	519

1 Average vehicle speeds from 26 sites.
2 Average vehicle speeds from 10 sites.
3 Motorcycles includes mopeds and other types of two wheeled motor vehicles.
4 Goods vehicles 3.5 tonnes gross weight and under.
5 Goods vehicles over 3.5 tonnes gross weight.

☎020-7944 6397

7.12 Journey time reliability measure[1] on the Strategic Road Network: England
      Years ending July 2005 to July 2008

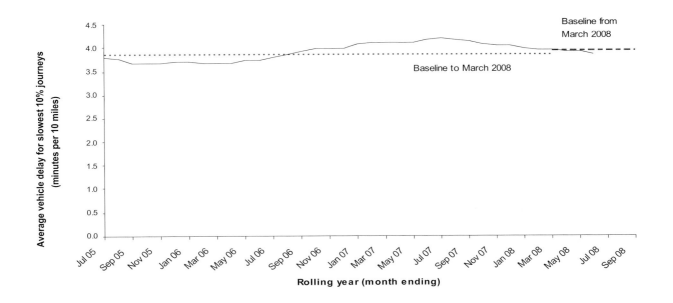

[1] Average vehicle delay for the slowest 10% of journeys.

☎020-7944 6392

7.13 Regional expenditure on roads: 2006/07

£ Million

	North East	Yorkshire and the Humber	North West	East Midlands	West Midlands	East of England	South East	London	South West	England
Motorways and trunk roads: [1]										
New construction/improvement and structural maintenance	46.7	73.3	200.5	199.9	255.8	226.2	307.4	20.2	290.9	1620.8
Current maintenance, including routine and winter maintenance [2]	18.6	26.7	67.6	54.8	69.8	65.1	86.9	5.4	87.1	482.0
DBFO shadow tolls [3]	34.0	75.5	-	16.3	-	27.8	33.6	-	54.8	242.1
Local Roads: [4]										
New construction/improvement for highways, lighting, road safety and structural maintenance [5]	146.7	287.6	333.7	236.0	301.9	363.1	358.7	411.7	290.5	2730.0
Revenue expenditure on bridge structural maintenance and strengthening	2.6	3.8	4.1	2.8	5.6	4.8	6.2	20.8	7.6	58.3
Routine and winter maintenance	38.2	96.9	135.1	78.8	92.7	107.0	169.3	250.0	100.9	1068.9
Revenue expenditure on road safety	10.9	13.7	22.8	16.2	32.3	24.4	29.8	237.1	12.4	399.6
Revenue expenditure on public lighting	39.4	43.9	66.7	31.3	43.7	37.6	50.2	57.9	36.9	407.5
All road expenditure	337.1	621.5	830.5	636.1	801.8	856.0	1042.1	1003.2	881.0	7009.2

1 Figures are now collected on a resource accounting basis and cannot be compared with data prior to 2001/02. ☎020-7944 4746
   Until 2001/02, associated costs of investment (including depreciation and capital costs) were not included within
   these figures. Apportionment between the Government Office Regions involves an estimation process.
2 Until 2001/02, this table showed figures for 'routine and winter maintenance and public lighting'
   Highways Agency is no longer able to separately identify this expenditure and this now falls within the wider category
   'Current maintenance, including routine and winter maintenance.'
3 Payments to contractors under Design, Build, Finance and Operate (DBFO) schemes.
4 Local authority expenditure excludes car parks.
5 Includes expenditure on 'patching'.

Source - Highways Agency Financial Accounts and local authority returns to DfT

7.14 Road construction tender price index: 1997-2007

1990=100

Year	1997	1998	1999	2000	2001	2002	2003	2004	2005	2006	2007
All roads	124	123	125	142	146	151	149	152	168	186	193 [p]

☎020-7944 3092
The figures in this table are outside
the scope of National Statistics

7.15 Road taxation revenue in 2006/07

(a) Vehicle Excise Duty classified by vehicle taxation group	Number of vehicles (thousand)	Road taxes (£million) Vehicle excise duty
Private and light goods	29,856	4,778
Motorcycles, scooters and mopeds	1,097	51
Buses and coaches	107	30
Goods	444	296
Other	2,095	64
All vehicles	33,599	5,220

(b) Fuel tax classified by propulsion type	Petrol	Diesel	Total
	11,610	11,600	23,210

☎020-7944 6386
The road tax figures in this table
outside the scope of National Statistics
Source - HMRC and DVLA

7.16 New road construction and improvement: motorways and all purpose trunk roads: England: 1997/98-2007/08

(a) Starts	1997/98	1998/99	1999/00	2000/01	2001/02	2002/03	2003/04	2004/05	2005/06	2006/07	2007/08
Route kilometres	0 [1]	10	20	23	5	21	51	30	69	65	59 [P]
Lane kilometres	0 [1]	65	126	95	18	65	195	82	153	178	104 [P]
(b) Completions											
Route kilometres	133	96	40	38	0 [1]	56	113	49	37	50	42 [P]
Lane kilometres	657	559	160	197	0 [1]	191	446	172	108	110	109 [P]

1 See comments on Table 7.16 in the Notes and Definitions.

☎020-7944 3092
The figures in this table are outside
the scope of National Statistics
Source - Highways Agency

135

8 Transport Accidents and Casualties:

Notes and Definitions

Road accidents and casualties: 8.1- 8.5

The statistics in these tables refer to personal injury accidents occurring on the public highway (including footways) in which at least one road vehicle or a vehicle in collision with a pedestrian is involved and which become known to the police within 30 days of its occurrence. The vehicle need not be moving and accidents involving stationary vehicles and pedestrians or users are included. One accident may give rise to several casualties. "Damage-only" accidents are not included in this publication.

Very few, if any, fatal accidents do not become known to the police. However, research conducted on behalf of the Department in the 1990s has shown that a significant proportion of non-fatal injury accidents are not reported to the police. In addition some casualties reported to the police are not recorded and the severity of injury tends to be underestimated. The Department is undertaking further research to investigate whether the levels of reporting have changed. The most recent work on levels of reporting was published by the Department in Article 6 of Road Casualties Great Britain: 2007 Annual report, which can be found at:

http://www.dft.gov.uk/pgr/statistics/datatablespublications/accidents/

Definitions of terms used in the tables:

Accident: Involves personal injury occurring on the public highway (including footways) in which at least one road *vehicle* or a *vehicle* in collision with a *pedestrian* is involved and which becomes known to the police within 30 days of its occurrence. The *vehicle* need not be moving and accidents involving stationary vehicles and pedestrians or users are included. One accident may give rise to several *casualties*. "Damage-only" accidents are not included in this publication.

Adults: Persons aged 16 years and over (except where otherwise stated).

Cars: Includes taxis, estate cars, three and four wheel cars and minibuses except where

otherwise stated. Also includes motor caravans prior to 1999.

Bus or coach: *Vehicles* equipped to carry 17 or more *passengers* regardless of use.

Casualty: A person *killed* or *injured* in an *accident*. Casualties are sub-divided into *killed, seriously injured* and *slightly injured*.

Children: Persons under 16 years of age (except where otherwise stated).

Drivers: Persons in control of *vehicles* other than *pedal cycles, motorcycles* and ridden animals (see *riders*). Other occupants of *vehicles* are *passengers*.

Failed breath test: Drivers or *riders* tested with a positive result, or who failed or refused to provide a specimen of breath.

Fatal accident: An accident in which at least one person is *killed.*

Goods vehicles: These are divided into two groups according to vehicle weight (see below). They include tankers, tractor units travelling without their semi-trailers, trailers, articulated vehicles and pick-up trucks.

> *Heavy goods vehicles (HGV)*: Goods vehicles over 3.5 tonnes maximum permissible gross vehicle weight (gvw).

> *Light goods vehicles (LGV)*: Goods vehicles, mainly vans (including car derived vans), not over 3.5 tonnes maximum permissible gross vehicle weight (gvw).

Killed: Human casualties who sustained injuries which caused death less than 30 days(before 1954, about two months) after the *accident.* Confirmed suicides are excluded.

Motorcycles: Mopeds, motor scooters and motor cycles (including motor cycle combinations).

Motorways: "M" roads and "A"(M) roads.

Other roads: All "B", "C" class and unclassified roads, unless otherwise noted.

Other vehicles: Other motor vehicles include ambulances, fire engines, trams, refuse vehicles, road rollers, agricultural vehicles, excavators, mobile cranes, electric scooters and motorised wheelchairs etc. Other non motor vehicles include those drawn by animal, ridden horses, invalid carriages without a motor, street barrows etc.

Passengers: Occupants of *vehicles*, other than the person in control (the *driver* or *rider*). Includes pillion passengers.

Pedal cycles: Includes tandems, tricycles and toy cycles ridden on the carriageway.

Pedal cyclists: Riders of *pedal cycles*, including any *passengers*. From 1983 the definition includes a small number of cycles and tricycles with battery assistance with a maximum speed of 15 mph.

Pedestrians: Includes *children* riding toy cycles on the footway, persons pushing bicycles, pushing or pulling other *vehicles* or operating pedestrian controlled vehicles, those leading or herding animals, occupants of prams or wheelchairs, and people who alight safely from vehicles and are subsequently injured.

Riders: Persons in control of *pedal cycles, motorcycles* or ridden animals. Other occupants of these *vehicles* are *passengers*.

Rural roads: Major roads and minor roads outside urban areas and having a population of less than 10 thousand.

Severity: Of an accident: the severity of the most severely injured casualty (fatal, serious or slight). Of a casualty: killed, seriously injured or slightly injured.

Serious accident: One in which at least one person is *seriously injured* but no person (other than a confirmed suicide) is *killed*.

*Serious injury: a*n injury for which a person is detained in hospital as an "in-patient", or any of the following injuries whether or not they are detained in hospital: fractures, concussion, internal injuries, crushings, burns (excluding friction burns), severe cuts, severe general shock requiring medical treatment and injuries causing death 30 or more days after the *accident*. An injured *casualty* is recorded as *seriously* or *slightly injured* by the police on the basis of information available within a short time of the *accident*. This generally will not reflect the results of a medical examination, but may be influenced according to whether the casualty is hospitalised or not.

Slight accident: One in which at least one person is slightly injured but no person is killed or seriously injured.

Slight injury: An injury of a minor character such as a sprain (including neck whiplash injury), bruise or cut which are not judged to be severe, or slight shock requiring roadside attention. This definition includes injuries not requiring medical treatment.

Speed limits: Permanent speed limits applicable to the roadway.

Urban roads: Major and minor roads within an urban area with a population of 10 thousand or more. The definition is based on the 1991 Office of the Deputy Prime Minister definition of urban settlements. The urban areas used for these tables are based on 2001 census data.

Users of a vehicle: All occupants, i.e. *driver* (or *rider*) and *passengers*, including persons injured while boarding or alighting from the *vehicle*.

Motoring offences: 8.6 - 8.7

Breath tests: Section 25 and Schedule 8 of the Transport Act 1981 amended the drinking and driving provisions of the Road Traffic Act 1972. These sections of the Act were renumbered (but otherwise unchanged) in the Road Traffic Act 1988. The police can require a person to take a screening breath test if they have reasonable cause to suspect that the person has been driving or attempting to drive or had been in charge of a vehicle with alcohol in his or her body, or that he or she has committed a moving traffic offence, or that he or she has been involved in an accident. A person failing to provide a breath test without reasonable excuse is guilty of an offence.

For the purposes of evidence in court, breath analysis was introduced in May 1983. The prescribed alcohol limit is 80 milligrams (mg) of alcohol in 100 millilitres (ml) of blood or 107mg per 100ml urine. The equivalent breath alcohol limit is expressed as 35 micrograms of alcohol per 100ml breath. In April 1996 the Association of Chief Police Officers recommended that drivers in all injury accidents should be breath tested.

An evidential breath test is required to be taken at a police station after a positive screening test, or where a screening test was refused or could not be provided. It may also be required after arrest for impairment or in certain other cases, e.g. where a person arrested for theft of a motor vehicle is suspected of having consumed alcohol.

A suspect will normally be asked to provide two specimens of breath to establish the amount of alcohol in his or her body. The lower result is taken as evidence of the person's breath alcohol concentration. Where the lower result is between 36 and 50 micrograms the suspect may request a blood or urine test. In certain limited circumstances a suspect can be required to provide a specimen of blood or urine instead of breath.

Findings of guilt at all courts: Includes all motoring offences which have resulted in a finding of guilt either after a summary trial at Magistrates' Court or else at the Crown Court. A person appearing in court can be dealt with for more than one offence at that appearance, and in this table the number of offences is counted, not the number of persons appearing at court.

Fixed penalty notices: A large number of motoring offences are dealt with by fixed penalty notices. Under the extended fixed penalty system introduced by the Transport Act 1982, now incorporated in Part III of the Road Traffic Offenders Act 1988, the police can issue fixed penalty notices for a wide range of offences. The court can automatically register an unpaid notice as a fine without any court appearance. Offences for which a fixed penalty notice cannot be given include causing death or bodily harm, dangerous driving, driving after consuming alcohol or taking drugs, careless driving, accident offences, unauthorised taking or theft of a motor vehicle, certain driving licence and record keeping offences, and vehicle test offences. When court proceedings are instituted following non-payment of a fixed penalty, the offence may be included twice in the table.

Written warnings: These include cautions given in lieu of prosecutions for offences where there would have been enough evidence to support a prosecution. Informal warnings and advice, whether oral or written, are not included.

Motor insurance (formerly 8.8)

The data previously published in table 8.8 are no longer routinely available. For further information see the Association of British Insurers web site at: www.abi.org.uk or

Standard and Poor's SynThesys Non-Life database of returns.

Railway accidents: 8.8 - 8.10

These tables give the number of train accidents and casualties on all railway undertakings in Great Britain. Railway undertakings are required to report accidents, failures and dangerous occurrences to the Secretary of State for Transport under the regulatory safety legislation. As well as Network Rail and London Transport railways, the tables also cover accidents on Eurotunnel, tram systems and minor railways.

Casualty figures in table 8.8 are shown in the categories below. Casualty figures are subdivided into casualties resulting from:
- Train accidents
- Accidents through movement of railway vehicles (but excluding train accidents) e.g. boarding or alighting from trains, opening or closing carriage doors at stations,
- Accidents on railway premises not connected with movement of railway vehicles e.g. falling on steps at stations, slipping on platforms,
- Injuries and fatalities of trespassers and suicides on railway land.

Table 8.9 is based on passenger casualties owing to train accidents and movement accidents. This is the basis for comparisons with other modes of transport. Under the new Accidents Reporting Regulations (RIDDOR 95) brought into force on 1 April 1996, there is no distinction between major and minor injury to members of the public. All injuries to members of the public are now shown as either minor injuries or killed. The reporting trigger for minor injuries is that the person is taken to hospital for treatment.

Table 8.10 shows the total number of train accidents (collisions, derailments etc) reported irrespective of whether personal injury was involved. The figures include accidents on non-passenger lines and lines closed to normal traffic while engineering work took place.

Due to European regulations on the reporting of rail transport statistics, the rail accidents data now covers calendar years, rather than financial years. As such, there is overlap between the 2002/03 data and the 2003 data, with accidents from 1 January 2003 to 31 March 2003 reported in both. However, each represents 12 full months.

8.1 Road accidents and casualties: 1950-2007

For greater detail of the years 1997-2007 see Table 8.2 or 8.3

Year	Accidents (thousands)	Casualties — Killed (number) Pedest-rians	Pedal cyclists	Motor cyclists	All other road users	All	Injured (thousands) Serious	Slight	All	All casualties (thousands)	Casualty rate per 100 million vehicle kilometres	All traffic (billion vehicle km)
1950	167	2,251	805	1,129	827	5,012	49	148	196	201	276	73
1951	178	2,398	800	1,175	877	5,250	52	159	211	216	272	80
1952	172	2,063	743	1,142	758	4,706	50	153	203	208	248	84
1953	186	2,233	720	1,237	900	5,090	57	165	222	227	265	86
1954	196	2,226	696	1,148	940	5,010	57	176	233	238	269	89
1955	217	2,287	708	1,362	1,169	5,526	62	200	262	268	281	95
1956	216	2,270	650	1,250	1,197	5,367	61	201	263	268	276	97
1957	219	2,225	663	1,425	1,237	5,550	64	205	268	274	284	96
1958	237	2,408	668	1,421	1,473	5,970	69	225	294	300	280	107
1959	261	2,520	738	1,680	1,582	6,520	81	246	327	333	283	118
1960	272	2,708	679	1,743	1,840	6,970	84	256	341	348	279	124
1961	270	2,717	645	1,544	2,002	6,908	85	258	343	350	262	133
1962	264	2,681	583	1,323	2,122	6,709	84	251	335	342	248	138
1963	272	2,740	589	1,279	2,314	6,922	88	261	349	356	246	145
1964	292	2,986	583	1,445	2,806	7,820	95	282	378	385	240	160
1965	299	3,105	543	1,244	3,060	7,952	98	292	390	398	234	170
1966	292	3,153	514	1,134	3,184	7,985	100	285	384	392	219	179
1967	277	2,964	463	920	2,972	7,319	94	269	363	370	199	186
1968	264	2,762	391	877	2,780	6,810	89	254	342	349	181	193
1969	262	2,955	402	791	3,217	7,365	91	255	346	353	179	197
1970	267	2,925	373	761	3,440	7,499	93	262	356	363	177	205
1971	259	2,939	411	800	3,549	7,699	91	253	344	352	163	216
1972	265	3,083	367	729	3,584	7,763	91	261	352	360	159	226
1973	262	2,806	336	750	3,514	7,406	89	257	346	354	149	238
1974	244	2,642	282	797	3,162	6,883	82	236	318	325	139	234
1975	246	2,344	278	838	2,906	6,366	77	241	319	325	138	236
1976	259	2,335	300	990	2,945	6,570	80	254	333	340	137	248
1977	266	2,313	301	1,182	2,818	6,614	82	260	341	348	138	253
1978	265	2,427	316	1,163	2,925	6,831	83	260	343	350	134	262
1979	255	2,118	320	1,160	2,754	6,352	80	248	328	335	128	260
1980	252	1,941	302	1,163	2,604	6,010	79	243	323	329	119	277
1981	248	1,874	310	1,131	2,531	5,846	78	241	319	325	115	282
1982	256	1,869	294	1,090	2,681	5,934	80	249	328	334	115	291
1983	243	1,914	323	963	2,245	5,445	71	233	303	309	105	294
1984	253	1,868	345	967	2,419	5,599	73	246	319	324	105	309
1985	246	1,789	286	796	2,294	5,165	71	241	312	318	101	316
1986	248	1,841	271	762	2,508	5,382	69	247	316	321	97	331
1987	239	1,703	280	723	2,419	5,125	64	242	306	311	87	356
1988	247	1,753	227	670	2,402	5,052	63	254	317	322	85	381
1989	261	1,706	294	683	2,690	5,373	63	273	336	342	83	412
1990	258	1,694	256	659	2,608	5,217	60	275	336	341	82	416
1991	236	1,496	242	548	2,282	4,568	52	255	307	311	75	417
1992	233	1,347	204	469	2,209	4,229	49	257	306	311	75	417
1993 [1]	229	1,241	186	427	1,960	3,814	45	257	302	306	74	416
1994	234	1,124	172	444	1,910	3,650	47	265	312	315	74	426
1995	231	1,038	213	445	1,925	3,621	46	261	307	311	71	434
1996	236	997	203	440	1,958	3,598	44	272	317	321	72	445
1997	240	973	183	509	1,934	3,599	43	281	324	328	72	454
1998	239	906	158	498	1,859	3,421	41	281	322	325	70	462
1999	235	870	172	547	1,834	3,423	39	278	317	320	68	471
2000	234	857	127	605	1,820	3,409	38	279	317	320	68	471
2001	229	826	138	583	1,903	3,450	37	273	310	313	65	479
2002	222	775	130	609	1,917	3,431	36	263	299	303	62	491
2003	214	774	114	693	1,927	3,508	34	253	287	291	59	495
2004	207	671	134	585	1,831	3,221	31	246	278	281	56	503
2005	199	671	148	569	1,813	3,201	29	239	268	271	54	504
2006	189	675	146	599	1,752	3,172	29	227	256	259	51	512
2007	182	646	136	588	1,576	2,946	28	217	245	248	48	517

1 See Notes and Definitions in Section 7 for details of discontinuity in road traffic figures from 1993 onwards.
   From 1993 the data has been estimated using the expansion factors and the new methodology for measuring road lengths, they
   are not directly comparable with the figures for 1992 and earlier.

☎020-7944 6595

8.2 Road accident casualties by road user type and severity: 1997-2007

											Number
	1997	1998	1999	2000	2001	2002	2003	2004	2005	2006	2007
Child pedestrians: [1]											
Killed	138	103	107	107	107	79	74	77	63	71	57
KSI [2]	3,954	3,737	3,457	3,226	3,144	2,828	2,381	2,339	2,134	2,025	1,899
All severities	18,407	17,971	16,876	16,184	15,819	14,231	12,544	12,234	11,250	10,131	9,527
Adult pedestrians: [3]											
Killed	835	803	760	750	712	688	695	589	604	602	585
KSI	6,925	6,592	6,221	6,112	5,745	5,644	5,422	5,005	4,847	4,894	4,900
All severities	26,223	25,827	24,806	24,481	23,463	23,258	22,531	21,404	20,725	19,774	19,676
Child pedal cyclists: [1]											
Killed	33	32	36	27	25	22	18	25	20	31	13
KSI	1,016	915	950	758	674	594	595	577	527	503	522
All severities	7,899	6,930	7,290	6,260	5,451	4,809	4,769	4,682	3,759	3,765	3,633
Adult pedal cyclists: [3]											
Killed	150	126	135	98	111	107	95	109	127	115	122
KSI	2,542	2,345	2,172	1,954	1,951	1,801	1,776	1,697	1,787	1,898	1,994
All severities	16,181	15,326	14,834	13,630	12,974	11,712	11,643	11,366	11,637	11,911	12,050
Motorcyclists [4] and passengers:											
Killed	509	498	547	605	583	609	693	585	569	599	588
KSI	6,446	6,442	6,908	7,374	7,305	7,500	7,652	6,648	6,508	6,484	6,737
All severities	24,492	24,610	26,192	28,212	28,810	28,353	28,411	25,641	24,824	23,326	23,459
Car drivers and passengers:											
Killed	1,795	1,696	1,687	1,665	1,749	1,747	1,769	1,671	1,675	1,612	1,432
KSI	23,191	21,676	20,368	19,719	19,424	18,728	17,291	16,144	14,617	14,254	12,967
All severities	211,448	210,474	205,735	206,799	202,802	197,425	188,342	183,858	178,302	171,000	161,433
Bus/coach drivers and passengers:											
Killed	14	18	11	15	14	19	11	20	9	19	12
KSI	601	631	611	578	562	551	500	488	363	426	455
All severities	9,439	9,839	10,252	10,088	9,884	9,005	9,068	8,820	7,920	7,253	7,079
LGV drivers and passengers:											
Killed	64	67	65	66	64	70	72	62	54	52	58
KSI	928	949	867	813	811	780	765	631	587	564	494
All severities	7,476	7,672	7,124	7,007	7,304	7,007	6,897	6,166	6,048	5,914	5,340
HGV drivers and passengers:											
Killed	45	60	52	55	54	63	44	47	55	39	52
KSI	573	560	540	571	500	524	429	406	395	383	363
All severities	3,302	3,444	3,484	3,597	3,388	3,178	3,061	2,883	2,843	2,530	2,476
All road users: [5]											
Killed	3,599	3,421	3,423	3,409	3,450	3,431	3,508	3,221	3,201	3,172	2,946
KSI	46,583	44,255	42,545	41,564	40,560	39,407	37,215	34,351	32,155	31,845	30,720
All severities	327,803	325,212	320,310	320,283	313,309	302,605	290,607	280,840	271,017	258,404	247,780

1 Casualties aged 0 -15.
2 Killed and seriously injured.
3 Casualties aged 16 and over.
4 Includes mopeds and scooters.
5 Includes other motor or non-motor vehicle users, and unknown road user type and casualty age.

☎020-7944 6595

8.3 Road accidents and accident rates: by road class and severity: 1997-2007

Number/*rate per 100 million vehicle kilometres*

	1997	1998	1999	2000	2001	2002	2003	2004	2005	2006	2007
Motorways											
Fatal	159	157	176	161	180	175	184	149	176	164	154
Fatal and serious	1,204	1,148	1,218	1,190	1,235	1,162	1,166	1,047	1,007	953	989
All severities	8,678	8,861	9,118	9,394	9,128	8,942	8,746	9,072	8,619	8,379	7,976
Rate [1]	*11*	*10*	*10*	*11*	*10*	*10*	*9*	*9*	*9*	*8*	*8*
Urban roads [2]											
A roads											
Fatal	693	576	566	590	601	615	616	519	483	517	462
Fatal and serious	10,147	9,570	8,880	8,996	8,608	8,316	7,750	7,025	6,359	6,528	6,339
All severities	69,713	68,837	67,064	68,170	66,350	63,192	60,806	56,962	53,078	49,811	47,969
Rate [1]	*84*	*84*	*81*	*83*	*81*	*76*	*74*	*68*	*64*	*60*	*59*
Other roads											
Fatal	535	544	564	532	547	479	509	495	504	486	445
Fatal and serious	12,064	11,521	10,923	10,533	10,348	9,985	9,417	8,725	8,580	8,541	8,279
All severities	84,628	84,277	83,153	82,450	80,193	77,442	74,060	71,609	70,580	67,177	63,798
Rate [1]	*82*	*80*	*77*	*76*	*73*	*68*	*64*	*62*	*61*	*58*	*54*
Rural roads [2]											
A roads											
Fatal	1,242	1,209	1,190	1,178	1,204	1,203	1,230	1,148	1,129	1,136	1,025
Fatal and serious	8,941	8,589	8,371	8,096	8,070	7,820	7,561	7,023	6,697	6,468	6,210
All severities	41,250	40,744	39,704	38,846	38,693	38,947	37,516	37,402	35,482	34,227	33,341
Rate [1]	*33*	*32*	*30*	*30*	*29*	*29*	*27*	*26*	*25*	*24*	*23*
Other roads [3]											
Fatal	663	644	602	624	611	648	706	665	621	623	628
Fatal and serious	7,200	6,855	6,743	6,579	6,316	6,304	6,230	5,891	5,286	5,380	5,218
All severities	35,567	35,680	34,480	33,612	33,445	32,686	32,642	32,205	30,889	29,542	29,018
Rate [1]	*55*	*58*	*56*	*54*	*54*	*50*	*50*	*48*	*46*	*42*	*40*
All roads [4]											
Fatal	3,298	3,137	3,138	3,108	3,176	3,124	3,247	2,978	2,913	2,926	2,714
Fatal and serious	39,628	37,770	36,405	35,607	34,764	33,645	32,160	29,726	27,942	27,872	27,036
All severities	240,287	238,923	235,048	233,729	229,014	221,751	214,030	207,410	198,735	189,161	182,115
Rate [1]	*53*	*52*	*50*	*50*	*48*	*45*	*43*	*41*	*39*	*37*	*35*
All A roads											
Fatal	1,939	1,788	1,782	1,782	1,826	1,821	1,847	1,669	1,612	1,653	1,487
Fatal and serious	19,128	18,201	17,388	17,204	16,761	16,168	15,328	14,055	13,063	12,997	12,550
All severities	111,165	109,807	107,474	107,544	105,548	102,378	98,436	94,429	88,599	84,050	81,316
Rate [1]	*53*	*52*	*50*	*51*	*49*	*47*	*44*	*42*	*40*	*37*	*36*
Other non-motorway roads											
Fatal	1,200	1,192	1,180	1,165	1,170	1,128	1,216	1,160	1,125	1,109	1,073
Fatal and serious	19,296	18,421	17,799	17,213	16,768	16,315	15,666	14,624	13,872	13,922	13,497
All severities	120,444	120,255	118,456	116,791	114,338	110,431	106,848	103,909	101,517	96,732	92,823
Rate [1]	*73*	*72*	*70*	*69*	*66*	*62*	*59*	*57*	*55*	*52*	*49*

1 Figures have been revised from those published in previous years, see Notes and Definitions in Section 7 for details.
2 The definition of urban and rural roads is different to that of built-up and non built-up shown in editions prior to 2003.
3 Urban and Rural accident figures for 1994-2004 have been revised.
4 Includes B, C and unclassified roads.
5 Includes cases where road class was not reported.

☎020-7944 6595

8.4 Casualties by hour of day: 2007

(a) Weekdays

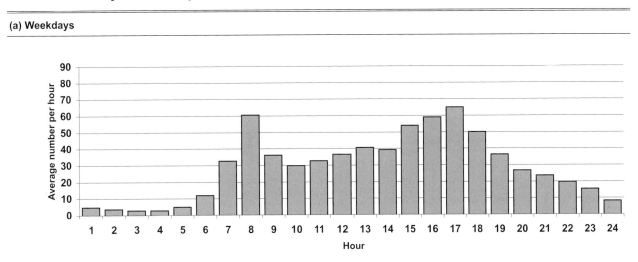

(b) Weekends

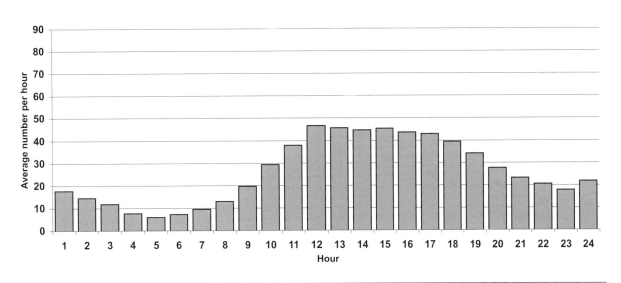

Note: The hours are defined as being the beginning of an hour, i.e 1 being between 1 am and 2 am, and 12 being between midday and 1 pm, etc.

☎020-7944 6595

8.5 Road accidents: breath tests performed on car drivers and motorcycle riders involved in injury accidents: Great Britain: 1997-2007

Number/*percentage*

	1997	1998	1999	2000	2001	2002	2003	2004	2005	2006	2007
Car drivers involved	338,924	337,794	329,866	329,846	321,900	314,568	299,333	291,842	281,810	267,991	255,891
Breath tested Number	157,373	173,610	175,916	172,840	163,540	159,782	151,442	149,430	149,687	146,564	146,024
Percentage of drivers involved	*46*	*51*	*53*	*52*	*51*	*51*	*51*	*51*	*53*	*55*	*57*
Failed breath test 1 Number	7,087	6,690	6,669	7,124	7,264	7,285	7,289	6,655	6,397	5,873	5,644
Percentage of drivers tested	*5*	*4*	*4*	*4*	*4*	*5*	*5*	*4*	*4*	*4*	*4*
Motorcycle riders involved	25,211	25,514	27,122	29,236	30,084	29,503	29,523	26,857	25,870	24,323	24,381
Breath tested Number	9,926	11,416	12,970	13,945	13,725	12,992	13,178	12,422	12,221	11,884	12,648
Percentage of riders involved	*39*	*45*	*48*	*48*	*46*	*44*	*45*	*46*	*47*	*49*	*52*
Failed breath test 1 Number	428	426	443	442	446	441	510	423	391	374	337
Percentage of riders tested	*4*	*4*	*3*	*3*	*3*	*3*	*4*	*3*	*3*	*3*	*3*

1 Failed or refused to provide a specimen of breath.

☎020-7944 6595

8.6 Motor vehicle offences: drinking and driving: summary of breath tests and blood or urine tests: England and Wales: 1997-2006

Number/percentage

	1997	1998	1999	2000	2001	2002	2003	2004	2005	2006
Screening breath test: number required (inc. refused/not able)	800,300 [2]	815,500 [2]	764,500 [2]	714,800	623,900	570,200	534,300	578,000 [3]	607,400	601,600
Of which: positive/refused[1]	103,500 [2]	102,300 [2]	94,100 [2]	94,600 [2]	99,500 [2]	103,500	106,300	103,000	104,300	105,700
Result (per cent)										
Positive	*13*	*13*	*12*	*13*	*16*	*18*	*20*	18	*17*	*18*
Negative	*87*	*87*	*88*	*87*	*84*	*82*	*80*	82	*83*	*82*
Refused/not able	..	..	..	..	..	..	..	..	..	..
Total	*100*	*100*	*100*	*100*	*100*	*100*	*100*	*100*	*100*	*100*

1 Includes persons unable to provide a breath test specimen.
2 Figures updated since publication of the TSGB 2007 edition.
3 Figures revised since publication of the 2004 bulletin.

☎020 7035 8855
Source - Minstry of Justice

8.7 Motor vehicle offences: findings of guilt at all courts, fixed penalty notices and written warnings: by type of offence: England and Wales: 1997-2006

Thousands of offences

	1997	1998	1999	2000	2001	2002	2003	2004	2005	2006
Offence type:										
Dangerous, careless or drunken driving etc	199	190	183	176	172	171	177	231	275	322
Accident offences	22	21	19	18	18	18	19	18	17	16
Speed limit offences	881	962	1,001	1,154	1,386	1,538	2,041	2,076	2,087	1,933
Unauthorised taking or theft of motor vehicle	37	37	36	32	32	32	30	27	25	23
Licence, insurance and record keeping offences	829	817	807	785	769	819	953	957	844	747
Vehicle test and condition offences	286	277	261	243	226	228	241	227	187	152
Neglect of traffic signs and directions and pedestrian rights	282	271	245	232	218	213	264	258	245	245
Other offences relating to motor vehicles (except obstruction, waiting and parking)	349	353	320	268	255	239	280	354	380	352
All offences (except obstruction, waiting and parking)	2,885	2,927	2,872	2,911	3,076	3,259	4,005	4,147	4,059	3,789
Obstruction, waiting and parking offences	2,219	2,139	1,828	1,611	1,341	1,180	1,059	896	584	499
All offences	5,104	5,066	4,700	4,523	4,417	4,439	5,244	5,043	4,643	4,288

1 These figures for 2003 have been revised

☎020 7035 8315
Source - Ministry of Justice

For further details on vehicle offences see Ministry of Justice Statistical Bulletin, "Motoring Offences and Breath Test Statistics" - England and Wales 2006 and associated Supplementary Tables - England and Wales 2006. Copies of this report and other RDS publications can be downloaded free from the Ministry of Justice website at: http://www.justice.gov.uk/publications/motoringoffences.htm

For further details on vehicle offences in Scotland see The Scottish Government Criminal Justice Series Statistical Bulletin Criminal Proceedings in Scottish Courts 2006-07 The Scottish Government ☎0131-244 2227

8.8 Railway accidents: casualties: by type of accident: 1997/98-2007

Number

		1997/98	1998/99	1999/00	2000/01	2001/02	2002/03	2003 [1]	2004	2005	2006	2007
Train accidents:												
Killed:	Passengers	7	0	29	10	0	6	0	5	0	0	1
	Railway staff	0	0	2	4	0	1	1	2	1	0	0
	Others	3	3	2	3	5	3	10	5	6	1 R	4
	Total	10	3	33	17	5	10	11	12	7	1 R	5
Major injuries:	Passengers	.	.	.	.	.	.	0	0	0	0	0
	Railway staff	2	2	3	6	6	0	0	5	0	2	3
	Others	.	.	.	.	.	.	0	0	0	0	0
	Total	2	2	3	6	6	0	0	5	0	2	3
Minor injuries:	Passengers	.	.	.	.	.	.	0	0	0	0	0
	Railway staff	37	29	20	36	17	23	12	21	20	17	10
	Others	.	.	.	.	.	.	0	0	0	0	0
	Total	37	29	20	36	17	23	12	21	20	17	10
Public injuries:	Passengers	190	40	290	178	21	128	53	76	22	20	94
	Railway staff	.	.	.	.	.	.	0	0	0	0	0
	Others	15	13	19	15	8	15	19	9	9	4	4
	Total	205	53	309	193	29	143	72	85	31	24	98
Accidents through movement of railway vehicles:												
Killed:	Passengers	15	17	14	7	10	14	8	3	5	4	4
	Railway staff	3	1	2	3	4	2	1	7	5	2	2
	Others	14	11	11	7	10	16	8	7	10	6	21
	Total	32	29	27	17	24	32	17	17	20	12	27
Major injuries:	Passengers	.	.	.	.	.	.	0	0	0	0	0
	Railway staff	34	35	37	25	26	26	35	48	28	25	33
	Others	.	.	.	.	.	.	0	0	0	0	0
	Total	34	35	37	25	26	26	35	48	28	25	33
Minor injuries:	Passengers	.	.	.	.	.	.	0	0	0	0	0
	Railway staff	215	246	289	296	293	313	299	328	311	333	262
	Others	.	.	.	.	.	.	0	0	0	0	1
	Total	215	246	289	296	293	313	299	328	311	333	263
Public injuries:	Passengers	617	668	569	610	573	556	584	547	580	525	526
	Railway staff	.	.	.	.	.	.	0	0	0	0	0
	Others	17	13	13	18	17	13	16	16	15	12	9
	Total	634	681	582	628	590	569	600	563	595	537	535
Accidents on railway premises:												
Killed:	Passengers	4	3	4	3	3	3	5	5	5	4	0
	Railway staff	0	3	1	1	1	4	3	1	0	2	0
	Others	2	1	0	1	2	1	1	0	1	2	0
	Total	6	7	5	5	6	8	9	6	6	8	0
Major injuries:	Passengers	.	.	.	.	.	.	0	0	0	0	0
	Railway staff	315	339	300	269	319	323	303	349	304	182	187
	Others	.	.	.	.	.	.	0	0	0	0	0
	Total	315	339	300	269	319	323	303	349	304	182	187
Minor injuries:	Passengers	.	.	.	.	.	.	0	0	0	0	0
	Railway staff	1,836	1,795	1,756	1,803	1,713	1,744	1,699	1,549	1,616	1,188	936
	Others	.	.	.	.	.	.	0	0	0	0	0
	Total	1,836	1,795	1,756	1,803	1,713	1,744	1,699	1,549	1,616	1,188	936
Public injuries:	Passengers	1,940	1,963	1,883	2,007	1,807	1,861	1,913	2,004	2,198	1,994	2,181
	Railway staff	.	.	.	.	.	.	0	0	0	0	0
	Others	95	75	53	51	67	55	60	44	36	57	38
	Total	2,035	2,038	1,936	2,058	1,874	1,916	1,973	2,048	2,234	2,051	2,219

8.8 (continued) Railway accidents: casualties: by type of accident: 1997/98-2007

												Number
		1997/98	1998/99	1999/00	2000/01	2001/02	2002/03	2003 [1]	2004	2005	2006	2007
Overall totals:												
Killed:	Passengers	26	20	47	20	10	23	13	13	10	8	5
	Railway staff	3	4	5	8	5	7	5	10	6	4	2
	Others	19	15	13	11	17	20	19	12	17	9 [R]	25
	Total	48	39	65	39	32	50	37	35	33	21 [R]	32
Major injuries:	Passengers	.	.	.	.	.	.	0	0	0	0	0
	Railway staff	351	376	340	300	351	349	338	402	332	209	223
	Others	.	.	.	.	.	.	0	0	0	0	0
	Total	351	376	340	300	351	349	338	402	332	209	223
Minor injuries:	Passengers	.	.	.	.	.	.	0	0	0	0	0
	Railway staff	2,088	2,070	2,065	2,135	2,023	2,080	2,010	1,898	1,947	1,538	1,208
	Others	.	.	.	.	.	.	0	0	0	0	1
	Total	2,088	2,070	2,065	2,135	2,023	2,080	2,010	1,898	1,947	1,538	1,209
Public injuries:	Passengers	2,747	2,671	2,742	2,795	2,401	2,545	2,550	2,627	2,800	2,539	2,801
	Railway staff	.	.	.	.	.	.	0	0	0	0	0
	Others	127	101	85	84	92	83	95	69	60	73	51
	Total	2,874	2,772	2,827	2,879	2,493	2,628	2,645	2,696	2,860	2,612	2,852
Trespassers and suicides:												
Deaths		265	247	274	300	275	256	252	242	280	321	270
Injured		136	149	144	177	179	137	132	132	127	140	122

1 Prior to 2003 data covered financial years. See Notes and Definitions section at start of Chapter 8.

R There have been revisions to data since the last TSGB publication

☎020 7944 8874
The figures in this table are outside the scope of National Statistics
Source - ORR, previously HSE

8.9 Railway movement accidents: passenger casualties and casualty rates: 1997/98-2007

											Number/rate per billion passenger kilometres
	1997/98	1998/99	1999/00	2000/01	2001/02	2002/03	2003 [2]	2004	2005	2006 [3]	2007
Casualties: [1]											
Deaths	22	17	43	17	10	20	8	8	5	4	5
Minor injuries	807	708	859	788	594	684	637	623	602	545	620
All casualties	829	725	902	806	604	704	645	631	607	549	625
Casualty rates:											
Deaths	0.5	0.4	0.9	0.4	0.2	0.4	0.2	0.2	0.1	0.1	0.1
Minor injuries	19.4	16.2	18.6	16.9	12.5	14.3	12.9	12.4	11.6	9.9	10.6
All casualties	19.9	16.6	19.5	17.3	12.7	14.7	13.1	12.5	11.7	10.0	10.7

1 Passenger casualties involved in train accidents and accidents occurring through movement of railway vehicles.

2 Prior to 2003 data covered financial years. See Notes and Definitions section at start of Chapter 8. The casualty rates continue to be calculated using financial year rail passenger kilometre data because calendar year data is not available for all sources.

3 Casualty rates have been revised because of a revision to national rail passenger kilometres.

☎020-7944 8874
The figures in this table are outside the scope of National Statistics
Source - ORR, previously HSE

8.10 Railway accidents: train accidents: 1997/98-2007

Number

	1997/98	1998/99	1999/00	2000/01	2001/02	2002/03	2003 [2]	2004	2005	2006	2007
Collisions	127	121	94	106	101	69	61	60	27	20	23
Derailments	93	117	89	93	88	67	63	62	64	46	47
Running into level crossing gates and other obstructions	680	690	753	693	557	495	433	523	480	503	486
Fires	344	343	340	301	291	292	271	323	187	163	141
Damage to drivers' cab windscreens [1]	619	564	617	607	665	498	409	368	299	328	309
Miscellaneous	0	0	2	1	2	0	0	0	0	1	.
All accidents	1,863	1,835	1,895	1,801	1,704	1,421	1,237	1,336	1,057	1,061	1,006

1 Category now reportable under RIDDOR 95.
2 Prior to 2003 data covered financial years.
  See Notes and Definitions section at start of Chapter 8.

☎020-7944 8874
The figures in this table are outside
the scope of National Statistics
Source - ORR, previously HSE

9 Vehicles:

Notes and Definitions

This section provides a range of data relating to vehicle registration and licensing, vehicle testing, driving license holding and car usage.

The following notes and definitions are relevant when considering the data presented within the section.

Vehicle registration and licensing: 9.1-9.8

Current taxation class groupings

The current taxation class groupings presented within this section are as follows:

Private and light goods (PLG):
This is by far the most common tax class, currently covering almost 89 per cent of licensed vehicles. This tax class primarily consists of cars and light vans but can include other vehicles used only for private purposes. Tax bands within PLG depend on engine size for vehicles first registered before March 2001, while for cars registered after March 2001, tax bands are based upon levels of CO_2 emissions, with lower rates for cleaner vehicles.

Motorcycles, scooters and mopeds:
This is a self-explanatory tax class, but excludes tricycles which have their own tax band. The rates of tax payable depend upon engine size.

Goods vehicles:
Vehicles that have a gross weight of over three and a half tonnes and are used for carrying goods are taxed in this class. Generally, the rate of tax payable depends on the maximum gross weight and the axle configuration of the vehicle. Since 1999, reduced rates have been available for vehicles that create less pollution.

Public transport vehicles:
This category covers buses and coaches with more than 8 seats (excluding the driver) used for commercial purposes. Vehicles not used for commercial purposes would be licensed in the PLG tax class. The rate of tax payable is dependent upon the number of seats in the vehicle. As for goods vehicles, since 1999 reduced rates have been available for vehicles that create less pollution.

Crown and exempt vehicles:
This group includes vehicles which are exempt from vehicle excise duty. This can be for a variety of reasons, including vehicles driven by disabled drivers, emergency and crown vehicles and vehicles manufactured before 1973.

Special vehicles group:
This group includes works trucks, road rollers, mobile cranes, digging machines and showman's vehicles.

Other vehicles:
This group includes three wheeled cars and vans, recovery vehicles, general haulage vehicles and tricycles.

Changes in the taxation system over time

There have been several changes to the vehicle taxation system in recent years which are particularly important when interpreting the time series presented in Tables 9.1 and 9.2. These are as follows:

From 1 October 1982:
All general goods vehicles weighing less than 1,525 kgs in unladen weight were transferred from the 'goods' taxation group to the 'private and light goods' group. This has resulted in a discontinuity in the data presented for both taxation groups between 1981 and 1982.

From 1 October 1990:
All general goods vehicles weighing less than 3,500 kgs in gross vehicle weight were transferred from the 'goods' taxation group to the 'private and light goods' group. This has resulted in a discontinuity in the data presented for both taxation groups between 1989 and 1990.

From 1 July 1995:
Major changes were made to the taxation system with the intention of simplifying the taxation structure. These changes included:
- farmers and showmen's vehicles were transferred from the 'goods' taxation group into the 'other vehicles' group.
- cars and motorcycles over 25 years of age were transferred from the 'private and light goods' and 'motorcycles' taxation group to the 'crown and exempt' taxation group.
- public service vehicles with fewer than 8 seats were transferred from the 'public

transport vehicles' taxation group into the 'private and light goods' taxation group.

Due to these numerous changes, there is a discontinuity between the figures presented in Tables 9.1 and 9.2 for all taxation groups between 1994 and 1995.

Methods of measurement

Licensed vehicles:
Since 1978, data relating to the number of licensed vehicles has been calculated through an analysis of the records held centrally by the Driver and Vehicle Licensing Agency (DVLA) as at 31 December each year.

Prior to this, statistics on licensed vehicles were calculated through a sample of vehicle records held by local taxation offices and included vehicles licensed for at least one month during the third quarter of the year.

Newly registered vehicles:
Statistics relating to new vehicle registrations are calculated through a complete analysis of new registrations and include all vehicles newly registered in the calendar year.

Vehicle testing: 9.9-9.13

The statistics presented within these tables have been provided by the Vehicle and Operator Services Agency (VOSA), contact: (☎0117 9543471.

Trailer tests:
Although there is no registration system for trailers which carry goods, there is still a requirement to have them tested each year under the DfT's plating and testing scheme.

MOT tests:
Since 2006/07, these statistics have been based on an analysis of all MOT tests carried out in the financial year. In 2005/06, the statistics were based on approximately 50 per cent of all tests carried out while, prior to this, the statistics were based on a 2 per cent sample of vehicle tests.

Passenger service vehicle tests:
EEC Directive 77/143 stipulated that all class VI (Public Service Vehicles) in use for more than one year must by 1 January 1983 have undergone a road-worthiness examination and be subject to an annual inspection thereafter. To meet this deadline, statutory testing of class VI vehicles commenced on 1 January 1982.

Heavy goods vehicle tests:
Vehicles subject to plating and testing have to undergo a test when they are 1 year old and are

tested annually thereafter; the term 'first test' refers to the first test of a vehicle in a particular year. The figures quoted cover the 52 week period ending on the Friday which precedes the first Monday in April.

Households with regular use of cars: 9.14

Data from 1961 onwards are derived from household surveys. Figures for earlier years are estimates. Also, see notes to Table 9.15.

Private motoring: 9.15 and 9.16

The mid-year estimates of the percentage of households with regular use of a car or van in Tables 9.15 (a) and (b) are based on combined data from the National Travel Survey (NTS), the Expenditure and Food Survey (previously the Family Expenditure Survey) and the General Household Survey (GHS), where available. The method for calculating these figures was changed slightly for 2006, to incorporate weighted data from the NTS and the GHS; previously these figures were based on unweighted data. Figures for 2005 have also been revised to incorporate weighted data.

Table 9.15 (c) by area type is based on data from the NTS only. Comparisons with Census data are also shown in Table 9.15 (a).

The percentage of driving licence holders in Table 9.16 is based on data from the NTS, and the estimated number of licence holders is based on the mid-year resident population estimates from ONS.

Annual mileage of 4-wheeled cars: 9.17

These figures are based upon annual estimates for each purpose (commuting, business and other private) per vehicle as reported by participants in the National Travel Survey (NTS). The data are for 4-wheeled cars only. Company cars provided by an employer for the use of a particular employee (or director) are included, but cars borrowed temporarily from a company pool are not.

Private motoring: 9.18

The statistics presented within these tables are provided by the Driving Standards Agency, contact: (☎02920 581218).

9.1 Motor vehicles licensed at end of year: 1950-2007

Thousands

Year	Private and light goods		Goods vehicles	Motor cycles etc	Public transport vehicles	Special machines/ Special concessionary[1]	Other vehicles	Special Vehicles group	Crown and exempt vehicles[1]	All vehicles
	Private cars	Other vehicles								
1950	1,979	439	439	643	123	262	24	.	61	3,970
1951	2,095	457	451	725	123	250	26	.	63	4,190
1952	2,221	477	450	812	119	270	29	.	86	4,464
1953	2,446	516	446	889	105	289	30	.	88	4,809
1954	2,733	566	450	977	97	307	32	.	88	5,250
1955	3,109	633	462	1,076	92	326	35	.	89	5,822
1956	3,437	685	471	1,137	89	336	37	.	95	6,287
1957	3,707	723	473	1,261	87	355	41	.	96	6,743
1958	4,047	772	461	1,300	86	367	46	.	96	7,175
1959	4,416	824	473	1,479	83	383	55	.	96	7,809
1960	4,900	894	493	1,583	84	392	65	.	101	8,512
1961	5,296	944	508	1,577	82	400	76	.	106	8,989
1962	5,776	1,002	512	1,567	84	401	83	.	107	9,532
1963	6,462	1,092	535	1,546	86	412	88	.	115	10,336
1964	7,190	1,184	551	1,534	86	421	90	.	120	11,176
1965	7,732	1,240	584	1,420	86	417	91	.	127	11,697
1966	8,210	1,283	577	1,239	85	399	87	.	142	12,022
1967	8,882	1,358	593	1,190	85	416	89	.	147	12,760
1968	9,285	1,388	580	1,082	89	409	92	.	157	13,082
1969	9,672	1,408	547	993	92	398	90	.	162	13,362
1970	9,971	1,421	545	923	93	385	89	.	121	13,548
1971	10,443	1,452	542	899	96	380	92	.	126	14,030
1972	11,006	1,498	525	866	95	371	95	.	128	14,584
1973	11,738	1,559	540	887	96	373	97	.	137	15,427
1974	11,917	1,547	539	918	96	380	96	.	149	15,642
1975	12,526	1,592	553	1,077	105	384	108	.	166	16,511
1976	13,184	1,626	563	1,175	110	387	117	.	156	17,318
1977	13,220	1,591	559	1,190	110	393	115	.	167	17,345
1978	13,626	1,597	549	1,194	110	394	111	.	177	17,758
1979	14,162	1,623	561	1,292	111	402	106	.	359	18,616
1980	14,660	1,641	507	1,372	110	397	100	.	412	19,199
1981	14,867	1,623	489	1,371	110	365	95	.	427	19,347
1982 [2]	15,264	1,624	477	1,370	111	371	91	.	454	19,762
1983	15,543	1,692	488	1,290	113	376	86	.	621	20,209
1984	16,055	1,752	490	1,225	116	375	82	.	670	20,765
1985	16,454	1,805	485	1,148	120	374	78	.	695	21,159
1986	16,981	1,880	484	1,065	125	371	73	.	720	21,699
1987	17,421	1,952	485	978	129	374	68	.	744	22,152
1988	18,432	2,096	502	912	132	383	83	.	761	23,302
1989	19,248	2,199	505	875	122	384	77	.	785	24,196
1990 [2]	19,742	2,247	482	833	115	375	71	.	807	24,673
1991	19,737	2,215	449	750	109	346	65	.	840	24,511
1992	19,870	2,198	432	684	107	324	59	.	903	24,577
1993	20,102	2,187	428	650	107	318	55	.	979	24,826
1994	20,479	2,192	434	630	107	309	50	.	1,030	25,231
1995 [2]	20,505	2,217	421	594	74	274	44	28	1,169	25,369
1996	21,172	2,267	413	609	77	254	40	48	1,424	26,302
1997	21,681	2,317	414	626	79	249	38	48	1,522	26,974
1998	22,115	2,362	412	684	80	243	37	47	1,558	27,538
1999	22,785	2,427	415	760	84	241	36	47	1,573	28,368
2000	23,196	2,469	418	825	86	233	34	46	1,590	28,898
2001	23,899	2,544	422	882	89	233	33	45	1,602	29,747
2002	24,543	2,622	425	941	92	.	32	46	1,855	30,557
2003	24,985	2,730	426	1,005	96	.	32	47	1,887	31,207
2004	25,754	2,900	434	1,060	100	.	32	50	1,929	32,259
2005	26,208	3,019	433	1,075	103	.	31	51	1,978	32,897
2006	26,508	3,137	446	1,094	107	.	31	54	1,991	33,369
2007	26,878	3,261	446	1,133	109	.	30	56	2,043	33,957

1 The "Special concession" vehicles form part of the "Crown and exempt" taxation class from 2002.
2 Changes to the taxation system have meant that there are some discontinuities in the series.

☎020-7944 3077

9.2 Motor vehicles registered for the first time: 1951-2007

Thousands

Year	Private and light goods	Goods vehicles	Motor cycles etc	Public transport vehicles	Special machines and special concessionary[1]	Exempt and Other vehicles[1]	All vehicles
1951	136	85	133	8	34	18	414
1952	188	82	133	5	35	16	459
1953	295	97	139	5	34	14	584
1954	386	110	165	6	35	17	718
1955	501	154	185	6	39	22	907
1956	400	148	143	5	32	23	751
1957	425	141	206	5	40	20	837
1958	555	173	183	5	47	19	982
1959	646	192	332	5	49	30	1,253
1960	805	226	257	6	43	33	1,369
1961	743	220	212	6	46	31	1,259
1962	785	192	140	6	43	27	1,192
1963	1,009	206	166	6	48	31	1,466
1964	1,191	229	205	7	46	34	1,711
1965	1,123	229	151	7	45	46	1,601
1966	1,065	227	109	7	48	36	1,494
1967	1,117	222	138	7	54	39	1,575
1968	1,117	232	112	7	57	37	1,562
1969	987	240	85	7	49	33	1,402
1969 [2]	1,133	94	85	7	49	33	1,402
1970	1,248	85	105	8	49	30	1,525
1971	1,462	74	128	10	38	30	1,742
1972	1,855	75	153	10	48	44	2,184
1973	1,851	83	194	10	50	43	2,230
1974	1,400	68	190	8	46	40	1,750
1975	1,317	67	265	8	49	45	1,750
1976	1,402	64	271	9	52	41	1,838
1977	1,445	69	251	9	48	40	1,862
1978	1,746	80	225	9	50	41	2,151
1979	1,892	91	286	9	48	44	2,370
1980	1,679	75	313	9	37	44	2,156
1980 [2]	1,699	55	313	9	37	44	2,156
1981	1,644	40	272	8	33	35	2,030
1982 [2]	1,746	41	232	7	39	40	2,104
1983	1,989	47	175	7	42	48	2,308
1984	1,933	50	145	7	40	64	2,239
1985	2,030	52	126	7	40	55	2,309
1986	2,071	51	106	9	35	62	2,334
1987	2,213	54	91	9	38	70	2,474
1988	2,437	63	90	9	45	79	2,724
1989	2,535	65	97	8	43	81	2,829
1990	2,180	44	94	7	34	78	2,439
1991	1,709	29	77	5	26	77	1,922
1992	1,694	29	66	5	24	84	1,902
1993	1,853	33	58	5	30	94	2,074
1994	1,992	41	65	7	35	110	2,249
1995 [2]	2,024	48	69	5	33	127	2,307
1996	2,093	46	90	7	26	150	2,410
1997	2,244	42	122	7	22	162	2,598
1998	2,368	49	144	7	15	157	2,740
1999	2,342	48	168	8	25	174	2,766
2000	2,430	50	183	8	24	176	2,871
2001	2,710	49	177	7	27	169	3,138
2002	2,816	45	162	8	-	199	3,229
2003	2,821	48	157	8	-	197	3,232
2004	2,785	48	134	8	-	211	3,185
2005	2,604	51	132	9	-	226	3,021
2006	2,499	48	132	8	-	227	2,914
2007	2,539	41	143	9	-	265	2,997

1 The "Special concession" vehicles form part of the "Crown and exempt" taxation class from 2002.
2 Changes to the taxation system have meant that there are some discontinuities in the series.

☎020-7944 3077

9.3 Motor vehicles licensed at end of year: by tax class, body type and engine size: 1997-2007

(a) Private and light goods tax class — Thousands

Year		1997	1998	1999	2000	2001	2002	2003	2004	2005	2006	2007
Body type cars classified by engine size												
Over	Not over											
	700cc	37	29	18	19	23	29	37	47	52	57	58
700cc	1,000cc	1,564	1,459	1,435	1,415	1,368	1,314	1,237	1,199	1,153	1,135	1,124
1,000cc	1,200cc	2,336	2,293	2,275	2,228	2,244	2,252	2,221	2,210	2,139	2,036	1,948
1,200cc	1,500cc	5,418	5,497	5,600	5,677	5,819	5,894	5,939	6,089	6,181	6,284	6,428
1,500cc	1,800cc	6,655	6,766	6,922	6,992	7,124	7,241	7,284	7,405	7,439	7,408	7,406
1,800cc	2,000cc	3,828	4,090	4,389	4,604	4,869	5,166	5,398	5,686	5,929	6,076	6,228
2,000cc	2,500cc	925	1,003	1,094	1,159	1,275	1,400	1,520	1,639	1,725	1,805	1,878
2,500cc	3,000cc	548	574	608	630	666	704	762	841	918	1,007	1,084
3,000cc		371	403	443	473	510	543	587	638	671	700	725
All engine sizes		21,681	22,115	22,785	23,196	23,899	24,543	24,985	25,754	26,208	26,508	26,878
Other vehicles		2,317	2,362	2,427	2,469	2,544	2,622	2,730	2,900	3,019	3,137	3,261
All private and light goods		23,998	24,477	25,212	25,666	26,443	27,165	27,715	28,654	29,226	29,645	30,139

(b) Motor cycles, scooters and mopeds tax class: by engine size

Over	Not over	1997	1998	1999	2000	2001	2002	2003	2004	2005	2006	2007
	50cc	96	102	117	141	154	155	159	161	153	144	139
50cc	125cc	143	143	148	160	172	177	182	189	192	199	211
125cc	150cc	1	1	1	1	1	1	1	1	1	1	1
150cc	200cc	12	12	12	13	13	14	16	16	16	15	15
200cc	250cc	44	42	41	38	35	33	33	33	32	32	32
250cc	350cc	10	10	9	9	8	8	9	9	8	8	9
350cc	500cc	54	57	61	62	62	70	74	75	74	72	71
500cc		265	317	371	403	437	482	531	576	599	623	653
All over 50cc		530	582	642	685	727	786	845	899	922	950	992
All engine sizes		626	684	760	825	882	941	1,005	1,060	1,075	1,094	1,133

☎020-7944 3077

9.4 Motor vehicles licensed by tax class in 2007: by method of propulsion

Thousands

Taxation class	Petrol	Diesel	Gas/Petrol-Gas	Gas Bi-Fuel/Gas Diesel	Hybrid-Electric	Other[1]	All
Private and light goods	20,522	9,529	30	27	32	-	30,140
ow: body type cars	20,320	6,482	28	16	32	-	26,878
Motor cycles, scooters and mopeds	1,131	1	-	0	0	-	1,133
Bus	1	108	-	0	0	0	109
Goods	1	445	-	0	0	0	446
Special vehicles group	-	54	1	1	-	-	56
Other non-exempt vehicles	12	18	-	0	0	-	30
Exempt vehicles	1,328	686	2	1	-	26	2,043
ow:							
former Special concessionary group	15	274	-	0	0	8	298
Total All Vehicles	22,997	10,839	34	28	32	27	33,957

1. Other comprises electricity, steam, new fuel technologies, electric diesel and fuel cells. ☎020-7944 3077

9.5 Body type cars licensed: by government office region:[2] 2007

	1997 (thousand)	2006 (thousand)	2007 Body type cars in all taxation classes			
			(thousand)	Per 1000 population	Average vehicle age	Percentage first registered in 2007
North East	800	1,015	1,029	403	6.0	7.7
North West	2,585	3,196	3,215	469	6.1	9.2
Yorkshire and The Humber	1,762	2,176	2,219	432	6.2	7.9
East Midlands	1,655	2,086	2,125	487	6.7	8.0
West Midlands	2,280	2,693	2,737	510	6.4	10.1
East of England	2,372	2,834	2,875	513	7.1	6.7
London	2,339	2,569	2,588	345	7.4	6.4
South East	3,590	4,403	4,467	542	6.9	8.2
South West	2,158	2,640	2,677	522	7.5	6.5
Total England	19,541	23,612	23,932	471	6.8	7.9
Wales	1,102	1,413	1,433	483	6.9	6.5
Scotland	1,726	2,173	2,216	433	5.8	8.8
Great Britain [1]	22,832	27,830	28,228	480	6.7	7.9

1 Totals for Great Britain include vehicles
  for which the region is unknown
2 Regions refer to location where each vehicle is registered

☎020-7944 3077

9.6 Goods vehicles over 3.5 tonnes licensed by body type:[1,2] 2007

Thousands

Body type	Over Not over	3.5 t 7.5 t	7.5 t 12 t	12 t 16 t	16 t 20 t	20 t 24 t	24 t 28 t	28 t 32 t	32 t 33 t	33 t 37 t	37 t 38 t	38 t	All weights
Rigid vehicles													
Box Van		61	4	6	17	1	3	-	-	-	-	-	92
Tipper		21	1	1	5	-	6	17	-	-	-	-	51
Dropside Lorry		12	1	1	5	-	3	-	-	-	-	-	23
Flat Lorry		8	1	1	4	1	5	1	-	-	-	-	20
Curtain Sided		10	1	1	8	1	4	-	0	-	-	-	24
Goods		5	-	1	2	-	2	1	-	-	-	-	12
Insulated Van		7	1	2	4	1	1	-	-	-	-	-	15
Refuse Disposal		1	-	-	2	2	8	2	0	-	-	-	15
Skip Loader		1	-	-	6	-	1	3	-	-	-	-	12
Panel Van		7	-	-	-	-	-	-	0	0	0	0	8
Tanker		-	-	-	2	-	3	1	-	-	-	-	8
Concrete Mixer		-	-	-	1	-	3	1	-	-	-	-	5
Street Cleansing		2	-	2	-	-	-	-	0	0	0	0	5
Tractor		-	-	-	-	-	1	-	-	-	1	2	4
Car Transporter		1	-	-	1	1	-	-	0	-	-	-	4
Livestock Carrier		3	-	-	-	-	-	-	0	0	0	-	4
Van		2	-	-	-	-	-	-	0	-	0	-	2
Luton Van		2	-	-	-	-	-	-	0	0	0	0	2
Special Purpose		1	-	-	-	-	-	-	0	0	-	-	2
Skeletal Vehicle		1	-	-	-	-	-	-	-	0	0	-	2
Truck		1	-	-	-	-	-	-	0	-	-	-	1
Specially Fitted Van		1	-	-	-	-	-	-	-	0	0	-	1
Tower Wagon		1	-	-	-	0	-	-	0	0	0	-	2
Pantechnicon		-	-	-	-	-	-	-	0	0	0	0	1
Motor Home/Caravan		1	-	-	-	0	0	0	0	0	0	0	1
Special Mobile Unit		-	-	-	-	-	-	-	0	0	0	0	1
Glass Carrier		-	-	-	-	-	-	-	0	0	0	0	-
Mobile Plant		-	-	-	-	-	-	-	0	0	-	0	1
Others/Unknown		2	-	1	1	-	1	1	0	-	-	-	5
Total		151	11	18	64	8	41	28	-	-	1	3	324
Articulated vehicles [3]													
Total		-	-	-	-	1	8	4	1	3	19	86	122
Rigid and articulated vehicles													
Total		151	11	19	64	9	49	32	1	3	19	89	446

1 Goods Vehicles identified by tax class
2 Figures may not sum due to rounding
3 There is insufficient reliable data to separate articulated vehicles by body type

☎020-7944 3077

9.7 Goods vehicles over 3.5 tonnes licensed by axle configuration at end of year: [1] 1997-2007

Thousands

| Year | Rigid vehicles | Articulated vehicles | | | All vehicles |
		Not over 28 tonnes	Over 28 tonnes	All	
1997	310	13	99	112	422
1998	310	13	98	111	421
1999	311	14	98	112	423
2000	311	14	100	114	425
2001	314	13	102	115	430
2002	316	12	104	117	433
2003	310	12	105	116	426
2004	316	11	107	118	434
2005	324	10	107	117	433
2006	325	10	111	122	446
2007	324	10	112	122	446

1 Goods vehicles identified by tax class. ☎020-7944 3077

9.8 Goods vehicles over 3.5 tonnes gross weight by axle configuration: [1] 2007

Thousands

| (tonnes) | | Rigid | | | | Articulated | | |
Over	Not over	2 axles	3 axles	4 axles	All rigid vehicles	2 axle tractive unit	3 axle tractive unit	All articulated vehicles
3.5	16	180.0	0.3	0.1	180.3	0.2	0.1	0.3
16	24	63.7	7.6	0.1	71.3	1.3	0.1	1.3
24	28	0.6	39.9	0.6	41.0	7.7	0.4	8.1
28	32	0.2	0.1	27.8	28.1	3.5	0.3	3.7
32	33	-	-	-	-	0.6	0.1	0.7
33	37	-	-	0.2	0.2	2.5	0.5	3.0
37	38	0.1	0.1	0.5	0.7	13.9	4.7	18.5
38		0.2	0.3	2.1	2.6	6.9	79.4	86.3
All weights		244.7	48.3	31.3	324.3	36.5	85.4	122.0

1. Goods vehicles identified by tax class. ☎020-7944 3077

9.9 Trailer tests by axle type: 1999/00-2007/08

National totals									Thousands
First / Annual tests in:	1999/00	2000/01	2001/02	2002/03	2003/04	2004/05	2005/06	2006/07	2007/08
1 axle	7.5	7.1	6.7	6.4	6.0	5.6	5.2	5.0	4.7
2 axle	89.8	82.2	74.1	68.9	63.9	58.4	53.9	49.0	45.9
3 axle	143.2	151.2	156.7	166.5	171.5	177.9	184.7	186.1	189.62
4 axle	0.1	0.1	0.1	0.1	0.1	0.2	0.2	0.2	0.2
5 axle	-	-	-	-	-	-	-	-	-
Total	240.6	240.6	237.6	241.9	241.5	242.1	244.1	240.3	240.46

☎01792 454296
The figures in this table are outside the scope of National Statistics
Source - VOSA

9.10 Road vehicle testing scheme (MOT): test results: 1997/98-2007/08

										Thousand/percentage	
(a) Motor cycles	1997/98	1998/99	1999/00	2000/01	2001/02	2002/03	2003/04	2004/05	2005/06	2006/07	2007/08
Tested	541.1	564.4	513.8	567.8	568.4	584.9	745.0 [1]	801.0	873.2	946.4	956.8
Failed	116.0	124.4	114.4	112.9	113.1	108.4	126.5	166.4	164.1	163.4	176.5
Percentage failed	21	22	22	20	20	19	17	21	19	17	18

(b) Cars, light goods vehicles, private passenger vehicles and other passenger vehicles

Cars and other passenger vehicles:											
Tested	21.5	22.2	22.0	22.8	22.8	22.8	22.5	20.7	22.7	26.3	27.2
Failed	7.8	7.9	7.4	7.2	7.3	7.1	6.6	6.0	7.5	8.7	9.6
Percentage failed	36	36	34	32	32	31	29	29	33	33	35
Light goods vehicles:											
Tested	0.3	0.2	0.3	0.3	0.3	0.4	0.5	0.6	0.4	0.5	0.6
Failed	0.1	0.1	0.1	0.1	0.1	0.1	0.2	0.2	0.2	0.2	0.2
Percentage failed	37	37	33	36	34	35	34	33	44	43	45
Private passenger vehicles: [2]											
Tested	0.03	0.03	0.03	0.03	0.03	0.03	0.04	0.03	0.05	0.05	0.05
Failed	0.01	0.01	0.01	0.01	0.01	0.01	0.01	0.01	0.01	-	-
Percentage failed	28	30	21	25	21	20	25	17	27	28	31

(c) All vehicles

Tested	22.3	23.0	22.9	23.7	23.7	23.8	23.8	22.2	24.0	27.8	28.8
Failed	8.0	8.1	7.6	7.4	7.5	7.3	6.9	6.3	7.9	9.1	10.0
Percentage failed	36	35	33	31	32	31	29	29	33	33	35

1 The overall increase in 2003/04 reflects an increase in small cc scooters,
 bikes and mopeds being tested
2 Vehicles with more than 12 passenger seats.

☎0117 9543382
The figures in this table are outside
the scope of National Statistics
Source - VOSA

9.11 Road passenger service vehicle testing scheme (PSV tests): 1997/98-2007/08

Thousands of tests and failure rates

Year	1997/98	1998/99	1999/00	2000/01	2001/02 [1]	2002/03	2003/04	2004/05	2005/06	2006/07	2007/08
First tests:											
Passed	64,769	62,950	67,219	67,016	65,899	65,458	67,528	67,425	69,270	69,447	70,777
Failed	11,001	12,332	11,216	11,583	14,290	14,515	13,832	13,045	12,086	12,237	11,046
Total tested	75,770	75,282	78,435	78,599	80,189	79,973	81,360	80,470	81,356	81,684	81,823
Re-tests:											
Passed	9,894	11,443	10,417	10,533	13,207	13,731	13,067	11,608	10,148	10,043	11,072
Failed	998	1,141	980	1,053	1,265	1,318	1,197	1,076	847	880	889
Total tested	10,892	12,584	11,397	11,586	14,472	15,049	14,264	12,684	10,995	10,923	11,961
Percentage failed:											
First test	*14.5*	*16.4*	*14.3*	*14.7*	*17.8*	*18.1*	*17.0*	*16.2*	*14.9*	*15.0*	*13.5*
Re-tests	*9.2*	*9.1*	*8.6*	*9.1*	*8.7*	*8.8*	*8.4*	*8.5*	*7.7*	*8.1*	*7.4*
All tests	*13.8*	*15.3*	*13.6*	*14.0*	*16.4*	*16.7*	*15.7*	*15.2*	*14.0*	*14.2*	*12.7*

1 Due to revisions of testing policy, from 2001/02 onwards fewer defects are now allowed to be rectified at the testing station, resulting in a decrease in passes, an increase in failures and an increase in re-tests.

☎01792 454296
The figures in this table are
outside the scope of National Statistics
Source - VOSA

9.12 Goods vehicles over 3.5 tonnes testing scheme (HGV Motor vehicles and Trailers): 1997/98-2007/08

Thousands of tests and failure rates

Year	1997/98	1998/99	1999/00	2000/01	2001/02 [1]	2002/03	2003/04	2004/05	2005/06	2006/07	2007/08
First tests:											
Passed	531.7	535.5	536.1	530.0	510.5	511.5	526.9	538.9	556.9	556.1	568.1
Failed	157.2	158.2	163.1	166.4	192.1	196.6	182.3	168.6	155.1	150.6	135.2
All	688.9	693.6	699.2	696.4	702.6	708.0	709.1	707.4	711.9	706.7	703.3
Re-tests:											
Passed	149.9	150.3	150.7	153.9	179.1	182.7	169.5	148.0	127.9	121.5	125.5
Failed	21.5	22.0	23.7	24.4	31.5	29.9	25.8	23.9	20.5	18.5	15.3
All	171.4	172.3	174.4	178.3	210.6	212.6	195.3	171.9	148.4	140.0	140.8
Percentage failed:											
First test	*22.8*	*22.8*	*23.3*	*23.9*	*27.3*	*27.8*	*25.7*	*23.8*	*21.8*	*21.3*	*19.2*
Re-tests	*12.5*	*12.8*	*13.6*	*13.7*	*15.0*	*14.1*	*13.2*	*13.9*	*13.8*	*13.2*	*10.9*
All tests	*20.8*	*20.8*	*21.4*	*21.7*	*24.5*	*24.6*	*23.0*	*22.0*	*20.4*	*20.0*	*17.8*

1 Due to revisions of testing policy, from 2001/02, fewer defects are now allowed to be rectified at the testing station, resulting in a decrease in passes, an increase in failures and an increase in re-tests.

☎01792 454296
Figures in this table are
outside the scope of National Statistics
Source - VOSA

9.13 Road vehicle testing scheme (MOT): percentage of vehicles failing: by type of defect: 1997/98-2007/08

Motor cycles: [1]											Percentage
	1997/98	1998/99	1999/00	2000/01	2001/02	2002/03	2003/04	2004/05	2005/06[7]	2006/07[7]	2007/08[7]
Brakes	7.9	7.4	8.6	6.5	6.1	5.7	5.7	7.1	5.9	5.2	7.68
Steering	8.3	8.9	9.2	7.9	6.6	6.7	6.7	7.4	2.7	2.4	2.96
Lights	10.7	11.4	11.6	10.1	9.8	9.5	9.1	9.5	10.0	9.7	10.44
Tyres	5.2	5.5	6.2	4.9	4.4	4.4	4.0	4.3	3.3	3.0	4.78
Other	7.5	7.2	5.9	6.4	6.2	5.8	5.4	6.2	.[6]	.[6]	.[6]
Cars and other passenger vehicles: [2]											
Brakes	15.1	14.3	13.4	12.4	12.4	12.0	11.1	10.6	11.8	12.0	18.2
Steering	16.8	16.8	15.8	14.4	13.9	13.5	12.3	11.4	2.7	2.6	3.6
Lights	18.4	18.0	17.6	15.9	16.1	15.8	15.7	14.9	16.4	16.7	19.0
Tyres	9.2	9.3	8.9	8.1	8.0	8.2	8.0	7.7	8.0	8.0	13.4
Petrol emission [3]	7.1	6.4	5.6	4.3	3.1	2.4	1.8	1.4	2.9	3.1	3.3
Diesel emission [3]	8.5	7.3	5.9	6.1	5.5	5.0	4.4	3.8	2.7	2.7	2.3
Other	16.4	15.6	14.0	12.8	12.1	11.2	9.9	9.0	.[6]	.[6]	.[6]
Light goods vehicles: [4]											
Brakes	18.7	18.1	14.2	16.8	15.9	16.4	14.9	14.1	23.3	23.5	32.0
Steering	21.2	20.3	17.3	19.3	17.0	19.1	16.3	16.0	6.6	6.4	8.1
Lights	22.5	22.4	18.7	21.2	19.9	20.5	20.4	19.0	26.1	27.1	29.8
Tyres	9.2	8.1	7.0	7.2	7.7	7.9	6.7	7.0	7.3	7.3	12.5
Petrol emission [3]	8.4	6.9	5.6	5.0	4.4	4.8	2.8	2.2	5.7	7.9	5.5
Diesel emission [3]	6.4	5.6	4.6	4.6	4.0	4.3	4.0	3.1	2.1	2.2	2.0
Reg. plates and VIN	2.0	1.8	2.1	1.9	1.7	1.7	2.0	1.6	2.0	2.0	2.3
Other	19.8	18.6	13.9	16.7	15.8	15.3	13.8	12.7	.[6]	.[6]	.[6]
Private passenger vehicles: [5]											
Brakes	13.0	9.7	7.8	7.8	7.1	6.4	10.6	6.2	11.1	12.1	17.5
Steering	10.6	10.8	8.1	7.6	7.5	6.7	9.3	6.2	3.0	3.2	4.6
Lights	12.7	12.3	10.0	9.8	8.2	8.4	14.0	8.9	12.4	13.8	16.0
Tyres	5.9	4.3	3.0	4.0	3.0	2.5	5.2	2.5	2.4	3.0	5.9
Petrol emission [3]	4.5	4.1	2.5	2.6	1.4	1.7	1.6	2.0	4.9	5.8	5.1
Diesel emission [3]	3.8	5.1	3.7	3.2	3.4	3.0	5.7	2.0	1.0	1.2	1.1
Other	14.1	19.2	12.6	10.7	8.9	10.2	11.6	8.3	.[6]	.[6]	.[6]

1 Emissions testing is not carried out on motorcycles.

2 Cars, 3 wheeled vehicles, motor caravans, vehicles with up to 12 passenger seats, taxis, goods vehicles not exceeding 3000kg gross weight

3 Petrol and diesel emissions tests are calculated individually as a percentage of petrol or diesel vehicles tested.

4 Gross weight over 3000kg up to 3500kg

5 Private passenger vehicles with 13 or more passenger seats (including community buses) etc

6 The failure category of Other is no longer applicable with the introduction of the MOT Computerised system

7 From 2005/06, the failure rates are taken from the new MOT Computerised system.

☎0117 9543382
The figures in this table are
outside the scope of
National Statistics
Source - VOSA

9.14 Households with regular use of car(s): 1951-2006

For details of household car ownership by region and area type, see Table 9.15

					Percentage
Year	No car	One car	Two cars	Three or more cars	All Households
1951	86	13	1	-	100
1952	84	14	1	-	100
1953	83	16	1	-	100
1954	81	17	2	-	100
1955	80	19	2	-	100
1956	78	20	2	-	100
1957	76	22	2	-	100
1958	74	24	2	-	100
1959	73	25	2	-	100
1960	71	27	2	-	100
1961	69	29	2	-	100
1962	67	30	3	-	100
1963	64	33	3	-	100
1964	62	34	4	-	100
1965	59	36	5	-	100
1966	55	39	6	-	100
1967	53	41	6	-	100
1968	51	43	6	-	100
1969	49	45	6	-	100
1970	48	45	6	1	100
1971	48	44	7	1	100
1972	48	44	8	1	100
1973	46	43	9	1	100
1974	45	44	10	1	100
1975	44	45	10	1	100
1976	45	44	10	1	100
1977	43	45	10	1	100
1978	44	45	10	1	100
1979	43	44	11	2	100
1980	41	44	13	2	100
1981	40	45	13	2	100
1982	40	44	13	2	100
1983	39	44	14	2	100
1984	39	44	14	3	100
1985	38	45	15	3	100
1986	38	45	15	3	100
1987	36	45	16	3	100
1988	35	44	17	3	100
1989	34	44	18	4	100
1990	33	44	19	4	100
1991	32	45	19	4	100
1992	32	45	20	4	100
1993	31	45	20	4	100
1994	32	45	20	4	100
1995	30	45	21	4	100
1996	30	45	21	4	100
1997	30	45	21	5	100
1998	28	44	23	5	100
1999	28	44	22	5	100
2000	27	45	23	5	100
2001	26	45	23	5	100
2002	26	44	24	5	100
2003	26	44	25	5	100
2004	25	44	25	5	100
2005[R]	25	44	25	5	100
2006	24	44	26	6	100

Note: Data from 1961 onward are derived from household surveys.
Figures for earlier years are estimates.

☎020-7944 3097
Source - Family Expenditure Survey, ONS;
General Household Survey, ONS;
National Travel Survey, DfT

9.15 Private motoring: households with regular use of cars

Historic details from 1951 are available in Table 9.14

(a) 1991-2006

Percentage

Combined survey data[1]	No car	One car	Two cars	Three or more cars	All Households
1991	32	45	19	4	100
2001	26	45	23	5	100
2002	26	44	24	5	100
2003	26	44	25	5	100
2004	25	44	25	5	100
2005[R]	25	44	25	5	100
2006	24	44	26	6	100
Census data					
1991	33	44	19	4	100
2001	27	44	23	6	100

(b) By Government Office Region: 2006 [1]

Percentage

	No car	One car	Two or more cars	All Households
North East	31	45	23	100
North West	27	43	31	100
Yorkshire and the Humber	25	45	30	100
East Midlands	19	45	36	100
West Midlands	23	42	36	100
East of England	17	42	41	100
London	36	46	18	100
South East	18	43	39	100
South West	17	45	37	100
England	24	44	33	100
Wales	22	45	33	100
Scotland	29	45	26	100
Great Britain	24	44	32	100

(c) By area type : 2007

Percentage/number

	Cars per Household	No car	One car	Two or more cars	All Households
London Boroughs	0.77	43	41	16	100
Metropolitan areas	1.01	31	42	27	100
Other urban areas with population:					
Over 250 thousand	1.08	27	44	29	100
25 to 250 thousand	1.16	23	44	32	100
10 to 25 thousand	1.17	22	46	32	100
3 to 10 thousand	1.31	19	42	40	100
Rural areas	1.54	10	38	51	100
Great Britain	1.14	25	43	32	100

1 Based on combined survey data sources - Family Expenditure Survey, ONS;
General Household Survey, ONS; National Travel Survey, DfT.

☎020 7944 3097

9.16 Private motoring: full car driving licence holders by age and gender: 1975/1976-2007

Percentage/number (millions)

Year	Age							All adults	Estimated number of licence holders
(a) All adults	17-20	21-29	30-39	40-49	50-59	60-69	70 or over		
1975/1976	28	59	67	60	50	35	15	48	19.4
1985/1986	33	63	74	71	60	47	27	57	24.3
1989/1991	43	72	77	78	67	54	32	64	27.8
1992/1994	48	75	82	79	72	57	33	67	29.3
1995/1997[1]	43	74	81	81	75	63	38	69	30.3
1998/2000	41	75	84	83	77	67	39	71	31.4
2002	33	67	82	84	81	70	44	70	31.9
2003	29	67	82	83	80	72	44	70	32.1
2004	27	65	82	83	80	72	46	70	32.2
2005	32	66	82	84	82	74	51	72	33.3
2006	34	67	82	84	82	76	50	72	33.7
2007	38	66	81	83	82	75	52	71	33.8
(b) Male									
1975/1976	36	78	85	83	75	58	32	69	13.4
1985/1986	37	73	86	87	81	72	51	74	15.1
1989/1991	52	82	88	89	85	78	58	80	16.7
1992/1994	54	83	91	88	88	81	59	81	17.0
1995/1997[1]	50	80	88	89	89	83	65	81	17.2
1998/2000	44	80	89	91	88	83	65	82	17.4
2002	35	71	88	90	89	85	68	80	17.5
2003	33	73	87	90	91	87	69	81	17.8
2004	30	68	87	89	90	86	72	79	17.7
2005	37	69	86	90	90	88	73	81	18.1
2006	37	71	86	89	91	90	76	81	18.4
2007	41	69	86	88	90	87	75	80	18.4
(c) Female									
1975/1976	20	43	48	37	24	15	4	29	6.0
1985/1986	29	54	62	56	41	24	11	41	9.2
1989/1991	35	64	67	66	49	33	15	49	11.1
1992/1994	42	68	73	70	57	37	16	54	12.2
1995/1997[1]	36	67	74	73	62	45	21	57	13.1
1998/2000	38	69	78	76	67	53	22	60	14.0
2002	31	62	76	78	73	55	27	61	14.4
2003	25	62	77	77	70	58	26	61	14.3
2004	24	62	77	77	71	58	28	61	14.5
2005	27	62	77	79	73	61	35	63	15.2
2006	31	63	78	79	74	63	31	63	15.3
2007	34	62	76	78	74	63	36	63	15.4

1 Figures for 1995 onwards are based on weighted data

☎020-7944 3097

9.17 Annual mileage of 4-wheeled cars by type of car and trip purpose: 2007

Miles/percentage

	Business Mileage	Commuting mileage	Other private mileage	Total mileage	Proportion of cars in sample
All company cars	8,060	6,100	5,830	19,990	5
Self-employed business car	5,030	3,640	4,580	13,260	3
Household car used for work	3,670	3,810	4,720	12,200	12
Other household car	60	2,320	5,080	7,460	80
All private cars	690	2,550	5,020	8,260	95
All cars	1,070	2,740	5,060	8,870	100

	Business Mileage	Commuting mileage	Other private mileage	Total mileage	Proportion of company cars in sample
All 4-wheeled cars:					
1995/1997[R]	1,710	2,830	5,160	9,700	7
1998/2000[R]	1,590	2,940	5,030	9,550	8
2002	1,250	2,780	5,140	9,170	7
2003	1,230	2,840	5,160	9,230	6
2004	1,140	2,850	5,170	9,160	6
2005	1,090	2,840	5,080	9,010	6
2006	1,040	2,770	4,960	8,770	5
2007	1,070	2,740	5,060	8,870	5

☎020 7944 3097

9.18 Private motoring: Car driving tests: 1997-2007/08

Thousands/rate

	1997[2,3]	1998/99	1999/00	2000/01	2001/02	2002/03	2003/04	2004/05	2005/06	2006/07	2007/08
Applications received [1]	1,206	1,286	1,205	1,263	1,315	1,468	1,526	1,675	1,847	1,883	1,878
Tests conducted	1,122	1,166	1,130	1,015	1,216	1,344	1,399	1,668	1,834	1,784	1,769
Passed:											
Male	257	267	256	229	273	300	304	365	411	405	412
Female	269	268	240	214	254	283	295	340	370	367	370
Total	526	535	496	443	527	583	598	706	781	773	782
Pass rate, by sex:											
Male	52	51	48	48	47	47	46	46	46	46	47
Female	43	42	40	40	40	40	40	39	40	41	41
Total	47	46	44	44	43	43	43	42	43	43	44

1   These are gross figures and take no account of applications
    which do not mature into a test due to cancellations etc.
2   Figures for 1996 and 1997 calculated on calendar year.
    Figures for following years calculated on financial years basis
3   Theory Test introduced

☎02920 581218
The figures in this table are outside
the scope of National Statistics
Source - DSA

10 International Comparisons:

Notes and Definitions

This section gives some broad comparisons between transport in the United Kingdom and transport in other major industrialised countries, based on statistics obtained from international publications. Although efforts have been made to achieve comparability, there are still hazards in international comparisons because of differences in the statistical methods and definitions, so the figures should be used with caution.

In most tables, the figures relate to either 1995 and 2005 or 1996 and 2006. For some countries recent data are not available and figures for earlier years are shown as best estimates with appropriate footnotes.

To ease comparisons, much of the data in the tables have been rounded, typically to three significant figures or fewer, but it should not be assumed that figures are always accurate to the precision shown.

Some United Kingdom (or Great Britain) figures differ from comparable tables in other sections of *Transport Statistics Great Britain*, as they conform to slightly different definitions for consistency with figures for other countries.

Data sources

The data are from a wide variety of sources. Population and Gross Domestic Product estimates are from *National Accounts (OECD)*. Other data come from the EU publication *Energy and Transport in Figures, and World Road Statistics (IRF)*, or from national statistics.

General Statistics: 10.1

Values at market exchange rates are series at current domestic prices converted to Euros by way of current exchange rates for those countries outside the Euro zone. Purchasing power parities are price relatives which show the ratio of the prices in national currencies of the same good or service in different countries relative to the EU27.

Road vehicles by type: 10.3

Stock of road vehicles: The number of road vehicles registered at a given date in a country and licensed to use roads open to public traffic. This includes road vehicles exempted from annual taxes or license fees; it also includes imported second-hand vehicles and other road vehicles according to national practices. The statistics should exclude military vehicles.

Passenger car: Road motor vehicle, other than a motor cycle, intended for the carriage of passengers and designed to seat no more than nine persons (including the driver). This, therefore, includes taxis and hired passenger cars provided that they have fewer than ten seats. This category may also include pick-ups.

Goods vehicle: Any single road motor vehicle designed to carry goods. This excludes articulated tractors and semi-trailers.

Motorcycle: Two-wheeled road motor vehicle with or without side-car, including motor scooter, or three-wheeled road motor vehicle not exceeding 400kg unladen weight. In most countries all such vehicles with a cylinder capacity of 50cc or over are included, as are those under 50cc which do not meet the definition of moped.

Moped: Two- or three-wheeled road vehicle fitted with an engine with a cylinder capacity of less than 50cc and a maximum authorised design speed in accordance with national regulations.

Buses and coaches: Passenger road motor vehicle (including mini-buses) designed to seat more than nine persons (including the driver).

Road traffic: 10.4

The Great Britain figures are gathered from traffic counts as described in Section 7 of this volume: for Great Britain, the traffic measured includes that by Great Britain registered (national) vehicles together with a small amount by foreign vehicles on British roads. Other countries' figures are generally for national vehicles, but comparable statistics are not always available since not all countries have a regular monitoring programme. Some countries rely on roadside interviews, fuel consumption and vehicle ownership data to derive the road traffic statistics.

For Great Britain, vehicle kilometres for buses and coaches relate to vehicles with bus and coach body types as opposed to just those taxed as hackneys with nine or more seats. This differs from Table 10.3 and may differ from other countries.

163

Freight Transport: 10.5

Road traffic: Figures relate to national and international freight carried by vehicles registered in the country. For most countries these are not comparable with those published previously, as earlier figures related to all freight moved regardless of the nationality of the vehicle.

Inland waterway traffic: Includes all transport loaded and moved on a country's inland waterways on inland waterway craft. It excludes traffic on vessels passing from the sea to an inland waterway.

Rail traffic: Includes all traffic on the country's network.

Passenger transport: 10.6

There are substantial differences in methods used to estimate passenger kilometres, so that results give only a broad indication of variation between countries.

Carbon dioxide emissions from transport: 10.7

This table is based on data from submissions by member states to the United Nations Framework Convention on Climate Change (UNFCCC). The full data can be found at:

http://unfccc.int/national_reports/annex_i_ghg_i nventories/national_inventories_submissions/ite ms/4303.php

The data follow the Intergovernmental Panel on Climate Change (IPCC) definitions of emissions, and are on the by source basis. Land Use, Land Use Change and Forestry (LULUCF) emissions have been excluded from the totals for international comparisons, because treatment of this category can vary between countries. The data in table 3.8(a) for UK 'net emissions all sources' includes LULUCF. Transport emissions of carbon dioxide are based on fuel purchases in the country in question.

Table 10.11 includes emissions from Crown Dependencies of Jersey, Guernsey and Isle of Man, and emissions from Overseas Territories. Table 3.7(a) includes emissions from Crown Dependencies but not from Overseas Territories.

Fuel prices: 10.8

The figures comparing the price of petrol and diesel are supplied by the Department for Business, Enterprise & Regulatory Reform, and are extracted from the IEA publication 'Energy Prices & Taxes'.

The use of the term Tax in part (b) of this table is necessary because some other European countries impose other taxes and fees on fuel. For the United Kingdom this includes just fuel duty and VAT.

The figures in Table 10.8 differ from those in Table 3.3 because of the differences in availability and timing of data collection. The international comparisons in Table 10.8 are based on averages over the year. Table 3.3 attempts to be as up to date as reasonably possible.

Principal fleets: 10.9

Fleets: Includes all trading ships of 100 gross tons and over, so that totals given here for the United Kingdom are not comparable with those given in Table 5.14 which includes trading ships in excess of 500 gross tons.

Airlines: 10.10

The figures in this table are supplied by International Civil Aviation Organisation (ICAO). A substantial proportion of the figures are estimated by ICAO on the basis of part-year data; the table therefore of use only as a guide. Airlines have been allocated to the country in which they are registered, apart from Cathay Pacific, which is based in Hong Kong, and which has been excluded from the United Kingdom figures. Traffic of the Scandinavian Airline System (SAS) has been divided 2:2:3 between Denmark, Norway and Sweden, respectively. The freight tonne-kilometres shown are those carried on freight-only flights.

Because they are not necessarily based on the same airlines each year, figures for some countries will not strictly be comparable over time.

Road deaths: 10.11

The data shown in this table are reproduced from the OECD International Road Traffic and Accident Database, International Transport Forum (ITF) and EU (CARE DATABASE).

International definition (Vienna Convention 1968) of road death: Any person who was killed outright or who died within 30 days as a result of the accident. Some countries use different definitions but adjustments are made for international comparability to a common 30 day basis.

10.1 General Statistics: 2006

	Population [2] (millions)	Area (1000 sq kms)	Population per square kilometre	Gross Domestic Product at current prices			
				At market exchange rates			At purchasing power parity [1]
				Euro (billion)	Euro per head of Population	1 Euro = [3]	Euro per head of Population
Great Britain	58.8	229	257	..	..	..	..
Northern Ireland	1.7	14	128	..	..	..	..
United Kingdom	60.6	243	250	1,910	31,500	0.68173	27,900
Austria	8.3	84	99	258	31,100	..	30,200
Belgium	10.5	31	344	317	30,000	1.956	28,900
Bulgaria	7.7	111	69	25	3,300	28.342	8,700
Cyprus	0.8	9	83	15	18,900	0.57578	21,900
Czech Republic	10.3	79	130	114	11,100	7.4591	18,600
Denmark	5.4	43	126	220	40,500	..	29,700
Estonia	1.3	45	30	13	9,800	15.6466	15,900
Finland	5.3	338	16	167	31,700	..	27,300
France	61.4	547	112	1,792	28,400	..	26,500
Germany	82.4	357	231	2,322	28,200	..	26,700
Greece	11.2	132	85	214	19,300	..	22,700
Hungary	10.1	93	108	90	8,900	264.26	15,300
Irish Republic	4.2	70	60	175	41,100	..	33,500
Italy	58.9	301	195	1,475	25,100	..	24,300
Latvia	2.3	65	36	16	7,100	0.6962	13,100
Lithuania	3.4	65	52	24	7,000	3.4528	13,500
Luxembourg	0.5	3	182	34	71,600	..	65,400
Malta	0.4	0	1,297	5	12,400	0.4293	17,700
Netherlands	16.3	42	390	534	32,700	..	31,000
Poland	38.1	313	122	272	7,100	3.8959	12,400
Portugal	10.6	92	115	155	14,700	..	17,500
Romania	21.6	238	91	97	4,500	3.5258	8,800
Slovak Republic	5.4	49	111	45	8,300	37.234	14,900
Slovenia	2.0	20	99	30	15,200	239.60	20,800
Spain	44.1	505	87	981	22,300	..	24,000
Sweden	9.1	450	20	306	33,700	9.2544	28,200
EU27	492.0	4,325	114	11,583	23,500	..	23,500
Norway	4.6	324	14	268	57,500	8.0472	44,000
Switzerland	7.5	41	182	309	40,900	1.5729	31,900
Japan	127.8	378	338	3,477	27,200	146.02	26,700
USA	299.4	9,827	30	10,509	35,000	1.2556	36,300

1 In terms of euros that have the same purchasing power over the whole of the EU calculated weighted average of the purchasing power of the national currencies of EU Member States.
2 Some figures provisional
3 Exchange rate: 1 Euro = in national currency in 2006

☎020-7944 4442
The figures in this table are outside the scope of UK National Statistics
Source - European Commission, Eurostat Yearbook, *European Economic Statistics; National Accounts (OECD) Population Trends (ONS)*

10.2 Road and rail infrastructure: 1995 and 2005

Thousand kilometres

	Road network						Rail network					
	All roads		ow: motorways		All roads per 1,000 square kilometres (kilometres)		In operation		ow: electrified		Rail network per 1,000 square kilometres (kilometres)	
	1995	2005	1995	2005	1995	2005	1995	2005	1995	2005	1995	2005
Great Britain	386	388	3.2	3.5	1,680	1,687	16.7	15.8	5.2	5.2	72	69
Northern Ireland	24	25	0.1	0.1	1,714	1,794	0.2	0.3 [1]	..	..	14	21
United Kingdom	410	413	3.3	3.6	1,682	1,693	16.9	16.1	5.2	5.2	69	66
Austria	130	134 [1]	1.6	1.7	1,550	1,596	5.7	5.7	3.3	3.5	68	68
Belgium	143	152	1.7	1.7	4,694	4,991	3.4	3.5	2.4	3.0	110	116
Denmark	71	72	0.8	1.0	1,653	1,676	2.8	2.6	0.4	0.6	66	61
Finland	78		0.4	0.7	230		5.9	5.7	2.0	2.6	17	17
France	893	951	8.3	10.8	1,641	1,748	31.9	29.3	13.7	14.8	59	54
Germany	642		11.2	12.4	1,798		41.7	34.2	17.7	19.4	117	96
Greece	117	118	0.4	0.9	886	890	2.5	2.6	..	0.1	19	20
Irish Republic	93	97	0.1	0.2	1,316	1,373	2.0	1.9	-	0.1	28	27
Italy	315		6.4	6.5	1,045		16.0	16.5	10.1 [1]	11.6	53	55
Luxembourg	5	5	0.1	0.1	1,975	2,010	0.3	0.3	-	0.3	106	106
Netherlands	122	134	2.2	2.3	2,940	3,234	2.7	2.8	2.0	2.1	66	68
Portugal	69	79	0.7	2.3	748	858	2.9	2.8	0.5	1.4	31	31
Spain	343		7.0	11.4	678		14.3	14.5	6.9	8.2	28	29
Sweden	211	425	1.3	1.7	469	945	10.9	11.0	7.2	7.7	24	24
Cyprus	..	..	0.2	0.3	..	..	..	..	-	-	.	.
Czech Republic	56	128	0.4	0.6	708	1,620	9.4	9.5	2.6	3.0	120	121
Estonia	15	57	0.1	0.1	332	1,261	1.0	1.0	..	0.1	23	21
Hungary	159	189	0.3	0.6	1,706	2,037	8.0	8.0	2.3	2.8	86	85
Latvia	60	70	-	-	930	1,081	2.4	2.3	..	0.3	37	35
Lithuania	63	79	0.4	0.4	959	1,219	2.0	1.8	..	0.1	31	27
Malta	2	..	-	-	.	.	..	..	-	-	.	.
Poland	372	..	0.2	0.6	1,191	..	24.0	19.5	..	11.9	77	62
Slovak Republic	42	44	0.2	0.3	870	896	3.7	3.6	1.4	1.6	75	74
Slovenia	15	38	0.3	0.6	731	1,896	1.2	1.2	..	0.5	59	60
Norway	90	93	0.1	0.3	278	287	4.0	4.1	2.4	2.5	12	13
Switzerland	71	71	1.2	1.4	1,720	1,726	3.2	3.4	..	3.4	78	82
Japan	1,142	1,193	5.7 [2]	7.4 [2]	3,022	3,156	20.3	20.1	11.9	12.2	54	53
USA	6,296	6,430	88.1	94.6	672	687	..	205.6	..	..	..	22

1. 2004 data.
2. National expressways

☎020-7944 3088

The figures in this table are outside the scope of UK National Statistics

Source - EU Energy and Transport in Figures (EUROSTAT); IRF
Ministry of Land, Infrastructure and Transport, Japan

10.3 Road vehicles by type, at end of year: 1996 and 2006

Thousands

	Cars and taxis		Goods vehicles [1]		Motorcycles [1,2]		Buses and coaches	
	1996	2006	1996	2006	1996	2006	1996	2006
Great Britain	22,272	27,873	2,555	3,472	769	1,240	158	181
Northern Ireland	547	794	63	110	13	30	5	6
United Kingdom	22,819	28,667	2,618	3,582	782	1,270	163	187
Austria	3,691	4,205	..	..	560	645	10	9
Belgium	4,339	4,976	457	670	212	360	15	15
Denmark	1,744	2,020	340	509	74	184	14	15
Finland	1,943	2,506	259	376	163	338	8	11
France	28,017	31,002	4,976	5,345	2,278	2,500 [3]	82	92
Germany	41,372	46,570	2,429	2,804	4,184	5,781	85	84
Greece	2,241	4,543	902	1,220	..	1,206	25	27
Irish Republic	1,057	1,802	147	319	24	35	6	8
Italy	29,911	35,297	3,000	4,332	6,391	10,239	78	96
Luxembourg	232	315	18	31	29	39	1	1
Netherlands	5,740	7,230	684	996	335	568	11	11
Portugal	2,750	4,290	970	1,320	241	559	16	15
Spain	14,754	20,637	3,057	5,033	1,308	4,385	48	58
Sweden	3,655	4,202	312	480	273	498	15	14
Cyprus	227	373	104	116	50 [4]	40	3	3
Czech Republic	3,193	4,109	225	491	915 [4]	823	21	21
Estonia	407	554	71	93	5	13	7	5
Hungary	2,264	2,954	303	444	..	130	19	18
Latvia	380	822	73	121	18	37	17	11
Lithuania	785	1,592	89	136	19	26	15	15
Malta	182	218	38	46	12	12	1	1
Poland	8,054	13,384	1,371	2,393	929 [4]	784	85	84
Slovak Republic	1,058	1,334	97	189	80	58	11	9
Slovenia	741	980	42	70	..	53	2	2
Norway	1,661	2,084	358	489	165	269	34	27
Switzerland	3,268	3,900	263	314	382	609	38	46
Japan	45,069 [4]	57,510	21,694	16,491	15,262	..	242	232
USA	129,728	135,399	76,147 [5]	107,944 [5]	3,871	6,679	697	822

1 There are differences in definitions between
   countries which limit comparisons.
2 Includes mopeds and three-wheeled
   vehicles but excludes pedal cycles.
3 Estimated by Eurostat.
4 1995 data.
5 Includes 2-axle, 4-tyre vehicles other than passenger cars.

☎020-7944 3088
The figures in this table are
outside the scope of UK National Statistics
Source - EU Energy and Transport in Figures (EUROSTAT)
Ministry of Land, Infrastructure and Transport, Japan
Highway Statistics, USA

10.4 Road traffic on national territory: 1995 and 2005

Billion vehicle kilometres

	Cars and taxis		Goods vehicles [1]		Motor cycles [2]		Buses and coaches	
	1995	2005	1995	2005	1995	2005	1995	2005
Great Britain	351.1	397.2	69.9	91.6	3.7	5.4	4.9	5.2
Austria	..	37.0	..	10.4	..	0.5 [3]	..	0.4 [3]
Belgium	91.2	79.6	1.8	13.2	..	1.1 [3]	62.3	0.8 [3]
Denmark	33.8	34.1 [3]	6.0	10.7 [3]	0.3	..	-	0.6 [3]
Finland	35.8	44.2	5.8	6.9	..	..	0.6	0.6
France	367.0	420.0	102.0	125.0	4.0	8.5	2.3	2.5
Germany	514.9	578.2	53.2	57.3	12.8	13.0	3.7	3.5
Greece	35.3	65.2 [3]	25.3	..	7.1	..	1.4	..
Irish Republic	22.5	..	4.8	..	0.3	..	0.3	..
Italy	187.1	..	33.6	..	..	..	..	..
Luxembourg	3.0	3.5 [4]	0.5	0.5 [4]	0.0	0.0 [4]	0.3	0.0 [4]
Netherlands	89.1	..	15.3	..	1.7	..	0.6	..
Portugal	38.4	..	39.0	..	1.2	..	0.7	..
Spain	108.0	..	18.9	..	0.7	..	2.1	..
Sweden	56.3	63.0	8.2	9.9	0.5	0.9	1.1	0.9
Cyprus	..	6.4 [3]	..	2.8 [3]	..	0.5 [3]	..	0.3 [3]
Czech Republic	24.5	..	2.4	..	0.6	..	10.4	..
Estonia	4.0	6.4	1.3	1.5	..	..	0.2	0.2
Hungary	..	..	..	..	..	..	..	..
Latvia	..	8.0	..	1.9	..	..	..	0.3
Lithuania	..	6.8	2.2	1.7	..	0.1	0.2	0.1
Malta	..	..	..	..	..	..	..	..
Poland	75.2	..	32.7	..	3.2	..	5.1	..
Slovak Republic	8.3	..	0.3	..	0.1	..	0.4	..
Slovenia	6.5	9.5	0.6	1.5	0.0	0.1	0.1	0.1
Norway	24.4	21.2 [4]	3.8	4.9 [4]	0.6	1.0 [4]	0.3	1.0 [4]
Switzerland	43.8	54.3	5.0	5.4	1.7	2.3	0.1	0.1
Japan	446.4	526.3 [3]	267.1	248.7 [3]	..	..	6.8	6.7 [3]
USA	2,315.7	2,719.7	1,558.1	2,063.9	15.8	17.3	10.3	10.7

1 Including light vans.
2 Including mopeds and three wheeled
   vehicles but excluding pedal cycles.
3 2004 data.
4 2003 data.

☎020-7944 3088
The figures in this table are outside the scope of UK National Statistics
Source - IRF
Federal Highway Administration, USA

10.5 Freight moved by mode: 1996 and 2006

Billion tonne-kilometres

	Road [1]		Rail		Inland waterway excluding coastal and one port traffic		Inland pipeline (Oil) 50 km long and over	
	1996	2006	1996	2006	1996	2006	1996	2006
Great Britain	..	..	15.1	23.1	0.2	0.2	11.6	10.8
Northern Ireland	..	..	-	-	-	-	-	-
United Kingdom	166.2	172.2	15.1	23.1	0.2	0.2	11.6	10.8
Austria	27.8	39.2	13.3	21.0	2.1	1.8	7.1	7.6
Belgium	41.8	43.0	7.2	8.6	5.7	8.9	1.5	1.6
Denmark	21.3	21.3	1.8	1.9	.	.	3.5	4.9
Finland	25.0	29.7	8.8	11.1	0.1	0.1	.	.
France	180.0	211.5	49.5	40.9	6.0	9.0	21.9	21.8
Germany	236.6	330.0	70.0	107.0	61.3	64.0	14.5	15.8
Greece	15.0 [2]	34.0	0.3	0.7	.	.	.	0.1
Irish Republic	6.3	17.5	0.6	0.2	.	.	.	.
Italy	175.5 [2]	220.4 [2]	21.0	24.2	0.1	0.1	10.1	11.2
Luxembourg	3.5	8.8	0.5	0.4	0.3	0.4	.	.
Netherlands	69.4	83.2	3.1	5.3	35.5	42.3	6.0	5.8
Portugal	33.6	44.8	1.9	2.4	.	.	.	.
Spain	102.0 [2]	241.8	11.1	11.6	.	.	6.1	10.1
Sweden	33.3	39.9	18.8	22.0	.	.	.	.
Cyprus	1.2	1.2	.	.	.	.	.	.
Czech Republic	30.1	50.4	22.3	15.8	0.1	0.0	2.3	2.3
Estonia	1.9	5.6	4.2	10.4	.	.	.	.
Hungary	14.3	30.5	7.6	10.2	1.4	1.9	2.4 [2]	2.7
Latvia	2.2	10.8	12.4	16.8	.	.	6.1	3.6
Lithuania	4.2	18.1	8.1	12.9	.	.	2.3	2.7
Malta	0.5 [2]	0.3	-	-	.	.	.	.
Poland	56.5	128.3	67.4	53.6	0.9	0.3	15.3	25.6
Slovak Republic	15.9	22.2	12.0	10.0	0.1	0.1	6.1	5.6
Slovenia	3.5 [2]	12.1	2.6	3.4	.	.	.	.
Bulgaria	.	13.8	7.5	5.4	0.5	0.8	0.4	0.4
Romania	19.7	57.3	24.3	15.8	3.8	8.2	2.7	2.0
Norway	9.7	19.4	2.8	3.3	.	.	5.1	4.6
Switzerland	11.4	10.7	7.9	12.4	0.1	0.0	1.2	0.3
Japan	306.0	334.9 [3]	25.0	22.8 [3]	..	..	..	..
USA	1,550.4	1,888.2 [3]	2,010.5	2,531.3 [3]	518.5	476.4 [3]	904.0	835.1 [3]

1 Freight moved by vehicles registered in the country on national and international territory.
2 Estimated
3 2005 Data

☎020-7944 3088
The figures in this table are outside
the scope of UK National Statistics
Source - EU Energy and Transport in Figures (EUROSTAT)
Ministry of Land, Infrastructure and Transport, Japan

10.6 Passenger transport by national vehicles on national territory: 1995 and 2005

Billion passenger kilometres

	Cars		Buses and coaches		Rail excluding metro systems		Total of these modes	
	1995	2005	1995	2005	1995	2005	1995	2005
Great Britain	618.0	674.0	44.3	49.0	30.0	43.2	692.3	766.2
Austria	62.2	70.6	8.7	9.3	10.1	9.1	81.0	89.0
Belgium	98.2	108.9	13.1	17.5	6.8	9.2	118.1	135.6
Denmark	48.7	52.7	7.3	7.4	4.9	5.9	60.9	66.0
Finland	50.0	61.9	8.0	7.5	3.2	3.5	61.2	72.9
France	640.1	727.4	41.6	43.9	55.6	76.5	737.3	847.8
Germany	815.3	856.9	68.5	67.1	71.0	76.8	954.8	1,000.8
Greece	44.0	85.0	20.2	21.7	1.6	1.9	65.8	108.6
Irish Republic	15.5	26.0	5.2	6.7	1.3	1.8	22.0	34.5
Italy	614.7	689.0	87.1	101.2	43.9	46.1	745.7	836.3
Luxembourg	4.7	6.3	0.5	0.8	0.3	0.3	5.5	7.4
Netherlands	131.4	148.8	12.0	11.8	16.4	14.7	159.8	175.3
Portugal	40.9	70.0	11.3	11.0	4.8	3.8	57.0	84.8
Spain	250.4	337.8	39.6	53.2	16.6	21.6	306.6	412.6
Sweden	86.8	97.3	9.7	8.8	6.8	8.9	103.3	115.0
Cyprus	3.4	4.8	1.0	1.3	-	-	4.4 [1]	6.1
Czech Republic	54.5	68.6	18.6	15.6	8.0	637.0	81.1	721.2
Estonia	6.3	10.2	2.0	2.7	0.4	0.2	8.7	13.1
Hungary	45.4	46.6	16.6	17.8	8.4	9.9	70.4	74.3
Latvia	7.5	14.0	1.8	2.9	1.4	0.9	10.7	17.8
Lithuania	16.0	34.8	4.2	3.7	1.1	0.4	21.3	38.9
Malta	1.7	2.0	0.4	0.5	-	-	2.1	2.5
Poland	110.7	197.3	34.0	29.3	26.6	17.9	171.3	244.5
Slovak Republic	18.0	25.8	14.4	8.5	4.2	2.2	36.6	36.5
Slovenia	16.3	22.5	2.5	0.9	0.6	0.8	19.4	24.2
Norway	44.7	53.0	3.8	4.3	2.4	2.7	50.9	60.0
Switzerland	75.5	83.3	5.5	5.7	11.7	16.1	92.7	105.1
Japan	640.0	751.0	100.0	86.0	396.0	385.0	1,136.0	1,222.0
USA	5,702.0 [1]	7,253.5 [1]	219.0	226.8	17.0	23.1 [2]	5,938.0	7,503.4

1 Including light trucks/vans.
2 2004 data.

☎020-7944 3088

The figures in this table are outside the scope of UK National Statistics
Source - EU Energy and Transport in Figures (EUROSTAT)
Ministry of Internal Affairs and Communications, Japan

170

10.7 Carbon dioxide emissions from transport: by source: 1996 and 2006

Million tonnes of carbon dioxide

	Road transport		Railways		Civil aviation		Navigation		All domestic transport[1]		All sources[2]		Memo items[3] International bunkers-aviation		International bunkers-navigation	
	1996	2006	1996	2006	1996	2006	1996	2006	1996	2006	1996	2006	1996	2006	1996	2006
European Union																
United Kingdom[4]	115.4	120.5	1.7	2.2	1.4	2.3	4.0	5.5	122.8	131.0	571.3	557.9	21.4	35.6	7.3	6.8
Austria	15.6	21.9	0.1	0.1	0.1	0.2	0.1	0.1	16.1	22.8	67.4	77.3	1.5	1.8	..	..
Belgium	21.6	24.4	0.2	0.1	-	-	0.4	0.5	22.4	25.2	128.0	119.1	3.3	3.7	15.9	27.3
Denmark	10.8	12.6	0.3	0.2	0.2	0.1	0.8	0.5	12.1	13.4	74.6	58.2	2.0	2.6	4.8	3.4
Finland	10.2	11.9	0.2	0.1	0.3	0.3	0.5	0.6	11.8	13.7	64.0	68.1	1.0	1.4	1.2	1.8
France	121.5	130.1	0.8	0.6	5.6	4.8	1.8	3.0	130.2	139.1	405.4	408.7	11.4	16.8	7.6	9.3
Germany	165.1	148.9	2.3	1.3	3.6	5.3	1.6	0.9	176.7	160.6	943.3	880.3	14.4	21.2	6.5	8.6
Greece	14.5	19.8	0.1	0.1	0.9	1.1	1.5	2.3	17.0	23.4	89.3	109.7	2.5	2.9	9.9	9.8
Irish Republic	6.7	13.1	0.1	0.1	0.1	0.1	0.1	-	7.1	13.5	37.1	47.3	1.0	2.8	0.5	0.4
Italy	104.5	118.3	0.4	0.3	1.9	2.8	5.7	6.1	113.2	128.5	439.3	488.0	6.0	9.2	2.9	6.5
Luxembourg	3.5	7.0	-	-	-	-	-	-	3.5	7.0	9.4	12.1	0.6	1.2	..	..
Netherlands	29.4	34.9	0.1	0.1	-	-	0.4	0.6	29.9	35.6	177.7	172.2	8.1	11.0	36.2	56.2
Portugal	13.1	18.5	0.2	0.1	0.3	0.4	0.2	0.2	13.7	19.3	50.3	64.0	1.5	2.3	1.2	1.7
Spain	64.3	95.1	0.3	0.3	3.8	7.2	1.6	2.8	70.1	105.6	243.0	359.6	6.6	10.0	14.7	26.2
Sweden	17.1	18.5	0.1	0.1	0.6	0.6	0.3	0.5	18.3	20.0	61.6	51.5	1.5	2.0	3.7	7.1
Bulgaria	5.3	7.6	0.1	0.1	0.2	0.1	-	..	6.6	8.6	65.0	55.1	0.5	0.5	0.7	0.3
Cyprus	..	..	..	..	..	..	..	..	..	..	6.0	8.0	..	1.1	..	..
Czech Republic	9.7	17.1	0.3	0.3	0.1	-	-	-	10.5	17.5	138.4	127.9	0.5	0.1	..	..
Estonia	1.4	2.1	0.1	0.1	-	-	-	-	1.7	2.4	18.7	16.0	-	0.7	0.3	0.7
Hungary	6.5	12.1	0.3	0.2	..	-	-	-	6.8	12.3	63.4	60.4	0.6	0.2	..	..
Latvia	1.7	3.1	0.2	0.2	-	-	-	-	2.0	3.3	9.2	8.3	0.1	0.2	0.3	0.6
Lithuania	3.0	4.2	0.3	0.2	-	-	-	-	3.3	4.4	15.8	14.5	0.1	0.2	0.4	0.4
Malta	..	..	..	..	..	..	..	..	..	..	2.0	3.0	..	..	..	..
Poland	29.3	36.2	0.7	0.5	0.1	0.1	0.1	-	31.7	37.4	374.9	330.5	1.1	1.2	0.7	0.9
Romania	10.2	12.0	0.9	0.2	-	-	0.1	-	11.2	12.3	135.4	111.0	0.3	0.4	0.4	0.1
Slovak Republic	4.1	5.7	0.2	0.1	-	-	..	..	4.3	5.8	42.4	40.0	0.1	0.1	..	..
Slovenia	4.2	4.6	-	-	..	-	..	..	4.2	4.6	15.7	16.9	0.1	0.1	..	0.1

1 Includes a small amount of emissions from other transport sources.
2 The Land Use, Land Use Change and Forestry (LULUCF) category has been excluded from the totals, because treatment of this category can differ between countries.
3 Categories not included in the national emissions total.
4 Figures for the UK are slightly higher than those in Table 3.8(a) due to the inclusion of emissions from Overseas Territories.

☎020-7944 4276

The figures in this table are outside the scope of UK National Statistics

Source - UNFCCC

10.8 (a) Petrol and diesel in the European Union: current retail prices: 1997-2007

Premium unleaded petrol (95 RON): per 100 litres											US Dollars
	1997	1998	1999	2000	2001	2002	2003	2004	2005	2006	2007
United Kingdom	101	108	113	121	110	110	125	147	158	168	188
Austria	97	90	87	87	81	82	99	118	130	137	154
Belgium	104	96	96	97	90	92	115	142	142	170	190
Denmark [1]	101	96	102	103	99	104	125	140	140	161	179
Germany	96	91	93	94	91	99	123	141	152	159	182
Finland	106	104	106	105	99	101	124	146	142	162	178
France	106	102	101	101	93	96	115	132	145	155	174
Greece	78	70	69	72	67	69	84	101	109 [R]	121 [P]	138
Irish Republic	89	84	80	82	80	81	98	118	129	140	153
Italy	107	101	102	100	94	99	120	140	152	161	178
Luxembourg	76	71	74	76	72	73	88	112	127	136	154
Netherlands	109	107	107	107	103	113	131	161	168	178	200
Portugal	93	90	86	80	81	83	109	128	142	164	181
Spain	79	74	75	76	73	77	92	108	119	128	142
Sweden	108	101	101	104	91	96	116	136	147	156	172

Lead replacement petrol [2,3]: per 100 litres											
United Kingdom	110	118	125	130	115	115	131	155	..	..	..
Austria	..	..	..	..	..	..	..	..	..	..	..
Belgium	112	105	103	101	97	99	..	..	..	..	..
Denmark	..	..	..	..	..	..	..	..	..	..	..
Germany	..	..	..	..	..	..	..	..	..	..	..
Finland	..	..	..	..	..	..	..	..	..	..	..
France	110	107	106	108	100	103	124	142	..	..	..
Greece	84	75	75	76	71	74	89	108	117 [R]	128 [P]	..
Irish Republic	98	98	95	96	..	..	..	..	..	..	..
Italy	113	107	107	104	98	..	..	..	..	..	..
Luxembourg	85	80	..	..	..	..	..	..	..	..	..
Netherlands	..	..	..	..	..	..	..	..	..	..	..
Portugal	96	93	89	..	..	..	..	..	..	..	..
Spain	82	78	79	81	77	82	100	117	130	140	..
Sweden	121	106	105	107	..	..	..	..	..	..	..

Diesel: per 100 litres											
United Kingdom	102	109	117	123	112	113	128	150	165	175	194
Austria	77	70	68	72	67	68	82	101	119	127	142
Belgium	75	69	68	75	70	68	84	109	109	135	150
Denmark	79	77	80	88	84	86	103	114	114	138	152
Germany	72	65	68	94	73	79	100	116	133	140	160
Finland	73	69	73	78	73	74	91	103	105	128	139
France	76	72	73	78	72	73	90	110	128	135	149
Greece	59	51	56	62	56	59	72	92	109 [R]	119 [P]	135
Irish Republic	85	79	75	78	73	73	91	110	129	137	148
Italy	85	79	81	82	78	81	99	117	138	146	159
Luxembourg	62	57	58	64	59	60	72	86	105	115	128
Netherlands	77	72	74	78	73	74	90	110	127	136	150
Portugal	64	59	58	60	60	61	80	98	116	133	150
Spain	87	79	60	64	62	65	78	94	111	119	131
Sweden	89	84	81	92	84	86	100	116	139	151	163

10.8 (b) Petrol and diesel in the European Union: Tax as a percentage of retail prices: 1997-2007

Premium unleaded petrol (95 RON) — Percentage

	1997	1998	1999	2000	2001	2002	2003	2004	2005	2006	2007
United Kingdom	77	81	81	75	76	77	76	74	69	67	67
Austria	65	68	68	61	63	64	64	62	57	56	57
Belgium	73	76	74	66	67	69	67	66	66	61	61
Denmark [1]	70	72	73	67	68	70	70	68	68	62	61
Germany	72	75	74	69	72	73	74	71	67	65	65
Finland	75	78	74	67	68	70	72	68	70	64	64
France	78	81	79	70	71	74	74	72	67	64	64
Greece	65	67	63	53	55	56	55	52	49 R	47 P	50
Irish Republic	67	68	68	59	56	64	64	64	60	57	57
Italy	72	75	73	65	66	68	68	66	63	61	60
Luxembourg	62	66	64	56	58	59	59	60	56	54	54
Netherlands	72	75	73	66	69	68	71	67	66	64	63
Portugal	70	73	68	49	46	69	68	67	63	60	61
Spain	65	69	67	59	59	62	62	59	55	53	52
Sweden	73	76	73	67	68	70	70	68	65	63	63

Lead replacement petrol [2,3]

	1997	1998	1999	2000	2001	2002	2003	2004	2005	2006	2007
United Kingdom	80	83	81	74	76	78	76	72	..	..	..
Austria	..	..	..	..	..	..	..	..	..	..	..
Belgium	74	77	76	64	64	67	..	..	..	..	..
Denmark	..	..	..	..	..	..	..	..	..	..	..
Germany	..	..	..	..	..	..	..	..	..	..	..
Finland	..	..	..	..	..	..	..	..	..	..	..
France	80	83	81	70	72	74	75	72	..	..	..
Greece	69	70	67	56	58	58	58	54	51 R	48 P	..
Irish Republic	67	70	69	61	..	..	..	..	..	..	..
Italy	74	76	74	66	68	..	..	..	..	..	..
Luxembourg	66	69	..	..	..	..	..	..	..	..	..
Netherlands	..	..	..	..	..	..	..	..	..	..	..
Portugal	73	74	67	..	..	..	..	..	..	..	..
Spain	68	71	69	60	60	63	62	59	55	52	..
Sweden	78	81	78	72	..	..	..	..	..	..	..

Diesel

	1997	1998	1999	2000	2001	2002	2003	2004	2005	2006	2007
United Kingdom	77	82	81	74	74	76	74	72	67	65	65
Austria	58	63	62	54	55	57	57	55	50	50	52
Belgium	61	64	63	53	54	59	58	55	55	48	47
Denmark	64	64	61	56	59	60	61	60	60	53	53
Germany	63	68	67	61	63	66	67	64	58	56	56
Finland	62	67	63	54	55	57	58	56	56	49	49
France	70	75	73	62	64	66	66	64	57	55	56
Greece	62	65	64	52	54	55	54	48	43	42 P	44
Irish Republic	63	64	64	55	48	57	58	59	53	51	51
Italy	68	71	70	60	61	64	63	60	54	52	53
Luxembourg	59	63	60	50	52	53	53	50	44	43	44
Netherlands	63	67	65	56	57	59	59	57	52	50	50
Portugal	61	64	63	52	51	57	57	55	50	49	50
Spain	60	64	62	53	54	56	56	53	47	45	45
Sweden	60	62	60	55	55	57	59	59	55	53	54

1 Regular unleaded (92 RON) prices have been used from 2000 to date.
2 Refers to Four star petrol in earlier years.
3 The sale of Lead Replacement Petrol has been discontinued in most EU Countries

☎020-7215 6935
The figures in this table are outside the scope of UK National Statistics
Source - Department for Business, Enterprise and Regulatory Reform

10.9 Principal trading fleets by type of vessel and flag at mid year: 1997 and 2007

Gross tonnage (million)

| | All trading ships of 100 gross tons and over | | *of which:* | | | | | | | |
| | | | Tankers | | Bulk carriers | | Container ships | | General cargo | |
	1997	2007	1997	2007	1997	2007	1997	2007	1997	2007
United Kingdom and Crown Dependencies	7.1	20.1	3.4	7.5	0.8	2.9	1.1	6.0	0.6	2.1
Denmark	5.3	8.9	1.5	2.1	0.5	0.3	2.1	5.5	0.7	0.5
France	4.1	5.8	2.4	3.1	0.4	0.2	0.5	1.6	0.3	0.1
Germany	5.5	12.1	0.2	0.6	0.0	0.2	4.1	10.8	0.9	0.3
Greece	26.5	33.6	13.5	19.6	9.9	10.0	0.9	2.3	1.1	0.4
Italy	6.1	12.6	2.3	3.7	1.5	2.1	0.4	1.2	0.8	2.4
Netherlands	4.5	6.3	0.9	0.5	0.2	0.2	1.1	1.4	1.7	3.0
Bahamas	24.5	40.6	12.1	18.8	4.4	7.7	1.0	1.9	5.7	6.4
Bermuda	4.0	8.3	2.3	3.7	0.9	1.8	0.5	0.8	0.2	0.2
China	15.5	22.6	2.2	4.6	6.5	9.6	1.4	3.2	5.2	4.8
Cyprus	23.5	19.3	4.0	4.1	12.3	9.5	1.7	3.4	4.9	1.9
Hong Kong	6.8	34.6	0.3	8.2	4.9	18.0	0.9	6.3	0.7	2.1
India	6.6	8.4	2.9	5.3	3.0	2.5	0.1	0.1	0.6	0.4
Japan	17.6	11.5	8.0	5.5	4.6	2.4	1.0	0.4	2.4	2.0
Liberia	59.1	71.9	32.1	34.5	17.3	12.5	3.8	21.2	4.3	3.7
Malaysia	4.5	6.4	1.9	4.8	1.3	0.4	0.5	0.7	0.8	0.5
Malta	20.6	25.2	8.3	7.9	8.0	12.2	0.6	1.3	3.4	3.4
Marshall Islands	6.1	33.8	3.4	20.8	1.6	7.5	1.0	3.9	0.1	1.4
Norway	21.7	16.7	12.9	9.0	4.1	2.5	0.1	0.2	3.7	4.2
Panama	86.1	160.2	25.4	41.1	36.6	69.5	8.6	25.6	14.1	21.1
Philippines	8.9	4.8	0.2	0.4	6.3	2.5	0.2	0.2	1.9	1.3
Russia	8.3	5.1	1.7	1.3	1.6	0.6	0.3	0.1	4.5	2.9
St Vincent and the Grenadines	7.7	5.6	1.4	0.3	3.1	2.3	0.1	0.1	2.9	2.8
Singapore	16.6	32.9	7.2	17.4	4.3	6.8	2.5	5.5	2.5	3.2
South Korea	7.0	10.5	0.6	1.5	3.7	6.4	1.7	1.2	1.0	1.2
Taiwan	6.1	2.6	1.0	0.8	2.6	1.2	2.4	0.4	0.2	0.1
Turkey	6.5	4.9	0.8	0.9	4.3	2.1	0.0	0.3	1.2	1.4
USA	12.2	10.4	5.5	2.6	1.3	1.2	2.7	3.1	2.6	2.8
World total [1]	492.2	716.4	177.9	256.7	160.9	210.3	44.8	117.8	90.3	101.4

1 Including other trading fleets not listed.

☎020-7944 4119
The figures in this table are outside
the scope of UK National Statistics
Source - Lloyds Register - Fairplay

10.10 Selected outputs of airlines: 1997 and 2007

State of airline registration	Scheduled services — International and domestic traffic								Non-scheduled services	
	Aircraft kilometres flown (million)		Freight [1] tonne-kilometres flown (billion)		Passenger kilometres flown (billion)		International passenger kilometres flown (billion)		International and domestic passenger kilometres flown (billion)	
	1997	2007	1997	2007	1997	2007	1997	2007	1997	2007
United Kingdom [2]	809	1,474	4.6	6.3	136.4	227.7	129.7	218.3	76.8	86.5
Austria	118	160	0.2	0.5	10.1	17.4	10.0	17.3	2.1	2.6
Belgium	122	124	0.3	0.8	11.3	7.8	11.3	7.8	0	0
Denmark	93	110	0	-	8.1	15.5	7.3	12.1	2.2	5.3
Finland	92	140	0.3	0.5	9.6	16.4	8.5	15.5	2.3	4.6
France	619	996	5.1	6.4	84.7	151.3	55.2	129.4	3.6	4.8
Germany	674	1,486	6.2	8.5	84.7	214.9	79.1	205.2	57.6	10.5
Greece	68	93	0.1	0.1	9.3	9.7	8.0	7.7	-	0.8
Irish Republic	44	436	0.1	0.1	7.3	64.2	7.2	64.2	0.1	-
Italy	339	440	1.4	1.6	38.0	52.3	29.3	39.1	2.6	8.8
Luxembourg	39	97	2.3	5.5	0.3	0.7	0.3	0.7	0.4	0.7
Netherlands	375	521	3.9	5.0	66.7	90.9	66.6	90.9	0.1	5.4
Portugal	107	199	0.3	0.3	10.5	21.4	9.0	18.9	0.6	2.0
Spain	305	639	0.7	1.2	37.2	88.4	23.6	62.4	16.5	14.0
Sweden	93	99	0.0	0.0	7.3	14.1	4.6	7.6	0.4	8.5
Bulgaria	23	18	0	0	1.8	1.4	1.8	1.4	0.2	0.4
Cyprus	20	34	-	0.1	2.7	4.5	2.7	4.5	-	0.2
Czech Republic	29	73	-	-	2.4	6.3	2.4	6.3	0.5	4.0
Estonia	5	10	0	0	0.2	0.8	0.2	0.8	0.1	0.3
Hungary	28	58	0	-	2.3	4.4	2.3	4.4	0.4	0.4
Latvia	6	26	0	-	0.2	1.5	0.2	1.5	0.1	0.5
Lithuania	9	13	0	0	0.3	0.6	0.3	0.6	0.1	0.9
Malta	20	27	-	-	1.7	2.7	1.7	2.7	0.6	0.3
Poland	45	92	0.1	0.1	4.2	7.3	4.1	7.0	0.5	0.1
Romania	24	51	0	0	1.7	3.7	1.6	3.6	0.2	0.3
Slovak Republic	2	25	0	0.1	0.1	2.9	0.1	2.9	0.1	1.2
Slovenia	0	18	0	0	0	0.9	0	0.9	0	0.3
Norway	115	121	0	-	9.1	17.5	5.0	8.3	0.7	4.3
Switzerland	239	178	1.8	1.1	26.5	25.2	26.2	25.0	8.0	4.5
Japan	777	862	7.5	8.4	151.1	147.6	84.1	77.5	0.4	1.9
USA	9,005	12,456	25.5	40.5	965.6	1,312.1	267.8	376.0	18.8	18.2
Russian Federation	480	868	0.8	2.2	49.3	82.3	18.1	34.7	7.3	28.6

1 Excludes mail.
2 Source - UK Civil Aviation Authority (CAA).

☎020-7944 3088
The figures in this table are outside the scope of UK National Statistics
Source - International Civil Aviation Organisation (ICAO)

10.11 International comparisons of road deaths for selected OECD countries: [1] **1996-2007**

	1996	1997	1998	1999	2000	2001	2002	2003	2004	2005	2006	2007 [2]	Rate of road deaths in 2007 per 100,000 population [3]
Great Britain	3,598	3,599	3,421	3,423	3,409	3,450	3,431	3,508	3,221	3,201	3,172	2,946	5.0
Northern Ireland	142	144	160	141	171	148	150	150	147	135	126	113	6.4
United Kingdom	3,740	3,743	3,581	3,564	3,580	3,598	3,581	3,658	3,368	3,336	3,298	3,059	5.0
Austria	1,027	1,105	963	1,079	976	958	956	931	878	768	730	691	8.3
Belgium	1,356	1,364	1,500	1,397	1,470	1,486	1,306	1,214	1,162	1,089	1,069	1,103	10.1
Denmark	514	489	499	514	498	431	463	432	369	331	306	407	7.5
Finland	404	438	400	431	396	433	415	379	375	379	336	382	7.1
France	8,541	8,444	8,918	8,487	8,079	8,160	7,655	6,058	5,530	5,318	4,709	4,620	7.3
Germany	8,758	8,549	7,792	7,772	7,503	6,977	6,842	6,613	5,842	5,361	5,091	4,949	6.0
Greece	2,157	2,105	2,182	2,116	2,037	1,880	1,634	1,605	1,670	1,658	1,657	1,580	14.4
Irish Republic	453	472	458	413	415	411	376	337	374	399	365	338	7.8
Italy	6,688	6,724	6,849	6,688 [4]	7,061 [4]	7,096 [4]	6,980 [4]	6,563 [4]	6,122 [4]	5,818 [4]	5,669	5,215	8.8
Luxembourg	71	60	57	58	76	70	62	53	50	45	36	43	9.0
Netherlands	1,180	1,163	1,066	1,090	1,082	993	987	1,028	804	750	730	709	4.3
Portugal	2,394	2,210	2,126	1,995	1,860	1,671	1,675	1,546	1,294	1,247	969	974	9.2
Spain	5,483	5,604	5,957	5,738	5,776	5,517	5,347	5,400	4,749	4,442	4,104	3,821	8.6
Sweden	537	541	531	580	591	554	532	529	480	440	445	471	5.2
Bulgaria	..	..	..	..	..	1,011	959	960	943	957	1,043	1,006	13.1
Cyprus	128	115	111	113	111	98	94	97	117	102	86	89	11.4
Czech Republic	1,568	1,597	1,360	1,455	1,486	1,334	1,431	1,447	1,382	1,286	1,063	1,222	11.9
Estonia	213	280	284	232	204	199	223	164	170	169	204	196	14.6
Hungary	1,370	1,391	1,371	1,306	1,200	1,239	1,429	1,326	1,296	1,278	1,303	1,232	12.2
Latvia	550	525	627	604	588	558	559	532	516	442	407	419	18.4
Lithuania	667	725	829	748	641	706	697	709	752	773	759	739	21.8
Malta	19	18	17	4	15	16	16	16	13	17	11	14	3.4
Poland	6,359	7,310	7,080	6,730	6,294	5,534	5,827	5,640	5,712	5,444	5,243	5,583	14.6
Romania	..	..	..	..	..	2,461	2,398	2,235	2,418	2,461	2,478	2,791	12.9
Slovakia	616	788	819	647	628	614	610	645	603	560	579	627	11.6
Slovenia	389	357	309	334	313	278	269	242	274	258	263	293	14.6
Norway	255	303	352	304	341	275	312	282	259	224	242	233	5.0
Switzerland	616	587	597	583	592	554	513	546	510	409	370	384	5.1
Australia	1,970	1,768	1,755	1,758	1,817	1,737	1,715	1,621	1,590	1,637	1,598	1,617	7.7
Canada	3,091	3,064	2,934	2,972	2,927	2,779	2,931	2,766	2,725	2,925	2,892	2,847	8.4
Iceland	10	15	27	21	32	24	29	23	23	19	31	15	4.9
Japan	11,674	11,254	10,805	10,372	10,403	10,060	9,575	8,877	8,492	7,931	7,272	6,639	5.2
New Zealand	514	540	502	509	462	455	404	461	436	405	391	422	10.0
Republic of Korea	14,551	13,343	10,416	10,756	10,236	8,097	7,222	7,212	6,563	6,376	6,327	6,166	12.7
USA	42,065	42,013	41,501	41,717	41,945	42,116	42,815	42,643	42,636	43,443	42,708	41,059	13.7

1 In accordance with the commonly agreed international definition, most countries define a fatality as one being due to a road accident where death occurs within 30 days of the accident. The official road accident statistics of some countries however, limit the fatalities to those occurring within shorter periods after the accident. Numbers of deaths and death rates in the above table have been adjusted according to the factors used by the Economic Commission for Europe and International Transport Forum, to represent standardised 30-day deaths: Italy (7 days) +8%; France (6 days) +5.7%; Portugal (1 day) +14%; Republic of Korea (3 days) +15%.

2 Provisional data

3 Population taken from the OECD's International Road and Traffic Accidents Database and EU Pocket Book and may differ from the figures in Tables 10.1 and 10.4.

4 Figures revised since publication of the TSGB 2007 bulletin.

☎ 020-7944 6595
Source - OECD, EUROSTAT, IRTAD and ITF

Chart 10.11 International comparisons: road deaths per 100,000 population: 2007 (Provisional)

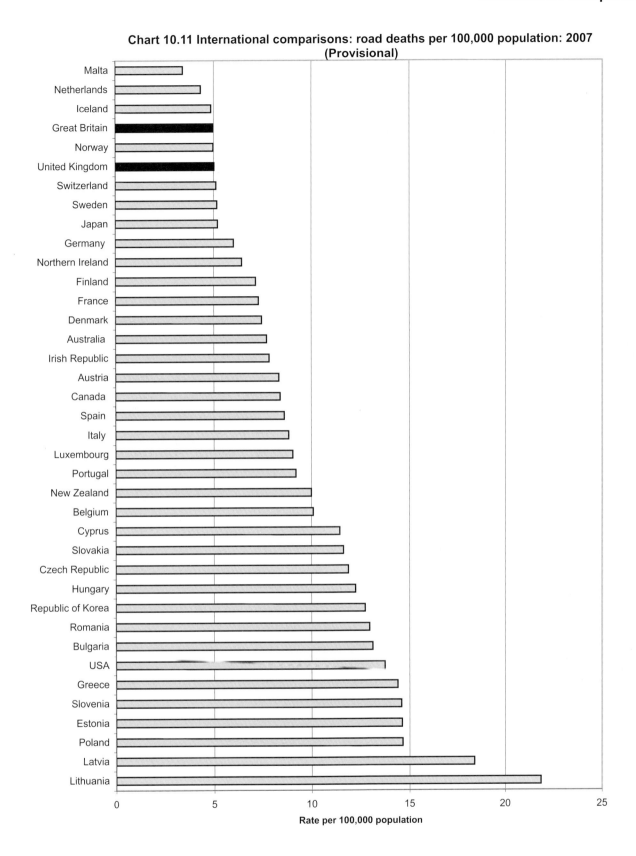

Rate per 100,000 population

Abbreviations used in Transport Statistics Great Britain: 2008 Edition

AAIB:	Air Accident Investigation Branch
ABI:	Association of British Insurers
ABP:	Associated British Ports
AES:	Annual Earning Survey
APEG:	Airborne Particles Expert Group
BAA:	British Airports Authority
BEA:	(French) Bureau Enquetes Accidents
BERR:	Department for Business, Enterprise and Regulatory Reform
BR:	British Rail
BRB:	British Railways Board
BRF:	British Road Federation
BSOG:	Bus Service Operators Grant
BW:	British Waterways
CAA:	Civil Aviation Authority
CfIT:	Commission for Integrated Transport
CLG:	Communities and Local Govt.
CPI:	Consumer Prices Index
CSRGT:	Continuing Survey of Road Goods Transport
CTRL:	Channel Tunnel Rail Link
CVTF:	Cleaner Vehicles Task Force
DBFO:	Design, Build, Finance and Operate (contracts)
DDA:	Disability Discrimination Act
DEFRA:	Department for Environment, Food and Rural Affairs
DfT:	Department for Transport
DLR:	Docklands Light Railway
DOE:	Department of the Environment
DPM:	Deputy Prime Minister
DiPTAC:	Disabled Person Transport Advisory Committee
DSA:	Driving Standards Agency
DVLA:	Driver and Vehicle Licensing Agency
EA:	Environmental Accounts
EC:	European Community
EEC:	European Economic Community

EPS:	European Passenger Services Ltd (ex-BR subsidiary)
EST:	Energy Saving Trust
ETC:	European Transport Council
ETS:	Emissions Trading Scheme
EU:	European Union
EuroNCAP:	EU New Car Assessment Programme
EUTC:	European Union Transport Council
FDR:	Fuel Duty Rebate
FFG:	Freight Facilities Grant
FTA:	Freight Transport Assn.
GDP:	Gross Domestic Product
GLA:	Greater London Authority
GMDSS:	Global Maritime Distress and Safety System
GMPTE:	Greater Manchester Passenger Transport Executive
GOL:	Gov. Office for London
Grt:	Gross registered tonnage
GT:	Gross Tonnage
gvw:	gross vehicle weight
HA:	Highways Agency
HERL:	Heathrow Express Rail Link
HGV:	Heavy Goods Vehicle
HMRC:	Her Majesty's Revenue and Customs
HSC:	Health and Safety Commission
HSE:	Health and Safety Exec.
ICAO:	Int. Civil Aviation Org.
ICC:	International Climate Change
Int:	International
IPCC	Intergovernmental Panel on Climate Change
IPS:	International Passenger Survey
IRF:	International Road Federation
IRFT:	International Rail Freight Terminal
KSI:	Killed or seriously injured
LA(s):	Local Authority(s)
LCA:	London City Airport
LCR:	London and Continental Railways
LDDC:	London Docklands Development Corporation

LEQ: Noise	Equivalent Continuous Level	RBSG:	Rural Bus Subsidy Grant
LFS:	Labour Force Survey	RDS-TMC:	Radio Data System - Traffic Message Channel
LGV:	Light Goods Vehicle	RID:	Regulations concerning the International Carriage of Dangerous Goods by Rail
LoLo:	Lift-on Lift-off		
LRT:	London Regional Transport		
LT:	London Transport	RITC:	Rail Industry Training Council
LTP:	Local Transport Plan	Ro-Ro:	Roll-on Roll-off
LU:	London Underground	RPI:	Retail Prices Index
MAIB:	Marine Accident Investigation Branch	RTFO:	Renewable Transport Fuel Obligation
MCA:	Marine and Coastguard Agency	RTRA:	Road Traffic Reduction Act
MMC:	Monopolies & Mergers Commission.	RVAR:	Rail Vehicle Accessibility Regulations
MML:	Midland Mainline (rail)	SACTRA:	Standing Advisory Committee on Trunk Road Assessment
MOT:	vehicle testing scheme		
MPV:	Multi-purpose vehicle		
NAEI:	National Atmospheric Emissions Inventory	SBG:	Scottish Bus Group
		SIC:	Standard Industrial Classification (of Economic Activity)
NATS:	National Air Traffic Services		
NBC:	National Bus Company	SMMT:	Society of Motor Manufacturers and Traders
NDLS:	National Dock Labour Scheme.		
NEG:	National Express Group	SPAD:	(train) Signal Passed at Danger
NET:	Nottingham Express Transit		
NEXUS:	Tyne and Wear Passenger Transport Executive	SPTE:	Strathclyde Passenger Transport Executive
		SRA:	Strategic Rail Authority
		STAG:	School Travel Advisory Group
NTO:	National Training Organisation		
		SYPTE:	South Yorkshire Passenger Transport Executive
NTS:	National Travel Survey		
OCJR:	Office for Criminal Justice Reform	TAG:	Track Access Grant
OECD:	Organisation for Economic Co-operation and Development	TCF:	Transport Card Forum
		TEN:	Trans European Network
		TfL:	Transport for London
ONS:	Office for National Statistics	TGWU:	Transport and General Workers Union
OPEC:	Organisation of Petroleum Exporting Countries	TMC:	Traffic Message Channel
		TRL:	Transport Research Laboratory
ORR:	Office of Rail Regulation	TSO:	The Stationery Office
OTIF:	International Railway Transport Organisation	TWA:	Transport and Works Act
		TWPTE:	Tyne and Wear Passenger Transport Executive
PAYE:	Pay (tax) as You Earn		
PCO:	Public Carriage Office		
PFI:	Public Finance Initiative		
PHV:	Private Hire Vehicle	UA:	Unitary Authority
PLG:	Private Light Goods (vehicle)	VAT:	Value Added Tax
		VED:	Vehicle Excise Duty
PPM:	Public Performance Measure	VI:	Vehicle Inspectorate
		VOSA:	Vehicle and Operator Services Agency
PPP:	Public-Private Partnership		
PSV:	Public Service Vehicle	WHR:	Welsh Highland Railway
PTA:	Passenger Transport Area	WYPTE:	West Yorkshire Passenger Transport Executive
PTE:	Passenger Transport Executive		

Index

Figures indicate table numbers.

183